Catholic Intellectuals
and Conservative
Politics in America,
1950–1985

Catholic Intellectuals and Conservative Politics in America, 1950–1985

PATRICK ALLITT

Cornell University Press

ITHACA AND LONDON

First published 1993 by Cornell University Press.

International Standard Book Number 0-8014-2295-7
Library of Congress Catalog Card Number 93-13515

Printed in the United States of America

Librarians: Library of Congress cataloging information
appears on the last page of the book.

⊗ The paper in this book meets the minimum requirements
of the American National Standard for Information Sciences—
Permanence of Paper for Printed Library Materials, ANSI Z39.48-1984.

For Toni, Frances, and Matthew

Contents

Preface

Conservatism, which dominated American political life during the 1980s, was a negligible influence thirty years before, and its political and intellectual development in the years after 1950 has not been fully explained. From its inception the American conservative movement has been a hybrid, born of contradictory ideological components and deeply divided on such issues as laissez-faire capitalism, individualism and the family, and the role of religion in society. The political crises of the 1960s and 1970s exposed many of the tensions in the growing conservative movement but the social dislocations of those decades strengthened its electoral appeal. Ideological conservatives, despite their unresolved theoretical dilemmas, came to power with the election of Ronald Reagan in 1980 and presided over national politics for the next twelve years.

This book explores one of the major strands in the development of the conservative intellectual movement, the fundamental role of Catholics. It implicitly challenges the view that evangelical Protestantism and libertarian economic theories were the chief components of the movement. Catholic laypeople worked out many of the principles of the new conservatism, beginning in the 1930s and 1940s, organizing journals in the 1950s and gradually winning the adherence of other intellectual and electoral groups. Not all U.S. Catholics were political conservatives, of course, but the church's hierarchy, traditions, and faith in the natural law were conducive to conservative thought in the cold war era. Even Catholic liberals in the 1950s were militantly anti-Communist and skeptical of the secular liberalism voiced by their non-Catholic contemporaries.

As the conservative movement gathered political momentum in the following decades, ironically, U.S. Catholicism itself underwent profound changes and lost much of its old conservative character. Hitherto a monolithic organization dominated by powerful bishops, who presided over a clearly defined social community with distinctive views, it became, in the 1960s and 1970s, contentious and fragmentary, no longer united on any religious, political, or social issue. Largely responsible for this transformation was the coincidence of the Second Vatican Council with America's social upheavals of the 1960s. After the council political and religious disagreement increased dramatically, widening divisions not only between liberals and conservatives but also among Catholic conservatives, with some linking their faith to a militant nationalism while others used it to condemn the nation for its sins. As a result of these disputes the centrality of Catholicism to the conservative movement diminished just as the movement itself was coming to power.

The Introduction outlines the principal elements of this story and examines the characteristic problems of conservative and Catholic history and historiography. Chapter 1 then draws an impressionistic picture of American Catholicism in the 1950s. It emphasizes Catholics' sense of distinctiveness, the importance of anticommunism as a rallying point for Catholics eager to exhibit their patriotic credentials, the first stirrings of liberal Catholicism, and Catholicism's intellectual and educational problems of the 1950s, which occasioned several controversies. Chapter 2 shows how, against this background, the new conservative movement took shape, chiefly through the efforts of William F. Buckley, Jr., and how it drew on themes in the work of an older generation of Catholic conservative intellectuals, including Ross Hoffman and Francis Graham Wilson. The movement's first crises, the 1956 Hungarian Revolution and Soviet leader Nikita Khrushchev's visits to the United States, provoked an all-but-unanimous anti-Communist outcry, whereas debates over the legitimacy of laissez-faire capitalism bore witness to a growing diversity of views.

Chapters 3 and 4 follow the fortunes of Catholic conservative intellectuals into the volatile 1960s. Chapter 3 shows how the election of John F. Kennedy, the civil rights movement, the decolonization of Africa, and Supreme Court decisions on prayer and Bible reading in public schools each occasioned alarm by seeming to contradict deeply held conservative principles. It shows, further, how the accelerating nuclear weapons race of the era prompted a Catholic debate about whether the nation could justifiably fight an annihilating nuclear war against the Soviet Union and whether God had chosen the United States as the citadel of Christendom. Chapter 4, on the later 1960s, demonstrates how the fallout from the social crisis of those years and from the Second Vatican Council created sharp divisions in American

Catholicism, as in the society at large. Those years witnessed the rise of a militant Catholic Left dedicated to direct protest actions against the American war in Vietnam and a no-less-militant Catholic conservatism dedicated to direct protest actions against liberalized abortion laws, while bewildered moderate nationalist conservatives struggled to come to terms with the spirit of the Vatican Council and the politics of upheaval.

In Chapter 5, I switch from an analytical narrative to a thematic discussion, in order to unravel the intricate Catholic response to the "sexual revolution" and to explain its philosophical, legal, and institutional consequences. Questions relating to sexuality and the family were central to Catholic controversy in the 1970s, eclipsing all other issues in their perceived urgency. The Supreme Court decision in Roe v. Wade set off a reconfiguration of Catholic conservative activists, some of whom dedicated themselves to antiabortion work as *the* issue for political action. The work of legal scholars, notably John T. Noonan, Jr., and Charles Rice, and the example of women who opposed abortion, notably Clare Boothe Luce and Ellen Wilson, are here singled out for illumination.

Chapters 6 and 7 are designed to explore more thoroughly some of the generalizations made in the narrative chapters. In each of them I compare the work of two men in the period from the early 1950s to the early 1980s to show how, in particular cases, Catholic conservatives could draw different lessons from the contingencies they faced. Chapter 6 investigates the work of John Lukacs and Thomas Molnar, two Hungarians who came to the United States as anti-Communist exiles after World War II. Both contributed to the international outlook of the new conservatism, and both used their faith to challenge conventional verities in their disciplines, Lukacs in history, Molnar in philosophy. Chapter 7 examines two indigenous Catholic conservatives, Garry Wills and Michael Novak, to show how similar events led them to opposite conclusions, Novak becoming more of a capitalist-nationalist, Wills moving in the opposite direction.

The Epilogue looks at the transformed face of American Catholicism in the 1980s, using as a symbolic episode the National Conference of Catholic Bishops' pastoral letter on nuclear weapons *The Challenge of Peace* (1983) and the resistance to its teaching by a lay Catholic group led by Michael Novak. It then surveys the new generation of Catholic traditionalists who have taken up the cause of orthodoxy, antiabortion, and profamily politics, writers dismayed by what seem to them worsening conditions of political, social, and intellectual life in contemporary America but eager, though they think it a forlorn hope, to stop the flood.

I have incurred many debts during the pleasurable research and writing of this book. First, I thank my graduate school teachers at the University of California, Berkeley, preeminently Richard Abrams. Thanks also to the faculty of the Harvard Divinity School, where I spent three enjoyable years as a postdoctoral fellow, especially Gordon Kaufman, Margaret Miles, William Hutchison, and Constance Buchanan. Thanks also to my fellow Luce Fellows there, Mary Segers and Timothy Weiskel. At the adjacent Weston School of Theology I learned a great deal about teaching and about John Courtney Murray from David Hollenbach, S.J. At Emory University, where it has been my privilege to work since 1988, I have benefited from the advice of several gifted and selfless colleagues, in particular James Roark, Frank Lechner, Randall Strahan, Margot Finn, and Thomas Flynn, each of whom read drafts of the book. Others who have been kind enough to read it and make suggestions for which I am most grateful are John Diggins at City University of New York, Graduate Center; James Fisher at Yale, himself the model of a modern Catholic historian; Wilfred McClay at Tulane; and Gerald Fogarty at the University of Virginia. The book is better for their advice. I also thank all the people, participants in this history, who granted me interviews, wrote letters, sent books and articles, and helped me to sort out what they did and did not think. Thanks, too, to Peter Agree at Cornell University Press for his continuing support and help. The largest of all my debts of gratitude I owe to my wife, Toni.

PATRICK ALLITT

Atlanta, Georgia

Abbreviations Used in the Notes

A	*America*
C	*Commonweal*
CHR	*Catholic Historical Review*
CM	*Catholic Mind*
CW	*Catholic World*
HLR	*Human Life Review*
MA	*Modern Age*
NCR	*National Catholic Reporter*
NOR	*New Oxford Review*
NR	*National Review*
R	*Ramparts*
SO	*Social Order*
T	*Triumph*

Catholic Intellectuals and Conservative Politics in America, 1950–1985

Introduction

American intellectual orthodoxy after World War II held that conservatism in this country was either negligible or nonexistent. Lionel Trilling in his famous introduction to *The Liberal Imagination* (1949) said that American conservatism was no more than a set of "irritable mental gestures which seek to resemble ideas," and Louis Hartz in *The Liberal Tradition in America* declared that conservative impulses were all but stillborn in a business-oriented society without any vestiges of an ancien regime. "The ironic flaw in American liberalism," he summarized, "lies in the fact that we have never had a real conservative tradition."[1] Trilling and Hartz were by no means uncritical champions of American liberalism as they found it at midcentury, but neither did they mean to take the conservative label for themselves. The new conservatism that developed in the 1950s and 1960s came from quite different sources. Outside or on the margins of academia, more religious than secular, and much more searching in its critique of liberalism than Trilling or Hartz, it encountered both practical and theoretical obstacles in its search for legitimacy and recognition, and its influence never matched that of such groups as the "New York intellectuals."

Religious tradition left a heavy imprint on both the radically disposed New York intellectuals, who were predominantly Jewish, and the new conservatives, who were mainly Catholic.[2] The Catholic laypeople who played a major role in founding and developing the new conservative movement drew very different lessons from their experience as outsiders in the older American mainstream, as compared to the New York intellectuals. They interpreted the liberal reforms of the New Deal and the Fair Deal not as supports to a maturing capitalist

1. Lionel Trilling, *The Liberal Imagination* (New York: Scribner's, 1949), ix; Louis Hartz, *The Liberal Tradition in America* (New York: Harcourt, Brace, 1955), 57.
2. On the New York Intellectuals, see Alexander Bloom, *Prodigal Sons: The New York Intellectuals and Their World* (New York: Oxford University Press, 1986).

system but as threatening evidence of incipient socialism at home. They saw the Soviet Union as the political and military center of a conspiracy dedicated to world conquest and harbored no benevolence toward any branch of Marxism. Fearing that the United States, at home and abroad, faced imminent disaster, these Catholic intellectuals joined other conservatives in advocating a more militant posture in the cold war and an end to domestic liberalism. They saw themselves as champions of Western civilization, the heritage of Christendom, and drew from their religious faith and tradition the principles they believed could alone draw that civilization back from the brink of catastrophe.

Earlier twentieth-century American conservatives had organized primarily around a defense of laissez-faire capitalism, often buttressed by a pseudoscientific evolutionary rhetoric of social Darwinism and progress. The Catholic new conservatism of the 1950s was based upon quite different convictions: first, that there is an unchanging human nature, capable of good actions but tainted by original sin and inherently imperfect; second, that the universe has an objective moral order to which human beings must try to orient themselves, their society, and its laws; third, that tradition and the cumulative wisdom of prior generations are the best guide for charting a course into the future. In many respects these principles were the opposite of laissez-faire evolutionary conservatism. While some of the Catholic new conservatives accepted American capitalism, they conceived of it as a means to preserve and nurture *families,* taken, according to the Catholic concept of natural law, as the basic units of society. From William F. Buckley, Jr.'s *God and Man at Yale* (1951) to Michael Novak's *Spirit of Democratic Capitalism* (1982), capitalism was justified and defended for its familism rather than its individualism, and where capitalism conflicted with familism, most believed capitalism should yield. In foreign policy the Catholic new conservatives of the 1950s forsook the isolationist tradition, favoring not merely "containment" of communism in Europe and Asia but an active "liberation" policy to rescue the "captive nations" from the thralldom of "atheistic communism." They saw themselves as champions of the West and the United States as Christendom's last great guardian. Their intellectual genealogy was dominated by European traditionalists: Edmund Burke, Cardinal John Newman, Alexis de Tocqueville, Georges Bernanos, G. K. Chesterton, Hilaire Belloc, and José Ortega y Gasset. Liberals, they believed, had made a fetish of relativism and pragmatism and so lacked the transcendent values to stand firm against the enemies of the West. The Catholic new conservatives therefore attacked American liberalism almost as remorselessly as they attacked communism.

George Nash, who wrote the first major history of the movement, notes that in the 1950s "much of the new conservatism seemed . . . Catholic in composition. Both Catholics and conservatives were outsiders. One is even tempted to say that the new conservatism was, in part, an intellectual cutting edge of the postwar 'coming of age' of America's Catholic minority."[3] Catholics were perhaps the one major population group whose adherence to a long, ostensibly unbroken tradition made them comfortable with the conservative label that many of their compatriots disliked. The two principal journals of the new conservatism, *National Review* and *Modern Age,* both founded in the mid-1950s, were not Catholic journals per se, but a striking number of Catholic writers worked for them. Among them were journalists William Buckley, L. Brent Bozell, James McFadden, Gary Potter, and Erik von Kuehnelt-Leddihn, political scientists Willmoore Kendall, Anthony Bouscaren, and Francis Graham Wilson, philosophers Frederick Wilhelmsen and Thomas Molnar, and historians Ross Hoffman, John Lukacs, Stephen Tonsor, and Garry Wills. Many of these men—Hoffman, Wilson, Kendall, Bozell, Potter, and later Russell Kirk, Frank Meyer and Jeffrey Hart—were converts who had found a special congruence between Catholicism and political conservatism and who took their new religion and its teachings with grave seriousness. Even non-Catholic contributors such as Will Herberg, James Burnham, and Peter Viereck expressed admiration for the Catholic church, which they described as an intrinsically conservative institution and a bulwark of Western civilization.

This history of Catholic lay intellectuals in the American conservative movement traces their early unity and subsequent fragmentation in the 1960s and 1970s. It describes and explains the previously neglected insights they brought to political and scholarly debate, the way they approached issues, and the influence of their religious tradition on their analysis. Their numbers were probably never large enough to be politically decisive (Buckley and Bozell, for example, both lost electoral campaigns in the mid-1960s). Indirectly, however, the influence of this small group of Catholic conservatives was considerable. Buckley, much the most publicity conscious and well known of the group, became a permanent feature of the political landscape; once the enfant terrible of television political debate, he was "mainstream" by the 1970s and a frequent adviser to President Reagan in the 1980s, as well as a

---

3. George Nash, *The Conservative Intellectual Movement in America since 1945* (New York: Basic, 1976), 80–81.

widely syndicated newspaper columnist.[4] Garry Wills and Michael Novak also carved out sizable reputations for themselves as columnists and commentators on public affairs, shining the light of their Catholic and conservative principles on current events. John Noonan, already a major figure in Catholic intellectual life in the 1960s, gained national renown among antiabortion activists, Protestant and Catholic alike, in the 1970s and was appointed by President Reagan to the federal appeals court circuit in 1987. Others, to be sure, such as the highly gifted but eccentric Frederick Wilhelmsen, Thomas Molnar, and John Lukacs, remained marginal in American intellectual life because their assumptions and principles were so remote from those of most contemporaries as to be unassimilable. Their work remains significant less for its direct influence than because it offers a running critique of familiar assumptions of intellectual discourse in their disciplines which they conscientiously declined to accept. Many of their insights have until now gone unremarked or unanswered.

The Catholic writers were joined by two other principal groups in the creation of the new conservatism. The first was libertarian capitalists—among them Murray Rothbard, Frank Chodorov, and Henry Hazlitt—whose philosophical orientation was usually quite different from the Catholics' but who at least shared an aversion to contemporary American liberalism and the growing reach of the state.[5] The most extreme form of libertarianism appeared in the fiction and manifestos of the Russian émigré Ayn Rand, but *National Review,* despite its principle of inclusiveness, denied that her brand of militantly atheistic and Promethean capitalism deserved the name of conservatism; she and Buckley, the journal's founder, shared an intense mutual dislike.[6] The second important group was the disillusioned former Communists now eager to fight against their erstwhile faith. Whittaker Chambers, author of *Witness* (1952), was the most famous; others included Max Eastman, James Burnham, John Dos Passos, and Will Herberg.[7] The Catholic traditionalists, the libertarians, and the ex-Communists had plenty of philosophical differences, but their antiliberal and anti-Communist convictions formed the nucleus of a political movement that

4. See John Judis, *William F. Buckley, Jr., Patron Saint of the Conservatives* (New York: Simon and Schuster, 1988).
5. On the libertarians, see Nash, *Conservative Movement,* 3–35.
6. Ibid., 156–59. See also Jerome Tuccille, *It Usually Begins with Ayn Rand* (New York: Stein and Day, 1971).
7. Whittaker Chambers, *Witness* (New York: Random House, 1952). On the Alger Hiss–Chambers case, see Allen Weinstein, *Perjury: The Hiss-Chambers Case* (New York: Knopf, 1978). On Burnham, Dos Passos, Eastman, and Herberg, see John P. Diggins, *Up from Communism: Conservative Odysseys in American Intellectual History* (New York: Harper and Row, 1975).

first came to wide popular notice with the presidential candidacy of Barry Goldwater in 1964. After a jolting reversal in that election the conservative movement as a whole went on to gather adherents under a "fusionist" umbrella of philosophical and practical ideas and came to power with the election of Ronald Reagan in 1980.

The success of the conservative movement, ably charted by Nash, was by no means echoed in the experience of lay Catholic intellectuals in the same period, however. Before 1950, few Catholic laypeople had been prominent in American intellectual life; rather, the church's separate educational apparatus had tended to produce an isolated cluster of intellectuals serving the Catholic community alone. By the 1950s, however, enough members of the laity had gained the education and the self-confidence to seek a place for their ideas in the wider American intellectual community and to argue that these ideas could benefit the country as a whole. Not all were conservatives, to be sure; some had derived liberal political ideas from Catholic tradition. Conservatives and liberals alike, however, demonstrating a new latitude of lay initiative and action, bore witness to the maturing of the U.S. Catholic community and its emergence from the preoccupations of an immigrant era.

In a church whose spokesmen had hitherto been bishops and priests the new lay voices raised controversies with religious as well as political consequences. They inaugurated a period of fragmentation which accelerated dramatically in the 1960s when church reforms initiated by the Second Vatican Council (1962–1965) coincided with social upheavals—secularization, civil rights, Vietnam, and the "sexual revolution"—in the United States. In 1950 the U.S. Catholic church spoke with one voice and regarded itself as a homogeneous body. By 1970 even the appearance of unanimity had vanished.

The fragmentation of American Catholicism was accompanied by the fragmentation of Catholic conservatism. Allen Guttman, writing in 1967, said that "the signs of the times seem to point towards a continued democratization of Catholic theory and practice. The bases on which to construct a conservative society continue slowly to erode."[8] Men and women who had shared compatible conservative views in the 1950s began to disagree with one another on the crucial religious and moral-political questions of the 1960s. Some, notably William Buckley and his fellow *National Review* editor Jeffrey Hart, believed that compromises with other conservatives and other Christians were

---

8. Allen Guttman, *The Conservative Tradition in America* (New York: Oxford University Press, 1967), 92.

essential to the welfare of the conservative political movement. For them practical political considerations outweighed doctrinal issues. Others, notably L. Brent Bozell and Frederick Wilhelmsen, dissented. In his Catholic loyalist journal *Triumph* Bozell declared in 1970 that a conflict between religious and political objectives must be resolved in favor of the religious, even if that resolution meant a virtual declaration of war against the state. *Triumph* itself suffered a split in 1970 when, after a period of growing tensions, half its editors moved on to create another new Catholic journal, *Rough Beast.* Many other responses to the challenges of the 1960s developed. For example Garry Wills, a former seminarian and anti-Communist journalist, isolated himself by voicing radical ideas on civil rights and the Vietnam War which dismayed his old comrades but which Wills considered true to Catholic and conservative principles properly construed. Other Catholic conservatives decided to devote themselves to specific issues. James McFadden, on the staff of *National Review* almost from its inception in 1955, set up the Ad Hoc Committee in Defense of Life and founded the antiabortion journal the *Human Life Review* after the Supreme Court decision in the case of Roe v. Wade (1973). Abortion politics turned the hitherto detached and scholarly conservative John Noonan into an active polemicist for the antiabortion cause. Others, for example, John Lukacs and Thomas Molnar, tried to exercise their influence through scholarship rather than direct action and advocacy journalism.

While the Catholic conservatives went their several ways in the 1960s, so too did the Catholic liberals. John Cogley, a prominent Catholic liberal of the 1950s and early 1960s, ultimately converted to Episcopalianism in exasperation at many of the church's policies. Another well-known liberal, Daniel Callahan, left the church while continuing to study the vital religious and ethical questions of his day. Some radical Catholic women, notably Mary Daly, abandoned Christianity completely, arguing that it was inherently repressive of women.[9] Rosemary R. Ruether, by contrast, undertook a far-reaching feminist reinterpretation of Catholic theology.[10] Of particular interest here, however, are Catholic liberals of the 1950s who moved in the opposite direction during the 1960s, reconsidered their political outlook, and belatedly attached themselves to the Catholic conservatives they had once an-

9. See, for example, Mary Daly, *The Church and the Second Sex* (New York: Harper and Row, 1968), written as a feminist critique of Catholicism from within, and *Beyond God the Father* (Boston: Beacon, 1973), written after Daley abandoned Catholicism.

10. See, for example, Rosemary Ruether, *New Woman, New Earth: Sexist Ideologies and Human Liberation* (1975; San Francisco: Harper and Row, 1988); Ruether and Eleanor McLoughlin, eds., *Women of Spirit: Female Leadership in the Jewish and Christian Traditions* (New York: Touchstone, 1979).

tagonized. The best example of such an odyssey is that of Michael Novak. A leading advocate of reform in the era of the Second Vatican Council, Novak was one of the first laymen publicly to advocate Catholic use of contraceptives and an outspoken opponent of U.S. involvement in Vietnam. By the 1970s, Novak had become identified with America's neoconservatives and was defending democratic capitalism, advocating nuclear deterrence, and opposing further experiments in the spirit of Vatican II.

This fragmentation can be understood as a stage in the breakdown of "ghetto" Catholicism or, to state it more positively, as a stage in the assimilation of Catholics into the U.S. mainstream. To be a Catholic in the 1950s was to be aware of oneself as a member of a minority group, set apart from the rest of society by a pattern of beliefs, ritual actions, liturgical practices, food taboos, and even a distinctive view of the nation's history and its place in Western civilization. A combination of pressures, generational, social, religious, and political, conspired to diminish greatly the sense of separateness and distinctiveness, and by the 1970s Catholicism no longer required the self-distancing actions its adherents had routinely performed twenty years before. The sociologist of religion Robert Wuthnow is one of many observers to note a fundamental rearrangement of religious forces in the United States in recent decades. From the polar antagonism of Protestants and Catholics, derived from the Reformation and still vividly apparent in the 1950s, emerged an alliance between conservative Protestants and conservative Catholics on such issues as school prayer and opposition to abortion and a matching alliance between liberal Protestants and liberal Catholics on a range of social and foreign policy issues.[11] Following the transformation at the level of intellectual history, to be sure, tells only part of the story. In this instance, however, the fragmentation of Catholic conservatism on the intellectual plane was paralleled at the popular level also and became a staple issue of American religious journalism throughout the 1960s and 1970s.

Traditionally, Catholic reasoning on political and moral issues was based on natural law, which has been defined by one of its students as "the belief that there exists in nature and/or human nature a rational order which can provide intelligible value-statements independently of human will, that are universal in application, unchangeable in their ultimate content, and morally obligatory on mankind. These statements are expressed as laws or as moral imperatives which provide a

11. Robert Wuthnow, *The Restructuring of American Religion: Society and Faith since World War II* (Princeton: Princeton University Press, 1988).

basis for the evaluation of legal and political structures."[12] In the 1950s almost all Catholic writers accepted natural law as the framework for moral reasoning, believed it was accessible and intelligible to all citizens, whether or not they were Catholic, and so considered it the appropriate basis for thinking about moral, educational, and political ideas. They were heartened to find non-Catholic authors, notably Robert Hutchins and Walter Lippmann, following their example by taking up natural law ideas as the basis of social and political analysis.[13]

The advantage of a natural law approach is that it offers distinct principles to apply to questions of, for example, medical or military ethics or the understanding of marriage. Logical syllogistic reasoning from natural law premises ought always to yield definite answers. Its disadvantage, however, which became increasingly obvious in the 1960s, is that natural law principles can in fact be made to yield multiple solutions to each problem, depending on which of the many available principles is granted salience for the particular issue under scrutiny. On the contested question of contraceptives during the 1960s, for example, Catholic adherents of the anticontraception position argued that each act of sexual intercourse was designed *by nature* to be open to the transmission of life and that to obstruct the intention of the act with contraceptives would be to act contrary to nature. Answering this argument, advocates of a reform in favor of contraceptives reasoned that the enjoyment of sex as a fulfillment of the sacrament of marriage was an equally *natural* function of marital intercourse, which was impaired if the couple feared an unwanted pregnancy. To use human ingenuity to thwart one function of marital sex in order that the other function might be enhanced, they said, does no violence to natural law.

As disputes over natural law proliferated, Catholics appealed to it less often after the 1950s though it has by no means disappeared. Natural law argumentation was unable to unify the Catholic intellectual community in the 1960s, nor did most other Americans recognize it as a reliable basis for moral reasoning. It is symbolically significant in this context, that John Noonan, editor of a journal on natural law questions, the *Natural Law Forum*, decided in 1969 to change its title to the *American Journal of Jurisprudence* and open it up to more non-Catho-

---

12. Paul Sigmund, *Natural Law and Political Thought* (Cambridge, Mass.: Winthrop, 1971), viii. See also H. L. A. Hart, "Positivism and the Separation of Law and Morals," *Harvard Law Review* 71 (1958): 593–627.

13. See, for example, Robert Hutchins, John Cogley, et al., Center for the Study of Democratic Institutions, *Natural Law and Modern Society* (Cleveland: World Fund for the Republic, 1963); Walter Lippmann, *Essays on the Public Philosophy* (Boston: Little, Brown, 1955), 83–85.

lic contributors. In his own work Noonan began to develop a synthesis of natural law and personalist ideas drawn from the French Catholic philosophers Gabriel Marcel, Etienne Gilson, and Jacques Maritain.

One of my concerns here is to bring together issues from American political and intellectual history with issues from American lay Catholic history, which are usually treated separately. Several fine studies of the new conservatism, by George Nash, John Diggins, Michael Miles, John Judis, and Melvin Thorne, have noted the Catholic component of the movement but have not integrated it into their analysis.[14] Conversely, most Catholic historians have until recently confined their studies to the church-related actions and writings of priests and bishops rather than the laity's religion-based actions in the secular world. Yet an important part of the story is the relative isolation of Catholic intellectuals and the relative subordination of the laity within the church until the 1950s, both of which ended in the 1960s. A brief consideration of recent Catholic historiography can clarify these issues.

Before the Second Vatican Council, American Catholic historiography was dominated by the history of the institutional church. Studies of bishops and their dioceses, their relations with Rome, and their organizational and financial problems received the lion's share of attention. Historians, most of them priests who shared the point of view of their predecessors, studied the Catholic laity much less closely except as its actions impinged on the hierarchy; they used the laity mainly as a statistical measure of population growth. The Catholic church in the United States remained a strongly centralized organization, dominated by powerful bishops. Catholic theology implicitly demoted the laity to a lesser status and regarded those in Holy Orders as nearer to God; Catholic historians followed suit.

Much Catholic theology of the early and mid-twentieth century explained and justified the claims of orthodoxy, to which clergy and laity alike should submit. Ironically the theology displayed less supernaturalism or mysticism than has been evident in some Catholic epochs and more orderly rationalism, just at a time when non-Catholic American intellectuals were starting to explore relativism, pragmatism, and existentialism.[15] The ahistorical assumptions of Catholic theology adversely influenced most Catholic historians. In the early twentieth century,

---

14. Nash, *Conservative Intellectual Movement*; Diggins, *Up from Communism*; Michael W. Miles, *The Odyssey of the American Right* (New York: Oxford University Press, 1980); Judis, *William F. Buckley, Jr.*; Melvin Thorne, *American Conservative Thought since World War II: The Core Ideas* (New York: Greenwood, 1990).

15. William Halsey, *The Survival of American Innocence* (Notre Dame, Ind.: University of Notre Dame Press, 1980), 8–19.

one commentator has noted, "Catholic historians were permitted to denounce as heretical those Catholic movements of the past that failed to anticipate subsequent doctrinal pronouncements." Worse, Catholic hagiographers, arguing from what a saint *should* have done in his or her lifetime, used pure deduction to write the "lives" of saints about whom they had no historical documentation.[16] This excessively rationalistic and ahistorical outlook served tolerably well for historians who confined themselves to recounting the story of institution-building, brick-and-mortar history, but it provided no framework for telling the history of American Catholic experience. The feelings and beliefs of laypeople, their actual experiences in contact with the non-Catholic population, and the ambiguities of American religious history went almost entirely unexplored.

American Catholic history entered a period of rapid change when Pope John XXIII summoned the Second Vatican Council and charged it with the task of *aggiornamento* (bringing the church up to date). The council devoted unprecedented attention to the laity. For the first time, lay status and married life were treated as vocations in their own right, of equal merit with the priesthood. The council also reconceptualized the church as a whole, defining it not by its hierarchy but democratically, as the people of God. The spirit of the council was a much-debated topic in the years that followed; experimental liturgy, debate on previously foreclosed topics such as contraception, and a new acknowledgment on the part of lay intellectuals that their church was historically conditioned influenced the ideas of Catholic historians. The council coincided with the first Catholic presidency and occurred at a time when the U.S. Catholic population in general was gaining in wealth, education, and social status. Although priests continued to play a dominant role in Catholic journals and universities, they no longer constituted the overwhelming majority of voices in either and have steadily yielded ground to the laity in the years since the council's close.[17]

Catholic historians, responding to the new mood and new self-understanding of the church and writing out of their own lay experi-

16. Eric Cochrane, "What Is Catholic Historiography?" *CHR* 61 (April 1975): 171.

17. On changes in American Catholic historiography, see Patrick Allitt, "A Big Catholic Monument," *Reviews in American History* 18 (Dec. 1990): 473–78. On the changing character of Catholic universities, see Robert Gannon, *Up to the Present: The Story of Fordham* (Garden City, N.Y.: Doubleday, 1967). Ross Hoffman discusses these changes in "Fordham Memoir" (unpublished manuscript in the form of letters to Gaetano Vincitorio, Aug. 13, 1973–Nov. 18, 1973, in the author's possession by courtesy of Mr. Vincitorio). On changes in Catholic intellectual life, see Philip Gleason, "In Search of Unity: American Catholic Thought, 1920–1960," *CHR* 65 (April 1979): 185–205.

ences, began to diversify the scope of their subject. David O'Brien, Philip Gleason, and Jay P. Dolan, for example, analyzed lay experience with more nuance than any predecessor; priest-historians such as James Hennesey, S.J., also abandoned some aspects of the old, clergy-centered institutional approach.[18] William Halsey and James T. Fisher wrote a new form of Catholic intellectual history which situated developments in Catholic thought alongside those of other American intellectuals, exploring their cross-fertilization rather than assuming a necessary antagonism or a hermetic mutual exclusion.[19] Their example is a model for much of what follows in this book.

In the 1990s the study of Catholic history, especially that of the last four decades, raises conceptual problems. In particular American Catholicism is no longer a clearly defined entity; its outlines have blurred in the years since Vatican II. In the 1940s and 1950s many Catholic scholars and journalists considered anything taking place within what they called the Catholic ghetto and any relations between it and the outside society to be fit subject matter. The ghetto provided a useful metaphor for a set of institutions and a distinctive way of life created partly by the prejudice of non-Catholics and partly by the shared needs and ritual requirements of Catholics themselves. It was especially appropriate when considering such aspects of Catholic self-segregation as the immense educational apparatus set up in parallel to that of the rest of society. But the metaphor could, if overused, become misleading. No other ghetto in European or American history contained tens of millions of inhabitants. No other ghetto was so geographically diverse; Catholics of the 1950s did not live in the limited, segregated enclaves of European Jewish ghetto tradition; neither did they suffer the legally supported segregation forced on U.S. blacks in their own ghettos. Moreover, Catholics misapplied the metaphor when they implied that their ghetto stood over against a homogeneous mainstream society. In fact, as Martin Marty has argued, no American in the 1950s could properly regard himself or herself as a member of the majority; the population consisted entirely of competing minorities, ethnic, religious, and political, each of which could claim for itself a ghetto status.

---

18. David O'Brien, *The Renewal of American Catholicism* (New York: Paulist Press, 1972); Philip Gleason, *The Conservative Reformers: German-American Catholics and the Social Order* (Notre Dame, Ind.: University of Notre Dame Press, 1968); Jay P. Dolan, *The American Catholic Experience: A History from Colonial Times to the Present* (Garden City, N.Y.: Doubleday, 1985); James Hennesey, S.J., *American Catholics: A History of the Roman Catholic Community in the United States* (New York: Oxford University Press, 1981).

19. Halsey, *Survival of American Innocence*; James T. Fisher, *The Catholic Counterculture in America, 1933–1962* (Chapel Hill: University of North Carolina Press, 1989).

Each might perceive its own ghettoization as unique, but the ubiquity of the phenomenon enjoins skepticism on subsequent historians.[20]

Nevertheless, I believe it is a defensible generalization to say that Catholics were a distinct component of the American population at least until the 1960s. Until then Catholics, whatever their differences, shared the sense of being members of an embattled minority in a more or less unfriendly environment. They may have been deluded in seeing their condition as exceptional and in perceiving a universal hostility from the outside world, but the fact that they did think in this way is itself an important historical datum. They also believed that their church alone spoke the truth of Christianity and offered hope of salvation; the pluralistic idea of multiple paths to salvation which is now so commonplace was, prior to Vatican II, condemned as the sin of indifferentism. When Catholics disputed one another, they often did so deferentially and circumspectly within the pages of Catholic journals, and they kept in clear sight the latent antagonism of their non-Catholic fellow citizens.

From the mid-1960s on, by contrast, on a wide range of issues, Catholic identity lost its determinative character. Anti-Catholicism as a respectable intellectual or social posture began to evaporate following the election of President Kennedy; ecumenism increased following Vatican II; and Christians of all varieties began to make alliances across denominational lines when they perceived common social or political interests. In the 1960s, for example, liberal Christians from all the churches, black and white, Protestant and Catholic, united behind the civil rights movement. In the late 1970s and 1980s, similarly, a coalition of evangelical Protestants and traditionalist Catholics worked together to protest legalized abortion. Under these conditions it becomes difficult for a historian to discuss "the Catholic position" on any issue, because Catholics themselves were voicing a wide diversity of opinions and often echoing the diverse opinions of their non-Catholic neighbors. Bishops and the Vatican Curia have tried to preserve a clearly defined orthodoxy, but it commands much less universal assent in the United States than it did before Vatican II. Likewise, the notion of the Catholic church as the people of God has enabled a wide variety of groups to claim that, even if the Vatican condemns their ideas, they are nevertheless voicing the sense of the people, and that the institutional church, rather than they themselves, is in error. The dispute over definitions has become acute. In the 1980s Pope John Paul II and the prefect

20. This issue is well treated by Martin Marty in "The Catholic Ghetto and All the Other Ghettos," *CHR* 68 (April 1982): 185–205.

of the Congregation for the Doctrine of the Faith, Cardinal Joseph Ratzinger, continued to claim an almost regal authority on political, moral, and ecclesiological questions and to treat Catholic laypeople throughout the world as their subjects. The U.S. episcopate, at the same time, shied away from such definition. It is noteworthy that the bishops' 1983 pastoral letter on nuclear weapons and the 1986 pastoral letter on the economy were addressed not simply to Catholics but to all Americans. It is noteworthy too that they made no formal claim on all Catholic consciences but left scope for a dissent that was not slow to develop within the Catholic community.

The gradual erosion of a Catholic intellectual distinctiveness and the declining appeal to theological categories and to the natural law tradition were observed at the time. In 1968, for example, Philip Gleason argued that a "crisis of Americanization" had arrived in which the blending of Catholics with the general population had caused Catholic intellectuals the same problems their non-Catholic counterparts had long endured. Contradicting the then-current vogue for "relevant" intellectual work, Gleason foresaw more problems than benefits for Catholics: "Nowadays the Church is being called upon to plunge into the 'mainstream' and make itself 'relevant.' Presumably it would not become especially relevant if it did nothing more than float with the tide. Yet spokesmen for the 'mainstream' policy have little to say about the distinctive additions the Church might make to the mainstream. Nothing that characterized the Church in its 'ghetto' days would seem to be acceptable."[21] Gleason noted that Catholic scholarly organizations, one by one, were questioning their own raison d'etre, with more militant spirits even arguing that to be a *Catholic* historian, sociologist, or philosopher, falsified or vitiated one's work into mere apologetics from the outset.[22]

Catholic identity, in sum, has become problematical since the mid-1960s and has made Catholic history a task whose boundaries and purposes are no longer as self-evident as they appeared to be forty years ago. For a history of Catholic laypeople, who were not constrained by the vows and the institutions of the clergy, the problems are still more acute. Catholic historians, aware of these difficulties, continue to debate their role, their methods, and the changing character of their discipline. One contributor to the debate, Eric Cochrane, noted in 1975 that the history of Catholicism and Catholic history are two different things. Anyone could study the history of Catholics, he

---

21. Philip Gleason, "The Crisis of Americanization," in *Catholicism in America*, ed. Gleason (New York: Harper and Row, 1970), 151.
22. Ibid., 141–49.

said, but only active members of the church could bring the assumptions of their faith to the study of that and other historical subjects. Catholic historians, he believed, still had important duties to fulfill and lessons to teach to other historians: taking theology and faith seriously as sources of human inspiration, refusing to obliterate behind "economic curves and social structures" human individuality as an agency of historical change, resisting the idea that religious motives could be "explained away" by "social, psychological, or economic determinants." Finally, Cochrane would resist the common twentieth-century heresy of nationalism. "As a member of a universal, multinational church, he [the Catholic historian] will never let himself be trapped within the confines of an 'American' or a 'German' school of historiography."[23] Catholic historians should also struggle to convey to their coreligionists, theologians above all, the sense that they live *in* history, because ahistoricity had been the curse of Catholic intellectual life for too long.[24] What is striking about Cochrane's program is its modesty; he conscientiously avoids all the strenuous claims for the truth of Catholic faith which were de rigeur for Catholic scholars before 1960. The program he presents will sound reasonable in almost all historians' ears; it is noncontroversial almost to the point of being anodyne, part of the Catholic scholars' retreat from the days when their sole and exclusive truth was cast in bronze.

To sum up: in writing the history of lay Catholic intellectuals in the American conservative movement I hope to show how a group of men and women, growing to maturity in the years before Vatican II, learned a pattern of attitudes and ideas from the Catholic church and carried them into their analysis of the wider American society. They regarded their faith not just as an accident of birth—many of them, indeed, were converts—but as central to their lives. They found in the intellectual traditions of their faith a way of thinking about the political, social, and economic environment in which they lived, and they believed that their faith offered solutions to their country's most pressing foreign and domestic crises. Most were "assimilationist" by disposition, addressing their ideas not simply to other Catholics but to Americans at large, whom they hoped to influence.

Despite the centrality of their faith, they were not, of course, merely Catholics. They were also citizens of the various states, holders of particular professional outlooks (professors, journalists, editors), and members of distinct generations whose educational formation had

---

23. Cochrane, "What Is Catholic Historiography?" 185–86.
24. Ibid., 188.

taken place under differing historical circumstances. In much of their work they voiced convictions that many non-Catholic conservatives, secular and religious, could echo more or less unchanged. My aim is to show how they approached their work *as Catholics* and to show that as the 1960s advanced it became progressively more difficult to isolate the Catholic element in much of that work.

Part of the tension and much of the complexity of this book are attributable to its proximity to the transformations that so suddenly exposed a long tradition of assumptions and explanatory devices to challenge or brushed them aside as inadequate. The nature of Catholicism itself, once widely believed inside and outside the church to be an unchanging essence, suddenly became a subject of dispute, as did many verities of the American political tradition. The fragmentation of Catholic conservatism, then, is part of a wider story: the transformation of American political, intellectual, and religious life in the 1960s and 1970s.

1

American Catholicism in the 1950s

The Catholic church presented a monolithic image to the rest of the nation in the years before Vatican II. Cardinal Francis Spellman of New York was then the most important figure in the American church: his chancery in New York was nicknamed "the powerhouse"; his influence over Catholic voters made him a man to be courted and revered by politicians; and he was one of a handful of bishops in the world to enjoy the confidence and have the ear of Pope Pius XII.[1] Vocations to the priesthood were plentiful; seminaries and convents were expanding; churches and parochial schools, Catholic colleges, and hospitals were all increasing to record numbers.[2] This was the period, as Will Herberg observed in his classic sociological study *Protestant, Catholic, Jew,* when the (white) population of the United States was still divided into the three principal blocs named in his title. Of the three, the Catholic bloc was the most homogeneous and most conscientious in its religious observance. Ethnic tensions among Poles, Germans, Italians, Irish, and Slavs which had riven American Catholicism in the early twentieth century were diminishing, while religious distinctiveness and high levels of endogamy remained.[3]

Preservation of Catholic unity was possible for a time after World

---

1. On Spellman, see Robert I. Gannon, *The Cardinal Spellman Story* (New York: Pocket Books, 1963); and John Cooney, *The American Pope: The Life and Times of Francis Cardinal Spellman* (New York: New York Times Books, 1984).

2. Jay P. Dolan, *The American Catholic Experience: A History from Colonial Times to the Present* (Garden City, N.Y.: Doubleday, 1985), 384–417.

3. Will Herberg, *Protestant, Catholic, Jew: An Essay in American Religious Sociology* (Garden City, N.Y.: Doubleday, 1955).

War II because of the hierarchical and clerical structure of the church and because of a long history of lay deference to the clergy. On questions of faith and morals Catholics were expected to regard the hierarchy, headed by an infallible pontiff, as beyond challenge. In the United States most laypeople, though theoretically entitled to express diverse views on other matters, had historically formed their opinions on the basis of church teaching and had respected and obeyed the declarations of their bishops and priests.[4] Characteristically, when Pope Pius XI encouraged greater lay activism in the 1930s under the program called Catholic Action, he expected the laypeople working in such movements to be guided by their priests.[5] The Legion of Decency, influential in U.S. film and theater censorship from the 1930s to the early 1960s, was the best-known example of Catholic Action.[6] The Catholic Worker movement, founded in the early 1930s by a lay convert, Dorothy Day, was very much the exception and involved only a tiny number of lay activists.[7]

Sociological factors, as well as the clerical tradition, contributed to a high degree of Catholic homogeneity in midcentury America. The majority of the Catholic population was urban and working class; most voted Democratic; most had attended Catholic schools for part or all of their education. There they had learned the importance of blending fidelity to their church with demonstrative loyalty to the nation. They fought vigorously when the country went to war, sometimes in response to direct episcopal instruction.[8] In consequence, Catholics were unlikely to declare themselves conscientious objectors during World War II; a significant Catholic isolationism, based among German and Irish Americans (who both had reasons for not wanting to help British interests) evaporated after Pearl Harbor.[9] Thousands of young Catholics volunteered to fight and earned distinguished war records. William F. Buckley, Jr., Catholic leader of the new conservatism, was never

4. On the power of midcentury bishops and the deference of the laity, see Edward Kantowicz, *Corporation Sole: Cardinal Mundelein and Chicago Catholicism* (Notre Dame, Ind.: University of Notre Dame Press, 1983).

5. Dolan, *American Catholic Experience*, 408–9.

6. Murray Schumach, *The Face on the Cutting Room Floor: The Story of Movie and TV Censorship* (New York: William Morrow, 1964), 84–93.

7. James T. Fisher, *The Catholic Counterculture in America, 1933–1962* (Chapel Hill: University of North Carolina Press, 1989), 25–69.

8. On clerical incitements to enlist and fight during World War I, see Ray Abrams, *Preachers Present Arms* (Scottsdale, Pa.: Herald Press, 1969), 73.

9. George Weigel, S.J., *Tranquillitas Ordinis: The Present Failure and the Future Promise of American Catholic Thought on War and Peace* (New York: Oxford University Press, 1987), 55–67. On the small band of Catholic conscientious objectors, see Gordon Zahn, "Catholic Conscientious Objectors in the United States" and "The Social Thought of the Catholic Conscientious Objector," in *War, Conscience, and Dissent*, ed. Zahn (New York: Hawthorne, 1967).

shipped overseas, but he went straight from school to an army commission in the last days of the fighting.[10] Anthony Bouscaren, another of the Catholic conservative intellectuals, flew missions as a pilot with the Marine Corps in the Pacific war and won multiple decorations.[11] After the war, many Catholic veterans, taking advantage of the GI Bill, gained higher education, better jobs than their parents, and upward social mobility, diversifying the sociological profile of American Catholicism as they did so.[12] Herein lay a source of later fragmentation.

Homogeneity was also assured in part by the presence of a vocal tradition of anti-Catholicism, against which most Catholics believed they must close ranks. After more than three centuries as a religious minority, facing recurrent hostility and persecution, the American Catholic community still felt embattled. In a nation whose history began with the adventures of militant Protestant settlers, most Catholics still felt the sting of old religious controversies and prejudice.[13] Indeed, in the late 1940s and early 1950s Paul Blanshard was writing influential attacks on Catholicism. In *American Freedom and Catholic Power* (1949), he cast doubt on Catholics' patriotic loyalty, claiming that it was compromised by their allegiance to the pope. He also charged that the Catholic hierarchy, like the Kremlin overlords, practiced a form of brainwashing on laypeople, whom he considered incapable of free thought.[14]

Anti-Catholicism—or resistance to Catholic priests, which Catholics interpreted as religious hostility—was apparent at many levels. Archbishop Spellman of New York and Eleanor Roosevelt got into a well-publicized squabble in 1948 when she accused him of bigotry on the issues of church-state separation and the use of taxes to support Catholic schools.[15] President Harry S Truman's decision to send an ambassador to the Vatican in 1951 in place of his personal presidential envoy, Myron Taylor, who had been there since 1939, occasioned a flurry of protests, even though his nominee, General Mark Clark, was a war

10. John Judis, *William F. Buckley, Jr., Patron Saint of the Conservatives* (New York: Simon and Schuster, 1988), 46–51.

11. *American Catholic Who's Who* (Grosse Pointe, Mich.: Walter Romig, 1964), 32.

12. Andrew Greeley, *The American Catholic: A Social Portrait* (New York: Basic, 1977), 50–68.

13. On the history of American anti-Catholicism, see Ray Allen Billington, *The Protestant Crusade, 1800–1860* (New York: Macmillan, 1938); and Barbara Welter, "From Maria Monk to Paul Blanshard," in *Uncivil Religion: Interreligious Hostility in America,* ed. Robert Bellah and Frederick Greenspan (New York: Crossroads, 1987), 43–59.

14. Paul Blanshard, *American Freedom and Catholic Power* (Boston: Beacon Press, 1949). See also Blanshard, *Communism, Democracy, and Catholic Power* (Boston: Beacon Press, 1951).

15. Cooney, *American Pope,* 177–85.

hero and a non-Catholic. Alarmed, the president backed off.[16] The presidential candidacy of John F. Kennedy in 1960 brought these issues to a head. Two ad hoc organizations, the National Conference of Citizens for Religious Freedom and Protestants and Other Americans United for Separation of Church and State, whose members included Norman Vincent Peale, Billy Graham, and Episcopal bishop James Pike, opposed the Catholic presidential candidate with a display of closely reasoned First Amendment arguments.

Because of this mix of politics and religious prejudice, many Catholic intellectuals in the 1950s found themselves repeatedly combating the accusation, implied or spoken, of divided loyalties. Candidate Kennedy was forced to do likewise before gaining the White House. In a speech to the Ministerial Assocation of Greater Houston in the fall of 1960 he declared: "I do not accept the right of any ecclesiastical official to tell me what to do in the sphere of my public responsibility as an elected official."[17] Thus Catholics found it necessary to reaffirm their political allegiance to the United States as well as their religious devotion to Rome. Some angrily denied the charge of disloyalty and made counter-accusations of bigotry; others, disliking confrontation, sought to explain away anti-Catholicism as a misunderstanding to be mitigated by calm discussion and the clarification of ideas on all sides.[18] Neither did any Catholic intellectuals accept the charge that they were "brainwashed" by the Vatican. They insisted instead that, though they voluntarily submitted to church guidance on many matters, there was a vast realm where, like all citizens, they must remain true to their consciences, exercise personal discretion, moral judgment, and political prudence. The church certainly trained their consciences, they said, but did not vitiate them.[19]

Given the sense of siege which public opposition generated, Catholic writers spent much of the 1950s trying to minimize their internal dis-

16. F. William O'Brien, "General Clark's Nomination as Ambassador to the Vatican: American Reaction," *CHR* 44 (Jan. 1959): 421–39.

17. John Cogley, *Catholic America* (New York: Dial Press, 1973), 118. Cogley helped draft the speech.

18. See, for example, John Cogley, "Call It 'the Thing,'" *C*, Nov. 9, 1951, 110, taking the indignant approach: Catholics "can remind non-Catholics that they often speak foolishly and intemperately about Catholic intentions. They often talk down to us as if we didn't know what it was to be an American, as if we were outsiders who had no appreciation or understanding of the traditions of the country, which is ours as well as theirs." See Bishop Robert Dwyer, "The American Laity," *CM* 53 (March 1955): 129–36, taking the conciliatory approach and advocating lay activism as an antidote to Blanshard's allegations.

19. See, for example, John Courtney Murray, S.J., "Catholics in America—a Creative Minority?" *CM* 53 (Oct. 1955): 590–97. Murray counseled that the Catholic population was so well established in America that it need no longer worry about Blanshard and his ilk. It was more important to cultivate intellectual life.

agreements. The disadvantage of keeping quiet in public was, of course, that it seemed to confirm non-Catholics' fears of a monolithic church. But in those days before Catholics looked favorably on ecumenism, it seemed the surest way to present a vision of unity and assurance against the perceived hostility of the outside world. Catholic authors at midcentury who disputed one another on political questions, accordingly, often remarked on the importance of preserving an internal comity lest non-Catholic adversaries exploit their latent divisions. By the end of the 1950s, however, maintaining a united front was becoming difficult for many Catholic writers because they disagreed profoundly on major political, economic, and cultural issues. The "monolithic" church Blanshard had thought he descried in the 1950s was already vulnerable to centrifugal forces that would greatly intensify in the 1960s.

CATHOLIC ANTICOMMUNISM

After the war, the issue of anticommunism provided the perfect rallying point for Catholics seeking to demonstrate their right to a central place in the national community, especially when the Korean War signaled open conflict against a Communist enemy. Aware that anti-Catholic nativists had often regarded them as un-American, some Catholics now took pleasure in declaring themselves champions of a "one hundred percent American" campaign against political leftists, rarely Catholic by birth, whose Americanism was now open to question.[20] J. Edgar Hoover's Federal Bureau of Investigation, a chief arm of the domestic anti-Communist movement, recruited heavily at Catholic colleges; Catholic journals supported the search for "security risks" in government; and the most famous Communist hunter of the era, Senator Joseph McCarthy, was himself Catholic and won widespread Catholic support.[21] His campaign and those of such other leading Communist hunters as Richard Nixon were encouraged and aided by Father John Cronin of the National Catholic Welfare Conference.[22] The only defense of McCarthyism that was even partially intellectually

20. On the history of American Catholic anticommunism, see Donald Crosby, *God, Church, and Flag: Senator Joseph R. McCarthy and the Catholic Church, 1950–1957* (Chapel Hill: University of North Carolina Press, 1978).

21. Vincent P. De Santis, "American Catholics and McCarthyism," *CHR* 51 (April 1965): 1–30. De Santis adds that Catholic support for McCarthy was by no means unanimous and that on a political issue of this kind the church as a body took no position.

22. On Cronin, see Thomas W. Spalding, *The Premier See: A History of the Catholic Archdiocese of Baltimore, 1789–1989* (Baltimore: Johns Hopkins University Press, 1989), 377–78, 434–36.

plausible was William Buckley's second book, cowritten with his broth-er-in-law L. Brent Bozell, *McCarthy and His Enemies.*[23]

Buckley is much the best known of the Catholic new conservatives, already the subject of several biographies.[24] His father had made a fortune in Mexican and Venezuelan oil drilling and was able to shelter his children from hardship throughout the Great Depression. Living principally in Sharon, Connecticut, the Buckleys, a large family, trav-eled extensively through Europe and the Americas, enjoying the ame-nities and privileges of wealth. Their devout Catholicism set them apart from their neighbors and generated a fierce sense of family loyalty comparable to that of the Kennedys, America's best-known rich Catho-lic family of the age. Young William Buckley, Jr., born in 1925, was drafted into the army straight from high school and served as a second lieutenant of infantry. World War II ended before he could be shipped to the battle zones, however, and from demobilization he entered Yale University.

At Yale, Buckley became influential on campus, a member of the debating team and, by the end of his junior year, editor of the *Yale Daily News.* The influx of veterans overburdened the faculty, and when he was still only a freshman, Buckley was hired as an instructor in Spanish, learned during his family's travels. As a student he became increasingly dissatisfied with the way in which most professors treated religion: few had any praise for Christianity, and even those who did emphasized doubt and ambiguity more than orthodoxy. He was no better pleased with the Keynesian, New Deal "collectivist" emphasis in the Yale economics department, and after graduation he wrote *God and Man at Yale,* a scorching attack on his alma mater for its neglect of orthodox faith and classical economics. It began with a ringing declara-tion: "I . . . believe that the duel between Christianity and atheism is the most important in the world. I further believe that the struggle between individualism and collectivism is the same struggle repro-duced at another level."[25] Publication of this book in 1951 brought him instant notoriety among American liberals and laid the foundations for his reputation as conservative young Turk, which, amply cultivated,

23. William F. Buckley, Jr., and L. Brent Bozell, *McCarthy and His Enemies* (Chicago: Henry Regnery, 1954).

24. See, for example, Charles Lam Markmann, *The Buckleys: A Family Examined* (New York: William Morrow, 1973); Mark Royden Winchell, *William F. Buckley, Jr.* (Boston: Twayne, 1984); Judis, *William F. Buckley, Jr.* The following summary is based on Judis's book and on my own interviews with Buckley, New York City, Jan. 6 and Sept. 29, 1986.

25. William F. Buckley, Jr., *God and Man at Yale: The Superstitions of "Academic Freedom"* (Chi-cago: Henry Regnery, 1951), xii–xiii.

would stay with him for the next fifteen years.[26] He spent a year working for the Central Intelligence Agency in Mexico, apparently unevent-
fully, but a love of public debate soon brought him back to the United
States and to McCarthyism, the biggest domestic controversy of the
early 1950s.

Brent Bozell at Yale had at first seemed an even more promising
student than Buckley. Bozell had been raised in Nebraska by Episcopalian parents who sent him to a Jesuit high school. He then served two
years in the Merchant Marine during the war.[27] On shore leave in San
Francisco in the last year of the war, he met his father, who had traveled
to the West Coast to announce his intention of converting to Catholicism. Bozell had independently reached the same conclusion; he too
planned to convert. His father died unexpectedly before carrying out
his resolve, but in 1946 Bozell formally joined the Catholic church.
During their student years together William Buckley introduced Bozell
to his sister Patricia; a romance ensued, and they were married in
1949, as Bozell began law school at Yale. From there Bozell went briefly
to a law practice in San Francisco, but his chief interest was conservative politics, and when he learned of an opening on Senator Joseph
McCarthy's staff, he returned to the East Coast to take it. After aiding
McCarthy's defense against a Senate censure resolution, Bozell stayed
on the senator's staff as a speech writer.

McCarthy and His Enemies, accordingly, benefited both from its authors' conservative convictions and from their personal acquaintance
with its principal subject. The book justified McCarthy's swaggering
attacks on government servants with the argument that even if many
of these men and women were not actual traitors, as McCarthy often
claimed, they were at least "security risks" who did not deserve their
privileged and strategically sensitive positions in government. Buckley
and Bozell took it as axiomatic that the United States was at war with
communism and that all Communists and their sympathizers were
ipso facto enemy agents. Against them, Americans must be resolute,
and this was a point, they believed, that McCarthy had grasped better
than his critics. Procedural protections of free speech should not be
extended even to those who would nullify that right in the name of
communism.

American "conformity" was a source of regret to many liberal intellectuals in the 1950s. David Riesman's influential book *The Lonely*

26. Liberal reviewers took the book as a serious affront. See, for example, McGeorge Bundy,
"The Attack on Yale," *Atlantic* 188 (Nov. 1951): 50–52.

27. This biographical summary is based on my telephone interview with L. Brent Bozell,
Feb. 26, 1991.

Crowd, for example, lamented the spread of social conformity and the displacement of the strong "inner-directed" personality by the pliant "other-directed" personality.[28] Buckley and Bozell, to the contrary, lauded conformity, arguing that if a society is to cohere, conformity to agreed-upon values must be upheld, even sometimes by the use of force:

> What we call the "institutions" of a society are nothing but the values that society has settled on over the years and now defends by sanctions. Most of us take a fierce pride in our society's institutions— quite reasonably, since it is our institutions that make us what we are. But it is well to remember that in exhibiting this pride, we are applauding just so many manifestations of conformity which were brought about by the practice of "thought control."[29]

The idiom here was Catholic, as was the authors' argument that Mc-Carthyism, by protecting the nation from an atheistic communism, was thereby promoting, rather than repressing, freedom of conscience.

Not all American Catholics supported McCarthyism; the major divide in the Catholic population was between anti-Communists who supported McCarthy and anti-Communists who criticized him. Historian Donald Crosby, S.J., has shown that Catholics could not present a united front on this issue. They argued the merits of McCarthyism and denounced each other as either "soft on communism" or "anti-democratic." It is significant, however, that most non-Catholic observers overlooked this disagreement and attributed pro-McCarthy sympathies to Catholics as a whole. Here is an instance in which the perception of unified Catholicism overrode empirical evidence to the contrary.[30]

For many non-Catholic Americans in the post–World War II era, militant anticommunism of this sort was a novelty. The "red scare" following World War I was almost thirty years past by then and the issue of communism had received only episodic attention in the intervening years.[31] President Franklin D. Roosevelt had granted the Soviet Union diplomatic recognition in 1933; interest in the Russian experiment and socialist ideas was widespread among intellectuals in the New Deal era; and the Soviet Union did not then appear to have

28. David Riesman, Nathan Glazer, and Reuel Denney, *The Lonely Crowd: A Study of the Changing American Character* (New Haven: Yale University Press, 1950).

29. Buckley and Bozell, *McCarthy and His Enemies*, 323.

30. Crosby, *God, Church, and Flag*, 228–44.

31. On the history of American anticommunism prior to the 1950s, see Richard M. Fried, *Nightmare in Red: The McCarthy Era in Perspective* (New York: Oxford University Press), 3–36.

an aggressively expansionist foreign policy. Moreover, in the interests of the wartime alliance with Stalin against Hitler, American war propagandists had portrayed the Russians as heroic allies and their leader as a determined, sincere, and patriotic man. As diplomatic relations between the victors worsened in the years after 1945, American images of Stalin changed rapidly; by 1950 most Americans regarded Stalin and communism with almost the same horror they had reserved for Hitler and nazism five years before.[32]

For American Catholics in the late 1940s, by contrast, zealous anticommunism was nothing new; Catholic schools and colleges had been teaching it for the best part of a century, and the wartime alliance with Stalin had not effaced it. In the late nineteenth century Pope Leo XIII had denounced socialism as an atheist and materialist creed that perverted natural law and made war against Christianity. Leo XIII's encyclical *Rerum Novarum* (1891), even as it criticized the social consequences of the industrial revolution, condemned socialism unequivocally and denied the acceptability of its proffered solution.[33] Pius XI reiterated the condemnation in another encyclical on social affairs, *Quadragesimo Anno* (1931), all the more vigorously as he now had the evidence of the Russian Revolution to cite. Catholic newspapers protested President Roosevelt's decision to open diplomatic relations with the Soviet Union in 1933 and welcomed an even sterner anti-Communist encyclical from Pius XI in 1937, *Divini Redemptoris*. They also vigorously protested Roosevelt's closeness to the anticlerical and leftist Mexican regime of the 1930s.[34]

The Spanish Civil War (1936–1939) intensified Communist-Catholic antagonism. Some American volunteers, many of them Communists, fought for the republic in the Abraham Lincoln Brigade. Most American Catholics, on the other hand, supported General Francisco Franco's war against the republic because they saw Franco as the savior of the Catholic church. Patricia Buckley Bozell recalled attending a dance when she was twelve years old and being astonished to find out that her Protestant contemporaries were learning to praise the republic and criticize Franco while she was learning just the opposite.[35] This faith in Franco was strengthened by the knowledge that the Soviet Union and Communist volunteers from other parts of the world were fighting

---

32. Some Americans other than Catholics (many fundamentalists, for example) remained anti-Communist during World War II. See George Sirgiovanni, *An Undercurrent of Suspicion: Anti-Communism in America during World War II* (New Brunswick: Transaction, 1990).

33. Dolan, *American Catholic Experience,* 334–36.

34. David O'Brien, *American Catholics and Social Reform* (New York: Oxford University Press, 1968), 82.

35. Telephone interview with Patricia Buckley Bozell, March 9, 1991.

for the republican side; indeed, Catholics treated Franco as the George Washington of Spain and interpreted his war by analogy with the American War of Independence. As the Catholic historian David O'Brien observes, "To the leaders of American Catholicism" the Spanish Civil War seemed a "clear confrontation of Christianity and civilization with Communism and barbarism."[36]

The degree to which the Catholic church supported fascism in the 1930s and 1940s remains a controverted issue, but it is indubitable, as O'Brien remarks, that when the church was forced to choose between fascism and communism, it chose fascism, which at least "allowed the Church to exist as a corporate teaching body," whereas communism represented "the ultimate expression of modern man's revolt against God, the Church, and civilization." Communism persecuted Christianity and tried to extirpate religion completely.[37] In general, fortunately, American Catholics were not obliged to make such a choice. Rather, they opposed all forms of totalitarianism, Communist and Nazi alike and, when war came in 1941, fought against the Axis as patriotic Americans. Catholic journals in the war years never waxed effusive about the Soviet Union, Stalin, or communism, however, despite the Grand Alliance. On the eve of the Soviet-American wartime alliance, indeed, Archbishop Francis Beckman of Dubuque warned that "the Christ-haters of Moscow and their international brethren . . . may well take note of the Church Militant when she becomes aroused."[38] George Sirgiovanni aptly summarizes the Catholic view: "Anyone who admired Communism had to hate religion, because the Communist millennium could not be achieved so long as organized religion endured." Hence, at the war's end, when public opinion in the United States was undergoing a jolting reorientation away from sympathy for Russia, the Catholic population was already fully prepared.[39]

The politics of anticommunism in the decade between 1946 and 1956 aroused bitter feelings on all sides.[40] Catholic intellectuals were all but unanimous in regarding communism as philosophically indefensible and the Communist movement as a ruthless international conspiracy bent on world conquest. Although they differed on techniques for fighting communism at home, with such liberal Catholic journals as

36. O'Brien, *American Catholics and Social Reform,* 86.
37. Ibid., 85, 82. On the associated issue of American Catholics' attitudes toward Italian fascism, see John P. Diggins, *Mussolini and Fascism: The View from America* (Princeton: Princeton University Press, 1972), 182–203.
38. Spalding, *Premier See,* 362–63.
39. Sirgiovanni, *Undercurrent of Suspicion,* 151.
40. See Fried, *Nightmare in Red; David Caute, The Great Fear: The Anti-Communist Purge under Truman and Eisenhower* (New York: Simon and Schuster, 1978).

Commonweal and *America* deploring Senator McCarthy while most of the diocesan press ardently supported him, no Catholics questioned the mendacity of communism itself. In that period, moreover, many Catholic writers regarded "reformed" Communists who had broken free of the party and now wanted to help destroy it as key figures in the struggle for the world, for knowing communism from the inside, they alone knew the full measure of its danger. If they were willing to name the names of their former comrades and expose all vestiges of Communist activity in the United States, they should be treated as heroes. Informers, under these circumstances, should be honored rather than vilified.[41]

The most famous apostate from communism was Whittaker Chambers. In 1948 he accused Alger Hiss, head of the Carnegie Foundation and once a ranking New Deal civil servant, of cooperating with him in a Soviet spy ring during the 1930s before Chambers left the party in 1937. Hiss was convicted of perjury in the resulting court case in 1950 despite his unwavering pleas of innocence.[42] Chambers's autobiography paints the struggle between communism and Western civilization in apocalyptic colors and warns that the ultimate conflict between them is imminent.[43] William Buckley found Chambers's brilliantly morbid vision inspirational, and Chambers became an occasional contributor to Buckley's *National Review* in the late 1950s.[44]

Chambers, though sympathetic to Catholicism as a bulwark of Western civilization, did not belong to the Catholic church. By contrast, another reformed Communist of the period, Louis Budenz, split from the Communist party and was received into the Catholic church on the same dramatic day, October 10, 1945, with much media fanfare. The proximate instrument of his reconversion was Monsignor Fulton Sheen, already a radio personality, renowned for bringing the journalist Heywood Broun and the industrialist Henry Ford II into the church. Budenz had been raised Catholic in Indiana but had left the church when he married a divorcee. He worked in the trade union movement in the 1920s, joined the Communist party in 1933, and served as an editor of its newspaper, the *Daily Worker*, throughout World War II. He gradually turned away from communism during the war and back to

41. In other parts of the population the opposite view prevailed and has continued to prevail. See, for example, Victor Navasky, *Naming Names* (New York: Penguin, 1980).

42. Allen Weinstein, *Perjury: The Hiss-Chambers Case* (New York: Knopf, 1978).

43. Whittaker Chambers, *Witness* (New York: Random House, 1952).

44. George Nash, *The Conservative Intellectual Movement in America since 1945* (New York: Basic, 1976), 102–6. After Chambers's death Buckley gathered his letters from the anti-Communist hero and published them as William F. Buckley, Jr., ed., *Odyssey of a Friend: Whittaker Chambers' Letters to William F. Buckley, Jr., 1954–1961* (New York: Putnam, 1969).

the church of his youth. On rejoining the church after a period of calculated deception of his Communist colleagues, he at once took up, by prearrangement, a professorship of economics at Notre Dame and settled down to write his autobiography, *This Is My Story* (1947). The book is written in the style of a sinner's confession, told when he is confident of his return to grace. Each set piece describes how Budenz acted as a Communist and how, as a Catholic, he *should* have acted. Every episode displays the supremacy of the church and denounces the wickedness of communism.[45] It was acclaimed a minor masterpiece by much of the Catholic press; one reviewer, apparently untroubled by its self-laudatory style, mentioned Budenz's "engaging humility" and said the book portrayed "a simple, straightforward idealist who writes without rancor toward anyone, and with especial sympathy for former comrades whose eyes have not yet been opened." Its depiction of communism was praiseworthy, the reviewer added, because it showed communism to be "utterly inhuman, in its indifference to justice, to mercy, to religion, even to logic."[46]

In 1947 Budenz became a professor of economics at Fordham University but spent much of his time between 1946 and 1952 testifying as an anti-Communist witness for the House Committee on Un-American Activities, for McCarthy's Senate Subcommittee on Internal Security, and in the Smith Act trial of the Communist party's leadership. Unlike McCarthy, who usually kept his religion in the background, Budenz frequently made explicit links in his testimony between Catholicism and anti-Communism. He wrote three more books, expanding his revelations about the workings of the Communist party, whose "party line" was always set by Moscow. Budenz emphasized that to treat American communism as an indigenous reform movement was a fatal error. Ironically, he reasoned that the accusation so often fallaciously made against the Catholic church—that it was the subversive agency of a foreign power—must be made in all seriousness against communism.[47] Budenz contributed to the tensions of the era by explaining to jurors in the Smith Act case *Dennis v. United States* (1949), that Communists often used "Aesopian" language, cloaking their real intentions in benign-sounding fables and even declaring mendaciously

45. Louis Budenz, *This Is My Story* (New York: McGraw-Hill, 1947). On Budenz, see also Herbert L. Packer, *Ex-Communist Witnesses: Four Studies in Fact Finding* (Stanford, Calif.: Stanford University Press, 1962), 121–77.

46. Joseph McSorley, untitled review of *This Is My Story*, in CW 165 (April 1947): 86–87.

47. Louis Budenz, *Men without Faces: The Communist Conspiracy in the USA* (New York: Harper, 1950); Budenz, *The Cry is Peace* (Chicago: Henry Regnery, 1952); Budenz, *The Techniques of Communism* (Chicago: Henry Regnery, 1954).

that their policy was the exact opposite of what it was in fact.[48] Budenz was a key witness in the case, in which eleven leaders of the American Communist party were convicted and imprisoned for conspiracy. He also played a role in the search for State Department "culprits" for the Chinese Revolution of 1949 and accused two State Department analysts, Owen Lattimore and Philip Jessup, of being "conscious agents of the Communist conspiracy."[49]

Anti-McCarthyite intellectuals hated Budenz. The Protestant journal *Christian Century*, for example, often home to anti-Catholic sentiments in the 1940s and 1950s, noted sourly: "It is not very surprising that a man who has been disillusioned about one totalitarian system which makes lofty claims as the defender of 'true freedom' by regimentation should seek refuge in another."[50] Columnist Joseph Alsop wrote a long article exposing fallacies in much of Budenz's testimony in the Lattimore case, and accusing him of lying.[51] Widely regarded as a cynical opportunist, a paid "professional witness" for anti-Communists, Budenz conspicuously retained the admiration of nearly all the Catholic press throughout the decade following his conversion and became a widely syndicated columnist in the diocesan press on cold war issues. On Budenz's behalf, for example, a furious Catholic author refuted Alsop's case in *Catholic World* and raised the familiar McCarthyite countercharge: If Alsop is defending accused Communists, maybe he's a Communist too.[52] The only prominent Catholic to attack Budenz was Senator Dennis Chavez (a Democrat from New Mexico), who accused him of using the cross of Christ as a "club" to beat his political adversaries and the church as a "shield and cloak" of false sanctity to hide his lies. Many Catholic journals and spokesmen reacted indignantly against Chavez, one calling him a "modern pharisee" and another declaring that his attack on Budenz was "unspeakably low."[53]

Catholic anticommunism was not confined to intellectuals; it also took on the characteristics of a popular, semireligious movement. The apparition of the Virgin Mary to a group of Portuguese children in 1917 (Our Lady of Fatima) to warn against the Russian Revolution was perhaps the first supernatural event of the cold war. But in 1950 a Catholic farmer's wife in Wisconsin reported that she too had been visited by the Blessed Virgin Mary with a stern message about the

48. Navasky, *Naming Names*, 31–32.
49. Caute, *Great Fear*, 318–19.
50. Editorial, "From Communist to Catholic," *Christian Century*, Oct. 17, 1945, 1180.
51. Joseph Alsop, "The Strange Case of Louis Budenz," *Atlantic* 189 (April 1952): 29–33.
52. Edward Heffron, "Alsop's Fables," *CW* 178 (Jan. 1954): 267–72.
53. Crosby, *God, Cross, and Flag*, 60–62.

danger of communism and the need to combat it with prayer. Despite skepticism from the hierarchy, thousands of pilgrims and curiosity seekers gathered to witness Mary Van Hoof receiving further intelligences from Our Lady of Necedah. Continuing a practice begun during World War II, some Catholic communities arranged novenas and retreats in which prayers were directed to the overthrow of communism and the conversion of the Russian people.[54]

As with the Spanish Civil War in the 1930s, so with the travail of Vietnam in the 1950s and early 1960s, many American Catholics understood the war as a fight to save the Christian Vietnamese from atheistic communism. The fact that Ngo Dinh Diem, leader of South Vietnam after the Geneva partition agreement of 1954, was Catholic accounts for much of his popularity among American Catholics in subsequent years. One such defender was Dr. Tom Dooley, a midwestern Catholic whose rise to fame coincided with the dawning of American awareness of Vietnam.[55] As a young navy doctor, aged only twenty-six, Dooley had the job of caring for Vietnamese refugees trying to escape from Haiphong after the Geneva agreement divided Vietnam into two temporary zones. Many of the two million refugees who fled the Communist-dominated northern zone were Catholics, Dooley noted, who had brought rosaries and crucifixes among their few poor belongings. At his camp one tent was reserved as a church, where the refugees "turned to the Mother of God, to the Blessed Virgin of Fatima," to pray for deliverance from their Communist persecutors.[56] The doctor's selfless and unstinting work with suffering Asians, first in Vietnam and later in Laos, colorfully described in a series of autobiographical best sellers, made Dooley, as an old school friend remarked, "a sort of anti-Communist Albert Schweitzer."[57] He worked near Communist insurgent lines in Laos in the late 1950s and endured a Chinese propaganda campaign which pictured him as an agent of American imperialism.[58] In a way (though not for reasons the Chinese mentioned) he was. Dooley voiced a boundless faith in America and Catholic Christianity as unequaled forces for good in the world. "American aid," he

54. Thomas Kselman and Steven Avella, "Marian Piety and the Cold War in the United States," *CHR* 72 (July 1986): 403–24.

55. The best and most detailed treatment of the life and work of Dooley can be found in Fisher, *Catholic Counterculture*, 131–204.

56. Thomas Dooley, *Deliver Us from Evil: The Story of Vietnam's Flight to Freedom* (New York: Farrar, Straus, and Cudahy, 1956), 77.

57. Thomas Dooley, *The Night They Burned the Mountain* (New York: Farrar, Straus, and Cudahy, 1960). Dooley's school friend was Michael Harrington; they grew up together in St. Louis. See Michael Harrington, *Fragments of the Century* (New York: Saturday Review Press/ E. P. Dutton, 1973), 13.

58. Dooley, *Night They Burned the Mountain*, 122–23.

said, "used wisely and generously . . . can create bonds of friendship that will be hard to sever. And we have several million willing American hands around the world, if we want to use them . . . in all the services overseas." These servicemen, with food, medicine, and good-will, could surely outweigh anti-American propaganda and teach the suffering peoples of the world about the "sympathy, generosity, and understanding that are hallmarks of the American Character."[59] The peaceful, humane world of Dooley's vision presupposed defeating communism and safeguarding Christianity, because Communists, he knew from personal experience, committed atrocities against Christians. Of a group of Catholic refugees from the Vietnamese province of Bao Lac he noted:

> The Communist Viet Minh often would tear an ear partially off with a pincer like a pair of pliers and leave the ear dangling. That was one of the penalties for the crime of listening to evil words. The Evil words were the words of the Lord's Prayer: "Our Father, Who art in heaven . . . Give us this day our daily bread . . . and deliver us from evil . . ." How downright treasonable, to ask God for bread instead of applying to the proper Communist authorities![60]

On another occasion, Dooley said he had encountered a Vietnamese priest who had been tortured by the Viet Minh by having nails driven into his head in parody of the crown of thorns.[61] Dooley's vivid symbolic appeal to Catholics and anti-Communists was annealed by his death, from melanoma, in 1961, when he was just thirty-four years old. *America* magazine saluted him as "a living symbol of Catholic youth ready to dedicate itself to the service of Church and country abroad."[62]

Anthony Bouscaren, a political scientist at Marquette University and Catholic conservative author on foreign policy questions, shared many of Dooley's assumptions about Vietnam. Bouscaren was horrified in 1955 when the English Catholic convert Graham Greene spoke in favor of a unified Vietnam under Ho Chi Minh. Greene must have forgotten, said Bouscaren, that Ho's victory in the north had already meant "death and torture to the Catholic defenders of Dien Bien Phu and the Catholic refugees in the North—millions and millions of them." Far from abandoning Diem, Bouscaren concluded, America must lend him

59. Dooley, *Deliver Us from Evil*, 18.
60. Ibid., 11.
61. Ibid., 182.
62. Editorial, "Splendid American," *A*, Feb. 4, 1961, 583.

support as wholehearted as that it gave to South Korea's Syngman Rhee and Nationalist China's Chiang Kai-shek.[63]

American Catholics' fervent support for the Catholic Vietnamese helped create the nation's foreign policy nightmare of the 1960s. For the non-Catholic majority of the Vietnamese population, the faith was tainted by French imperialism. The conversions of mandarins seeking advancement under the French were seen as defections to the enemy. Ngo Dinh Diem, Nguyen Cao Ky, and Nguyen Van Thieu, the South Vietnamese rulers whom the Americans attempted to prop up, one after the next, between 1955 and 1975, were all Catholics, and all bore the taint of colonialism. Their indulgence in bribery and corruption on a Wagnerian scale, coupled with their reluctance to fight for an independent South Vietnam, intensified the hatred they engendered and eviscerated any possibility of a permanent independent South Vietnam. The lesson, however, was learned only with agonizing slowness in the United States.[64]

McCarthyism, popular piety, admiration for Louis Budenz and Dr. Dooley, and anxiety over the fate of the Catholic Vietnamese were all aspects of the American Catholic anticommunism in the 1950s. The issue was vigorously exploited by Catholic politicians and prelates. Archbishop Michael Curley of Baltimore, for example, had been denouncing communism as "this most dangerous of all heresies" since the mid-1930s.[65] In the 1940s he encouraged John Cronin, a Sulpician priest from his diocese, to collaborate with the FBI in seeking out Communists in the Baltimore shipyards and in the 1950s enabled him to become Vice-President Nixon's speech writer.[66] This was one part of the setting in which the Catholic new conservatives moved. It is obvious that in their rhetoric, they felt comfortable with strident anticommunism, perhaps because they were so securely anchored in the faith that was communism's polar antagonist. Anticommunism, to them, represented firm ground. To this extent they were in the company of all their coreligionists.

Two Liberalisms

The second worst threat to Western civilization in the view of the Catholic new conservatives was American liberalism, for liberalism and

63. Anthony Bouscaren, "France and Graham Greene versus America and Diem," *CW* 181 (Sept. 1955): 414–17.

64. See Neil Sheehan, *A Bright Shining Lie: John Paul Vann and America in Vietnam* (New York: Random House, 1988), 136–42, 173–76.

65. Cited in Spalding, *Premier See,* 361.

66. Ibid., 376–77.

communism shared common philosophical roots in the Enlightenment and a common political heritage dating from the French Revolution. American liberals in the twentieth century, Catholic conservatives believed, had made a fetish of pragmatism and relativism, so that they lacked the firm intellectual foundations on which to stand in the coming war for civilization; thus they provided, either knowingly or unwittingly, an entering wedge for communism. At a practical level, meanwhile, the expansion of the federal government during the New Deal, World War II, and the Fair Deal and the assumption that the state ought to concern itself with a growing range of social problems appeared to these conservatives to exemplify creeping socialism that would erode the outward distinctions between American freedom and Soviet statism. Worse, the willingness of presidents Roosevelt, Truman, and Eisenhower to accord the Soviet Union diplomatic recognition and to look for ways of peaceful coexistence, they said, showed that both major parties were in the hands of men who had failed to recognize the unbridgeable gap between communism and "the West." By underestimating the mendacity and determination of the Communists and by failing to grasp that the conflict was ultimately a spiritual struggle, liberals were paving the way for the defeat of Western civilization.

Just as all faithful Catholics opposed communism, so all opposed philosophical liberalism, which had fought a protracted war against the church since the eighteenth century. But here a crucial complication arises, for many American Catholics were enthusiastic supporters of the New Deal, the trade unions, and the agenda of the Democratic party, their liberal influences notwithstanding.[67] The influential Monsignor John A. Ryan of the National Catholic Welfare Conference, himself a prominent New Dealer, for example, did not trace the philosophical roots of the New Deal to liberal theory; he considered it a bold excursion along the lines laid down by Pope Pius XI's economic encyclical *Quadragesimo Anno*.[68] Besides, as "liberal" Catholics began to argue with growing confidence in the 1950s, American liberalism as it had developed in the nineteenth and twentieth centuries was quite distinct from the French or continental anticlerical liberalism that a succession of popes had condemned. The laypeople who edited *Commonweal* and *Cross Currents* and the Jesuits who edited *America* showed

---

67. O'Brien, *American Catholics and Social Reform*, 41–57.

68. On Ryan, see ibid., 120–40. See also Francis Broderick, "The Encyclicals and Social Action: Is John A. Ryan Typical?" *CHR* 55 (April 1969): 1–6.

that this distinction had profound consequences both for Catholicism in the United States and for the church as a whole.[69]

Prominent liberal Catholics, among them John Cogley, Joseph Cunneen, and Donald Thorman, polemicized against what they called "secular liberalism" and the philosophical heritage of the French Enlightenment as ardently as the Catholic new conservatives. They believed, nontheless, that much of the historic political achievement of liberalism was defensible and valuable and should not be discarded solely because it had been accomplished by people who were, for other reasons, adversaries of Catholicism.[70] They particularly welcomed the growth of political democracy in the United States, which they sharply differentiated from the "totalitarian democracy" of the French Jacobin tradition. Whereas in the continental system the state took ontological priority over the citizens and became the fount of all rights, in the American system, democracy was simply a means for choosing representative legislators and governors in which the state remained ontologically subordinate to the population and confined by constitutional restrictions and natural law.

In a moment of introspection on the thirtieth anniversary of the founding of *Commonweal,* the journal's editors stated their position:

> The editors of this magazine clearly tend to be "liberal," not in the nineteenth-century European sense but in the modern American sense of the word. We are deeply committed to the idea of political democracy, and we have little patience with Catholic writers who discuss political questions as if nothing had happened between the French Revolution and the present. . . . We are deeply concerned with genuine measures to fight Communism—moral, economic, military, and psychological—and completely uninterested in "anti-Communist crusades." We think Catholics have not given enough thought to what it means to live in a pluralistic society and we consider it imperative that they repair this omission.

Despite some of the adverse connotations of the word *liberal,* they

69. The distinction was most fully explained by John Courtney Murray, S.J., to whom I will return. His colleague at Woodstock Seminary, Gustave Weigel, was also an influential exponent of this distinction. See his "Religious Tolerance in the World Community," in *Pope Pius XII on the World Community,* ed. Charles Keenan (New York: America, 1954), 26–30.

70. See, for example, John Cogley, "On the Left," C, March 7, 1952, 534; Joseph Cunneen, "The 'Religious Issue' and the Limits of National Purpose," *Cross Currents* 10 (Fall 1960): 313–16; Donald Thorman, "Conservatives, Liberals, and Catholicism," in Thorman, *The Emerging Layman: The Role of the Catholic Layman in America* (Garden City, N.Y.: Doubleday, 1962), 172–81.

therefore concluded, they would accept the label and continue to fight for the "good causes" it represented in the years to come.[71]

Discrimination among types of liberalism was worked out most fully by the famous Jesuit professor John Courtney Murray in a series of articles during the late 1940s and the 1950s and in his book *We Hold These Truths: Catholic Reflections on the American Proposition* (1960).[72] Murray reversed many old assumptions of Catholic political theology. He argued that the United States had preserved the political-philosophical heritage of medieval Christendom better than any European nation, even the ostensibly Catholic monarchies of France and Spain. The European nations fell prey to monarchical aggrandizement in the era of the absolutist ancien regimes, he said, but the American founding fathers upheld an older wisdom rooted in classical and Catholic traditions by creating a constitution based on balance of power, limited government, and natural law. Hence, by a historical paradox, a militantly Protestant nation had faithfully carried the heritage of Catholic Christendom into the mid-twentieth century.[73] Far from being latently disloyal, as nativist anti-Catholics had long claimed, Catholics were the nation's firmest adherents and longest-serving defenders, not merely in practice but also in theory! Taking a certain amount of license with the historical record, Murray pictured Roger Williams as a defender of the Catholic tradition of church-state separation, described Thomas Aquinas as "the first Whig," and claimed that Andrew Jackson had anticipated the themes of Leo XIII's social encyclical letter *Rerum Novarum* by fifty years. He blended the best of American and Catholic traditions in order to emphasize their harmony.[74]

Murray set himself the task of showing that even popes Pius IX and Leo XIII had acknowledged and advanced the Catholic political tradition of balanced constitutional powers at the same time that they condemned many aspects of liberalism and modernity usually associated with the United States. Murray was thus able to engage his critics on their own ground (the words of these nineteenth-century pontiffs) and to suggest, circumspectly, that the contemporary Vatican was not

71. Cited in Thorman, "Conservatives, Liberals, and Catholicism," 174–75.

72. On Murray, see Donald Pelotte, *John Courtney Murray: Theologian in Conflict* (New York: Paulist Press, 1975); Patrick Allitt, "The Significance of John Courtney Murray," in *Catholic Polity and American Politics*, ed. Mary Segers (New Haven: Garland, 1990), 53–67; John C. Murray, S.J., *We Hold These Truths: Catholic Reflections on the American Proposition* (New York: Sheed and Ward, 1960).

73. John C. Murray, S.J., "The Church and Totalitarian Democracy," *Theological Studies* 13 (1952): 525–63.

74. Murray, *We Hold These Truths*, 56–63, 32; John C. Murray, S.J., "Leo XIII: Two Concepts of Government," *Theological Studies* 14 (1953): 556–57, 559.

fully cognizant of its own history. With a superbly balanced rhetorical style, Murray on the one hand sought to convince skeptical Americans that Catholic tradition shared the basic premises of the Declaration of Independence (hence his title *We Hold These Truths*) and on the other hand tried to convince the Vatican that it need have no fears of Americanism but rather should acknowledge the United States constitutional system as the ideal modern setting for the church. "Catholic participation in the American consensus," he declared,

> has been full, free, unreserved and unembarrassed, because the contents of this consensus—the ethical and political principles drawn from the tradition of the natural law—approve themselves to the Catholic intelligence and the Catholic conscience. Where this kind of language is talked, the Catholic joins the conversation with complete ease. It is his language. . . . The ideas are expressed in a way native to his own universe of discourse. Even the accent, being American, suits his tongue.[75]

Murray was perhaps disingenuous in claiming "complete ease," especially in view of the interfaith tensions of the 1950s; but the claim, perhaps here only a wish, was to be borne out in subsequent decades.

Up to the mid-twentieth century, Catholic theological disputants usually cited the pontifical words they considered most apt for their needs without reference to the circumstances in which the popes had uttered them—a technique Michael Novak, then a liberal, described as "non-historical orthodoxy."[76] Murray, by contrast, reintroduced historical considerations into Catholic political theology. He scrupulously placed Pius IX and Leo XIII in their historical contexts to demonstrate which events (generally of European history) had provoked their condemnations of "totalitarian democracy" and "liberalism." He observed, for example, that although "the Roman advisors of Leo XIII knew their Rousseau, they had probably never heard of the *Federalist Papers*." The nineteenth-century popes, though concerned with politics, "apparently had no interest in the most striking and successful political realization of modern times, despite the fact that the philosophy behind it was of linear descent from the central political tradition of the West, which the Church herself had helped fashion."[77] In other words, the Vatican had neglected to follow developments in America in the heat of its nineteenth-century battles against the Jacobins and their heirs.

75. Murray, *We Hold These Truths*, 41.
76. Michael Novak, *The Open Church: Vatican II, Act II* (New York: Macmillan, 1964), 66.
77. Murray, "The Church and Totalitarian Democracy," 554.

The U.S. Constitution, Murray repeated, must not be understood as part of that Jacobin heritage. Instead, the Bill of Rights, especially the crucial First Amendment, marked the United States as a nation whose state authority confined itself solely to temporal affairs and prescinded completely from judging affairs of the spirit. The Constitution, like the medieval Catholic church, recognized that church and state were two distinct "societies," each with its proper sphere of operation, united only to the degree that persons belong, by nature, to both. In certain areas the natural spirituality of human beings permits the church to intrude into the temporal sphere (in facilitating public worship, for example), but in no area should the state override its exclusively temporal character and intervene in spiritual affairs.[78] Where the state tried to buttress the church, as in Spain with the notorious case of the Inquisition, it violated the principle of the two societies. In an age when most American Catholics were enthusiastic supporters of Spanish Catholicism and Franco's defense of the church, Murray regarded Spanish history as an object lesson in how not to conduct church-state relations. He believed the Inquisition itself had contributed to the rise of "that peculiarly militant form of unbelief which . . . tends to ensue upon government efforts to suppress unbelief."[79]

Murray's second important task, adumbrated in his strictures on Spain, was to justify on the basis of Catholic principles and tradition a position of religious toleration for non-Catholics. One reason for the widespread suspicion of Catholics was the old assertion that there was no salvation outside the church, that religious toleration, though acceptable so long as Catholics were a minority, was theoretically objectionable and should be eliminated once Catholicism predominated. John Ryan, for all his liberal reputation, had himself reiterated the point in a 1924 seminary textbook, providing high-caliber ammunition to Paul Blanshard and other foes of the church (though Ryan modified his view in 1928).[80] Theory and practice on the issue were clearly at variance in midcentury America. For many Catholic citizens, living and working side-by-side with Protestants, Jews, agnostics, and atheists, the principle of intolerance and the threat of damnation for everyone outside the church seemed like old embarrassments. Catholics had never been a majority and most could foresee no prospect of their becoming one. Proud of their church, sure of its unique religious mis-

---

78. John C. Murray, S.J., "St. Robert Bellarmine on the Indirect Power," *Theological Studies* 9 (1948): 291–334; Murray, *We Hold These Truths*, 197–217.

79. Murray, "Leo XIII: Two Concepts of Government, II," 14.

80. John A. Ryan and Moorehouse F. X. Millar, *The State and the Church* (New York: Macmillan, 1924).

sion, they were nevertheless vexed by a doctrine that could win them only ill will.[81] Murray's reasoning on the two societies established that church coercion of consciences and especially state aid for such coercion violated venerable Catholic principles; he was able to provide theoretical justification for a position of religious toleration.[82]

For a time in the mid-1950s the Jesuit order felt sufficiently alarmed by the direction of Murray's work in political theology that it denied him the imprimatur for two articles and discouraged him from publishing further articles on the church-state question. His historically astringent analyses of Vatican conduct, they believed, tended toward a relativization of the truth.[83] Murray's censure was short-lived, however, and his fortunes took a turn for the better at the end of the 1950s. John Kennedy's speech writer Theodore Sorensen solicited Murray's advice before Kennedy delivered a speech on church-state relations to a gathering of Protestant ministers in Houston during his 1960 campaign. Murray's views on religious liberty also won a sympathetic hearing at the Second Vatican Council. After being omitted from the U.S. delegation to the first session, Murray was subsequently included and found his views vindicated in *Dignitatis Humanae*, the council's declaration on religious liberty, which he helped to draft.[84]

During Murray's lifetime and since his death in 1967 his heritage has been claimed not only by liberal Catholics but also by Catholics in the conservative intellectual movement. When William Buckley edited an anthology of conservative writings of the twentieth century, he used one of Murray's essays (from *We Hold These Truths*) to illustrate conservative thinking on church-state relations.[85] The two of them had become acquainted at Yale in the early 1950s when Buckley was writing *God and Man at Yale* and Murray was teaching there for a year; they lunched together on the day it was published.[86] Murray's conviction that a binding consensus must underlie society ("We hold these truths to be self-evident . . .") echoed Buckley's reasoning on conformity in *McCarthy and His Enemies*. Russell Kirk, founding editor of *Modern Age*, another journal of the new conservatism, also published Murray in

81. Occasionally bishops silenced priests who preached "extra ecclesiam nulla salus" ("outside the church there can be no salvation") too vigorously. Such was the fate of Father Leonard Feeney of the Saint Benedict Center, Harvard, in 1948.

82. Allitt, "Significance of Murray," 62–64.

83. The case against Murray was made by (for example) Joseph Fenton in "The Theology of Church and State," *Proceedings of the Catholic Theological Society of America* 2 (1947): 15–46.

84. Dolan, *American Catholic Experience*, 425.

85. John C. Murray, S.J., "E Pluribus Unum," in *Did You Ever See a Dream Walking? American Conservative Thought in the Twentieth Century*, ed. William F. Buckley, Jr. (Indianapolis: Bobbs-Merrill, 1970), 37–51.

86. Interview with Buckley, New York City, Jan. 6, 1986.

an early edition.[87] Murray's actual political sympathies are not easily discerned, however; he avoided advocacy journalism and made few direct contributions to the political debates of the 1950s and 1960s. Whatever his personal views, however, the treatment subsequently accorded him is revealing.

Paradoxically, as their use of Murray might suggest, the Catholic new conservatives were themselves in some respects liberal Catholics. They were laypeople eager to establish themselves without clerical props and certainly without deferring to clerical control and censorship. Most of them favored political collaboration with members of other faiths, and they usually avoided making "triumphalist" claims. Many of them were educated at secular universities; some were married and hoped for a reform of Catholic teaching against contraception. Almost all of them wanted to climb out of the Catholic ghetto and play a fuller role in the mainstream of American intellectual life. In all these ways they were comparable to the politically liberal Catholics against whom, nevertheless, they polemicized vigorously. In tracing the intra-Catholic disputes of the 1950s and early 1960s, it is worth emphasizing that the overt antagonism between Catholic liberals and conservatives on political and economic questions was undergirded by several common interests and hopes.

The principal journals of liberal Catholicism were *Commonweal, Cross Currents, Jubilee* ("the first national picture magazine for a Catholic audience"),[88] and *America,* and articles in the *Catholic World, Sign, Ave Maria,* and *Social Order* also often exhibited a liberal Catholic sensibility. One frequent contributor to *Commonweal,* briefly one of its editors, was John Cogley, whom many contemporaries considered the liberal Catholic par excellence; Michael Novak recalled that in his days as a seminarian in the late 1950s Cogley had been an intellectual inspiration, almost a "father figure."[89] As a columnist for *Commonweal,* Cogley wrote frequent articles on the importance of interreligious harmony and mutual deference, refuted charges of Catholic intolerance, and on one occasion toured the politically volatile Middle East on a goodwill mission with a Protestant clergyman and a rabbi, a decade before such missions became commonplace.[90] Despite an unbending anticom-

87. John C. Murray, S.J., "The Freedom of Man in the Freedom of the Church," *MA* 1 (1956): 134–45.
88. *Jubilee* was the creation of Thomas Merton's friends Edward Rice and Robert Lax—a sort of Catholic version of *Life* magazine, featuring liturgical woodcuts, illustrated articles on church art and architecture, fiction, and profiles of prominent American Catholics of the day.
89. Interview with Michael Novak, Washington, D.C., April 9, 1985.
90. For Cogley on interreligious harmony, see, for example, "Patriot vs. Prelate," *C,* March 6, 1953, 546. Refuting allegations of Catholic intolerance, see, for example, Cogley, "Each His

munism, Cogley was one of the most prominent Catholic opponents of Senator Joseph McCarthy.[91] He supported Democratic party initiatives and candidates, including Kennedy, and praised the political and social heritage of the New Deal. His journalism often implicitly appealed to a non-Catholic audience (some of his columns were reprinted in the secular press) or asked Catholic readers to consider how their non-Catholic neighbors might misconstrue controversial Catholic actions.[92]

From *Commonweal*, Cogley moved into increasingly "mainstream" institutions, working for several years with the Ford Foundation's Fund for the Republic under the tutelage of Robert Hutchins.[93] Hutchins, son of a Protestant minister and former president of the University of Chicago, was attracted to the Catholic natural law tradition and the work of Thomas Aquinas. Cogley nurtured his interest, and in 1961 they published *Natural Law and Modern Society* with the help of John Courtney Murray and other participants in Fund for the Republic seminars.[94] Cogley subsequently became religion editor of the *New York Times*, the first Catholic to hold that position. His rapid career advancement indicates the possibilities open to a gifted layman by the 1950s.

Other liberal Catholic authors joined Cogley in espousing the laity as a rising force in the church. In keeping with the familiar paradox of American Catholicism, one of these advocates was a priest, Father Leo Ward, who noted in an enthusiastic survey of 1959 that the "status of lay leadership and a lay vocation is beginning to give at least to some lay people a new sense of importance and dignity in the life of the Church" even though the era of lay initiative was "hardly yet out of the baby stage."[95] Laypeople echoed the sentiment, among them Donald Thorman, editor of *Ave Maria*, who collected his essays on the theme for a book called *The Emerging Layman* (1962). Thorman emphasized that Catholicism had massive resources in its laity which it could not afford to waste. Too often, he lamented, laypeople remained silent when they should be joining vigorously in political debate. When fed-

Own," *C*, May 2, 1952, 86. On touring the Middle East, see Cogley, "The Battle against Time," *C*, Dec. 18, 1953, 276–79. The Protestant minister was Harold Fey of *Christian Century*, and the rabbi was Morris Lazarou of *Jewish Newsletter*.

91. See, for example, John Cogley, "Draw Your Own Conclusions," *C*, Oct. 16, 1953, 29–30; and Cogley, "Extreme Partisanship," *C*, March 5, 1954, 546.

92. For example, Cogley, "Archbishop and Ambassador," *C*, Nov. 16, 1951, 134.

93. The following biographical passage is based largely on Cogley's autobiography, *A Canterbury Tale* (New York: Seabury, 1976).

94. Robert Hutchins, John Cogley, et al., Center for the Study of Democratic Institutions, *Natural Law and Modern Society* (Cleveland: World/Fund for the Republic, 1963).

95. Leo Ward, C.H.C., *Catholic Life, USA: Contemporary Lay Movements* (New York: Herder and Herder, 1959), 6, 4.

eral aid to education was at issue, for example, "'the Catholic position' was presented by priests—as if there was only one acceptable Catholic view on the whole matter," so that "the non-Catholic on the outside looking in could hardly be blamed if he formed the opinion that in this matter Catholics were tools of the clergy and were being whipped into line by the bishops and priests."[96] Like Cogley, Thorman was uncomfortably aware of how Catholic actions might look in the eyes of outsiders. Another assertion that the laity was "rising" came from Michael Novak. In the late 1950s, just before he was scheduled for ordination, Novak decided not to become a priest. His faith was undiminished, however, and he set about demonstrating the possibilities of a lay vocation in writing and Catholic activism throughout the following decades.[97]

Together with the liberals, the Catholic church also included what James Fisher has called a Catholic counterculture, comprising no more than a handful of adherents through the 1930s, 1940s, and 1950s. Though its members were few, its moral example was to become influential in the 1960s as a source of inspiration to the Catholic "New Breed" of that decade.[98] Its most prominent lay figure was Dorothy Day (1897–1980), a Greenwich Village bohemian in the World War I years, who wrote news and stories for the *Masses*, had several sexual affairs and an abortion, and gave birth to an illegitimate daughter (1926). She then converted to Catholicism and opened the House of Hospitality in New York, to which the destitute were invited to come at no cost for indefinite periods of time to enjoy her ungrudging welcome. With a French anarchist and visionary, Peter Maurin, she ran a newspaper, the *Catholic Worker*, and tried without much success to organize rural communes. The Catholic Worker movement, through which John Cogley and many other Catholic liberals passed as young people, refused to support Franco in the Spanish Civil War and scandalized most American Catholics by taking an absolute pacifist stand in the war against Hitler. It refused to cooperate with New York's nuclear air-raid drills in the 1950s and became an early center of opposition to the Vietnam War in the 1960s.[99]

In Harlem, meanwhile, Baroness Catherine de Hueck ran Friendship House, a project comparable to Day's House of Hospitality, but for

96. Thorman, "Conservatives, Liberals, and Catholicism," *Emerging Layman*, 165.

97. His early work on this theme was collected in Michael Novak, *A New Generation: American and Catholic* (New York: Herder and Herder, 1964).

98. Fisher, *Catholic Counterculture*, 249–50. The following summary is based on this work.

99. On Day and the Catholic Worker movement, see also William Miller, *Dorothy Day: A Biography* (San Francisco: Harper and Row, 1982); Mel Piehl, *Breaking Bread: The "Catholic Worker" and the Origins of Catholic Radicalism* (Philadelphia: Temple University Press, 1982).

African Americans. Through it in 1939 passed Thomas Merton, a convert from a dissolute, purposeless life to the disciplines of Catholicism and en route to his vocation in a Trappist monastery.[100] As Fisher observes, these Catholics were not, like many of their working-class co-religionists, trying to move toward middle-class respectability; instead, they were trying to get away from it with a socially marginal Catholicism as their chosen vehicle of escape.[101] They and, still more, such stray Catholics as the novelists Ammon Hennacy and Jack Kerouac lived lives of heroic impracticality.[102] One group in the Catholic counterculture, founders of the Marycrest Christian commune in rural New York, expressed their radicalism by following Catholic prohibitions on birth control unswervingly; the twelve couples gave birth to seventy-nine children.[103] The Catholic counterculture was not large, but it offered auguries of things to come and indicated that Catholic tradition contained potentially explosive elements as well as sources of conservatism and conformity.

CATHOLIC EDUCATION AND INTELLECTUAL METHOD

Closely associated with the development of a new role for the laity, the rise of a self-conscious liberal Catholicism, and the emergence of a small, yet visible Catholic counterculture was a debate on the quality and the purposes of Catholic higher education. The debate, which had smoldered through the previous decades caught fire when the Catholic historian John Tracy Ellis published his article "American Catholics and the Intellectual Life" in 1955. Ellis observed that never in history had the church devoted so much money and energy to building an educational apparatus as it had in the United States since the Third Plenary Council of Baltimore (1884). How meager its intellectual results had proved! Distinguished Catholic scholars nurtured in the system were few and far between. Declining to blame the prejudice of outsiders, Ellis held that a "defensive" Catholic outlook, lack of strong Catholic intellectual traditions in the United States, and a pervasive intellectual unadventurousness were to blame for this state of affairs.

---

100. Thomas Merton, *The Seven Storey Mountain* (New York: Harcourt, Brace, 1948), 340–48.

101. This theme is particularly clear in Fisher's treatment of the Marycrest community in *Catholic Counterculture*, 101–29. But see also his analysis of Dorothy Day's use of her new religion: "Day's genius resided in her ability to reverse the trajectory of the conventional American conversion narrative. . . . Day offered deconversion, or breakdown, as a permanent state of grace" (32).

102. Ibid., 251–52, 205–11, 218–22.

103. Ibid., 101–29.

Catholic educators had become afraid of the vital scientific and philosophical developments taking place in the twentieth-century world; nor had they excelled even in scholasticism. They had imitated many of the worst frivolities of the secular educational system without benefiting from its strengths. Many of the brightest stars in the Catholic firmament, to make matters worse, were converts who had been educated outside the fold, rather than being reared within it: "In the case of practically all of these convert scholars Catholic education can take no credit whatever, for they were what they were and are, intellectually speaking, when the grace of the Holy Spirit illumined their minds and led them to find a lasting place amongst us."[104] To be reinvigorated, said Ellis, Catholic scholars must get beyond their "self-imposed ghetto mentality" and take the same risks as any other scholars, must question themselves remorselessly and defer no longer to dogmatic authorities.[105]

Ellis's article generated much soul-searching by Catholic writers during the late 1950s; many, especially on the liberal Catholic side, fleshed out the skeleton of his mea culpa, describing wasted opportunities in Catholic schools, overattention to sports instead of scholarship, the use of apologetics in courses where they held no relevance, even the sorry paucity of Catholic Rhodes scholars since the Rhodes scheme began.[106] It is noteworthy that many of the new conservative Catholics had themselves been educated wholly or in part outside the Catholic educational system and had perhaps benefited from the greater vigor of non-Catholic schooling. William Buckley, for example, attended Yale as an undergraduate, as did Brent Bozell; Garry Wills was a graduate student at Yale after leaving the Jesuit seminary; John Noonan was a Harvard graduate. Ross Hoffman, a convert, had been an undergraduate at Lafayette College, a graduate student at the University of Pennsylvania, and a professor at New York University before his conversion led him to accept a post at Fordham instead. Francis Wilson, another convert in the movement, was a professor at the University of Illinois, trained first at the University of Texas, then at the University of California and Stanford. One of his graduate students at Illinois, Willmoore Kendall, in turn converted to Catholicism, but he too worked at Yale, outside the Catholic educational system.

104. John Tracy Ellis, "American Catholics and the Intellectual Life," *Thought* 30 (1955): 382. For a non-Catholic analysis of Catholicism as "unintellectual," see R. H. Knapp and H. B. Goodrich, *Origins of American Scientists*, 2 vols. (Chicago: University of Chicago Press, 1953).
105. Ellis, "American Catholics," 386.
106. The scale and variety of responses to the Ellis article are reviewed in Thomas F. O'Dea, *American Catholic Dilemma: An Inquiry into the Intellectual Life* (New York: Sheed and Ward,

It would be wrong to imply that American Catholicism had no intellectual life or that a Catholic collegiate education represented a disqualification for an intellectual career. Indeed, the journal in which Ellis published his famous article, *Thought*, emanating from Fordham, had enjoyed a vigorous existence for two decades and attracted some notice beyond Catholic circles. It was joined after 1940 by *Theological Studies*, where much of John Courtney Murray's work was first published, and Notre Dame's distinguished *Review of Politics. Cross Currents*, founded in 1950, was a self-consciously "highbrow" Catholic quarterly, which introduced Americans to the work of prominent European Catholic intellectuals (among them Pierre Teilhard de Chardin, Yves Congar, Henri de Lubac, and Gabriel Marcel) and made early ecumenical gestures with articles by and about prominent Protestants (Paul Tillich, Karl Barth, Emil Brunner) and Jews (Martin Buber and Abraham Heschel).

Catholic high schools and colleges were sometimes also fine in their way. Michael Harrington, a student at Holy Cross College of Worcester, Massachusetts, in the 1940s and subsequently a powerful analytical writer in the socialist movement, described the mix of rigor and archaism in his college career: "We followed a classic curriculum that had its antecedents in the *Ratio Studiorum*, the traditional Jesuit theory of education formulated in 1559. . . . we took four years of Latin and two of Greek. . . . our knowledge was not free-floating; it was always consciously related to ethical and religious values." Such a curriculum, as Harrington, Ellis, and a growing body of Catholic authors observed, scanted the understanding and mastery of new phenomena, new disciplines, and the crucial developments in science and philosophy of the previous century: "Philosophy and theology were regarded as the sovereigns of the sciences, infinitely superior to physics and mathematics, which only dealt with proximate, not with last, causes."[107]

Despite these criticisms, Russell Kirk and other conservative observers believed that, insofar as it resisted the relativism common in secular schools, the Catholic college still offered many advantages.[108] In *God and Man at Yale* William Buckley made the point at length, illustrating the severe disadvantages of secular schools for a young Christian. John Lukacs, a professor at Chestnut Hill College in Philadelphia and a Catholic conservative, agreed that Catholics must be wary of emulating

---

1958). The episode is reexamined and the "myth" of Catholic intellectual inferiority exploded by Andrew Greeley in *American Catholic*, 69–89.

107. Harrington, *Fragments of the Century*, 10–11.

108. Russell Kirk, *The Intemperate Professor* (Baton Rouge: Louisiana State University Press, 1965), 39–55.

the intellectual habits of their secular contemporaries. Ellis had lamented that "the vast majority of American Catholics remained relatively impervious to the intellectual movements of their time," to which Lukacs answered: "But is this necessarily bad? . . . Had the Catholic population remained quite impervious to Deism, majoritarianism, scientism, social Darwinism, Marxism, Freudism, pragmatism, positivism, moral relativism, existentialism, nihilism, National Socialism, Fascism, Communism, all prominent 'intellectual movements,' there would be more gain than loss." He warned against overlooking the moral dimensions of intellectual life, adding that what Catholic education most needed was not big-name intellectual celebrities but cultivation in students of the "intellectual virtues."[109]

Anthony Bouscaren, though himself educated at Yale and the University of California, became a Catholic university professor and took a similar line, with an anti-Communist turn. "Perhaps we have not produced more Oppenheimers," he admitted, naming a scientist who had lost his government security clearance on suspicion of disloyalty, "but it might also be held that less well-known but more stable and logical scientists are preferable."[110] Buckley's jeremiad, Lukacs's denigration of many intellectual trends, and Bouscaren's warning about loyalty bear witness to the Catholic conservatives' ambivalence about educational change. They certainly favored rigorous higher education, but only so long as it promoted what they regarded as right thinking on crucial matters. Such an education would not be easy to attain, they said, so long as American universities were dominated, as they believed they were, by academic liberals. Mere learning, they believed, could as well promote disaster as avert it, especially when learning lost its secure mooring in natural law.

In addition to the appeal to natural law, Catholic conservatives' intellectual work in the 1950s showed other distinctive characteristics. One was a mistrust of scientific method, especially when it was extended beyond the provenance of the physical and biological sciences. The social sciences, with their claims of objective social knowledge, were a prime target. John Lukacs lamented, "In the history of human reason, the story of the scientific illusion of progressive objectivity has become a sorry tale; and nothing is sorrier in it than the modern belief that the further we remove ourselves from the object, the more accurate our knowledge of it. The purpose of human knowledge," he added,

109. John Lukacs, "Intellectuals, Catholics, and the Intellectual Life," *MA* 2 (Winter 1957–58): 45, 52.

110. Anthony Bouscaren, "Catholics and Intellectualism: A Dissent," *CW* 187 (May 1958): 124.

"is understanding rather than accuracy."[111] Opposing understanding and accuracy in this way rather than assuming that the two are harmonious, marked Lukacs's detachment from the epistemological assumptions of most secular contemporaries.

Frederick Wilhelmsen, a passionate Catholic traditionalist, concurred with Lukacs and added that scientific and technological knowledge was of value only to those intent on transforming the world, not to those who sought understanding: "Paradox though it may be" said Wilhelmsen, "it remains a brutal truth; scientific power over a thing is had in proportion to the failure to know the thing as it is."[112] Educators, Wilhelmsen believed, should not try to appear "scientific" or objective, offering the detached observations of the anonymous observer; rather, teaching "demands attachment and engagement . . . thinking involving the whole man whose role in life demands of him assent and commitment."[113] Thomas Molnar, like Lukacs a Hungarian Catholic refugee in the American conservative movement, added that the development of the social sciences in the late nineteenth century, growing up in the shadow of social Darwinism and under the influence of John Dewey, had had pernicious consequences for the ideas of tradition and permanence in education. Dewey and his successors, Molnar noted, "have made the concept of change and the preparation for change veritable articles of faith. Henceforward, no philosophy may be credited with enough truth value to warrant its adoption as a common system of reference."[114]

For William Buckley, objectivity and "value-neutral" education likewise bespoke not a desirable evenhandedness but a shying away from the vital issues of the day. He believed that teachers should be indoctrinators in the sense that they should conscientiously implant the traditional wisdom of civilization in, and extirpate error from, the minds of their students. He noted wryly that the oft-touted "free marketplace of ideas" metaphor had been tacitly abandoned by the educators charged with the denazification of German education after World War II, who certainly did not offer young Germans Nazi literature along with the possible alternatives.[115] Buckley and Russell Kirk contributed to the vigorous academic-freedom debate of the 1950s, stirred up by the loyalty oath controversy, by McCarthyism, and by Buckley's own *God and Man at Yale*. They both believed that while academic freedom

---

111. John Lukacs, *A History of the Cold War* (Garden City, N.Y.: Doubleday, 1961), 261.
112. Frederick Wilhelmsen, "Technics and Totalitarianism," *C*, April 23, 1954, 58–61.
113. Frederick Wilhelmsen, "The Professor's Vocation," *C*, June 26, 1959, 319–21.
114. Thomas Molnar, *The Future of Education* (New York: Fleet Education, 1961), 70.
115. Buckley, *God and Man at Yale*, 159.

liberated researchers to pursue their convictions and theories in private, wherever they might lead, it did not entitle them as teachers to teach whatever they happened to consider true. Rather, teachers must defer to the traditional wisdom of their society and transmit the established truth to the new generations in their charge until such time as their own new claims won general intellectual acceptance.[116]

Buckley and his colleagues believed that education, to be worthy of the name, must lead students to sure knowledge of the permanent truths. "Millenniums of intellection," said Buckley, "have served an objective purpose. Certain problems have been disposed of. Certain questions are closed, and with reference to that fact the conservative orders his life." He added: "All that is finally important in human experience is behind us. . . . Whatever is to come cannot outweigh the importance to man of what has gone before."[117] The assumption that life's most important questions had been answered once and for all placed Catholic conservative intellectuals firmly at odds with the pragmatic liberal tradition in education, which assumed, as David Hollinger puts it, "the durability of inquiry, on the one hand, and the tentativeness, fallibility, and incompleteness of knowledge on the other."[118] The Columbia sociologist Robert MacIver, in a characteristic declaration of the pragmatic faith, answered Buckley with the assertion that "when a scholar says something is true, he means true so far as our knowledge goes and no further. His truth has no finality; it is never absolute."[119]

These philosophical differences regarding educational purpose and intellectual method led the Catholic new conservatives to pay educational issues close attention. Buckley's column in early editions of *National Review,* "The Ivory Tower," and Russell Kirk's column, "From the Academy," kept readers in close touch with developments on the major college campuses and in the schools; both men recognized the power of education in the formation of new generations.

Two emblematic incidents at Ivy League universities illustrate the conflict between Catholicism and secular education in the postwar years. The best known is the case of Leonard Feeney, the Jesuit chaplain at the St. Benedict Center near Harvard in the late 1940s. Feeney denounced the Harvard undergraduate curriculum, which found no

116. Russell Kirk, *Academic Freedom: An Essay in Definition* (Chicago: Henry Regnery, 1955).

117. William F. Buckley, Jr., *Up from Liberalism* (1959; New York: Bantam, 1968), 154.

118. David Hollinger, "The Problem of Pragmatism in American History," in Hollinger, *In the American Province* (Bloomington: Indiana University Press, 1985), 30.

119. Robert MacIver, *Academic Freedom in Our Times* (New York: Columbia University Press, 1955), 4.

room for the Bible. With breathtaking oratory he converted two hundred students to Catholicism and insisted that there was no salvation outside the church. His intolerance and zeal led to complaints from Harvard, from more conciliatory Catholics, and ultimately from Archbishop Richard Cushing of Boston himself, who silenced the recalcitrant Feeney.[120]

Less publicized was the slightly later case of Hugh Halton, Catholic chaplain to Princeton. Appointed in 1952, he, like Feeney, breached the interreligious civilities his predecessors had observed. He too preached the orthodox but by then usually muted line that there was no salvation outside the church and that the salvation of their souls was of supreme importance to Princeton's Catholic men. He also did what he could to convert non-Catholic undergraduates and preached a fervent anticommunism. He led a public protest against the university's decision to let Alger Hiss, newly released from jail, speak about his ordeal, describing Hiss as an "unrepentant perjurer."[121] In 1956 Halton denounced relativism in philosophy, declaring that "the teachings of some professors at Princeton are doing more harm than all the writings of Karl Marx taken together." He singled out the philosopher Walter Stace and the ethicist Joseph Fletcher for condemnation.[122]

After several years of escalating incidents, Princeton's president, Robert Goheen, withdrew Halton's faculty privileges in 1957 and asked the local bishop to replace him with a more temperate Catholic chaplain. The bishop refused, and in the ensuing standoff, Catholic journalists anxiously debated the rights and wrongs of the Halton case. John Cogley in *Commonweal* deplored Halton's bad manners and unseemly provocation of confrontations. He feared Halton would reinforce the anti-Catholic stereotype, but still Cogley did not think Princeton's president entirely justified: "Paradoxically, the idea of the university should be broad enough to shelter dissent even against the idea itself."[123] William Buckley saw the case as a symbolic confrontation. He shared Halton's concern that so many Catholic undergraduates in Ivy League colleges abandoned their religion. "The man who views with apostolic concern the faith of the students he is there to look after," said Buckley, "will do everything in his power to guard that faith, and he will begin by patiently asserting the intellectual legitimacy of

---

120. On the Feeney case, see Catherine Goddard Clark, *The Loyolas and the Cabots* (Boston: Ravensgate, 1950). See also Mark Silk, *Spiritual Politics: Religion and America since World War II* (New York: Simon and Schuster, 1988), 70–87.

121. *U.S. News and World Report*, May 4, 1956, 67.

122. *New York Times*, Sept. 24, 1957, 34.

123. John Cogley, "The Princeton Affair," C, Oct. 18, 1957, 73.

religion," even if that meant criticizing philosophical relativists. The defense of faith sometimes demanded militancy, and a college chaplain could not always promise quiescence and pliability if he was to be taken as something more serious than a mere "spiritual jester."[124] Here, as in *God and Man at Yale,* Buckley was more concerned with religion in general than with Catholicism per se. He feared that Christianity of all varieties was being undermined by relativism and materialism, and that Christians might soon have to overlook their internal distinctions in order to face their common foes. In this belief, Buckley anticipated what was to become the dominant opinion among religious conservatives in the 1960s, 1970s, and 1980s, when intrachurch splits along political lines would replace interdenominational rivalries as the major American cleavage.

The Halton confrontation was resolved at last when the Dominicans, Halton's order, withdrew him from Princeton and sent him to Oxford University in England to teach law, his previous academic speciality. One of his many declarations in the course of the controversy aptly summarized the Catholic conservatives' outlook on the crisis of Western and U.S. civilization by the mid-1950s. "Princeton and America," said Halton, "were conceived and developed by men who adhered to the spiritual, moral, intellectual and cultural convictions inherent in the Judeo-Christian tradition. Princeton's eminence, and America's prestige, are intelligible only in this context."[125] It was in order to preserve and revivify these convictions against their liberal and Communist challengers that Catholic new conservatives went into battle.

124. William F. Buckley, Jr., "The Role of the College Chaplain," *NR,* Jan. 11, 1958, 41.
125. *U.S. News and World Report,* May 4, 1956, 67.

2

Catholic Conservatives and the 1950s

Many of the dominant figures of the new conservative movement in the 1950s, including its chief publicist, William Buckley, were born between 1925 and 1935 and became politically active in the decade after World War II. Their early work was a reaction to the legacy of the New Deal and to the great-power confrontation of the cold war. Just as Catholic anticommunism had a history in the early twentieth century, however, so did several of the other salient themes of the new conservatism. Two precursors of the movement, both converts to Catholicism, were the historian Ross J. S. Hoffman and the political scientist Francis Graham Wilson, whose work in the 1930s and 1940s laid part of the intellectual groundwork for the movement. They saw the post-World War II years as affording Catholics a special opportunity to lead a conservative revival and believed such a revival necessary if the civilization of the Christian West, with the United States now its chief guardian, was to be preserved.

Hoffman, descended from a German family in America since before the Revolution, was born in Harrisburg, Pennsylvania, in 1902, and graduated from Lafayette College in 1923. He had no formal religious education as a child and recalled that a few fragments of Christian Science teaching he had imbibed from his aunts were extinguished in college. "I left college" he wrote, "hardly doubting that supernatural religion was a thing suitable only for quite feeble and unemancipated minds." His political views at that time were mildly socialist.[1] The

1. Ross Hoffman, *Restoration* (New York: Sheed and Ward, 1934), 24. Biographical details of his early life are based on his unpublished typescript memoir, in the author's possession, "As Life Used to Be: A Memoir of Youth, 1902–23."

decision to return to graduate school began an intellectual, political, and religious transformation. Hoffman studied for the history Ph.D. under William Lingelbach at the University of Pennsylvania, and his first book, *Great Britain and the German Trade Rivalry, 1875–1914*, based on his doctoral dissertation, won the George Beer Prize of the American Historical Association.[2] The book was devoid of explicitly ideological or religious content, and its enthusiastic reception helped him win a job as an assistant history professor at New York University.

Although he concentrated on nineteenth-century European history, graduate school courses had also introduced him to the Catholic Middle Ages, in which he found much to admire, "a vigor and health . . . passion, heroism, and hard thinking" that he had not previously associated with any era prior to the Enlightenment. That positive impression inspired him to take a renewed interest in the Catholicism of his own day, especially once he had married a Catholic woman of Irish descent. He discovered that the papal encyclical letter *Rerum Novarum* laid out a program for industrial reconciliation and social justice which he found more palatable than anything the secular politicians of his day had to offer, and he concluded that it was, in its way, "a more revolutionary document than the Communist Manifesto." In time, he recalled, he came to believe that the church "was a great kingdom at war with all the enemies against whom I had ranged myself. . . . It went to the root of all social injustice; absence of charity. It sought to deliver men from industrial slavery and defended liberty against its major enemy, the modern absolutist state."[3]

Hoffman's conversion to Catholicism was the fruit of growing conviction rather than sudden transformation. It resulted not only from these reflections on church history and teaching but also from close study of Scripture. Hoffman, in the face of critical remarks from colleagues at NYU who regarded his conversion as atavistic, insisted that in joining the church he had not surrendered his intellectual freedom but rather increased its range immeasurably. Conversion in fact "brought me a kind of intellectual shame for having been so long content to live in a very little universe."[4] In his outward life he bore witness to the power of conversion by moving to the Jesuits' Fordham University in New York. He was to work there for the rest of his life, devoting himself

2. Ross Hoffman, *Great Britain and the German Trade Rivalry, 1875–1914* (Philadelphia: University of Pennsylvania Press, 1933).

3. Hoffman, *Restoration*, 35, 42–43.

4. Ibid., 49.

to war against intellectual relativism and to improving the quality of Catholic historiography.[5]

It was common in the early twentieth century for Catholic scholars to laud the Middle Ages with special fervor as the culmination of Catholic Christendom. Hoffman warned against this attitude because it appeared reactionary in the eyes of non-Catholics and because it bespoke an anxiety about the universality of the Catholic message. Catholicism can flourish in all ages, he asserted, and Catholic historians are uniquely well equipped, because of their knowledge of humankind, to understand all periods of the past without recourse to apologetics.[6] Hoffman's concern with how Catholic historiography would be viewed by historians beyond the church anticipated a dominant concern of Catholic intellectuals twenty years later.

Hoffman's work during the 1930s, all the same, carried the vivid imprint of his conversion in its zeal against the whole non-Catholic world. At first he remained opposed to capitalism, on the grounds that it was based upon greed, fueled by usury, and led to a perversion of science in the interest of technological transformation. That is not to say that he retained any allegiance to socialism; rather, he now condemned both alternatives as materialistic systems that occluded the spiritual dimensions of life. Instead, he sympathized with "distributism," an economic theory based on papal teaching and developed by the English Catholic writers G. K. Chesterton and Hilaire Belloc.[7] Distributism favored the broadest possible distribution of property ownership to give dignity and independence to families, which in Catholic thought make up a healthy society. It would emphasize handcrafts and would use a guild system to regulate whatever industries were necessary. Not surprisingly, distributism was always vulnerable to attack for its anachronistic resistance to industrialization and cities and a tendency to glorify the Middle Ages. Hoffman avoided overly close identification with it by arguing for what he called the "organic state," which would provide genuine national unity without eliminating the characteristic features of modernity. He wrote several articles on the political and economic crisis of the 1930s for the *American Review* and later published them as *The Organic State.*[8]

5. Ross Hoffman, "Fordham Memoir," unpublished manuscript in the form of letters to Gaetano Vincitorio, Aug. 13, 1973–Nov. 18, 1973, in the author's possession.

6. Ross Hoffman, "Catholics and Historismus," *CHR* 24 (Jan. 1939): 401–12. See also Hoffman, *Tradition and Progress, and Other Historical Essays in Culture, Religion, and Politics* (Milwaukee: Bruce, 1938).

7. Ross Hoffman, *The Will to Freedom* (New York: Sheed and Ward, 1935), 137.

8. Ross Hoffman, *The Organic State: An Historical View of Contemporary Politics* (New York: Sheed and Ward, 1939).

The *American Review,* which John Diggins has described as "a journal noted for the perversity of its brilliance,"[9] was a continuation of the *Bookman,* which throughout the 1920s had been a platform for the "new humanist" authors, Paul Elmer More and Irving Babbitt. As one of their historians has observed, the new humanists were precursors of the new conservatism; new humanism produced the first outline of an intellectual conservatism in twentieth-century America. Its proponents were cultural traditionalists, defensive of classical principles in art, deeply skeptical about human nature, and neo-Burkean in their political and social views.[10] Rebelling against both a romanticism that exalted individualism over the common elements of human society and a naturalism that "overstated man's ties to his environment and pictured him the mindless victim of his animal impulses," the new humanists, most of them literary critics, enjoyed only a small, mainly academic, audience.[11] Throughout the 1920s they were steadily opposed by more influential contemporaries, Van Wyck Brooks, Walter Lippmann, H. L. Mencken, and Edmund Wilson. The leading New Humanists, moreover, were not churchpeople. Irving Babbitt was sympathetic to Catholicism as an organization but maintained philosophical and institutional reservations. Paul Elmer More became increasingly preoccupied by traditional Christianity in the later years of his life, sharing his friend T. S. Eliot's yearning for a traditionalist Christian culture, but never going quite so far as to join the church.[12]

Under the editorship of Seward Collins, the *American Review* of the 1930s shifted away from the largely literary interests of Babbitt, More, and the *Bookman* in response to the crisis of the Great Depression. Collins brought together a group of social critics to enrich the literary and aesthetic protest against modernism. Among them were Chesterton and Belloc, the English distributists; neoscholastic Catholics such as Hoffman, Charles Ronayne, and Christopher Dawson; second-generation new humanists such as Norman Foerster and George Ray Elliott (also a Catholic convert); and several of the "southern agrarians," including Allen Tate (another Catholic convert), John Crowe Ransom, and Donald Davidson.

The great political hope of *American Review* conservatives, including Hoffman, was for a revival of the "organic" or "corporate" state, to

9. John P. Diggins, *Mussolini and Fascism: The View from America* (Princeton: Princeton University Press, 1972), 211.

10. J. David Hoeveler, *The New Humanism: A Critique of Modern America, 1900–1940* (Charlottesville: University Press of Virginia, 1977), 3.

11. Ibid., 4.

12. Ibid., 153–76.

replace the contractual, competition-based system of democratic capitalism. Several contributors believed that Mussolini's fascism had created the best model for the corporate state, "a new form of Democracy . . . in which the interests of the people, and especially of the people as producers, are duly represented in a single, patriotic, corporate body which is an expression of their will; not the will or a compromise between the many wills of each separate class or personal political group."[13] Monarchy of some form, in which the people were unified through an elected, hereditary, or even self-appointed leader (like Mussolini), they believed, was the only way of restoring a society that could express a common will, as opposed to the factionalism and selfishness endemic in parliamentary democracies. Hoffman visited Rome in 1936, was delighted by much of what he saw, and came close to a full endorsement of Mussolini's experiment, especially since it had made a concordat with the Vatican in 1929.[14]

By contrast, Hoffman detested the "paganism" of German Nazism and the "pedantic quackery" of Hitler's racial theories, just as he detested the "barbarism" of Soviet Russia.[15] Where the American Left of the 1930s drew a distinction between communism, on the one hand, and fascism and nazism, on the other, Hoffman made the crucial distinction between fascism, on the one hand, and communism and nazism, on the other, treating these latter two as twin anti-Christian heresies. He traced them back to the nineteenth-century cult of science—scientific history in the case of communism and scientific racism in the case of the Nazis. The two ideologies vividly illustrated the dangers as well as the benefits of science, he said, an issue on which Catholics had long been outspoken.[16] For Hoffman, then, the idea of fascism brought to mind images of economic recovery, national unity, and religious freedom; it did not denote aggressive militarism, certainly not the street-action "shirt" movements. He was badly misguided about the nature of Italian fascism and subsequently repented his early enthusiasm, recalling after World War II that he "had some measure of hope that Mussolini would manage to cut loose from the Axis alliance." When, to the contrary, the Italians joined the Germans, his "Italian bubble . . . exploded."[17]

Like many Catholic converts before and since, Hoffman had little

---

13. Harold Goad, "The Principles of the Corporate State," *American Review* 1 (April 1933): 85.

14. Hoffman, *Organic State*, 81–87.

15. Ibid., 76, 79.

16. Ibid., 108.

17. Hoffman to Vincitorio, Aug. 28, 1973, "Fordham Memoir."

sympathy for other branches of Christianity during the 1930s. At the door of Protestantism, indeed, he laid the blame for most of the ills of the contemporary world. Protestants, he argued, had first upset the exquisite balance of faith and works in Catholicism by insisting on salvation by faith alone. By the twentieth century they had done a volte-face and seemed to be relying solely on salvation by works: that at least was true in the case of the social gospel movement.[18] He also criticized Protestantism for breaking the tradition of submission to church authority and for exalting the individual conscience to Promethean heights. Only Catholicism, he warned, could rescue the world because it alone was in no way tainted or compromised by the Great War, capitalism, and now the Great Depression—all of which Hoffman claimed he could trace to the Reformation. Catholicism alone held in unbroken line a sense of tradition and continuity from the time of Christ.[19] As the threat of the dictators worsened in the later 1930s, however, Hoffman began to moderate his anti-Protestant tone; it seemed possible that the Christian nations, if they were to survive at all, would have to find common ground against a dreadful common foe. It was an inkling of the political rapprochement across devotional boundaries which was to mark the Catholic new conservatives of the 1950s and to become almost universal in American religion from the 1970s.[20]

Many Catholics, especially those whose Irish heritage made them anti-British, supported American isolationism in the years between Hitler's invasion of Poland and the Japanese attack on Pearl Harbor. Hoffman, however, again anticipating the postwar Catholic conservatives' loyalties, was antiisolationist and pro-British, though his convictions angered many Catholics and brought a spate of rude letters through his mailbox.[21] Never mind that Britain was a predominantly Protestant nation, he said; it had now become, by default, the leader of the remnants of Christendom against its worst enemy since the era of militant Islam. Whereas the League of Nations had been based on an imagined world community and thus had crumbled in the face of

18. Hoffman, *Restoration,* 126.

19. Ibid., 127–33.

20. For this development in his thought, see Hoffman, *The Great Republic: A Historical View of the International Community and the Organization of Peace* (New York: Sheed and Ward, 1942).

21. For example, Rev. Joseph Luther wrote to Hoffman, Sept. 18, 1941, denouncing him as "stupid" for advocating intervention to aid Britain and adding, "The best advice that can be given men like yourself is to bundle yourself off to Britain and help defend a sottish empire which has enslaved half the world, persecuted the Church of Christ, given us every silly ism, and now linked itself with atheistic Communism in a vain effort to escape the decadence and degeneration which has emasculated its manhood." Uncataloged letter in Hoffman's papers, quoted by courtesy of Mary-Ellen Flinn, Hoffman's daughter.

its first major crisis, Christendom, though still incomplete, was the only actual international community yet to exist and it would have to form the nucleus of the postwar order.[22] During the war, Hoffman wrote extensively on the need both to ally with the Soviet Union for the defeat of Germany and yet to avoid the expectation of permanent amity with it. The overwhelming Nazi and Japanese threats justified this alliance of convenience, he believed, but disagreements among the victors were fully to be expected; certainly this war would *not* bring warfare itself to an end; Wilsonian illusions were to be resisted.[23]

Hoffman described the nations of Christendom as "the great republic," and in a book of that title, published during the war, he traced the history of the Christian political order since the decline of Rome. By the thirteenth century, he argued, the theory of the two societies, church and state, had been worked out, after which the church eschewed all efforts to establish a theocracy. Instead, it permitted the proliferation of multiple states, each distinct and specific to its region, yet all united in the one faith under the spiritual guardianship of the papacy. The church, he emphasized, had long recognized the independence and dignity of the political order as ordained by God.[24] Hoffman's "great republic" was strongly reminiscent of John Courtney Murray's reasoning about church and state. Both men used Catholic history to argue that the secular U.S. republic fulfilled, rather than challenged, the requirements of Catholic political theology. In this way both men anticipated the reasoning embodied in the Vatican II declaration on religious liberty and helped show the perfect consonance of the United States and Catholicism.

In 1945, as the war neared its conclusion, Hoffman founded the Burke Society of Fordham University, which undertook to revive "the principles, values, and traditions which are the heritage of the political and international society of Christendom."[25] Shortly thereafter he and fellow Fordham professor Paul Levack brought out an edition of Edmund Burke's writings and speeches which embodied the most topical of Burke's ideas. Their own age, the editors declared, was one of catastrophic dissolution, just like the revolutionary era in which Burke had lived. He was the first and greatest critic of the French Revolution and of the heretical Jacobinism it spawned, from which the modern

22. Hoffman, *Great Republic*, 150–56.
23. Ross Hoffman, *Durable Peace* (New York: Oxford University Press, 1944).
24. Hoffman, *Great Republic*, 13–15.
25. Description given by William Schlaerth, S.J., in his preface to *Alexis de Tocqueville's Democracy in America: Symposium*, ed. Schlaerth (New York: Fordham University Press, 1945), i, an early symposium of the society.

revolutionary spirit was descended.[26] Burke's wisdom was, therefore, extremely timely for these dawning years of the cold war. Burke, though much studied and widely admired in the century and a half since his death, had often been taken as a supremely practical politician, a pragmatic virtuoso. To the contrary, Hoffman and Levack insisted, Burke, though he certainly knew how to compromise when necessary, actually stood in the great tradition of political philosophy which ran from the classics through Saint Thomas Aquinas. They depicted this Anglican writer, an exponent of natural law, as a sort of Catholic manqué in whom twentieth-century American Catholic conservatives could find an almost ideal model.[27] Burke's greatest virtue, according to Hoffman, was that he had repudiated politics based upon abstract blueprints—utopianism—and had understood the complexities of sinful human nature. In all these principles Burke was a perfect foil for the fallacies of contemporary liberals and radicals.[28]

In a subsequent anthology of letters and papers from the early 1770s, when Burke acted as political agent in London for the Colonial Assembly of New York, Hoffman observed that his sympathy for the colonists in the years before 1776 was consistent with his later vehemently anti-revolutionary attitude toward the France of 1789.[29] The American Revolution, according to Hoffman, was a conservative reaction against the presumptions and follies of George III and a succession of rash and incompetent ministers. The contrast between the two revolutions, as Hoffman summarized it elsewhere, was perfectly apparent in the events of the year 1789, "when we cemented our revolutionary union by ratifying a constitution drafted by sagacious men behind closed doors, the while political lunatics in open and tumultuous convention tore the French state to pieces."[30] Here too was a recurring theme of the new conservatism in the 1950s: that the American Revolution should be understood as a conservative event utterly different from the French Revolution. The *Burke Newsletter,* first an adjunct of *Modern Age,* later a journal in its own right, was an important theoretical publication of the new conservatives. Other Catholics, among them Peter Stanlis,

26. Ross Hoffman and Paul Levack, Introduction to *Burke's Politics: Selected Writings and Speeches of Edmund Burke on Reform, Revolution, and War,* ed. Hoffman and Levack (New York: Knopf, 1949), xii–xv.

27. Ibid., xvi. Levack notes that Hoffman himself wrote the topical and polemical introduction to this collection. Telephone interview with Paul Levack, June 21, 1990.

28. Hoffman and Levack, Introduction to *Burke's Politics,* xxiii.

29. Ross Hoffman, ed. *Edmund Burke: New York Agent, with His Letters to the New York Assembly and Intimate Correspondence with Charles O'Hara, 1761–1776* (Philadelphia: American Philosophical Society, 1956), 189–93.

30. Ross Hoffman, *The Spirit of Politics and the Future of Freedom* (Milwaukee: Bruce, 1950), 25–26.

Carl Cone, Thomas Mahoney, Morehouse Millar, and Francis Canavan, contributed to the Burke revival along the natural law lines laid out by Hoffman.[31]

In *The Spirit of Politics and the Future of Freedom* (1950) Hoffman summarized his hopes for a conservative revival led by Catholic Americans and guided by the spirit of Burke. The horrifying events of the foregoing decades had made the need for conservative renewal clearer than ever before. Since 1914 the world had been chastened by the experience of permanent revolution, "an evil so great that it sums up almost all the evils abounding in the nightmare of horror which has tortured the world during the past few decades. Lenin, Trotsky, and Stalin, Hitler, and Goebbels, have been its outstanding practitioners. . . . It is the black art of sending the human race upon an endless adventure into a promised land that is never reached; the perpetual sacrifice of today for a future that never becomes a present."[32] Restoration was a project, then, not for Catholics alone but for the entire nation, with the object of benefiting Christendom as a whole. Hoffman believed American Catholics were best able to lead this revival, however, because their church was free, wealthy, and thriving and because they alone among Americans were untainted by the ideologies of liberalism and pragmatism. He took it as an encouraging sign that the years following the Nazi defeat had witnessed a renewed interest in the question of human rights. "It seems unlikely," he noted, "that men can long continue talking about human rights without asking themselves why humans have rights and so raising again the great questions concerning human nature which an evolution-minded generation ignored."[33]

Ross Hoffman had by 1950 expressed many of the convictions that were to guide the Catholic new conservatives in the coming decades. His faith that Catholics would lead the conservative movement was borne out at first, though their leadership became problematic when the movement began to fragment in the 1960s. Yet Hoffman had also anticipated several aspects of Vatican II Catholicism. In his historical method, resistant to hagiography and apologetics, he adumbrated a major theme of postconciliar scholarship.[34] In the ecumenism he had

31. See, for a sampling of this Catholic Burke scholarship, Peter Stanlis, *Edmund Burke and the Natural Law* (Ann Arbor: University of Michigan Press, 1958); Francis Canavan, *The Political Reason of Edmund Burke* (Durham: Duke University Press, 1960); Thomas Mahoney, *Edmund Burke and Ireland* (Cambridge: Harvard University Press, 1960).

32. Hoffman, *Spirit of Politics*, 46.

33. Ibid., 79.

34. Patrick Allitt, "Ross Hoffman and the Transformation of American Catholic Historiography," paper presented to American Catholic Historical Association, April 5, 1991, Oxford, Miss.

developed by the 1950s out of an earlier anti-Protestant zeal, he again anticipated the pan-Christian alliances of the postconciliar era, when Protestants and Catholics would often make common cause on such political issues as support for school prayer and opposition to abortion.

Francis Graham Wilson, though less passionate, led a career in many ways comparable to Hoffman's. Born in 1901 in Texas, he converted in 1924 from Episcopalianism. Afterward, he continued his academic career in non-Catholic institutions, gaining a Stanford Ph.D. in 1928, then teaching first at the University of Washington and later at the University of Illinois.[35] As with Hoffman's, much of his academic work addressed recent history and U.S. political phenomena. Wilson too derived from his faith a critical and disengaged perspective on his country which enabled him to see it as part of the West, rather than a distinct and unassimilable entity; both men eschewed the long American tradition of historiographical exceptionalism. A series of Wilson's 1949 lectures, published as *The Case for Conservatism* (1951), adumbrated many of the principles the Catholic new conservatives elaborated in the following years. Tracing American conservatism from Burke and *The Federalist* rather than from explicitly Catholic sources, Wilson nevertheless emphasized their continuity with the longer tradition of Christendom and their consonance with natural law.

Wilson described five distinct propositions underlying the conservative political disposition: first, that there is an intelligible pattern in history, not a mere succession of intrinsically unrelated events; second, that human nature is imperfect and corruptible; third, that "there is a moral order in the universe in which man participates and from which he can derive canons or principles of political judgment"; fourth, that government must be closely circumscribed; and fifth, that private property is the foundation of civilization. Elaborating on these themes, he emphasized how knowledge of the imperfectibility of human beings had emerged out of the Judeo-Christian doctrine of sin and how all the other principles were linked in the Christian conception of life. Even Christians who rejected the legitimacy of economic laissez-faire, Wilson argued, should accept the legitimacy of private property because it nourished families. "If one believes in the Christian principle of the family, one can easily believe that property is a natural adjunct to the moral function of the family." It is a point, he added, that the "Catholic encyclicals have defended . . . as a means of preserving the independence and the standard of living of the family." Wilson aimed

---

35. For biographical details on Wilson, see *American Catholic Who's Who,* 1956–57 (Grosse Pointe, Mich.: Walter Romig, 1957), 483.

his remarks not only at Catholic audiences. Rather, he believed that Protestants, finding the civilization they had built in the United States assailed on all sides by liberalism and communism, needed the aid of Catholics and Jews alike: "Today our problem is not the defense of Protestantism with its philosophy of history, but the defense of religion at all." The three Judeo-Christian faiths alone could "keep alive the humanitarian tradition that belongs to the religious traditions of the West."[36]

Wilson singled out John Dewey, the pragmatic philosopher and progressive reformer, as an emblem of contemporary liberalism whose work threatened the conservative verities. (Probably no man suffered more frequent attack from the Catholic new conservatives in the following years than Dewey, whose ideals were the antithesis of their own.) Dewey, said Wilson, purported to study society scientifically, blending a naive faith in science and progress with a Darwinian materialism. This approach falsified human realities by omitting the spiritual dimension that separates human beings from all other natural phenomena.[37] Dewey's philosophical principles had influenced the new behavioral scientists, too, who prescinded entirely from questions of truth and faith. In historical studies using behavioral science principles, Wilson observed, "ideas are functional and forceful and they are reflective of interests, classes, and groups, but the possibility of theoretical advance outside of empiricism is denied." The possibility of truth was disappearing, he feared, and under these assumptions, "intellectual history, and its subcomponent, political philosophy, will be on the way to oblivion as the center of the study of the science of politics."[38]

Wilson made a forceful case for the consonance of Catholicism and American conservatism. They shared, he said, an abhorrence of the French and Russian revolutionary traditions, both of which were, "first of all, destroyers of Christian society" and had tried to extinguish "the Great Tradition of Institutional Christianity and Christian philosophy." Neither conservatives nor Catholics were opposed to all forms of revolution, however, as the American Revolution and Catholic support for it had demonstrated. Catholic conservatives, therefore, should avoid bringing the European theorists of reaction, Louis de Bonald, Joseph de Maistre, and Prince Metternich, to their aid, but they could profit-

---

36. Francis Graham Wilson, *The Case for Conservatism* (Seattle: University of Washington Press, 1951), 12, 22, 63.

37. Francis Graham Wilson, "The Foremost Philosopher of the Age," *MA* 2 (Winter 1957–58): 54–62.

38. Francis Graham Wilson, "The Behaviorist's Persuasion," *MA* 3 (Summer 1959): 312–13.

ably call upon the tradition of Burke and *The Federalist*. Wilson mentioned that the political-theological elements of this rapprochement were being worked out by John Courtney Murray. The Anglo-American conservative tradition accepted representative government, justified rebellion against tyranny, and avoided utopianism, again in a way consonant with Catholic tradition. "Neither the Mystical Body, nor natural law, nor original sin," Wilson remarked, "gives one the right to assume that a perfect political society can be realized within history." The limited government advocated by the new conservatives, protest against the growing reach of the federal government over the states and localities, and prudent defense of the free market, he concluded, made the new conservative movement a "congenial political atmosphere" for Catholics. Both groups "operate on the principle of an objective moral order and reject secularism based on pragmatic and neo-utilitarian philosophy."[39]

COLD WAR DEVELOPMENTS

Catholic lay conservatives coming of age in the 1950s generally shared the views of Hoffman and Wilson, believing that opposition to communism, foreign and domestic, was their most immediate vital task. Communism was for them what the French Revolution had been to Burke. Many of them understood the contest with the Soviet Union not simply as a political standoff in which troops, aircraft, industrial capacity, and military resolve would be decisive. Rather, they believed the cold war must be seen as an eschatological struggle in which Christian Western civilization, the preserver of truth and faith, confronted its demonic nemesis. Brent Bozell argued that the West had been "vouchsafed the truth about the nature of man and his relationship with the universe" and that "the West asserts a God-given right, and thinks of it as a God-given duty, to conserve and spread its truth," of which the churches were "the principal custodians."[40] Frank Meyer added, borrowing the idiom of Saint John's Gospel: "Communism, in actual and objective fact, does represent an absolute black, and the West, as a civilization *in its essence*, as close to an absolute white as is possible in the subdued light which illuminates this imperfect world."[41]

39. Francis Graham Wilson, "Catholics and the New Conservatism," *SO* 6 (June 1956): 247, 248, 249, 252.

40. L. Brent Bozell, "The Strange Drift of Liberal Catholicism," *NR*, Aug. 12, 1961, 81.

41. Frank Meyer, *The Conservative Mainstream* (New Rochelle, N.Y.: Arlington House, 1969), 119.

William Buckley launched *National Review* in November 1955, and the journal showed this intense preoccupation with communism from the start. Some contributors emphasized the dangers of Soviet Russia in strategic great-power terms and others focused on the implacable mendacity of the ideology itself. The conservatives' suspicions of the Soviet Union were confirmed by the Hungarian crisis of 1956, when Hungarian revolutionaries overthrew their Soviet puppet government, declared Hungary a neutral nation, and called on the Western powers for assistance. Radio Free Europe, a U.S. propaganda operation, had been encouraging such actions by broadcasting news of the Dwight Eisenhower–John Foster Dulles policy of "rollback," which implied that the United States would aid anti-Communist rebellions.[42] In the event, however, no American aid arrived and the Hungarian rebellion was crushed by Soviet tanks and troops.

From first to last, Catholic conservatives understood the Hungarian Revolution as a political event freighted with religious significance. During the late summer of 1956, when one Hungarian Communist ruler was replaced by another, the nationalist Imre Nagy, *National Review* watched suspiciously and described the exhumation of four Hungarian patriots who had been executed seven years before but were now to be buried with honor in the national pantheon: "The godless religion of Communism is driven to complete the symbolic cycle of its black inversion of true religion. To its myriad rites of crucifixion it now adds a blasphemous resurrection."[43] Gradually the editors realized the magnitude of the events taking place in Hungary, dropped this scornful tone, and celebrated what appeared to be the overthrow of communism there. The release of Cardinal Joszef Mindszenty, primate of the Hungarian Catholic church, who had been imprisoned after a show trial in 1949, they greeted with "prayerful thanksgiving." They also urged that the United States and the United Nations make good on their rhetoric of self-determination and rollback by intervening decisively against a Soviet attack.[44]

Despite Catholic conservatives' hopes, however, and despite their support for Senator William Knowland's idea of a "crusade for freedom," the United States took no action and stood by as the revolution was crushed. They were dismayed. The destruction of the rising, wrote one, "is, excepting the drama of the Warsaw rising of 1944, the most

42. On the events of 1956 in Hungary, see Bennett Kovrig, *Communism in Hungary: From Kun to Kadar* (Stanford, Calif.: Hoover Institution Press, 1979), 285–316.

43. Editorial, "The Ghosts Are Restless," *NR*, Oct. 20, 1956, 4.

44. Untitled editorial, *NR*, Nov. 10, 1956, 3; editorial, "Next Stage in Eastern Europe," ibid., 6–7.

monstrous single happening in modern history."[45] The pusillanimity of the government seemed inexcusable to Brent Bozell, since its inaction sent a message to the Soviet Union that the United States would not intervene in the internal affairs of any Warsaw Pact country. "The significance of the Hungarian revolution," he wrote: "is not merely that the United States failed to implement its highly touted liberation policy when rebellion occurred, but that the transformation of rebellion from hypothesis to reality so terrified U.S. policy makers as to lead them to support measures which would insure the integrity of the Communist empire." Bozell knew that without Soviet support, United Nations intervention in Hungary would provoke the dissolution of the UN, but like most of his colleagues he assigned dubious value to the international organization; it was, he said, "expendable, especially if it were to expire in the cause of freedom."[46]

What made the U.S. government's quiescence in the Hungarian Revolution all the more shameful, in Catholic conservatives' eyes, was that it coincided with the Anglo-French-Israeli attempt to retake the Suez Canal from Egypt, which had seized it earlier that year. In the Suez crisis the United States supported a United Nations condemnation of the three powers' attack, and American pressure on Britain and France brought their armies to a halt. *National Review* regarded this action as a sin of commission as unpardonable as Eisenhower's sins of omission in Hungary. President Gamel Abdel Nasser of Egypt, it editorialized, was a "willing tool of Communist imperialism" who had shown himself perfectly willing to commit his own acts of "imperial aggression." For the United States to act in concert with the Soviet Union in the United Nations to condemn Britain and France was a shameful betrayal of Western civilization. "Over the humiliated forms of our two oldest and closest allies we clasp the hands of the murderers of the Christian heroes of Hungary." Again biblical analogies drove home their sense of outrage: "Britain and France are not stones that can be freely cast but flesh that can only be torn out of the living body of which we also are an organic part. In denying them—as in every ultimate betrayal—it is ourselves we deny. At dawn the cock will crow."[47] Throughout its first year of publication, *National Review* had criticized President Eisenhower's foreign policy of de facto coexistence with the Soviet Union, which it regarded as too conciliatory; some contributors had already urged conservatives not to vote for Eisen-

---

45. Erik von Kuehnelt-Leddihn, "Hungary: The West's Darkest Hour," *NR*, Nov. 24, 1956, 11.

46. L. Brent Bozell, "Foggy Bottom Gets the Jitters," *NR*, Dec. 15, 1956, 8.

47. Editorial, "Abstractions Kill the West," *NR*, Dec. 8, 1956, 7.

hower in the election of 1956. After Hungary, the split with Eisenhower was sharper than ever.[48]

To escape his persecutors when the Hungarian rising failed, Cardinal Mindszenty fled to the sanctuary of the U.S. embassy in Budapest. Mindszenty had once been tortured by the Nazis for aiding Hungarian Jews. He was tortured again, brainwashed, and imprisoned after a show trial by the Hungarian Communists in 1949, and there was every reason to suppose that he would suffer as bad or worse fate if he was recaptured. Accordingly, the U.S. government permitted him to stay in the embassy, but in conditions scarcely better than those of a prisoner. To U.S. Catholics he became the living embodiment of uncompromising Christian opposition to totalitarianism behind the Iron Curtain in the following years. Mindszenty societies, politicoreligious education and pressure groups, sprang up in many Catholic parishes in the late 1950s and early 1960s. Mindszenty himself stayed in the embassy until 1972, when, finally, in an era of "detente," Pope Paul VI asked him to leave, and the Hungarian government guaranteed him safe conduct out of the country.[49]

Reflecting on the Hungarian Revolution, Catholic conservatives shared the view that only a supernatural faith could have inspired the rising against such desperate odds. Frederick Wilhelmsen, one of the most impassioned of the group, noted that political analysts had predicted in the foregoing years that "revolution behind the Iron Curtain not only could not succeed but that it could not even get under way. What they forgot," said Wilhelmsen, "was that the Faith is not of this world."[50] Stanley Parry, a priest, echoed Wilhelmsen's views and said the revolution "can be grasped only in the perspective of the struggle between Michael and Lucifer, between Christ and Satan." He speculated that by demonstrating the heroism of the Hungarians to the irresolute West, "God perhaps is offering Christendom a last chance to be worthy of its redemption."[51] Erik von Kuehnelt-Leddihn, a Catholic contributor writing from Europe, added that the faith and determination of the Hungarian workers, students, and peasants in the rising "has taught a lesson not only to Moscow but also to certain flabby-minded and muddled Christians in the West." They had shown Western Christians who still doubted it, he said, that Christianity and communism were utterly irreconcilable.[52] In the following years, *National*

48. On voting for Eisenhower, see "Should Conservatives Vote for Eisenhower? James Burnham, Yes; William Schlamm, No," *NR*, Oct. 20, 1956, 12–15.
49. See Joszef Mindszenty, *Memoirs* (New York: Macmillan, 1974).
50. Frederick Wilhelmsen, "The Meaning of Hungary," *NR*, Dec. 1, 1956, 9–10.
51. Rev. Stanley Parry, "The Meaning of Hungary," *NR*, Dec. 1, 1956, 10.
52. Erick von Kuehnelt-Leddihn, "Exploded Myths," *NR*, Jan. 5, 1957, 13.

Review used tributes to Cardinal Mindszenty as sticks with which to beat the government for what they regard as its neglect of the "captive nations" and the "Church in chains."[53]

Two prominent figures in the new conservative movement were Hungarian Catholics who had come to the United States after World War II. For both men, John Lukacs, professor of history at Chestnut Hill College, Philadelphia, and Thomas Molnar, professor of French at Brooklyn College, Hungary had been their home as children and young men, and they felt strongly about the tragedy of the uprising. Lukacs, who had left Hungary in 1946 at the age of twenty-three, described himself as a "bourgeois" Hungarian Catholic and noted the contrast between himself and the "proletarian" Hungarian refugees he met ten years later at Fort Kilmer, New Jersey, as they flooded into the United States after the revolution failed.[54] By then Lukacs was well established, married to an American wife, contributing to Catholic journals, and playing an active role in the conservative intellectual revival.[55]

Lukacs had already published a historical account of the misconceptions that governed Western attitudes toward Eastern Europe in the interwar years and the dangers consequent upon American lack of resolve, *The Great Powers and Eastern Europe.* In the late 1940s, he argued, U.S. diplomatic firmness could have hindered Soviet domination of Eastern Europe. Stalin had moved carefully at first because "he did not quite realize how full and uncontested was his grasp of his new domains." Alas, too many "muddled liberal illusions" had acted as "deadweights" on U.S. policy makers and permitted them to let Eastern Europe slip out of their grasp and into complete Stalinist domination by 1950. In an elegiac lament for a region slipping into barbaric Communist darkness Lukacs held out one hope for Eastern Europe: "Only the magnetic force of a rejuvenated, remade, and truly united Western Europe, one that has recovered the erstwhile spiritual greatness of that Christian continent, can eventually develop enough attraction to penetrate the steely barriers separating the West from Eastern Europe's modern police states."[56] But there was little sign of this spiritual rejuvenation in 1953, and U.S. paralysis in the 1956 crisis

53. See, for example, M. Stanton Evans, "The World's Most Orphaned Nation," *NR*, Jan. 15, 1963, 36; Alice Leone Moats, "Can Anyone Free Cardinal Mindszenty?" *NR*, June 18, 1963, 491–93; editorial, "Cardinal Mindszenty," *NR*, March 1, 1974, 248–49.

54. John Lukacs, "Lessons of the Hungarian Revolution," *Commentary* 24 (Nov. 1957): 224.

55. This section is based in part on my interview with John Lukacs, Nov. 8, 1990, in Phoenixville, Pa.

56. John Lukacs, *The Great Powers and Eastern Europe* (Chicago: Henry Regnery, 1953), 691, 697, 699.

confirmed Lukacs's view that the West was in fact decaying spiritually. Decay was manifest in the rise of juvenile delinquency, the demagoguery of politicians, the welfare state, and "the transformation of American society in an increasingly regimented, standardized, military, and centralized direction."[57] "The trouble with the West," he reflected in the aftermath of the Hungarian Revolution, "is that it long ago lost its confidence in the efficacy of its own moral standards," so that, ironically, it fell to "Poles and Hungarians, to remind us of the inherent superiority of Western morality."[58]

Indeed, unlike most of his American-born colleagues, Lukacs tended to denigrate the force of communism itself; he treated it as an exhausted ideology that the Soviet Union used cynically, which had had almost no influence on the peoples of Eastern Europe, so that "except for a few aged Marxists huddled in New York there are few truly international Communists left."[59] Without in any way diminishing the magnitude of the cold war, Lukacs saw it more as a national than as an ideological conflict. Dismayed by the "immoral and unchristian implication of ideological crusades," he warned conservatives against apocalypticism.[60] And in an early Catholic expression of revulsion against nuclear weapons, when Catholic opinion still generally accepted them as guardians of American security, he noted how they had proven a two-edged sword, working as much against U.S. interests as for them. From the moral point of view, Lukacs grieved that the makers of the bomb, "puny men who no longer believe in the virtue of imitating Christ," had "arrogated to themselves the part of gods." From the strategic point of view, too, he recognized how knowledge of the possibility of nuclear war had disabled the response to the Hungarian Revolution. Nuclear weapons could act not only as "a defense of freedom but also as a restriction of freedom." They were, he concluded, "instruments of utmost potency as well as of historic impotence."[61] Later, in the 1980s, American Catholicism as a whole was to be riven over the question of the legitimacy, moral and military, of nuclear weapons.

Thomas Molnar was another Hungarian American who became prominent in the ranks of Catholic conservative intellectuals. Born in 1921, raised partly in Budapest and partly in Romanian Transylvania,

57. John Lukacs, *A History of the Cold War* (Garden City, N.Y.: Doubleday, 1961), 190.
58. Lukacs, "Lessons of the Hungarian Revolution," 230.
59. Ibid., 226.
60. Lukacs, *History of the Cold War*, 208–9; Lukacs, "The Question of Crusades," C, Oct. 16, 1953, 43.
61. Lukacs, *History of the Cold War*, 280, 136.

he became a Catholic resistance worker during World War II, was imprisoned at the Dachau concentration camp by the Nazis, but managed to survive the war.[62] Escaping the postwar Communist domination of Hungary, he traveled first to Belgium and then to the United States, where he earned a doctorate in modern languages at Columbia in 1952.[63] He taught briefly at St. Mary's College in northern California, a Catholic school, but then returned permanently to New York as a professor at Brooklyn College. A restless intellect, he wrote in the following years on a diversity of issues, among them the end of European imperialism in Africa, the crisis of American education, changing conditions in U.S. Catholicism, and the phenomenon of utopianism. Like Lukacs, Molnar became a frequent contributor to Catholic and conservative journals and wrote an extensive analysis of American foreign policy and its illusions in the crucial area of Eastern Europe. In *The Two Faces of American Foreign Policy* (1962), the differences between the two scholars are clear. Molnar was less willing than Lukacs to accept coexistence even temporarily, more willing to justify imperialism as a positive force of civilization, and more willing to countenance the use of nuclear weapons.[64] But both men believed that the cold war had an underlying religious significance and that victory presupposed a revivified, united Christian Europe. The "basic unity of Western philosophy, rooted in the Judeo-Christian religion," said Molnar, "is one of the half dozen pillars on which an orderly world rests" (145).

American liberals, Molnar believed, were chronically liable to utopian delusions, among them the notions that imperialism was always an evil and that such supranational organizations as the United Nations would soon be able to displace national sovereign states. Like Lukacs again, Molnar denied the American-born anti-Communists' conviction that the Soviet Union was locked into its own ideology and unswerving in its pursuit of world conquest. Rather, said Molnar, it was the U.S. liberals who had become trapped by their illusions, whereas the Soviets "have not been lulled by their own slogans" and so were better able to "advance by the use of common sense" (49). The fate of Eastern Europe in the twentieth century provided, in his view, the perfect example of how liberals fell prey to pious abstractions instead of hard policy considerations. Woodrow Wilson's "impatience"

62. This section is based in part on my telephone interview with Thomas Molnar, Jan. 15, 1991.

63. George Nash, *The Conservative Intellectual Movement in America since 1945* (New York: Basic Books, 1976), 78–79; Thomas Molnar, "Growing Up in Eastern Europe," *HLR* 16 (Spring 1990): 63–71.

64. Thomas Molnar, *The Two Faces of American Foreign Policy* (Indianapolis: Bobbs-Merrill, 1962), 228.

to "smash the Habsburg Empire to pieces" at the end of World War I had opened "a fatal power vacuum—a temptation for both Germany and Russia—in the most vulnerable part of Europe" (59). The United States was still paying the price for this mistake; the captive nations of Eastern Europe were paying a still higher price.

Molnar derided containment policy and the faltering steps taken by Presidents Eisenhower and Kennedy in their conduct of the cold war: "The Eisenhower administration talked big and carried a small stick" (65–66). The great moments in the cold war, he said, had both been achieved by President Truman: first, the Berlin airlift of 1948 (66) and, second, the rapid and decisive response to the invasion of South Korea in 1950 (185). In each case, forceful action had led to a Communist retreat. Since then, as so often in the past, U.S. policy makers had vacillated between self-interest and idealism and had been too willing to indulge shifting popular opinion: "Our very wavering between soft-ness and a show of power resulted in using force either much too late (as in the thwarted invasion of Cuba [i.e., the Bay of Pigs]) or much too ruthlessly (as in using the atomic bomb over Hiroshima and Nagasaki)" (63).[65] In the case of the Hungarian Revolution Molnar believed that "a quick decision to dispatch a team of observers from the UN to Buda-pest immediately after the Nagy government's proclamation of seces-sion from the Soviet bloc would have decisively embarrassed the Russians" and prevented their bloody repression of Hungary (209). So long as policy makers remained vulnerable to what he considered their utopian illusions, Molnar saw little hope of victory. "There is some-thing rotten about all these pious prayers for a change of heart, a change of nature, a transcendence of history," he exclaimed. "Pascal's words apply to our intellectuals: he who wants to act like an angel, ends by acting like a beast" (167). These were the themes the prolific Molnar would develop in the coming decades as he and Lukacs pre-sented a brilliantly eccentric view of American and European events from their position on the margins of both.

Three years after the Hungarian rising, in September 1959, Soviet leader Nikita Khrushchev visited the United States at the invitation of President Eisenhower. Members of both major political parties and many liberal intellectuals believed a policy of permanent coexistence with the Soviet Union was now possible; they noted that Khrushchev had denounced Stalin at the Twentieth Communist Party Congress in 1956 and that he seemed to embody "communism with a human face,"

65. Walter Lippmann also noted the dangerous effect of popular opinion on consistency in foreign policy, in *Essays on the Public Philosophy* (Boston: Little, Brown, 1955). Molnar, however, regarded Lippmann as too "soft," too willing to temporize with communism.

to use a common catchphrase of the era. Given the fearsome threat of nuclear weapons, they also thought coexistence necessary, believing that closer diplomatic relations and cultural exchanges were important avenues of communication between the potential belligerents. By contrast, Americans who understood the conflict of East and West as a spiritual struggle were dismayed by the Khrushchev visit. The Catholic bishop of St. Augustine, Florida, invoked the memory of the "heroic Hungarian freedom fighters" in denouncing Khrushchev's visit and said he would never welcome "one whose hands are crimson with the blood of our fellow Christians."[66] Catholic lay conservatives, like this prelate, interpreted the visit as analogous to the European appeasement of Hitler at the end of the 1930s. Khrushchev, "the butcher of Budapest,"[67] as the *National Review* called him, was the servant of an ideology of world conquest; he did not suffer under the illusion that permanent coexistence was possible. He might be able to use a visit to the United States and protestations of goodwill to further Soviet propaganda, but the conservatives considered it axiomatic that he would not have agreed to the visit unless he anticipated some strategic advantage from it. Sooner or later, they believed, he did indeed intend to "bury" the West as he had threatened just weeks before.

Protesting the Khrushchev visit, Catholic conservatives aimed most of their fire against the administration and its apologists for assuming, with perhaps fatal consequences, that the visit could benefit U.S. interests. William Buckley addressed an anti-Khrushchev protest rally at Carnegie Hall and criticized the administration both for inviting the Soviet leader and for urging Americans to greet him warmly. If Eisenhower's words of welcome really echoed the thoughts of the American people, he said, "the people have lost their reason, and we cannot hope to live down the experience until we have recovered our reason and regained our moral equilibrium." Ultimately, America's spiritual resources would prevail because the religious heritage of the West was more than a match for Communist atheism: "Khrushchev cannot take permanent advantage of our temporary disadvantage, for it is the West he is fighting. And in the West there lie, however encysted, the ultimate resources, which are moral in nature. Khrushchev is not aware that the gates of Hell shall not prevail against us."[68]

National Review columnists Brent Bozell and Frank Meyer agreed that despite the vast superiority of its spiritual resources, the West was

66. "Archbishop Joseph Hurley to the Priests of His Diocese," *NR*, Sept. 12, 1959, 318.

67. Editorial, "Even the Legion," *NR*, Sept. 12, 1959, 319.

68. William F. Buckley, Jr., "The Damage We Have Done to Ourselves," *NR*, Sept. 26, 1959, 351.

suffering a terrible short-term defeat at Khrushchev's hands. "Without the firing of a shot we have suffered the greatest defeat in our history" wrote Meyer. By recognizing communism and its world leader, "we have surrendered our honor, betrayed our moral duty to the enslaved people of the world, and—the character of Communism being what it is—we have immensely assisted it on its road to world conquest."[69] Bozell traced the apparent willingness to appease Khrushchev to the idea that war had become unthinkable lest it destroy the world. This attitude, he said, was understandable from the point of view of "atheist materialists" such as the Communists, who had no life after death to anticipate, but should not prove decisive in the Western tradition, which "puts a high value on human life, but . . . provides for something else when life is gone." This argument ought in fact to be the West's "trump" against communism: "The terror—the specter of a lifeless planet—is, by all rights, *our* weapon." Bozell added that a morally reoriented American leadership ought to conduct the cold war incrementally, for Western advantage, until such time as it realized defeat or open war were the only remaining alternatives. At that point it should launch a surprise attack on the Soviet Union "in the middle of the night" and do it "with the serenity with which spiritually free men always choose good over evil; with the knowledge that when the right is pursued, it is God who ordains the cost."[70]

A fourth Catholic critic, Garry Wills, joined the chorus against Khrushchev in *National Review*. As a Jesuit seminarian Wills had first submitted an unsolicited article to Buckley's journal in 1957. Buckley liked the article so much that he offered Wills, then aged twenty-three, a summer internship.[71] Wills decided against ordination to the priesthood and took up graduate study in the classics at Yale. He wrote regularly for *National Review* in the following years, first as a graduate student, later as an assistant professor of classics at Johns Hopkins. In the controversy over Khrushchev's visit Wills argued that President Eisenhower and those who supported his invitation of Khrushchev were guilty of cowardice, the same cowardice that had allowed "the cry of Hungary" to go "unanswered" and refused "to see in Chiang Kai-shek's little garrison [i.e., on Taiwan] a desperate romance of courage." Unable to overcome this cowardice because of spiritual irreso-

69. Frank Meyer, "They Cry 'Peace, Peace,' When There Is No Peace," *NR*, Oct. 10, 1959, 391. Meyer, an ex-Communist, was not at this time a Catholic. He was a deathbed convert from Judaism, but by the late 1950s he shared the Catholic idiom on this issue.

70. L. Brent Bozell, "They Gave the Orders, II," *NR*, Oct. 24, 1959, 419.

71. On Wills's early encounters with Buckley and *National Review*, see his *Confessions of a Conservative* (Garden City, N.Y.: Doubleday, 1979), 3–59.

lution, said Wills, the apostles of coexistence bore witness to "the morbidity of the modern soul," which "reflects a paralysis in the face of evil." To call war "unthinkable" was to deny oneself sound preparation for war when it did, inevitably, arrive. Anyone who believed that the new scale of destruction signified by nuclear weapons made war impossible was "ignorant of the moral history of mankind." This was not to say that war was imminent, "but if we will not think of it, we shall infallibly suffer it. Sin always thrives on neglect."[72]

These Catholic conservatives were in practice powerless to prevent Khrushchev's visit. Indeed, he returned a year later to speak at the United Nations. Editorializing on behalf of the Committee for the Freedom of All Peoples, founded in protest against Khrushchev's visit, the *National Review* recommended that the Soviet leader be greeted with "silence or jeers," that "church services be held for the oppressed peoples in the captive lands, that the press ignore his presence," and that "all flags be flown at half mast."[73] The committee's open letter to Khrushchev, edged in black, accused him of violating natural law: "We regard you as a predator; your regime as a barbarism outside the international community; your revolution as total war against the human race."[74] Catholic conservatives were correspondingly angry to learn that a prominent businessman, Cyrus Eaton, had actively promoted Khrushchev's visit, thrown a luncheon party on his behalf, and welcomed him to American soil; they saw his actions as contemptuous abuse of the freedom given him by "the nation that protects him."[75]

The preoccupation with the cold war and the active participation of Eastern Europeans in the movement indicate how different new conservatism was from earlier forms of American conservatism, which had tended strongly toward isolationism and exceptionalism. The concept of Christendom gave Catholic new conservatives a wider sphere of concern than earlier, nativist conservatives had shown. They also differed from earlier conservatives in their approach to capitalism.

CAPITALISM

Among Catholics in general, and to some extent within the ranks of Catholic new conservatives, the 1950s witnessed a debate over the degree to which they could in good conscience support and defend

72. Garry Wills, "Nero in Our Camp," *NR*, Sept. 12, 1959, 332–33.
73. Editorial, "Against the Khrushchev Visit," *NR*, Sept. 24, 1960, 165, 167.
74. Statement by Committee for Freedom of All Peoples, *NR*, Sept. 29, 1960, 166.
75. Untitled editorial, *NR*, Oct. 8, 1960, 197.

the capitalist order in the United States. They displayed a spectrum of views on these questions, some ardently in favor of capitalism, others giving qualified approval, others rejecting many of its most characteristic attributes as incongruent with their faith. The debate pivoted about two sets of issues. First, what were the aspects of the economic order about which questions must be asked? These included the legitimacy of private property, entrepreneurial initiative, government regulation of business, laissez-faire and the free market, and the role of technology in capitalism; different authors accorded these various factors different degrees of legitimacy. Second, how did the Vatican approach economic issues, and what papal declarations must be studied in making one's decision about them? The papal encyclicals *Rerum Novarum* and *Quadragesimo Anno* were the two documents most closely scrutinized, but their ambiguities gave rise to as many debates as they closed; the argument was to intensify, as will be seen, after publication of a third economic encyclical, *Mater et Magistra*, in 1961.

In their everyday lives all Catholics were, to some degree, involved in the workings of the economy. Some princes of the church, notably Cardinal Joseph Mundelein of Chicago and Cardinal Francis Spellman of New York, were adept businessmen in their own right. Mundelein sold shares in "Catholic Bishop of Chicago, Inc.," on the open market, which kept their value even in the worst days of the Great Depression.[76] Catholic statements defending the pattern of the American economy were not uncommon, especially as it became clear, following World War II, that the nation was not going to sink back into the depression conditions of the 1930s but was, instead, becoming the first great "affluent society." One widely read reassurance for postwar Catholics was Father Edward Keller's *Christianity and American Capitalism* (1953), which followed each assertion of support for capitalism with extensive quotations from the two papal letters in an attempt to show that its author was not deviating in any way from papal writ. Keller justified the American economy largely because of its actual successes in generating and distributing wealth and because government controls already restrained radical laissez-faire. The church, he said, condemned only "Manchesterian" individualism, which subordinated the moral law to the law of the market; the church defended "that individualism which is socially and morally responsible." American capitalism, Keller wrote, "is founded on the basic institutions of private property, freedom of competition, freedom of enterprise, and

76. Edward Kantowicz, "Cardinal Mundelein of Chicago and the Shaping of Twentieth-Century Catholicism," *Journal of American History* 68 (June 1981): 61–62.

freedom of contract. The social encyclicals do not condemn these institutions." Like an experienced welfare capitalist, Keller advocated good business-labor relations and high wages to facilitate widespread property holding, but he firmly denied that the papal letters could be read to support a then-current Congress of Industrial Organizations plan for labor comanagement of factories. Such a scheme "would be revolutionary" and would render the basic institutions of capitalism "meaningless." They would also, he added, usher in a form of socialism and so violate the strictest prohibitions of Pope Pius XI.[77]

Keller knew that the United States had undergone a transformation from competitive capitalism to corporate oligopoly since the mid-nineteenth century and that its economy was now competitive only in some spheres. But just as results showed that "free competition is productive of much good," so too the morality of the new corporate economy must be judged by its fruits: "The big corporations pay the highest wages, have the best working conditions, guarantee the workers the greatest stability of employment and economic security." Unconvinced by arguments that their existence threatened the common good, Keller maintained that "the burden of proof is upon those who would break up these naturally big corporations into many small competing units." The "gigantism" of big government, in his opinion, presented a far greater danger to society than that of big business.[78]

Father Keller's voice was not isolated. Endorsing his approach, Father John Dinneen, a Jesuit priest, found in favor of the system whose workings had made the United States the world's richest nation. He considered it both economically and politically benign, "a competitive system hedged in by institutional safeguards, that is, ordered capitalism in contrast with anarchical or historical capitalism." It represented, to his satisfaction, "true democracy in action." In the contemporary world, he believed, the only actual alternative was the "coercive economy" prevalent behind the Iron Curtain, which the church had condemned unequivocally. By contrast, the church "has . . . been an ardent supporter of capitalism in its essential structure, recognizing that it is based upon man's natural right to private property." So successful had capitalism been that it had created for "the American people as a whole that minimum of material abundance which is necessary for the practice of virtue."[79] Another Catholic journalist, Arnold McKee, endorsed this last point, noting that by safeguarding private

77. Edward A. Keller, C.S.C., *Christianity and American Capitalism* (Chicago: Heritage Foundation, 1953), 40–42, 18, 15, 50, 54–55.

78. Ibid., 50.

79. John A. Dinneen, S.J., "'Capitalism' and Capitalism," *CW* 180 (Jan. 1955): 294, 295.

property and resisting excessive state intervention, U.S. capitalism conformed "to the requirements of human nature and dignity and to the purpose and ends of the economy as part of society."[80] These examples could be multiplied at will with citations from most of the American Catholic media of the 1950s.

It was no dramatic innovation, therefore, for William Buckley to express enthusiastic support for capitalism in two books from the 1950s, *God and Man at Yale* and *Up from Liberalism*. Some commentators on Buckley have tended to exaggerate the novelty of his claims and have treated him as philosophically eccentric for defending Christianity and capitalism side by side.[81] Buckley, like Keller, wrote in favor of the free-market economy not in the abstract but as part of a protest against the increasing reach of the state and what he perceived as the overbearing power of trade unions. In the intervention of the government, especially its coercive taxation, he saw a greater threat to citizens than in the pursuit of wealth by separate individuals, because the state was more likely to abridge citizens' freedoms than any corporation. Private property and private enterprise should be understood as barriers against political tyranny. "It is part of the conservative intuition," he wrote, "that economic freedom is the most precious temporal freedom, for the reason that it alone gives to each one of us, in our comings and goings in our complex society, sovereignty—and over that part of existence in which by far the most choices have in fact to be made."[82]

At the same time, Buckley insisted that support for economic individualism did not entail either philosophical materialism or consent to the idea that capitalism depends upon selfishness. He repudiated the "anarcho-capitalist" or radical libertarian theorists Murray Rothbard and Ayn Rand, who touted "the virtue of selfishness" and regarded altruism as folly, and he had no sympathy for social Darwinian metaphors that treated economic competition as a survival struggle. Instead, Buckley emphasized the social benefits accruing to all citizens in a capitalist society and the benignity of such arrangements. "Support for the weak," he noted, "is an automatic result of the free enterprise system because no one can bring prosperity to himself without bringing it to others (except where prosperity is due to government

---

80. Arnold McKee, "Selling American Capitalism," *CM* 55 (July–Aug. 1957): 317.

81. See, for example, John P. Diggins, *Up from Communism: Conservative Odysseys in American Intellectual History* (New York: Harper and Row, 1975). Diggins says that Buckley's "halfhearted attempt to assimilate papal doctrine with Ludwig von Mises ended in frustration" and that "conservatism, capitalism, and Christianity present . . . an impossible synthesis" (407).

82. William F. Buckley, Jr., *Up from Liberalism* (1959; New York: Bantam, 1968), 156.

subvention)."[83] Conversely, the trend toward "collectivism," which he believed was being assiduously fostered in Yale's department of economics, was deplorable because it trampled individuals' rights and eroded their most important "temporal" freedoms. Economics directed by state intervention abridged personal choices by assuming "that the economic ass can be driven to Point A most speedily by the judicious use of carrot-and-stick, an approach that supersedes the traditional notion . . . that we are not dealing with asses, and that Point A cannot possibly, in a free society, be presumed to be the desired objective of tens of millions of individual human beings."[84]

Buckley brought *Up from Liberalism* to a rhetorical close with a declaration that can be read, and was often read at the time, as an assertion of radical libertarianism: "I will not willingly cede more power to anyone, not to the state, not to GM, not to the CIO. I will hoard my power like a miser, resisting every effort to drain it away from me." As it stands, the statement tastes indeed of radical laissez-faire individualism. But the paragraph continues in a way that crucially modifies this impression. Buckley wants to be an isolated economic operator not on ultimate philosophical grounds but only because he sees it as the surest foundation for yet more important issues: "I mean to live my life as an obedient man, but obedient to God [and] subservient to the wisdom of my ancestors."[85]

Among the Catholic new conservatives of the 1950s, Buckley was one of the most ardent defenders of free enterprise, albeit on nonmaterialist grounds. Other Catholic new conservatives defended capitalism more equivocally. Stanley Parry, reviewing *Up from Liberalism* in *Modern Age*, found its argument "bracing" as a short-term goad to political conservatives but regretted that Buckley had turned the conflict between liberals and conservatives into a policy affair rather than emphasizing its spiritual dimensions. Buckley, he said, had skirted the issue of "whether freedom of choice alone is sufficient to make a man free." He agreed with Buckley that conservatives had to build an "ordered society," without which a free market could not operate, and he agreed that "liberal collectivism, with its brutal imposition of order through the power of the state," had failed to create such a society. But still, "there are some grave limitations to a straight private property approach to the problem of freedom." Buckley's manifesto, he concluded, was useful as an "early attempt" to rebuild a coherent, spiritually ori-

83. William F. Buckley, Jr., *God and Man at Yale: The Superstitions of "Academic Freedom"* (Chicago: Henry Regnery, 1951), 53.
84. Buckley, *Up from Liberalism*, 122.
85. Ibid., 176.

ented conservatism, but a "long and arduous task" still lay before conservatives.[86] Brent Bozell, similarly, favored free-market capitalism less
for its own positive benefits than as a check against the power of "big
government" and powerful trade unions. Eisenhower's "New Republicanism," he said, had overridden both constitutional balance and natural law: "The American Constitution is full of can'ts. . . . The natural
law is also full of can'ts . . . [but] the New Republicanism rejects the
theory of limited government and adopts as its very own the first
principle of totalitarianism, that the state is competent to do all
things."[87] The Democratic party, meanwhile, was dominated by the
unions, and before long, Bozell believed, "organized labor will achieve
supreme political power" and make "Walter Reuther the most important man in America."[88] A free-market revival, in Bozell's view,
would restrain both Republican and the Democratic aberrations and
safeguard natural law.

Francis Graham Wilson was another Catholic conservative who,
under conditions then prevailing, believed that capitalism was defensible, if not worthy of enthusiasm. His approach might be compared
to Irving Kristol's later "two cheers for capitalism," as support for the
best of the actual alternatives in the contemporary world.[89] Wilson
noted that the primary concern of Catholics had always been to assure
the "freedom of the person in both the political and the economic
order" and that the church had long recognized that differing historical
circumstances demanded different political and economic systems.
Guardedly he continued: "The test of legitimacy of an economic order
would be its fulfillment of primary moral conditions. It might seem,
then, that a Catholic conservative may defend capitalism on the ground
that it provides the conditions of a possible Christian life." This hypo-
thetical Catholic conservative "might also argue prudentially and with
wisdom that the free market system, or some form of capitalism, will
provide and has provided elsewhere a basic economic protection of
the family."[90]

Frederick Wilhelmsen and Garry Wills were exceptional among the
Catholic lay conservatives of the 1950s in denying entirely that conservatives should support capitalism. Each of them regarded capitalism
as inseparably linked to the philosophical tradition of liberal individu-

---

86. Stanley Parry, "Conservatism and the Social Bond," *MA* 4 (Summer 1960): 306–11.
87. L. Brent Bozell, "Repeal of the Constitution," *NR*, Dec. 25, 1956, 9–10.
88. L. Brent Bozell, "Reuther Schemes for Power," *NR*, Oct. 20, 1956, 8–9.
89. See Irving Kristol, *Two Cheers for Capitalism* (New York: Basic, 1978), an influential "neoconservative" manifesto of the 1970s and 1980s.
90. Wilson, "Catholics and the New Conservatism," 251.

alism, and they emphasized that capitalism had done more to transform the world and shatter its traditional forms than any other phenomenon in world history. Like their predecessor Ross Hoffman, they based their approach to economic questions on the "distributism" of Belloc and Chesterton. The distributists had regarded capitalism as the rule of the moneylender (Belloc's theorizing took on a distinctly anti-Semitic cast) and industrialism as the rule of the machine. They favored craftsmanship rather than mass production as a nonalienating form of manufacture.[91] Hence, turning Buckley's principles around, distributist Catholics could argue that capitalism undermined rather than preserved the widespread distribution of private property. Despite respectful treatment of distributism in his study of Chesterton, Garry Wills recognized that the quest for a distributist economy in midcentury America was quixotic, and he paid little further attention to economic issues; most of his early conservative journalism was devoted to debunking what he regarded as the follies of contemporary liberalism.[92]

Wilhelmsen was hardly more optimistic than Wills about recovering the organic agrarian community of Christendom, but he wrote extensively against the capitalism that had overpowered it. "It would" he believed, "be an abuse of language to label as conservative or Rightist attempts to defend the vestiges of the nineteenth-century laissez-faire order."[93] Like Belloc, of whom he wrote an appreciative study (and in one sense like Belloc's contemporaries Max Weber and Richard H. Tawney), Wilhelmsen traced capitalism to the rise of Protestantism and regarded it as a continuing manifestation of Calvinism. Medieval Christendom, he claimed, had lived in harmony with nature, but the Reformation had encouraged an instrumental and exploitative approach to the natural world. "With Calvinism, the unity of all things in the bosom of traditional life was shattered for all time. Power fell to the 'godded men' who looked upon temporal society as nothing but an instrument to bring about the golden world wherein the Lord would dwell in the midst of his Saints."[94] Unlike Buckley, Kirk, Wilson, and other Catholic theorists of the new conservatism, Wilhelmsen hammered at the theme of the Reformation as the ultimate source of present woes. "The Calvinist revolution," he believed "has altered the

91. R. P. Walsh, "Distributism," *New Catholic Encyclopedia* (New York: McGraw-Hill, 1967), 4:912.

92. On distributism, see Garry Wills, *Chesterton, Man and Mask* (New York: Sheed and Ward, 1961), 176–80.

93. Frederick Wilhelmsen, "The Conservative Catholic," *C*, Feb. 20, 1953, 491–93.

94. Frederick Wilhelmsen, "The Conservative Vision," *C*, June 24, 1955, 295–99.

structure of our civilization far more deeply than either the French Revolution or the Communist Manifesto."[95] Protestantism was an "eschatological" faith, whereas Catholicism was "incarnational." Catholicism permitted an appreciation of "being," whereas Protestantism and its secular descendant, liberalism, glorified only "becoming" and transformation. This transformative approach to the world had undergirded the industrial revolution and generated all its baleful consequences. For Wilhelmsen, "a thoroughly technologized society, one governed by the rhythm of the machine, would be a sin against the human spirit."[96]

Wilhelmsen appears to have had relatively little influence among Catholic philosophers or conservative authors either in the 1950s or subsequently. He is, nevertheless, an interesting figure, worthy of some attention, because he demonstrates the persistence of the most militant Catholicism in postwar America. What one historian said of Belloc applies equally to Belloc's eulogist, Wilhelmsen: "No spark of ecumenism exists in his flaming apology for the Faith."[97] He continued to voice in the 1950s and 1960s attitudes that had been commonplace in the work of Ross Hoffman and other orthodox apologists for Catholicism in the early twentieth century. In that respect he was a holdover from an earlier period of militant Catholicism. Ironically, he augured several themes voiced by the American anticapitalist Left in the 1960s. Hatred for the alienating scale of capitalism and the inexorability of a machine-driven society were common themes in the social critique of Tom Hayden, Staughton Lynd, and other voices of the new Left. Wilhelmsen was, moreover, one of the first Americans to take an interest in Marshall McLuhan (subsequently an icon of the new Left), praising him in 1956 for demonstrating the "depersonalizing effects of [advertising's] trafficking in the human psyche."[98]

Wilhelmsen's unsettling presence and theologically rigorous argumentation, both in the popular press and in journals of scholastic theology, demonstrate the difficulty of aligning Catholics along a simple left–right spectrum of political ideas. The same difficulty that is so conspicuous in Wilhelmsen's case arises in analyzing other intellectuals in recent Catholic history. Garry Wills, for example, later expressed ideas abhorrent to many conservatives, which he said grew out of his conservative convictions and his Catholic faith.

Opinions about capitalism among the Catholic new conservatives

95. Frederick Wilhelmsen, "In the Name of Sanity," *SO* 5 (Jan. 1955): 25.
96. Frederick Wilhelmsen, "Technology: Limited or Unlimited?" *A*, Oct. 20, 1956, 66–68.
97. M. A. Hart, "Hilaire Belloc," *New Catholic Encyclopedia* 2:257–58.
98. Wilhelmsen, "Technology: Limited or Unlimited?" 67.

were, to sum up, mixed but generally favorable. At the same time, liberal Catholics drew a much darker picture of capitalism and insisted that it was incompatible with their faith. Throughout the first half of the twentieth century, working-class Catholics had played a vigorous role in the trade union movement, and they tended to regard the capitalists, the bosses, with jaundiced eyes, as exploiters rather than benefactors of humankind.[99] Liberal Catholic reviewers of Keller's and Buckley's defenses of capitalism, therefore, argued that their authors were ignorant of conditions among American workers and that their arguments for capitalism failed to account for the poverty and oppression still widespread in the United States. Reviewing *God and Man at Yale,* for example, Christopher Fullman noted that Buckley "rightly fears the totalitarian state but what does he know of the totalitarianism of the mining patches of West Virginia?" Fullman went on to cite examples of tyrannical capitalist power and to argue that more measures along the lines of the New Deal and the National Labor Relations Act, not less, were needed to safeguard workers against bosses. As for Buckley, Fullman remarked, "in chapter one he is all for Christ," but "in the rest of the book he seems to be all for Adam Smith," and the two were irreconcilable.[100] Another reviewer feared that Buckley had fallen into the trap of thinking that capitalism and collectivism were the only two economic alternatives available. He had, alas, failed to judge Yale's teaching of economics "in the light of Catholic social teaching." Accordingly, his sensible strictures on academic freedom were mitigated by his faulty economic reasoning, which "contravene[s] Catholic moral doctrine as applied to economics and politics on almost every topic he takes up."[101] Keller suffered a similar rebuke. One reviewer accused him of citing only those passages from the papal encyclicals which supported his basic contentions and passing over in silence those that were incompatible with them. "It is perfectly clear," the reviewer declared, "that the Holy Father attributes depersonalization and the domination of the individual to the organization of modern life around industrial production." For this alienation capitalism must take the blame. "When the collective state arises, it simply capitalizes on a situation that industry has already created."[102]

Perhaps the key point of difference between liberal and conservative Catholics on the economic issue was disagreement over the degree to

99. See, for example, Marc Karson, *American Labor Unions and Politics, 1900–1918* (Carbondale: Southern Illinois University Press, 1958), 212–84.

100. Christopher Fullman, "God, Man, and Mr. Buckley," CW 175 (May 1952): 104–8.

101. Editorial, "God and Free Enterprise," A, Nov. 17, 1951, 173.

102. Joseph P. Fitzpatrick, S.J., "The Encyclicals and the United States," CM 53 (Jan. 1955): 8.

which they should model their opinions on the words of the papal encyclicals, as opposed to adapting themselves to the exigencies of their practical situation. Conservatives acknowledged the encyclicals as helpful guides to the principles at issue, but no more than that. One remarked: "Papal pronouncements are directives in principle; it would be ridiculous to suppose that they apply equally in every respect to, let us say, proletarianized France and an essentially bourgeois America."[103] Some liberal Catholics disliked such an approach, which they believed left individuals too much scope to make prudential judgments in favor of capitalism. One angry opponent of the "ultra-conservative Catholic" who supported capitalism said that such a man was usually "the wealthy employer type," whose support could be explained only by his "ignorance. . . . He is unacquainted with Catholic social teaching."[104]

In taking a more distanced and contextual approach to the economic encyclicals rather than aiming to reduplicate them as nearly as possible, the Catholic lay conservatives were following in economics the principles John Courtney Murray used in his political theology. They emphasized that the church is a historical institution, changing from one age to the next and unable to avoid the exigencies of historical transformation. A papal declaration, accordingly, had to be considered not simply as a disembodied statement valid in all times and at all places but rather as a historically conditioned document. As Murray had shown, the encyclical letters of the later nineteenth century could best be understood in the context of the European politics of their age, and historical contextualization permitted a more nuanced interpretation: thus, Murray was able to rediscover a long-submerged Catholic political tradition. In his case, as I have suggested, his use of the historical principle does not mean that he was a particularly accurate historian; his purposes lay elsewhere. While Murray was working on the issue of political theology in the mid-1950s, however, a young lay scholar named John T. Noonan, Jr., was bringing a greater rigor to Catholic historiography and contributing in vital ways to the debate over economics. His findings proved highly congenial to the conservative position. Ten years later, ironically, Noonan would become a central intellectual figure for both liberals and conservatives in the Catholic controversy over contraception.

Noonan was born in 1926 in Boston, graduated from Harvard in the class of 1947, and then earned a Ph.D. from the Catholic University of

---

103. George Gent, "Liberal, Conservative, Catholic," *CW* 184 (Nov. 1956): 102.
104. Ralph Gorman, C.P., "The Ultra-Conservative Catholic," *CM* 53 (Nov. 1955): 655.

America in Washington, D.C.[105] He returned to Harvard for law school, graduated in 1954, and spent a year working with President Eisenhower's National Security Council at the time of the partitioning of Vietnam and the Quemoy-Matsu Islands crisis. From government he returned to Boston once more and for a while in the mid-1950s worked with a Boston law firm while serving as the elected chair of the Brookline Redevelopment Corporation. Following publication of a book based on his doctoral dissertation, however, Noonan was offered a professorship of law at Notre Dame and began to work there in 1959.

Noonan's book, *The Scholastic Analysis of Usury,* was far too solid and studious to cause any sensation, but in its way it marked a new departure in Catholic historical scholarship. Its message was that Catholic teaching on usury had gone through several stages and had been completely transformed between the Middle Ages and the twentieth century. Beginning with a strict prohibition on the charging of interest in the high Middle Ages, scholastic theologians had repeatedly modified and mitigated the rigors of this principle in subsequent centuries. And yet, said Noonan, this development had been almost universally overlooked, both by Catholic historians wedded to a view of the church as infallible and transtemporal and by secular historians eager to denigrate the church as backward looking and inflexible. Whereas most analysts of Catholicism and capitalism up to that time had merely gathered pertinent statements on the issue, Noonan insisted on a chronological approach that appreciated the long development of the theory. "No error is more widespread," he noted "than treatment of the theory as if it had been immutable. Reputable economic historians will see no incongruity in citing thirteenth- and seventeenth-century writers together for a proposition although the analytical context in which the later writer speaks may have substantially altered the significance of the language he shares with the earlier authority."[106]

In his treatment of the scholastic theorists and the changing Vatican attitude toward banking, moneylending, and commerce, Noonan showed an acute sensitivity to the way in which words themselves are historically conditioned and shift in meaning in response to new conditions, changing as they do so the understanding of the issues they are used to portray. The meaning of "fair" in the concept of the "fair price," for example, had changed radically in light of changing perceptions of economic justice. *The Scholastic Analysis of Usury* gained

105. This section is based in part on personal interviews with John T. Noonan, Jr., Berkeley, Calif., June 10, 20, and 24, 1985.

106. John T. Noonan, Jr., *The Scholastic Analysis of Usury* (Cambridge: Harvard University Press, 1957), 6.

mixed reviews, some Catholics revolting against Noonan's implicit message that Catholicism had laid the foundations of capitalism. One critic who found Noonan's message unpalatable simply denied that it was true: "The Roman Church has never felt free to adopt the insouciant tones of Noonan. . . . to this day the Church has not dared to assert the propositions that Noonan so blithely assumes."[107] Others took the message to heart and found both the research and the developmental principle to constitute sound scholarship. Catholic medievalist David Herlihy realized the book's importance: "The implications of his findings . . . seem clear; they add up to a thesis which might be called 'The Scholastic Ethic and the Rise of Capitalism.' They seem to show that Calvinism does not bring with it a leap from an anticapitalist medieval ethic that lives on in Catholicism."[108] Stephen Tonsor, intellectual historian and another Catholic contributor to the new conservative journals, concurred; Noonan, he believed, had revealed "that the medieval writers in many respects were economic realists who sought to harmonize what we believe to be economic law with the ethical demands of Christianity."[109] In itself, Noonan's work had nothing to contribute to the detailed economic policy questions confronting midcentury America, but in demonstrating a long Catholic prehistory to the capitalist era, it gave both comfort and intellectual plausibility to the Catholic new conservatives.

To sum up, in their approach to the cold war, the Catholic new conservatives took a militant anti-Soviet and anti-Communist position. They also wrote extensively about the need to maintain the sort of pressure against domestic Communists which Senator Joseph McCarthy had led; early issues of *National Review* lamented the apparent relaxation of the internal security apparatus in the years after McCarthy's Senate censure and premature death.[110] They understood communism as a Christian heresy, viewed the events of the cold war in religious terms, and believed themselves to be the new defenders of the heartland of Christendom, defenders of God's truth, while showing a special solicitude for the Christians of the "captive nations" behind the Iron Curtain and the "Bamboo Curtain." Many of them believed that the final struggle for the world was imminent, that a third world war, heavy with theological as well as political significance, had, in effect,

107. Benjamin Nelson, review of Noonan, *Scholastic Analysis,* in *American Historical Review* 64 (1959): 618.

108. David Herlihy, review of Noonan, *Scholastic Analysis,* in *Journal of Economic History* 19 (Dec. 1959): 638.

109. Stephen Tonsor, letter to the editor, *MA* 4 (Winter 1959–60): 110.

110. Editorial, "Communists Know Their Enemy," *NR,* Jan. 31, 1959, 481; editorial, "There Ought to Be a Law," *NR,* May 9, 1959, 39, 41.

already begun. In this struggle, they believed, American liberals would be a nuisance rather than a source of strength. The best of the liberals, Catholic conservatives agreed, still held the values of the West at heart but had sundered them from the faith that gave them life. The worst of the liberals had promoted the idea of tolerance and the cult of scientific method above all the substantive spiritual truths of civilization, and they constituted a hazard to the West. "Tomorrow's battle for the soul," said Frederick Wilhelmsen, "will be fought without that hypocritical tolerance which drained the modern world of honor and clogged the soul with deceit. The old world hoped to retain the values but not the faith of Christ. The new world will be more honest. The battle between Christ and Antichrist will be a naked and clean struggle between giants stripped of all finery."[111]

As part of their apocalyptic view of the international situation, the Catholic lay conservatives worked to maintain the United States in a situation of readiness for war. Many of them championed a regulated capitalist economy, finding it consonant with church teaching, enriching for the population as a whole, and benign rather than predatory, especially compared to the collectivist alternative. In taking this approach to the economy, they accepted church teaching as a useful guide but, for the most part, never denied themselves a latitude of action at points where the two might seem to conflict. As manifestations of the new "liberal Catholicism," they acted in confident independence of their hierarchy, cooperated in journalistic ventures with non-Catholics, and began to forgo the apologetic and defensive outlook that Catholic intellectuals in the wider society had hitherto displayed. They were, to be sure, "liberal Catholics" only in a limited and paradoxical sense. Few identified themselves as such at the time. The self-proclaimed liberal Catholics feared and mistrusted them throughout the 1950s, and at the opening of the 1960s, smoldering tensions between the two groups burst into flames.

111. Frederick Wilhelmsen, Introduction to Romano Guardini, *The End of the Modern World*, trans. Joseph Theman and Herbert Burke (New York: Sheed and Ward, 1956), 11.

3

Transformations of the Early 1960s

America's Catholic community was in transition before the 1950s came to an end. The growing self-confidence of lay intellectuals and the signs of a cleavage between conservative and liberal Catholics seemed likely to continue in the coming years, as did the increasing prosperity of the Catholic population as a whole. The events of the early 1960s, however, accelerated these trends and inaugurated a period of rapid, unprecedented change in American Catholicism. First, the successful presidential election campaign of John F. Kennedy demonstrated that Catholicism was no longer an insuperable obstacle to gaining the White House. It sparked a vigorous debate not only between Catholics and the members of other faiths but also within the Catholic community. Second, in the years of Kennedy's presidency, Supreme Court decisions against prayer and Bible reading in public schools confirmed perceptions about the secularization of American life and provoked disputes about the religious foundations of the nation. At the same time, paradoxically, the African-American civil rights movement won successive triumphs under a charismatic religious leadership. Catholic liberals regarded Martin Luther King and his followers as "prophetic" figures in a sinful America; most Catholic conservatives, to the contrary, treated the civil rights movement leaders as either Communist dupes or apostles of anarchy.

Along with these domestic developments, meanwhile, came a great upheaval in the church. After the aristocratic Pope Pius XII died in 1958, his successor, Angelo Roncalli, who took the name John XXIII, had been on Saint Peter's throne for only three months when he called an ecumenical council, dedicated to aggiornamento of the Catholic church. The consequences of his decision to "open a window" onto the modern world were to be immense. In 1961, the year before the council began, John XXIII published the encyclical letter *Mater et Magistra*, over whose significance American Catholics squabbled publicly in a way not previously seen. One observer of the 1960 election and subsequent events spoke of "the newly discovered, nonmonolithic shape of Catholic opinion."[1] Another added that "the 1960s may see a deeper division of American Catholics into warring ideological factions than has occurred in the past."[2] Centrifugal forces were at work as old issues of ghetto Catholicism were left behind. Moreover, from this time forward the Catholic conservative group began a fragmentation of its own; tensions already apparent in the 1950s became fractures as some favored the "liberalization" of their religion and others tried to hold on to the ancient verities.

THE KENNEDY CAMPAIGN

The prospect of a Catholic stepping into the Oval Office seemed so remote in the middle and late 1950s that some of the few writers who addressed the issue believed it scarcely merited discussion; Protestant anti-Catholicism, in their judgment, was still far too widespread. As late as March 1960 the editor of the *Catholic World* raised the issue but concluded, "I would say that the American people are unwilling to vote for a Catholic president." The tradition of anti-Catholicism was too strong for "the majority of voters," who, he believed, were "not emotionally and psychologically mature enough to conquer bias and cast a ballot for a Catholic." Moreover, he thought, this might be just as well for the present because a Catholic president "would work under the intolerable strain of prying, lynx-eyed scrutiny from censors who would smell Vatican influence in every Presidential utterance."[3] Kennedy's strong showing in the 1960s primaries, however, soon reawakened the issue, dormant since the Al Smith campaign of 1928, and such remarks were heard no more. For our purposes three contending voices on the religious question can be distinguished in the 1960 debate: first, anti-Catholic; second, pro-Kennedy Catholic; and third,

---

1. Alan Westin, "The John Birch Society: Fundamentalism on the Right," *Commentary* 32 (Aug. 1961): 103.

2. Patricia Barrett, R.S.C.J., "Religion and the 1960 Presidential Election," *SO* 12 (June 1962): 281–82.

3. John Sheerin, "How Fair Are Kennedy's Critics?" *CW* 190 (March 1960): 333–35.

anti-Kennedy Catholic. The intra-Catholic points of disputation reflected growing divisions among Catholic intellectuals, partly along party-political lines, but partly on deeper substantive issues.

First, the anti-Catholic position: several organizations worked against the Kennedy candidacy frankly because of his religion. Among their leaders were such well-known figures as the nation's chief positive thinker, Norman Vincent Peale, and the Episcopal bishop of California, James Pike.[4] Two anti-Kennedy pressure groups, Protestants and Other Americans United for the Separation of Church and State (POAU) and the National Council of Citizens for Religious Freedom (NCCRF), each argued that a Catholic president was bound by the nature of his faith to violate the First Amendment and to seek preferential treatment for his coreligionists.[5] These organizations were composed largely of educated urban Protestants, but their anti-Catholicism was more than matched by rural Protestant groups. As one historian of southern religion has shown, the United States was, in the opinion of Southern Baptists, "locked in mortal combat with the Vatican as well as with the Kremlin." One minister declared: "*No Power* is harder at work bidding for the supremacy of our free country than the Vatican-controlled Catholicism here in America."[6] In November 1959, Baptist state conventions in Alabama, Arizona, Arkansas, and Texas all voted to oppose a Catholic presidency.[7] In speeches and campaign literature that exploited themes made familiar by Paul Blanshard in the 1950s (many of which Blanshard himself had recently underlined in *God and Man in Washington*)[8] these campaigners emphasized that Catholics had never endorsed the principle of religious liberty. Catholics were prepared to take shelter under conditions of religious toleration so long as they were a minority, but they would convert the state to Catholicism and eliminate religious freedom as soon as they gained power.[9] It was a reprise of the argument that had given so much trouble to Al Smith in 1928. Other frequently voiced objections against Kennedy were that

---

4. On the religious aspects of the 1960 campaign, see Lawrence Fuchs, *John F. Kennedy and American Catholicism* (New York: Meredith, 1967), 164–88. James Pike, *A Catholic in the White House* (Garden City, N.Y.: Doubleday, 1960), was a book-length attack on the possibility.

5. NCCRF was founded Sept. 7, 1960, by Protestant journal editors Daniel Poling, L. Nelson Bell, Harold Ockenga, and Norman Vincent Peale, and was more hostile to Kennedy than POAU. See Fuchs, *John F. Kennedy*, 173, 177–78.

6. Andrew M. Manis, *Southern Civil Religions in Conflict: Black and White Baptists and Civil Rights, 1947–1957* (Athens: University of Georgia Press, 1987), 46–47.

7. Lawrence Fuchs, "The Religious Vote: Fact or Fiction?" *CW* 192 (Oct. 1960): 9–14.

8. Paul Blanshard, *God and Man in Washington* (Boston: Beacon, 1960).

9. On the historical persistence of this argument, see Barbara Welter, "From Maria Monk to Paul Blanshard," in *Uncivil Religion: Interreligious Hostility in America*, ed. Robert Bellah and Frederick Greenspan (New York: Crossroads, 1987), 43–59.

he was incapable of making up his own mind, deferring in all things to Catholic dogma, and that he would surrender American sovereignty to an Italian prelate.[10]

These arguments against a Catholic presidential candidate, which pointedly failed to distinguish between theoretical and practical ideals, were by no means unanimously endorsed by Protestants; Reinhold Niebuhr and John C. Bennett, leading Protestant theologians from Union Seminary, New York, condemned POAU in indignant mixed metaphors, for "opening the floodgates of bigotry clothed in the respectability of apparently rational argument." On September 12, 1960, one hundred leading Protestants, Catholics, and Jews issued an ecumenical statement defending the legitimacy of the Kennedy candidacy.[11] Catholic writers, not surprisingly, also united in deploring the religiously motivated attacks on a Kennedy candidacy. The editor of the *Catholic World* declared that Bishop Pike of POAU was no more than an anti-Catholic "agitator," trying to sow religious dissension, not, as he claimed, defending religious freedom. Catholic journal editors nevertheless spent much of 1960 painstakingly refuting the charges that Catholics favored religious persecution and enjoyed no true freedom of conscience and citing examples of internal divisions to belie the claim of a servile and monolithic Catholic population.[12] Others took the offensive by showing that America's Protestants, not Catholics, were the intolerant group; one Jesuit conducted an expedition into the history of church-state relations which demonstrated how religiously intolerant the early Protestant colonies had been by contrast with Maryland's Catholic founders, whose 1633 declaration of religious toleration survived only until the Protestants, becoming a majority in 1704, passed antipopery laws.[13] Much of the American press sympathized with Kennedy's claim that his faith was no bar to office, and as 1960 advanced, the probability of his victory increased steadily.[14] For Catholics sympathetic to Kennedy's policy positions, the campaign was an exhilarating experience; each obstacle crossed brought the White House closer. "The election of a Catholic president," one commented,

10. On the issue of Catholicism in the 1928 election, see Francis L. Broderick, "When Last a Catholic Ran for President," *SO* 10 (May 1960): 198–210.

11. Cited in Barrett, "Religion and the Election," 272.

12. John Sheerin, C.S.P., "Birth Control: Whose Dilemma?" *CW* 190 (Jan. 1960): 204–6; "Bishop Pike Asks Another Question," *CW* 190 (Feb. 1960): 273–79; George Kelley, "Catholics: In 1960 and Later," *A*, June 4, 1960, 337–38.

13. See, for example, Edward Duff, S.J., "Church and State in the American Environment: An Historical and Legal Survey," *SO* 10 (Nov. 1960): 385–402.

14. On the Catholic response to the Kennedy campaign, see also Theodore White, *The Making of the President, 1960* (New York: Atheneum, 1961), 355–58.

"would be a turning point not just in American Constitutional development but in the history of America as a civilization."[15] A month before
the election, a group of 166 lay Catholics issued a statement extolling
the principle of religious freedom. At a press conference their leader,
William Clancy, justified his decision not to have any priests' signatures
on the document as a way of refuting the idea that "Catholic laymen
are afraid of opening their mouths without consulting a priest." The
signatories, he said, were exercising their rights as citizens and expressing their convictions "quite confident of our orthodoxy."[16]

Catholic conservatives, though they despised Kennedy's political
views, defended the principle of a Catholic for president and, as usual,
took the offensive against its critics. The notion that Kennedy might
abolish religious freedom, they remarked, was no more likely than the
idea that Richard Nixon, the Republican candidate, might surrender
to the Soviet Union under pressure from his pacifist Quaker coreligionists. Confirming that Catholics have free conscience on nearly all issues, certainly all the issues germane to the forthcoming election, they
said that "Catholics are totally free to reject the political asides that
issue from Vatican spokesmen" and are bound in conscience only on
questions of faith and morals. They also rejected Norman Vincent
Peale's assertion that the ideal president was an autonomous man who
acted exclusively upon his own judgments. "God save us from the
event. Most of us are guided prescriptively—by tradition, by habits of
mind, and conscience and morals, by rules fashioned by others," for
which we should be grateful.[17] L. Brent Bozell agreed that no man
should be disqualified from the presidency because he was a Catholic—quite the contrary—but here he seized the opportunity to criticize
liberal Catholics and Kennedy himself as well as anti-Catholic
spokesmen. Bozell disliked the way in which many Catholic defenders
of Kennedy had set about their task. In the press debate of mid-1960,
for example, "no one saw fit to acknowledge the differences among
the faiths and to try to impart to the public an informed, dispassionate
understanding of them," though to him these differences seemed vast
and vitally important. Candidate Kennedy himself was partly to blame;
he was in a position to "produce salutary consequences for all concerned by spending less of his time dissociating himself from his
Church and more of it explaining those teachings and practices that

15. Victor Ferkiss, "Why Not a Catholic President?" *CW* 190 (Feb. 1960): 279.
16. Edward Duff, S.J., "Religion and Politics," *SO* 11 (Jan. 1961): 1–6.
17. Editorial, "A Little Positive Thought for Norman Vincent Peale," *NR*, Sept. 24, 1960,
168–69.

give concern." Instead, Kennedy had tried to make religion seem altogether a matter of indifference, said Bozell.[18]

Catholic conservatives disliked Kennedy's record as a senator and anticipated no improvement from him if he reached the White House. His apparent dedication to the domestic New Deal tradition they found abhorrent: his guiding ideas "were drab pickings from the decadent Liberalism he claimed to espouse," wrote Bozell.[19] Moreover, his willingness to coexist with the Soviet Union in foreign affairs made him, in their eyes, as bad as Eisenhower.[20] The best they could say of him was that "as a Catholic he could hardly capitulate to Communism. That *would* be letting his coreligionists down!" So although his prospective election was to be regretted, they felt confident that "conservatives, under a Kennedy regime, [will] live to fight again."[21] They treated Kennedy's coterie of Harvard advisers as the high priests of liberalism, and quipped that Kennedy was nullifying the ostensible benefits of a youthful candidacy by expressing outmoded ideas in weary clichés, as though he were old before his time.[22] As the campaign neared its end, they also suspected Kennedy of taking advantage of the Catholic issue and using it to raise votes from citizens afraid they might otherwise seem prejudiced. *National Review*'s last issue before the election carried on its cover a cartoon of Kennedy with the word "Reuther" (that is, trade union leader Walter Reuther) stamped across his chest and the text: "If I can only keep the Catholics who don't want to vote for me thinking they're renegades, and the non-Catholics who don't want to vote for me thinking they're bigots, maybe everybody will forget about whose vest-pocket I'm in."[23]

Following Kennedy's election, the *National Review* group and other conservatives continued to polemicize against his policies at home and abroad, and against his advisers. One Catholic conservative, Neil McCaffrey, denied that the election bore witness to a Catholic "coming of age," an overworked phrase of the time. Kennedy, he argued, was far too negligent in his observance to give any pride to Catholics, and his campaign had been "predicated on Catholic gullibility." McCaffrey even suggested that Catholics had disseminated anti-Catholic litera-

18. L. Brent Bozell, "The Catholic Issue," *NR*, Sept. 24, 1960, 171.
19. L. Brent Bozell, "Behind Mr. Truman's Attack," *NR*, July 16, 1960, 12.
20. Frank Meyer, "Principles and Heresies," *NR*, Feb. 11, 1961, 81.
21. John Chamberlain, "The Chameleon Image of JFK," *NR*, April 23, 1960, 261–63.
22. Bozell, "Behind Truman's Attack," 12; Noel Parmentel, Jr., "Hax, Fax, Jax, Pax," *NR*, June 4, 1960, 360, 375.
23. *NR*, Nov. 5, 1960, cover.

ture, hoping for a favorable backlash.[24] That these conservatives were willing to turn so openly against Kennedy is itself evidence of their self-confidence; they felt no need to huddle with coreligionists in defense of one of their own, and indeed actively worked to prevent his election. Of course, Catholic politicians were nothing new; Catholic congressmen, senators, and judges had taken their seats from the late eighteenth century on and represented all political parties. But the symbolic significance of the presidency—its central place in what Robert Bellah termed the nation's "civil religion"—made 1960 a crucial moment in both U.S. and Catholic history.[25] The issue of a Catholic president was settled and never subsequently reemerged, though it is perhaps worth remarking in passing that since 1960 neither party has chosen a Catholic as its presidential candidate.

Intra-Catholic Disputes

As the new conservative movement established itself in the American media, and as its figurehead, William F. Buckley, Jr., became increasingly well known in print, on radio, and on television, Catholic journals began to debate the significance of his brand of conservatism and its congruence with their faith. They applauded his outspoken defense of Christianity, even while some lamented his political and economic proposals. For example, in 1957, after watching Buckley on television, defending Catholicism because he said it was true, John Cogley remarked that his performance was "arresting . . . because so many people no longer think of religion in terms of truth or falsehood. Millions have stopped considering religion as something to engage the rational side of man." Cogley balanced this accolade with dismay at how Buckley linked the defense of Christianity to militant anticommunism: "I found myself agreeing often with his premises and balking like a mule at the conclusions he reached."[26] From the beginning of his public career, Buckley had caused eyebrows to rise among liberal Catholic reviewers; the Jesuit journal *America*, in particular, criticized *National Review* from its inception. Having previously frequently ac-

---

24. Neil McCaffrey, untitled review of Patricia Barrett, *Religious Liberty and the American Presidency*, in *NR*, April 9, 1963, 293.

25. Robert Bellah, "Civil Religion in America," *Daedalus* 96 (Winter 1967): 1–21, reprinted in *Secularization and the Protestant Prospect*, ed. J. F. Childress and D. B. Harned (Philadelphia: Westminster, 1970), 93–116. The article includes a detailed exegesis of Kennedy's inaugural address as an example of "civil religious" discourse.

26. John Cogley, "A Television Shocker," *C*, April 12, 1957, 38.

cepted articles for publication from Russell Kirk and Erik von Kuehnelt-Leddihn, *America's* editors changed their minds and refused them
when it found the pair were contributing to the new conservative journal, which they accused of treating their own former editor, Robert
Hartnett, S.J., disrespectfully.[27]

At the end of the 1950s and in the first years of the 1960s Buckley
frequently debated Catholic liberals on the issues of the day—desegregation, communism, and the welfare state—often before Catholic college audiences. A series of debates on Catholic liberalism versus
Catholic conservatism in which Buckley took on William Clancy (leader
of the Catholic laymen's delegation for Kennedy) began "ringing bells
all over the Holy Name Society circuit" in 1960, "pumping large doses
of Geritol into the sluggish bloodstream of the old art of public debate."[28] This kind of debate between two laymen was itself, one priest
noted, "a truly remarkable pioneering lay venture."[29] Several of these
debates appeared in print, with Catholic editors analyzing Buckley's
remarks in the light of church teaching, noting particularly their consonance or dissonance with the papal "social encyclicals," *Rerum Novarum* and *Quadragesimo Anno.* The most frequently sounded notes in
the controversy were Buckley's claim that Catholic liberals were "soft
on communism" and too willing to join antireligious secular liberals
in extending the welfare state and liberal Catholics' retort that they
were loyal to papal encyclical teaching while Buckley was escalating
international tensions and voicing a mongrelized version of the old
Manchester laissez-faire liberalism, which had no legitimacy in Catholic tradition. "I grieve," said Kevin Corrigan in a characteristic exchange, "that Mr. Buckley does not yet appear to have risen above so
mean a social philosophy as nineteenth-century liberalism."[30]

Buckley was eager to match his antagonists on religious as well as
political grounds. To deal with complex and sometimes arcane issues of
Catholic doctrine and tradition, in which he had no formal theological
training, he created an informal "brain trust" of sympathetic New York
Catholic priests, monsignors Florence Cohallen (a New York seminary

27. Editorial, "On Editorial Policy," *NR*, Dec. 28, 1955, 6–7.
28. Editorial, "Wring Out the Old," *A*, Jan. 7, 1961, 438–39.
29. William J. Smith, S.J., letter to the editor, *A*, Feb. 11, 1961, 634–35.
30. William F. Buckley, Jr., "The Catholic in the Modern World: A Conservative View," and William Clancy, "A Liberal View," *C*, Dec. 16, 1960, 307–13; Kevin Corrigan, "God and Man at *National Review*," *CW* 192 (Jan. 1961): 207–12; William F. Buckley, Jr., "A Very Personal Answer to My Critics," *CW* 192 (March 1961): 360–65; James Schall, S.J., "Mr. Buckley at Santa Clara," *CW* 195 (Aug. 1962), 275–80. Other critical Catholic appraisals of Buckley from this period include Thomas P. Neill "Up from Liberalism," *Sign* 39 (Dec. 1959): 69; Francis McMa-hon, "An Approach to Anarchy," *A*, Oct. 17, 1959, 76–78; Kevin Lynch, "Up from Liberalism," *CW* 190 (Nov. 1959): 132–33.

teacher), Eugene Clark (subsequently press officer of the New York archdiocese), and Roger Pryor (later director of schools in the New York archdiocese).[31] Buckley learned from them and from other Catholics who wrote for *National Review* (Frederick Wilhelmsen, Garry Wills, Erik von Kuehnelt-Leddihn, Colin Clark, Arnold Lunn, Stanley Parry, and others) to cite papal encyclicals in support of his positions, to venerate the Catholic decentralizing principle of "subsidiarity" ("To call us subsidiarists anti-Catholic is about as convincing as calling the Popes anti-Catholic"[32]), to deny that he was a radical libertarian, and to confirm the Catholic principle that the state was ordained by God for human governance. In one exchange he explained: "When we conservatives curse the state we do not mean we would be without it altogether. . . . The state is a divine institution. Without it we have anarchy, and the lawlessness of anarchy is counter to the natural law; so we abjure all political theories which view the state as necessarily evil."[33]

Tempers were worsening on both sides of this discussion to such a degree that the editor of *Ave Maria*, Donald Thorman, proposed a truce in 1961 while Catholic conservatives and liberals worked out a minimal program behind which all could unite in public.[34] Buckley, too, sometimes insisted that, as Catholics, liberals and conservatives should agree to disagree on political questions. Angered over accusations of disloyalty to the church, he denied that differing opinions over the welfare state, for example, made members of either side "deficient in their allegiance to the moral authority of the Church."[35] But on other occasions he dropped conciliation for pointed antagonism of Catholic liberals. Once he described Dorothy Day, widely admired leader of the Catholic Worker movement, as a "good-hearted woman" whose ideas were "slovenly, reckless, intellectually chaotic, [and] anti-Catholic."[36] Catholic liberals, he added, in the same inflammatory speech, were secretly ashamed of their own heritage and so "grope for reassurance by seeking a symbiotic relationship with the Left . . . propitiating the liberals with an imprudent and incontinent enthusiasm for progressive nostrums."[37] No wonder Buckley suffered angry counterattacks, accu-

31. This brain trust is described in Garry Wills, *Confessions of a Conservative* (Garden City, N.Y.: Doubleday, 1979), 60.

32. Buckley, "A Very Personal Answer," 365.

33. Ibid.

34. Buckley's answer to Thorman is printed as "Catholic Liberals, Catholic Conservatives, and the Requirements of Unity," in his *Rumbles Left and Right* (New York: Putnam, 1963), 142–52.

35. Ibid., 115.

36. Buckley, "The Catholic in the Modern World," 307.

37. Ibid., 308.

sations of deliberate misrepresentation, and the charge of being "vehemently negative" toward modern civilization, thereby forsaking "the Christian's second vocation, which is to adapt the truths he has conserved to the unique needs of the present."[38]

One weapon in the hands of Catholic liberals during this debate was the expanding presence of the John Birch Society. Founded in 1958 by Robert Welch, a sometime candy manufacturer, it dedicated itself to the eradication of communism and endorsed methods almost as pernicious as those for which it condemned the Communists. Organized in cells along strictly hierarchical lines the society was a breeding ground for rumors and suspicions and soon drew headlines with its declaration that senior American officials, President Eisenhower not least among them, were themselves Communist agents. The society also initiated agitation for the impeachment of Supreme Court Chief Justice Earl Warren for his judicial activism. Its scattershot imputations of treason were as reckless as those made by the recently deceased Senator Joe McCarthy, but the organization grew rapidly and demonstrated the continuing appeal of anticommunism as a popular movement into the early 1960s. By 1961 half its members were Catholics, and a ferociously anti-communist Catholic columnist, Richard Ginder, formerly a champion of McCarthy, was a member of its central board. Alan Westin explained right-wing Catholics' enthusiasm for the John Birch Society: "Some influential Catholics are complaining bitterly that President Kennedy has joined the 'Liberal Establishment,' that he has been 'selling out' Catholic Church interests, and that the administration of the first Catholic president may go down in history as the 'softest on Communism.'" Under these conditions, Westin noted presciently, "the old super-loyalist element in the American Catholic community" might "bridge the chasm of the Reformation" and create an alliance of Catholic and Protestant "fundamentalists."[39] Such a shift was indeed to be one of the most important changes in America's religious-political landscape during the two following decades.

The Catholic conservatives around *National Review,* however, had recognized early that association with the John Birch Society could only damage their cause by aligning them with antidemocratic extremism, and Buckley editorialized against Welch from the beginning. Russell Kirk jibed: "Eisenhower is not a Communist: he is a golfer."[40]

38. Clancy, "A Liberal View," 313.
39. Westin, "John Birch Society," 104.
40. Eugene Lyons, "Folklore of the Right," *NR,* April 11, 1959, 645–47; editorial "The Question of Robert Welch," *NR,* Feb. 3, 1962, 83–88. On Buckley's relations with the society, see also John Judis, *William F. Buckley, Jr., Patron Saint of the Conservatives* (New York: Simon and Schuster, 1988), 193–200.

Buckley also denigrated Ayn Rand, the Russian émigré novelist and darling of libertarians, whose *Atlas Shrugged* (1957), was a right-wing cult classic in the late 1950s and early 1960s. Although a few *National Review* contributors admired Rand's glandular celebration of capitalism, Garry Wills voiced the majority opinion when he condemned it for its cold philosophical materialism and its icy contempt for the human community and all affairs spiritual.[41] Thenceforward, Rand declared a personal war against Buckley. Nevertheless, proximity on many political questions to the John Birch Society and to Rand's "Objectivists" hampered the Catholic intellectual conservatives' claim to respectability; Catholic liberals routinely yoked them together in their anticonservative polemics.[42]

Two disputes intensified public ill-feeling between Catholic liberals and conservatives in 1961. On the seventieth anniversary of Leo XIII's *Rerum Novarum*, Pope John XXIII published a new social encyclical letter *Mater et Magistra* ("Mother and teacher"). Like all encyclicals, it dealt mainly with general principles upon which Catholics should guide themselves in approaching social tasks; it did not spell out a specific political program. It appeared to press commentators, however, to offer comfort to liberal Catholics by endorsing industrial cooperation between managers and workers, urging developed nations to devote more of their wealth to aiding underdeveloped nations, and avoiding the issue of East-West ideological polarization (which, to conservatives, was of course all-important). Historically American Catholics had greeted each new encyclical with reverence and respectful expressions of assent. Father John Cronin, though a veteran anti-Communist crusader, received the encyclical in the old deferential way, describing it as a "majestic document," noting that Pope John XXIII had gone "far beyond Pope Pius XI in endorsing worker participation in the activity of the enterprise," and enthusing over a "realistic, moderate and progressive" document that placed "implicit trust in labor and its leaders" even as it reiterated that private property was "the sound foundation of social order."[43]

41. Garry Wills, "But Is Ayn Rand Conservative?" *NR*, Feb. 27, 1960, 139. Whittaker Chambers had also written an anti-Rand review for Buckley: "Big Sister Is Watching You," *NR*, Dec. 27, 1957, 594–96. The pro-Rand view was expressed by E. Merrill Root, "What about Ayn Rand?" *NR*, Feb. 13, 1960, 116–17.

42. See, for example, Stanley Rothman, "American Catholics and the Radical Right," *SO* 13 (April 1963): 5–9, 37. Buckley retaliated in 1962 by claiming that the editors of *America*, which had condemned the John Birch Society, were as intolerant as Welch. "Anyone who disagrees" with *America*, he claimed, they treated as "not really a good Catholic; at best he is a heathen-symp." William F. Buckley, Jr., "*America's* Bull," *NR*, March 27, 1962, 192.

43. John Cronin, "*Mater et Magistra*: Social Teaching Updated," *SO* 11 (Sept. 1961): 289–95.

In light of this traditional reverence for encyclicals, *National Review* was more than a little provoking when it greeted *Mater et Magistra* with a short, unceremonious editorial on the Vatican's "vast, sprawling document," which, by its neglect of communism as the worst obstacle to the world's social development, would "be seen by some as a venture in triviality coming at this particular moment in history."[44] It joked that conservatives were telling one another "Mater Si, Magistra No!" (a parody of Fidel Castro's slogan, "Cuba si, Yanqui no!").[45]

The sequel to these remarks illuminates many American Catholics' sense of unease in a period of rhetorical transition. The editors of *America* magazine tried at first to take the joke lightly, remarking that "our friend Bill Buckley" must surely have let this editorial slip past him unnoticed.[46] But unable to maintain the levity, they went on to express horror at what seemed to them an unpardonable disrespect. "We resent the insult to fellow Catholics. We consider the statement slanderous." They also expressed the hope that, although *Mater et Magistra* could "scarcely be reconciled" with the conservatives' economic principles, they would nevertheless accept it "with filial respect."[47] *Commonweal* cautioned conservatives that "no one should take the statement that *Mater et Magistra* is not ex cathedra [i.e., delivered infallibly] to mean that the principles it enunciates can be lightly dismissed or easily evaded."[48] The *Catholic World* echoed that infallibility was not the issue here: "The Catholic cannot stand off at a distance and cast a cold eye on papal statements, dismissing them as optional because not necessarily infallible."[49] Criticism was not confined to Catholic journals. Two weeks later the Catholic bishop of Charleston, South Carolina, Paul Hallinan, joined in the chorus of dismayed criticism and declared that if Catholic conservatives found *National Review*'s remarks amusing, "then the work facing our chaplains and student leaders is more extensive than we thought."[50]

Buckley answered that *National Review* was not a Catholic journal and so could not be held to the standards appropriate for *America* and *Commonweal*. Rather than let it go at that, however, he began to worry the issue, as though afraid that he had in fact overstepped the bounds of propriety. He noted that *National Review* followed the tradition enunciated in *Quadragesimo Anno* of subsidiarity—that the smallest possible

---

44. Untitled editorial, *NR*, July 29, 1961, 38.
45. The remark was first made by Garry Wills. See Wills, *Confessions*, 44.
46. Editorial, "William F. Buckley, Jr.," *A*, Aug. 19, 1961, 624.
47. Editorial, "Affront to Conservatives," *A*, Aug. 19, 1961, 622.
48. Editorial, "A Venture in Triviality," *C*, Aug. 25, 1961, 461.
49. John Sheerin, "The Reaction to *Mater et Magistra*," *CW* 193 (Sept. 1961): 341.
50. Editorial, "Venture in Negativism," *A*, Sept. 16, 1961, 727.

unit of society, individual, family, or local community, should deal with social problems wherever possible rather than involve the state and higher political organizations—a principle seemingly at a discount in liberal Catholics' interpretation of *Quadragesimo Anno*.[51] In an "Open Letter" to *America*'s Jesuit editor, Thurston Davis, Buckley lauded the papal encyclical tradition in general as "the most important literature in behalf of the highest claims of humankind that has been generated out of any single modern source" and added that "if—God forbid—I should ever be tempted to defy the teaching authority of the Church, whose cause I have taken seriously ever since I was in my teens, I should not announce my apostasy in doggerel." Despite these obeisances, however, he refused to apologize for the editorials and affirmed his regret at the pope's emphasis and timing in the encyclical. He then moved over to the offensive, accusing *America* of "ideological sectarianism" for its unremitting opposition to all that *National Review* represented. He warned the Jesuits that by ignoring conservative strictures about the absolute centrality of the Soviet threat they were undermining the defenses of the Christian West. "When we stand together, as well we may, in that final foxhole," he told Father Davis, "you will discover, as we pass each other the ammunition, that all along we had the same enemy, and that if we had acted in concert we might have spared ourselves that final encounter under such desperate circumstances."[52] Davis refused to print the open letter; so Buckley put it into the pages of his own journal instead.

Other Catholic journals commented on this fracas and tried to adjudicate in the light of the history and theology of encyclicals. Neil McCaffrey, the young Catholic conservative who had denigrated the significance of the Kennedy election in 1960, decided to collect the articles in which the issue was being debated and bring them out in a single volume. When several contributors withdrew from the project, however, he encouraged Garry Wills, one participant, to elaborate on his article, and the first full-length English-language study of papal encyclicals, *Politics and Catholic Freedom*, was the result.[53]

Wills began by summarizing the 1961 dispute but soon moved into rigorous historical and theological analysis of encyclical letters. He demonstrated that these were usually advisory and informative rather than dogmatic; although they outlined Catholic principles for conduct, they did not specify how the principles should be realized in the pru-

---

51. William F. Buckley, Jr., "The Strange Behavior of *America*," *NR*, Aug. 26, 1961, 114–15.

52. William F. Buckley, Jr., "An Open Letter to Thurston Davis, S.J.," *NR*, Sept. 23, 1961, 187–88.

53. On the germination of the project, see Wills, *Confessions*, 61–62.

dential realm of politics. He quoted Pope Leo XIII's encyclical *Immortale Dei* on this precise point:

> In matters merely political, as, for instance, the best form of government, and this or that system of administration, a difference of opinion is lawful. Those, therefore, whose piety is in other respects known, and whose minds are ready to accept in all obedience the decrees of the apostolic see, cannot in justice be accounted as bad men because they disagree as to subjects we have mentioned; and still graver wrong will be done them if—as We have more than once perceived with regret—they are accused of violating, or of wavering in, the Catholic faith.[54]

Indeed, it was to seek illumination on nondogmatic issues that Pope Benedict XIV had introduced encyclical letters in 1740 as consultative documents (52). Wills emphasized that on particular historical and political questions, the popes were (and had often recognized themselves as being) as fallible as any individual citizen. Thus if historical material was included in the text of an encyclical, for example, it might well be misleading because the pope could err by being falsely informed (83). Although passages from *Quadragesimo Anno* and *Mater et Magistra* could certainly be taken as presumptive evidence of papal approval for trade unions, "one should say that Popes are 'for' unions only with the understanding that they are for certain principles of social action and organization." To claim that the pope favored a specific union or its policies, Wills emphasized, "is an inference from the principle, not a mere rephrasing of it" (205). Clearly *Politics and Catholic Freedom* was a vindication of Buckley's 1961 dissent to *Mater et Magistra* and an affirmation that on political questions there was no such thing as "the" Catholic position.

Politics and Catholic Freedom was a daring book for its time (written 1962), both in its developmental theory of the church and in its half-submerged attempt to pare down Vatican power and authority—techniques that became commonplace among American Catholic writers only several years later. "Even Christ grew in wisdom and knowledge and grace in the sight of men," Wills remarked in one of many arguments for a developmental view of the church. "Is the Church to avoid, or hide, the historical task of learning from experience, correcting itself, maturing in consideration of this problem or that?" (120–21). The answer to this rhetorical question had been, through much of the twentieth century, yes. For Wills it was no, and he argued against the kind of Catholic "fundamentalism" that would attribute divine perfection to everything spoken by the church. This was, ironically, the error of contemporary liberal Catholics, he said, who appeared to believe that "Providence acts in a manifest and final way in the very order of history, so that hesitation about those enlightened political enthusiasms which lay claim to papal warrant is a repudiation of God's divine government in time" (128). Here was Wills's rarefied and theologically rigorous rebuke to *America* for its challenge to Buckley.

As Wills noted later in his intellectual autobiography, this dispute had an ironic aftermath. Catholic liberals, enthusiastic about the apparent emphases of *Mater et Magistra*, urged Catholic conservatives to submit in docility and act in ways the letter seemed to indicate. In 1968 the positions were to be reversed when Pope Paul VI issued the encyclical *Humanae Vitae* upholding traditional church teaching against contraception. Catholic liberals (and by then radicals too) greeted *Humanae Vitae* with dismay and apparently flouted it in large numbers; even among the conservatives, only a minority was willing to submit to its teaching. It was Wills, working on behalf of conservatives, who laid the theoretical groundwork for dissent to *Humanae Vitae* in the *Mater et Magistra* controversy. By then, however, it hardly mattered. The deferential and studious tones of debate still evident in the early 1960s had given way to stridency; as Wills said, the two sides were "effaced" in the later 1960s.[55]

The controversy over *Mater et Magistra* was further evidence of lay assertion within American Catholicism and was interpreted as such by some observers at the time. There was certainly no intention to challenge the church as a whole, however. As James O'Gara, a liberal journalist with no sympathy for Buckley, observed, "Even those who say 'Mater si, Magistra no' are not really in the tradition of European anticlericalism." They showed, rather, that the community of "God's holy people at work in the world" still required much teaching. The church's task now, he argued, using the rhetoric of aggiornamento, was to "develop informed and apostolic laymen."[56]

The 1961 encyclical controversy had scarcely begun when Brent Bozell set off a second controversy with a polemic called "The Strange Drift of Liberal Catholicism," written from El Escorial in Spain, whence he had retreated with his family in pursuit of an ideal, integral Catholi-

55. Wills, *Confessions*, 62.
56. James O'Gara, "Lay-Clerical Tension," C, July 6, 1962, 373.

cism.[57] He deplored recent articles by Father George Dunne, S.J. and other liberal Catholics who thought of America as a sick and racist society and argued, to the contrary, that the Christian West, now guarded primarily by U.S. military might, had been appointed by God as His instrument of salvation. "The West makes this claim over against the rest of the world," Bozell declared, "that it has been vouchsafed the truth about the nature of man and his relationship with the universe, and has been commissioned to construct and preserve an earthly city based on this truth." Accordingly, "the West asserts a God-given right, and thinks of it as a God-given duty, to conserve and spread *its* truth, to judge political and economic systems according to its lights, to change and improve them under its authority."[58] To fulfil its divinely appointed task, the West must guard not only against its external enemies but also against internal paralysis of the will, which seemed to Bozell all too common among American liberals, Catholics not least among them. Efforts at conciliation with the Soviet Union and other Communist regimes, the diversion of government funds into poverty relief and foreign aid programs, and the effort, proposed by Father Dunne, to admit the justice of some third-world revolutionaries' claims, would be to betray God's trust and hasten the fall of civilization. The following month, in a review of Paul Ramsay's *War and the Christian Conscience*, Bozell elaborated on these themes, arguing that God, having anointed the West, would not permit it to succumb in war against the Soviet Union. America's nuclear weapons might yet be God's instruments of salvation. "We must keep our 'ultimate' weapons *and be disposed to use them with good conscience* . . . if this becomes the only way to save the Christian West." Otherwise, a "Soviet triumph" would "destroy Christian civilization."[59] In making these claims Bozell was, of course, contradicting the tenor of John Courtney Murray's argument, in *We Hold These Truths*. Murray had emphasized the circumscribed secular purposes of U.S. constitutional government, stressing that it had no religious mission to fulfill in itself, so long as it protected the religious freedom of its citizens. In contrast, Bozell, then enjoying life in the heart of Franco's Spain, wanted to confer a religious significance and an apocalyptic duty on the American nation.

Bozell's claims set off an angry debate. *America* and *Commonweal* condemned him for an "unbelievably misguided" attempt to baptize the state and its military power. "To speak of the West as God's civilization

57. This section is based in part on telephone interviews with L. Brent Bozell, Feb. 26, 1991, and Patricia Buckley Bozell, March 9, 1991.

58. L. Brent Bozell, "The Strange Drift of Liberal Catholicism," *NR*, Aug. 12, 1961, 83.

59. L. Brent Bozell, "Nuclear War and the Moral Law," *NR*, Sept. 23, 1961, 197–98.

is almost blasphemous," one editorial declared, while the idea of the West's asserting itself over the rest of the world just as the era of Western imperialism was ending in Asia and Africa was "dangerous and foolish."[60] The church, not the West, is God's instrument on earth. Father Norris Clarke, S.J., criticized Bozell for assuming, anachronistically, that a consensus of values based on Christian revelation now bound the West together. "I fear," he wrote, "that Mr. Bozell has not yet really accepted the fact that, like it or not, we no longer live in the world of the Holy Roman Empire, of Philip II's Spain, or even in the select club of Christian European kings and princes who agreed with each other at least on the ultimate, if not the immediate, destiny of man." Clarke foresaw that other civilizations, now aborning, might pick up the mantle of Christianity's protector hitherto worn by the West.[61] Other critics added that "the West is not the true end and nature of the Catholic Church," especially not in the United States, where capitalism and industrialization represented the antithesis, not the fulfillment, of Christianity.[62]

The debate did not stop after one round. Frank Meyer (subsequently a deathbed convert to Catholicism and already adept in natural law argumentation and citation of papal literature) upheld Bozell's claims and affirmed that the West's role in preserving Christianity was of "transcendent" rather than merely earthly significance. "It is sad to have to remind Catholics," Meyer lamented, "that this is a sacramental, not a Manichean world, that our secular actions as ordinary men partake of the sacred when we act with good faith and motive and grace towards truth and good." Meyer echoed Bozell's assurance of righteousness in a holy war: "Communism, in actual and objective fact, does represent an absolute black, and the West, as a civilization, is, *in its essence*, as close to an absolute white, as is possible in the subdued light which illuminates this imperfect world."[63] Garry Wills, too, in a long, densely reasoned letter to *Commonweal*, complete with quotations from Aristotle, Aquinas, Dante, and Newman, supported Bozell's contentions and argued that Christ's incarnation demonstrated the transcendent significance of worldly events. History showed, moreover, that "the organized earthly body of the Church is defended by secular means." To believe that a disembodied spirit of Christianity could re-

60. Editorial, "God and the Cold War," *C*, Sept. 8, 1961, 483. For another angry response, see Rev. James O'Leary, "God Save Father Dunne: A Public Confession to L. Brent Bozell," *A*, Sept. 9, 1961, 703.

61. Norris Clarke, S.J., "Is the West 'God's Civilization'?" *A*, March 31, 1962, 855.

62. Edward T. Welch, "A Matter of Principle," letter to *NR*, Nov. 18, 1961, 354–56.

63. Frank Meyer, "*Commonweal* Puts the West in Its Place," *NR*, Oct. 7, 1961, 234.

place the actual institution of the church in the West, all its imperfections notwithstanding, was to fall prey to a form of gnosticism. "The whole of the West's resources of thought and language have been recruited in the formulation and protection of Christ's teachings," said Wills, so that the religious, intellectual, and political destinies of the West remained inseparable.[64] Even on the issue of nuclear weapons, Bozell found support from other Catholic conservatives. Father Vincent Miceli, S.J., affirmed that Soviet communism was an evil so immense that the weapons were justified.[65]

This debate indicates the development of two distinctive Catholic approaches to the U.S. role in world affairs. Some conservatives still believed in a special religious destiny for the nation, with corresponding duties, whereas most liberals (never "soft on communism" despite frequent allegations) declined to vest themselves or their fellow citizens with a divine mission. *Commonweal*'s editors sharply summed up the controversy from the liberal point of view: "That Communism is a very great and dangerous evil is perfectly clear to all Christians. What we oppose categorically is the conservative attempt to turn the struggle of free men throughout the world against Communism into a struggle only for the preservation of Western values." They refused to endorse Bozell's claim that the civilization of Western Europe and North America had been singled out for any divine mission and emphasized that the universal church might equally hereafter carry on its mission from another culture.[66]

The luminaries of the new conservative movement did not all share Bozell's crusading outlook. While most were either pillars of the church or at least sympathetic supporters from outside (flying buttresses?), a notable exception was Max Eastman. Early in his life he had belonged to the American Socialist party, had been editor of the *Masses*, had briefly sojourned in the Communist party, and then had had a long career in the anti-Stalinist Left; by the 1950s he had come full circle in his political ideas to support militantly anti-Communist conservatism.[67] A member of the editorial board of *National Review*, Eastman

64. Garry Wills, "An Exchange of Views: God and the Cold War," *C*, Oct. 21, 1961, 95–98.
65. Vincent Miceli, S.J., "The Morality of Nuclear Weapons," review of Walter Stein, ed., *Nuclear Weapons: A Catholic Response*, in *NR*, Oct. 9, 1962, 276–77. This debate foreshadowed the Catholic nuclear weapons debate of the 1980s, on which see George Wiegel, S.J., *Tranquillitas Ordinis: The Present Failure and the Future Promise of American Catholic Thought on War and Peace* (New York: Oxford University Press, 1987), 261–85.
66. Editorial, "God and Man at *National Review*," *C*, Oct. 27, 1961, 108.
67. On the career of Max Eastman, see John P. Diggins, *Up from Communism: Conservative Odysseys in American Intellectual History* (New York: Harper and Row, 1975); Daniel Aaron, *Writers on the Left* (New York: Harcourt, Brace, and World, 1961).

was made uneasy by the religious orientation of many of its contributors. Finally, in early 1964 he announced his retirement from *National Review* and specified in a parting article that he could not countenance the religiously motivated ideas of Buckley, Bozell, Wills, Meyer, and many of the others. His remarks indicated that for Eastman, "freedom," the rhetorical icon of all conservatives in their fight against communism, signified absence of external restraints, whereas for the religious conservatives it signified conformity with natural law. "To advocate freedom and then lay down the law as to how men 'should' use it," Eastman declared, "is a contradiction in terms. It is a reversion not to classic liberalism, but to pre-liberal ecclesiastical authoritarianism. I don't strive to understand an objective moral order or move towards it because I don't think any such moral order exists."[68]

Buckley was sad to witness Eastman's departure; his skill as a writer and his wide reputation in American letters had made him a valuable asset to the journal from the beginning. Commenting upon the retirement, Buckley tried to explain the relationship between conservatism and Christianity and concluded that those who had been denied the "gift" of faith, though they could be precious allies in the fight against liberals and Communists, were ultimately deficient in their own sense of what it was they must fight for. "The pro-religious conservative can therefore welcome the atheist as a full-fledged member of the conservative community even while feeling that at the very bottom the roots do not interlace, so that the sustenance that gives a special bloom to Christian conservatism fails to reach the purely secularist conservatism."[69]

WILL HERBERG AND CONSERVATIVE ECUMENISM

Eastman was the exception rather than the rule; religion remained central to the conservative project of the early 1960s, but its scope began to broaden. Brent Bozell and Frederick Wilhelmsen considered Catholics the group best fitted to defend the West. Others were increasingly willing to admit that there were plentiful Jewish and Protestant allies for this cause, equally committed to the preservation of a Judeo-Christian nation.[70] The early 1960s, with the issue of a Catholic

68. Max Eastman, "Am I a Conservative?" *NR*, Jan. 28, 1964, 57–58.

69. William F. Buckley, Jr., "What Is Conservatism?" in Buckley, *The Jeweler's Eye* (New York: Putnam, 1968), 28.

70. On this concept, see Mark Silk, "Notes on the Judeo-Christian Tradition in America," *American Quarterly* 36 (Spring 1984): 65–85.

presidency apparently settled once and for all, witnessed some reconciliation of Catholic conservatives with conservatives of other faiths,
especially those, such as evangelist Fred Schwartz of the Christian
Anti-Communist Crusade, who shared in the anti-Communist fervor.[71]
National Review began in the early 1960s to take note of conservative
evangelical theology too, observing of Carl Henry's *Basic Christian Doctrines*, for example, that "it disproves the theory that in Protestant
theology intellectualism can only be synonymous with liberalism."[72]
Other Catholics were expressly willing to put aside continuing religious differences to pursue common goals.[73]

In 1961, consonant with this broadening of outlook, *National Review*
took on a religious affairs editor, Will Herberg. Like Max Eastman,
Herberg was a former Communist who now regarded communism as
the West's deadliest enemy. Tempted to convert to Christianity in the
early 1950s following his exit from the Communist party, he was reas-
sured by Reinhold Niebuhr that his native Jewish tradition could nurture him equally well; this conversation was itself a landmark in the
history of American ecumenism.[74] In the following years, many of
them spent as a professor of religion at Drew University, Herberg established a reputation for critical scholarship on religious questions. His
sociological study *Protestant, Catholic, Jew* (1955) was widely admired
at the time and became the classic account of the interplay of religion
and ethnic identity in American history. In it, Herberg questioned the
depth of the 1950s religious revival and lamented the conventionality
and shallowness of many Americans' faith.[75] By contrast, his *Four Existentialist Theologians* (1958) celebrated the intellectual intensity and
philosophical relevance religious faith could still call forth from powerful minds in Protestantism, Catholicism, Eastern Orthodoxy, and Judaism.[76]

71. See, for example, the pro-Schwartz editorial, "The Mad Attempt to Get Schwartz," *NR*,
July 31, 1962, 53–54.
72. D. B. Lockerbie, untitled review of Carl Henry, *Basic Christian Doctrines*, in *NR*, April 23,
1963, 330.
73. See, for example, the letter from Catholic John P. McCarthy, editor of *New Individualist
Review* (a libertarian journal), to *America*, June 24, 1961, in response to a critical article. McCarthy justified himself: "I am willing to cooperate with people whose social philosophies are
not truly compatible with Catholic social thought, in order to achieve certain objectives which
are. . . . The furtherance of Catholic social philosophy demands that American Catholics stop
writing just for themselves and begin to collaborate with those who are not as orthodox as
we" (453).
74. On the earlier career of Herberg, see Diggins, *Up from Communism*, 118–59, 269–302.
75. Will Herberg, *Protestant, Catholic, Jew: An Essay in American Religious Sociology* (Garden
City, N.Y.: Doubleday, 1955).
76. Will Herberg, *Four Existentialist Theologians* (Garden City, N.Y.: Doubleday, 1958). Its
subjects are Jacques Maritain (Catholic), Martin Buber (Jewish), Paul Tillich (Protestant), and
Nicolas Berdayev (Russian Orthodox).

Herberg had his doubts about Catholicism in the 1950s. Writing as a "friendly outsider" in 1953 he argued that Catholic natural law thinkers were too apt to see simple black and white where a dose of Niebuhrian ambiguity would make better sense of complicated issues. U.S. Catholics he found prudish, standoffish, and uncreative by comparison with their European coreligionists. And like many non-Catholic contemporaries, he feared that, given the chance of majority power, they would repeal the First Amendment. At the same time Herberg had to admit, "In an age of spiritual chaos and disorientation, Catholicism stands forth as the keeper of an enduring tradition that has weathered the storms of the past and stands unshaken amidst the disasters of our time." It held forth a "universalist" promise in an age of baleful particularisms, rocklike in its steadiness while the Protestants vacillated.[77] These were not small virtues for Herberg, bereft of his old certainties.

By the early 1960s, as Herberg's conservative convictions intensified, he spoke in much more glowing terms of U.S. Catholicism as the nation's (and the world's) presumptive anti-Communist leader. As an outsider, he was able to spell out the advantages Catholicism enjoyed as chief guardian of the West more systematically than many of the Catholic conservatives themselves ever did. In one of his first columns there, for example, Herberg noted that many *National Review* editors were Catholics and added that "even the non-Catholics feel high reverence for the Papacy and Church as a great conservative force and a mighty bulwark against the totalitarian subversion of western freedom and culture."[78] A few years later he noted that after years of careful study of religion he "had come to the conclusion that religiously and culturally, socially, and even politically, the Roman Catholic Church was the most significant positive force of the West. . . . I could not help admiring the way the Church had held out against the secularizing, 'liberalizing,' and 'progressivizing' madness of the nineteenth century . . . in order to preserve the fundamental truths about the spirituality, the dignity and destiny of the human person and of mankind as a whole." He had often been described as an apologist of the church "in partibus infidelium. And I still am," said Herberg.[79] He admired the church partly because it had resisted the "cardinal error" of the Protestant social gospel tradition. Always engaged in works of charity, Catho-

---

77. Will Herberg, "A Jew Looks at Catholics," *C*, May 22, 1953, 174–77. See also editorial, "Sectarian Conflict," *C*, Dec. 12, 1952, 249, in which Herberg wins Catholic praise for criticizing anti-Catholicism.

78. Will Herberg, "Controversy over an Encyclical," *NR*, Nov. 4, 1961, 299.

79. Will Herberg, "The Limits of Papal Authority," review of Garry Wills, *Politics and Catholic Freedom*, in *NR*, Aug. 25, 1964, 730–34.

lics had yet never believed that social work was central to Christianity. The social gospel's emphasis on charity as Christ's love, by contrast, he saw as overweighted against the demands of God's justice, which was an imperative for any religion purporting to guide a way of life.[80]

In a marked change from his views in the early 1950s, the Will Herberg of the early 1960s believed that the Catholic balance of love and justice *depended* on the natural law tradition of scholarship which he had once denigrated. Natural law, he now argued, was the best guide for practical action and judgment in this world which nevertheless kept in sight the City of God. Based on Aristotelian and Ciceronian models, the Thomist synthesis of natural law and Christian tradition had enriched Catholic thought in the high Middle Ages. It had then fallen under attack by Luther and Calvin, who did not deny the idea of natural law completely but saw human beings as too depraved by sin to be able to discern it sufficiently for their guidance. Protestants, Herberg implied, had been left with too few intermediate structures between themselves and God, so that the absolute demands of God came to them "vertically from above" and made them vulnerable to an ad hoc political and moral "situationism."[81] Herberg speculated that the rejection of natural law by the Protestant neo-orthodox theologians of the early twentieth century, notably Reinhold Niebuhr in the United States and Karl Barth in Germany, had deprived them of a standpoint from which adequately to condemn the rising totalitarian regimes of Stalin and Hitler. Meanwhile, social gospel ministers in the interwar years (whom Niebuhr too had criticized) had been in a far worse situation, advocating peace in the face of a rising hurricane and underestimating the human propensity to sin. "Were the advocates of 'patience and understanding' with Nazi Germany the spokesmen of Christian responsibility?" Surely not. There were times when Christians must show anger and belligerence, as Herberg's new Catholic colleagues certainly did today.[82]

After the war, Herberg argued, when "legal positivism" and "cultural relativism" had shown themselves insufficient in the struggle against tyranny, "something very close to a natural law ethic and a natural law jurisprudence re-emerged as a defense against the great Leviathan."[83] In modified form, this was the kind of argument Ross

80. Will Herberg, "Again the Social Gospel," *NR*, Feb. 13, 1962, 96, 109.

81. Will Herberg, "Conservatives, Liberals, and the Natural Law, I," *NR*, June 5, 1962, 407, 422; and "Conservatives, Liberals, and the Natural Law, II," *NR* June 18, 1962, 438.

82. Herberg, "Again the Social Gospel," 96.

83. Herberg, "Conservatives, Liberals, and the Natural Law, I," 407. Herberg even argued that Niebuhr should be understood as a Burkean conservative and proposed his inclusion in

Hoffman had been making from within the Catholic church while the war was in progress, though Hoffman had taken a less ecumenical view than Herberg now proposed. Herberg recognized that Protestant dependence on Scripture and Catholic natural law tradition could not be reconciled without great intellectual stress and that this difference placed an obstacle in the path of consensus among religious conservatives: "Varying interpretations of the higher law are possible, and may even be ultimately irreconcileable, as perhaps are the two conceptions of the higher law most familiar to us, one of which sees the source of the higher law in the revealed word of God, and the other in the rational structure of man's nature."[84] Nevertheless he hoped these differences were not too great to prevent a Protestant-Catholic alliance in the defense of the West.

Such a sterling defense of Catholicism and natural law by an American Jew was not without its paradoxes. Herberg's aim, however, was to reconcile conservatives from all the American faiths while seeking out special strengths where he could locate them. "Conservatism . . . has always found in religion—the traditional religions of the community—both the basis and the pinnacle of the culture," he declared. These traditional faiths provided the spring of civic virtue and moral coherence, but in addition, they always held out a challenge to the status quo, demanded self-scrutiny, and forestalled the development of a "pseudo-religion" of the secular state itself. "To have seen this so clearly," Herberg believed, "constitutes the great merit of the so-called 'reactionary' papal encyclicals of the nineteenth century." Herberg wanted to avoid the imputation that religion was merely being put to work to make conservatism a strong secular force. In the early 1960s, it seemed to him, secular-minded liberals were trying to expel religion from public life while secular-minded conservatives were trying to yoke it to defense of the social order. "The man of faith," Herberg warned, "must protest against both."[85] Religion, in other words, was highly desirable to conservatives of whatever conviction but remained in tension with and stood in judgment over all political programs.

Others shared Herberg's conclusions and also promoted the possibility of reconciling conservatives from the different faiths. Now that the Second Vatican Council was in session, debating a new place for their church in the modern world, Catholics of all political persuasions were seeking allies. Catholic educator Harold Gill Reuschlein made a charac-

---

the new conservatives' pantheon. Will Herberg, "Reinhold Niebuhr, Burkean Conservative," *NR*, Dec. 2, 1961, 379.

84. Herberg, "Conservatives, Liberals, and the Natural Law, II," 438.
85. Will Herberg, "Conservatives and Religion: A Dilemma," *NR*, Oct. 7, 1961, 230, 232.

teristic pitch for such groupings in 1963: "The real danger to Catholicism is not Protestantism; it is not Judaism; it is an anthropocentric humanism on the march." As far as the Catholic layman was concerned, said Reuschlein, "this must mean that he has an affirmative duty to enter into an alliance with his God-centered brethren of whatever religious persuasion against the common threat of secular humanism."[86] Francis Graham Wilson, one of the first Catholic spokespeople of the new conservative movement and himself a convert, argued in the early 1960s not simply that Catholic-Protestant alliance was necessary but even that Protestants—he had once been one himself—had some special qualities from which Catholics might benefit. Observing the beginnings of a new conservatism in Spain at the start of the 1960s, Wilson said that the peoples of Catholic countries "need to regard their work as an expression of moral personality, and they need to develop the Protestant respect for the law." Combining these two Protestant qualities with Catholic faith, he believed, would facilitate "conservative progress" not only in Spain but throughout the anti-Communist world.[87]

CHURCH-STATE TENSIONS

If the United States was to be the fortress of the Judeo-Christian tradition, however, its religious underpinnings must be made as explicit as possible in public institutions and in the training of each new generation. This conviction formed the background to conservatives' reception of the Supreme Court decision *Engel v. Vitale* (June 1962), when, to their dismay, the court ruled against prayer in public schools. At issue in the case was the New York Board of Regents' nondenominational and noncompulsory prayer: "Almighty God, we acknowledge our dependence upon Thee, and we beg Thy blessings upon us, our parents, our teachers and our country." A more anodyne invocation of the Omnipotent would be hard to imagine, but the American Jewish Committee, Ethical Culture, the Unitarian church, and other amici curiae litigated against it on First Amendment grounds.[88] The Supreme Court, in a six-to-one decision, found that the prayer violated the estab-

86. Harold Gill Reuschlein, "The Future Belongs to the Articulate," *CW* 196 (Jan. 1963): 245.
87. Francis Graham Wilson, "The New Conservatives in Spain," *MA* 5 (Spring 1961): 149–60. Here Wilson also endorses Ross Hoffman's proposal for a reconciliation of Catholic conservatism with the Burkean tradition (160).
88. On the background and history of the case, see Robert S. Alley, *The Supreme Court on Church and State* (New York: Oxford University Press, 1988), 194–203.

lishment clause of that amendment, and the following year, in *Schempp* v. *Abington Township* and *Murray* v. *Curlett*, the Court extended the ban to prayers from any source and to Bible reading in public schools.[89] Just at a time when many conservatives were trying to make the case for the Christian West or at least the Judeo-Christian tradition as explicit as possible, the Supreme Court seemed to be trying to undermine the nation's sacred mission.

Most Catholics deplored the decisions. Cardinal Spellman of New York said that "it strikes at the very heart of the godly tradition in which America's children have for so long been raised."[90] The editors of *America*, the Jesuit magazine, fresh from their controversy with Buckley over *Mater et Magistra*, described *Engel* as "a stupid decision, a doctrinaire decision, an unrealistic decision that spits in the face of our history, our tradition and our heritage as a religious people." It would, they predicted, prompt more Catholic parents to send their children to parochial schools, where they could avoid "the enslaving limitations of secularistic dogma."[91] The editor of the *Catholic World* agreed that the decision would "gravely disturb the peace and harmony of the local and national community" and that it had "aided the John Birchers' mad campaign against the Court."[92] *America* took the same line in a second furious editorial on the issue, noting that the Warren Court, already under attack by opponents of its judicial activism, would lose further credibility and cast doubt on such noble decisions as *Brown* v. *Board of Education*. The editor cited the complaint of an Alabama congressman—"They've put the Negroes in the schools, and now they've driven God out"—as an omen of things to come. *America* blamed the American Jewish Committee, especially its counsel Leo Pfeffer, and warned that the "Jewish agencies" that hailed these decisions had won a victory that would be "rather costly in terms of community relations."[93] That sounded like a threat of anti-Semitism to Pfeffer, and a heated exchange of letters followed, with ecumenical courtesies strained to the limit.[94] *America* generated a further exchange of recriminations by criticizing Dean Kelley, director of the National Council of Churches, the leading mainstream Protestant group, for refusing to

89. Ibid., 204–24.

90. Cited in Charles Rice, *The Supreme Court and Public Prayer* (New York: Fordham University Press, 1964), 5.

91. Editorial, "Black Monday," *A*, July 7, 1962, 456.

92. John Sheerin, "The Ban on Public Prayer," *CW* 195 (Aug. 1962): 261–65.

93. Editorial, "After June 25, 1962," *A*, July 14, 1962, 483–84.

94. See, in particular, editorial, "To Our Jewish Friends," *A*, Sept. 1, 1962, 665–66; and letter, "To Our Catholic Friends," *A*, Sept. 8, 1962, 679–80. *America*'s rebuttal came in an editorial, "The Main Issue," *A*, Sept. 15, 1962, 713.

condemn the decision.[95] Ironically, one of the few Catholics to publish arguments in support of the decisions was himself a Jesuit; Robert Henle argued that the "neutral secularism" embodied in the Court's findings was acceptable to Catholics, that only a "positive secularism" enjoined by the state would be intolerable.[96]

William Buckley took a measure of satisfaction from the Jesuits' discomfiture at *America,* but he too condemned the Court's findings. He declared that they signaled the need for a constitutional amendment designed to "outlaw any preferential treatment given to a single religion" but "permit[ting] religion to continue to be a part of public life; a part, if you like, of the official American image."[97] This theme of "official image" was central in his opinion. Under no illusion that the regents' prayer, a few verses of the Bible, or the Ten Commandments, could of themselves revive the faith of a generation, he nevertheless believed them to be of great ritual importance in aligning the nation's public institutions behind religious symbols. Will Herberg agreed that references to God on the currency, in the Pledge of Allegiance, and by congressional chaplains might look like forms of taking the Lord's name in vain; nevertheless, he favored them as symbols that forestalled the development of a cult of the state.[98] Like most conservative commentators on the issue, he believed the Court had erred in so explicitly contradicting Justice William O. Douglas's declaration in the *Zorach* case of 1952: "We are a religious people, whose institutions presuppose a Supreme Being."[99] Russell Kirk, in his regular *National Review* educational affairs column, praised schools that continued to pray and read the Bible in violation of the Court's finding, and speculated jeeringly that the American Civil Liberties Union would next try to "prescribe certain deletions from the Declaration of Independence, if the pure minds of the rising generation must not be exposed to that notorious theocratic manifesto."[100]

That Catholics should so fervently protest the Court's decision was itself a sign of a changed mood in Catholicism. In the nineteenth century Catholic prelates had fought bitter campaigns to get prayer and

---

95. Editorial, "Roundup on Prayer Cases," *A,* July 28, 1963, 541–42; letter from Dean Kelley, *A,* Aug. 11, 1962, 575, in which Kelley described the watered-down school prayers as "the ultimate profanity" and said they were "superficial, pretentious, unscriptural, and unworthy of Christians," adding, "It seems singular to me that some Christians should feel it an exercise of *their* religious freedom to *make others watch them worship!*"
96. Robert Henle, S.J., "Dilemmas of the Prayer Decision," *SO* 13 (March 1963): 32–48.
97. William F. Buckley, Jr., "Take a Vote, Gentlemen," *NR,* Sept. 11, 1962, 177.
98. Will Herberg, "Religious Symbols in Public Life," *NR,* Aug. 28, 1962, 145.
99. Will Herberg, "The 'Separation' of Church and State," *NR,* Oct. 23, 1962, 315.
100. Russell Kirk, "Now I Lay Me Down to Sleep," *NR,* Sept. 25, 1962, 230.

Bible reading *out* of public schools, on grounds that Catholic children were subjected to Protestant propaganda from the King James version and Protestant prayers. Now, as one commentator has noted, this "important group switched sides; after more than a century of opposition to religious exercises with a Protestant orientation in the public schools, the Catholic Church now favored almost any means that would prevent the schools from becoming completely secularized."[101] Here again was evidence of shifting priorities in the encounter with the non-Catholic world. Catholics were beginning to realize that agnosticism and indifference might be worse adversaries than Protestantism.

The Becker Amendment, intended to restore prayer and Bible reading in schools and to preserve other religious symbols in public life ("In God We Trust" on currency, "under God" in the Pledge of Allegiance, and military chaplains) made progress through Congress in the following years, won simple majorities, but was never able to get the necessary two-thirds majority to send it to the states for ratification. Catholic conservatives wrote extensively and angrily on the issue. Charles Rice, for example, a professor at Fordham Law School, wrote a book-length study of the issue, *The Supreme Court and Public Prayer*, making what seemed to prayer advocates an overwhelming case, historical and judicial, for the preservation of religious observance in public education. Until 1962, said Rice, "the United States Constitution was concededly based upon a profession that, in fact, there is a God and there is a divine law to which men and nations are subject." The Court had now denied that premise "by enjoining upon government a rule of neutrality . . . on the very question of whether there is a God at all."[102] Rice denied that this new position was in fact neutral. Rather, he argued, it instituted religious agnosticism as national faith. But the struggle against communism, Rice believed, "requires an affirmation that indeed there is a God" and that "even the state is subject to His law" (xii). Just when the religious dimensions of the cold war needed to be made as explicit as possible, the government of Christendom's protector was trying to minimize them.

Rice, in addition to denouncing the *Engel, Schempp,* and *Murray* cases through rigorous arguments based on precedent and U.S. legal history, emphasized that there were practical benefits to be gained "from governmental promotion of recognition of God." Foremost among them was a safeguarding of constitutionalism and limited government. The

---

101. James Reichley, *Religion in American Public Life* (Washington, D.C.: Brookings Institution, 1985), 146.
102. Rice, *Supreme Court,* ix.

child who saw his or her teachers "affirm the existence of God and His law over all," he declared, "is less likely to follow the demagogue who asserts . . . the final power to ordain what is right and wrong" (126).[103] Equally beneficial, affirming God's rule would encourage a sense of order and personal responsibility, qualities Rice believed lacking in modern students. Like many fellow conservatives he traced the decline of educational standards and the rise of juvenile delinquency to twentieth-century "progressive" educational orthodoxy and its philosophical underpinnings in pragmatism, all of which seemed to him hostile to religion. "The tiny seed of pragmatic doubt sown in the 1920s has borne bitter fruit in a generation of students, too many of whom are indolent under instruction, docile under indoctrination, rebellious under correction, and scornful under exposure to principle in the slightest degree" (122–23). As a solution at least to the immediate political dilemma, if not to juvenile delinquency, Rice argued for a revival of judicial restraint, "a wholesome timidity in the judiciary" (131)—a doctrine that seemed to him more honored in the breach than in the observance by the Warren Court—and for a constitutional amendment "not to change the Constitution, but to restore it" (157).

Civil Rights

Simultaneously with the school prayer decisions and the Kennedy presidency, the activist phase of the nonviolent civil rights movement was gathering force; these were the years of the sit-ins, the freedom rides, and major demonstrations in Washington, Selma, Birmingham, and elsewhere. Historians of the movement have recognized that its leadership in the first decade, 1955–1965, was clergy dominated.[104] Martin Luther King, Jr., Ralph Abernathy, Andrew Young, Jesse Jackson, and others blended a language of political progress with biblical references familiar both to their own evangelical congregations and to their white listeners, creating a rhetorical bridge between their two audiences. Presenting political liberation as a religious issue, moreover, reinforced the movement's sense of purpose and justification. White churches followed the African-American ministers' lead with varying degrees of enthusiasm. In 1958 the Catholic hierarchy joined in by issuing a pastoral letter, "Discrimination and the Christian Con-

103. Herberg made the same point in "Religious Symbols in Public Life," 145, 162.
104. See, for example, David Garrow, *Bearing the Cross: Martin Luther King, Jr., and the Southern Christian Leadership Conference* (New York: Random House, 1986), 20–24, 97.

science," which James O'Gara termed "a hard-hitting condemnation of discrimination and segregation."[105] The bishops acknowledged that as a matter of historical fact "segregation in our country has led to oppressive conditions and the denial of basic human rights for the Negro." Catholics, they said, should now work carefully to end this shameful situation, though always remembering "to steer prudently between 'a gradualism that is merely a cloak for inaction' and 'ill-timed and ill-considered ventures.'"[106]

The emergence of black civil rights as a major political issue came as a shock to the sensibilities of many liberal Catholics. Father Louis Twomey, S.J., for example, admitted his shame on realizing that throughout his life until this point he had been thoughtlessly "part of a vast conspiracy, coldly calculated to deprive our Negro fellow-men of the spiritual and material goods to which under God they have an inalienable right."[107] Liberals agreed that this was a religious question. "As Christians," one noted, the leading figures in the civil rights movement "are making an appeal of conscience to their white brothers against the sin of segregation."[108] Matthew Ahmann, director of the National Catholic Council for Interracial Justice, called racism a "heresy."[109] *Commonweal, America, Jubilee,* and the new *National Catholic Reporter,* another lay initiative of the early 1960s, enthused about the movement's self-disciplined nonviolence in the face of white provocation, and treated King as a prophet whose witness brought shame on whites who had acquiesced so long in racial segregation.[110] The "blend of courage and dignity" shown by King and the National Association for the Advancement of Colored People, said *America,* "has helped arouse the consciences of many moderate whites."[111] The editors of these journals praised the demonstrators and condemned the police. When in Birmingham, Alabama, police used dogs and fire hoses against a desegregation demonstration in 1963, *Commonweal* said that "it was . . . the police who should have been arrested, both for ob-

105. Editorial, "Bishops Condemn Racial Injustice," *A,* Nov. 29, 1958, 264; James O'Gara, "Getting Nowhere Fast," *C,* May 8, 1964, 194.

106. "Bishops Condemn Racial Injustice," 264.

107. Louis Twomey, S.J., "Autobiographical Notes on the Race Problem," *SO* 13 (Jan. 1963): 1–4.

108. William Shannon, "The Crisis in Birmingham," *C,* May 24, 1963, 238–39.

109. Matthew Ahmann, "Catholics and Race," *C,* Dec. 2, 1960, 247–50.

110. See, for example, "Mississippi Malaise," *Jubilee* 11 (July 1963): 14–21; Martin Luther King, Jr., "Love and Non-violence," ibid., 22–23; editorial, "The Saints without Names," *NCR,* Nov. 4, 1964, 3.

111. Editorial, "Negro Gains," *A,* Feb. 18, 1961, 652. See also "In This Issue," *Jubilee* 11 (July 1963): 1: "He [King] speaks to the conscience of white Americans, North and South, pointing out that when one man humiliates another he inevitably demeans himself."

structing justice and for vicious assault."[112] Priests and nuns in growing numbers began to join King's demonstrations against segregation
and racial discrimination, seeking active roles in transforming racial
relations in American cities north and south. Sometimes their superiors supported them. When Father Robert McDole of Oklahoma City
was arrested for disorderly conduct in a 1960 antidiscrimination rally,
for example, a local judge dismissed the charge, expecting the priest
to be disciplined by his bishop. But Bishop Victor Reed defended and
praised the priest, maintaining that "in the absence of sufficient lay
activity the clergy may take direct action in these matters."[113]

The civil rights movement had international repercussions. The Soviet Union made propaganda capital out of enforced segregation,
which made American declarations of universal freedom and equality
ring hollow. Catholic supporters of the civil rights movement, accordingly, pointed out the foreign policy benefits of desegregation. It
would, they argued, improve the country's image in the eyes of newly
decolonized African nations whose leaders perceived themselves as
facing the choice of Western or Soviet client status. To critics who
believed that the civil rights movement was Communist inspired, they
answered that, properly understood, desegregation would help *combat*
communism. "It can never be stressed enough," said *America* in 1960,
"that racism is not only villainous and sinful. In a world of many races,
most of them colored, a crime against our American Negroes is also
the most explosive propaganda bomb we can hand our enemies to use
against us."[114] Fear that American racial policy would tempt the new
African nations into the arms of the Soviet Union certainly played a
role in the Kennedy and Johnson administrations' approach to civil
rights and their gradually increasing willingness to back up rhetoric
with federal intervention, first judicial, later legislative. At the same
time, however, fear of breaking up their solid white electoral base in
the South acted as a constant brake on the Democratic presidents. Like
these presidents, the Catholic church as a whole dragged its feet and,
as *Commonweal* noted in 1963, showed none of the "concreteness or
urgency" it displayed on questions of sexual morality.[115] With the inspiring exception of a few dedicated activists, such as Dorothy Day,
Josephite priest Philip Berrigan, and Jesuit John Lafarge, Catholic intel-

---

112. Editorial, "Birmingham, a City," C, May 17, 1963, 212–13.
113. Editorial, "Priestly Leadership," A, Feb. 4, 1961, 582.
114. Editorial, "Subversive Segregationists," A, Dec. 10, 1960, 360. See also editorial, "Playing into Red Hands," A, Oct. 1, 1960, 2.
115. Editorial, "A Sad Chapter," C, May 1, 1963, 163–64.

lectuals followed rather than led throughout this period of dramatic social change.[116]

If the liberal Catholic intellectuals were followers rather than leaders in the civil rights movement, Catholic laypeople were sometimes active opponents of desegregation. About 500,000 African Americans were Catholic in the mid-1950s; many of them lived in Louisiana. The most glaring case of a gulf between the bishops' theory and the liberals' hopes, on the one hand, and the laity's practice, on the other, came in New Orleans, where an attempt to desegregate parochial schools in the interest of this large minority led to massive resistance from Catholic whites. Already in a 1955 incident a black priest, Father Gerald Lewis, had been forcibly prevented by white parishioners from conducting Mass at Jesuit Bend, Louisiana; the whites refused to relent even when Archbishop Joseph Rummel of New Orleans closed their church. When the school desegregation plan was announced in 1960, prosegregation Catholics demonstrated in the streets, intimidated blacks who tried to attend the schools, swore to defy the order, and launched a white supremacist newspaper, the *Catholic Warrior*.[117] Four out of five leaders of the New Orleans White Citizens' Council were Catholics, and one segregationist zealot, Leander Perez, was ultimately excommunicated for his intransigence. Another excommunicated Catholic, Jackson Ricau, Jr., ran the segregationist *Citizens' Report*, while Emile Wagner, Jr., founder of Roman Catholics of the Caucasian Race, was aided by Monsignor Carl Schutten, editor of *Catholic Action of the South*.[118] John LaFarge, on the staff at Loyola University of New Orleans, ruefully admitted that "the Catholic schools cannot be integrated for fear of mass withdrawal of white pupils to the public school system . . . as well as withdrawal by the angry laity of financial support for the Church and Church institutions."[119] This was the downside of encouraging activism by the "new layman"; New Orleans was a vivid example, said LaFarge, of "a total capitulation of the Church to a militant laity."[120] Northern white Catholics also, for the most part, lacked enthusiasm for the civil rights movement. Louise Day Hicks, a Catholic

116. On Berrigan, see Francine DuPlessix Gray, *Divine Disobedience: Profiles in Catholic Radicalism* (New York: Knopf, 1970). On Day, see William Miller, *Dorothy Day: A Biography* (San Francisco: Harper and Row, 1982). On John Lafarge, S.J., see his *Catholic Viewpoint on Race Relations* (Garden City, N.Y.: Hanover House, 1956); also Joseph O'Neill, S.J., ed., *A Catholic Case against Segregation* (New York: Macmillan, 1960).

117. James Lawrence (pseud.), "Scandal of New Orleans," *C*, Feb. 3, 1961, 475–76; John Beecher, "Magnolia Ghetto," *R* 3 (Dec. 1964): 45–50.

118. Beecher, "Magnolia Ghetto," 47.

119. John LaFarge, "American Catholics and the Negro, 1962," *SO* 12 (April 1962): 156.

120. Ibid., 156.

member of the Boston school board, built a political career in the 1960s on her intransigent opposition to busing programs to integrate schools there.[121]

The Catholic new conservatives' attitude toward the civil rights movement was generally unenthusiastic. Rarely openly racist like the New Orleans white laypeople who opposed desegregation, they were, rather, skeptical of the methods used to end American apartheid. They disliked judicial activism and opposed the growing reach of the federal government. Conservatives condemned the crucial Supreme Court decision *Brown* v. *Board of Education of Topeka, Kansas* (1954), which had set this phase of the civil rights movement in motion, as "one of the most brazen acts of judicial usurpation in our history," adding that it was "shoddy and illegal in analysis and invalid as sociology."[122] They defended the Montgomery Bus Boycott of 1955–1956, but only on the narrow, businesslike grounds that citizens dissatisfied with a service should be free to use or decline it as they wished, and it was up to the vendor to offer better service.[123] As strong defenders of states' rights (who often couched their defense in the language of subsidiarity), conservatives opposed federal intervention in southern states' internal affairs: "Support for the southern position rests not at all on the question of whether negro and white children should, in fact, study geography side by side; but on whether a central or a local authority should make that decision."[124] *National Review* carried justifications of segregation from Georgia Senator Richard Russell and the former southern agrarian author Donald Davidson, who argued against violating the deeply set folkways of the south's "organic" community.[125] In 1959 Buckley himself opined that the disfranchisement of blacks in the South could be justified on grounds of their lack of education and civilization. "In the South, the white community is entitled to put forward a claim to prevail politically because, for the time being anyway, the leaders of American civilization are white."[126] On the lecture circuit, where prointegration Catholics quoted these passages to reproach him, Buckley sometimes added that Mississippi's problem was not too few black voters but too many white voters, many of whom

121. Howard Husock, "Boston," in *Busing, USA,* ed. Nicolaus Mills (New York: Teacher's College, Columbia, 1979), 334–48.

122. Editorial, "Segregation and Democracy," *NR,* Jan. 25, 1956, 5.

123. Untitled editorial, *NR,* March 14, 1956, 6.

124. Editorial, "The South Girds Its Loins," *NR,* Feb. 29, 1956, 5–6.

125. Sam Jones, "Voice of the South" (interview of Richard Russell), *NR,* July 27, 1957, 105–6; Donald Davidson, "The New South and the Conservative Tradition," *NR,* Sept. 10, 1960, 141–46.

126. William F. Buckley, Jr., *Up from Liberalism* (1959; New York: Bantam, 1968), 111.

ought also to be barred from the franchise; the remark was consistent with his view that the United States should not be a plebiscitary democracy but should require evidence of education and reflectiveness from its citizens before granting them the vote.[127] "It is more important for a community, wherever situated geographically, to affirm and live by civilized standards," he said, "than to labor at the job of swelling the voting lists."[128]

On this issue Brent Bozell disagreed with his brother-in-law. He pointed out that efforts to thwart the operation of the Fifteenth Amendment would undermine respect for the rule of law, exactly what he disliked about the *Brown* decision. And he added, "The evidence is far from conclusive that southern civilization hangs on the thread of negro disenfranchisement or even that white southerners believe it does."[129] By 1964 Buckley was coming around to agreement with Bozell. Racist attacks on civil rights workers, the bombing of black churches in Mississippi, the murder of Medgar Evers, and transparent miscarriages of justice in all-white local southern courts showed him that states' rights, the issue about which he cared most, was being used simply as a fig leaf of respectability and legality by die-hard segregationists. Ironically, it was the lawlessness of the segregationists that made federal intervention by Congress and the courts inevitable, hastening the decline of the states' rights tradition.[130] Buckley remained, however, a widely disliked symbol of resistance to desegregation; at a Communion breakfast for New York Catholic policemen in 1965 he spoke about another violent civil rights confrontation, at Selma, Alabama, and although he did not justify the police violence, he did try to mitigate the officers' culpability by arguing that they had been under excessive stress in a long confrontation with demonstrators. Buckley's remarks were favorably received by New York's finest, but they set off a flurry of accusations in the liberal press that he was conniving at racism.[131]

Martin Luther King, Jr., was not warmly received by most of the new conservatives. Will Herberg found even King's nonviolent resistance

127. For one such debate, see William J. Kenealy, S.J., "Desegregation," *SO* 12 (June 1963): 249–56. Kenealy, a professor of law at Loyola of Chicago University, had debated Buckley in Fairfield, Conn., April 16, 1963.

128. Buckley, *Up from Liberalism*, 112.

129. L. Brent Bozell, "The Open Question," *NR*, Sept. 7, 1957, 209.

130. On bombing of churches, see editorial, "What Says the South?" *NR*, Oct. 20, 1964, 898–99. On Evers and the attempted assassination of James Meredith, see William F. Buckley, Jr., "How Guilty Is the South?" *NR*, June 28, 1966, 611.

131. Buckley wrote extensively about the affair in the book that describes his 1965 campaign for mayor of New York City: William F. Buckley, Jr., *The Unmaking of a Mayor* (1966; New York: Bantam, 1967), 9–28.

"seriously deviant and heretical" and without justification in Christian tradition. "The early Christians, under the teaching of the apostles," he pointed out, "were enjoined to obey the laws of the state, a pagan state, mind you, whether they held these laws to be just or unjust." Only worship of the emperor had been forbidden to the early Christians; they were otherwise obliged to submit to the laws. Herberg added: "Strange as it may seem to Dr. King, the very purpose of government is to make us obey laws of which we do not approve."[132] In Herberg's view, disobeying laws in the name of a "higher law" was a recipe for disaster. Garry Wills, without calling King subversive, wrote a critical review of his "Letter from Birmingham Jail," faulting its scholarship and, in places, its logic. "King is so convinced that all right and justice and truth are attuned to the civil rights movement," he said, after a harsh summary of King's errors of interpretation, "that he reaches out toward anything that calls up noble emotions . . . and appropriates it without further thought."[133] King's burning assurance that he was right seemed to Wills at this time almost idolatrous. By contrast, Wills was impressed by Malcolm X and the Black Muslims' ability to create a hardworking, self-disciplined, self-helping community out of former drug addicts and criminals. "Robbed of honor," he observed, "these negroes, by a tour de force, take the very badge of their inflicted inferiority, their blackness, and make it a symbol of pride. . . . The muslim community is a living refutation of the old charge that the negro cannot live a life of sobriety, industry, and pride in himself." Self-sufficiency rather than dependence on government was the way to advancement for African Americans, he was convinced. He added in 1964 that the surest way to guarantee peaceful resolution to the civil rights crisis was for blacks and whites alike to vote for Barry Goldwater.[134]

AFRICAN DECOLONIZATION

The entire world, not merely the United States, was experiencing demands for liberation and political assertion by hitherto disadvantaged races in the early 1960s. These were the years when, according to British prime minister Harold Macmillan, a "wind of change" was blowing through Africa; the British, French, Spanish, Belgians, and

132. Will Herberg, ".A Religious 'Right' to Violate the Law?" *NR*, July 14, 1964, 579–80.
133. Garry Wills, "Dr. King's Logic," *NCR*, Aug. 4, 1965, 8.
134. Garry Wills, "Who Will Overcome?" *NR*, Sept. 22, 1964, 818–20.

Portuguese were either turning their colonies over to self-government or else coming under intense pressure from world opinion to do so. On decolonization, as on the issue of civil rights, Catholic opinion makers in the United States sharply disagreed. The most controversial cases were those of the Congo, a former Belgian colony going through a complex decolonization process in the early 1960s, and Algeria, a French colony in a state of civil war since the mid-1950s. As Catholic liberals told it, Belgian imperialism in the Congo was a story of unalleviated tyranny and rapacity on which the curtain could hardly come down too quickly. The Congolese, wrote one reporter, hated the Belgians as fiercely, and with as good cause, as Eastern Europeans hated the Russians. The West, with Auschwitz and nuclear weapons to its credit, should not be too censorious about the occasional cruelties of the new Congolese leaders in the difficult transition period. Rather, "patience, forbearance, charity, and above all freedom from the taint of race prejudice are required before we can expect the new black leaders of the Congo to forgive us the sins committed against them."[135] As for Algeria, Catholic liberals looked on approvingly at President Charles de Gaulle's decision in 1961 to grant it self-government and to withdraw French forces. "His recognition that decolonization offers the only way out," wrote *Commonweal*, along with "his vision, his patience, and his firmness, inspire a degree of confidence that is remarkable in our times."[136]

Catholic conservatives had a completely different view of Africa. Western imperialism appeared to them benign; it had brought to a close the era of ceaseless tribal warfare, had introduced Western medicine, had begun programs of universal education. Thomas Molnar traveled throughout Africa in the early 1960s to investigate the state of the continent. His reports, published regularly in *National Review* and the basis for two books, justified white dominance, condemned the "abstraction" of national self-determination as an example of liberal utopianism, and criticized the United Nations for encouraging delusions about the capacity of many areas of Africa to act as "nations."[137] Erik von Kuehnelt-Leddihn found much about imperialism to praise, even in the Congo, where, he said, the Belgians had done "an excellent, and in a way selfless, job," especially by eradicating diseases. He warned that the lack of an educated native elite would mean disaster

---

135. Daniel Friedenberg, "Harvest in the Congo," *C*, Sept. 23, 1960, 511–13.
136. Editorial, "Algerian Hopes," *C*, March 17, 1961, 624.
137. Thomas Molnar, *Africa: A Political Travelogue* (New York: Fleet, 1965); Molnar, *South West Africa: The Last Pioneer Country* (New York: Fleet, 1966).

for the area, not liberation, if the colonizing power were to leave.[138] Nevertheless, it left, and a new state came into being, created, said *National Review*, "ex nihilo out of Wilsonian abstractions and by Belgian funk." Just as conservatives believed Martin Luther King to be either a Communist agent himself or at least a Communist dupe, so did they interpret the new African nations as destined to succumb to the everspreading red stain of the worldwide Communist conspiracy. The Congo, after all, contained cobalt, uranium, and diamond mines that made it strategically significant.[139] In the civil wars that tore the region in the following years, Catholic conservatives found confirmation of their worst fears, and they regarded every disorder as evidence of Communist infiltration.[140]

Katanga, one province of the old Belgian Congo, site of the most productive mineral mines, declared independence from the new nation under the leadership of the pro-Western, "pro-Catholic and conservative party" of Moise Tshombe.[141] Conservatives justified the Katangan split, whereas the United Nations tried forcibly to prevent it and to maintain national coherence under the leadership of Patrice Lumumba. A period of Byzantine political maneuvering ensued, marked by frequent assassinations and allegations of torture and cannibalism from both sides. Catholic conservatives, already skeptical of the United Nations, came to consider it hardly more than an instrument of Soviet policy. A divided Congo, wrote one observer, would be comparable to a divided Korea, Vietnam, or Germany: at least half "free." But the United Nations exclaimed, "How dreadful! We prefer it unified, united . . . Like Christian Hungary, and Christian Poland."[142] Another remarked that "all over Africa Christian civilization is in retreat because nobody seems any longer to believe in it" enough to defend its vital interests.[143]

Conservative Catholics were not entirely uncritical of the white presence in Africa, even though they thought it, by and large, a force for good. Kuehnelt-Leddihn, for example, was dismayed by the flagrant racism of South African apartheid, "a policy which is not merely segre-

138. Erik von Kuehnelt-Leddihn, "Letter from the Congo," *NR*, June 18, 1960, 393–94.

139. Editorial, "Whose Drums on the Congo?" *NR*, July 16, 1960, 7.

140. For example, see editorial, "Grand Guignol," *NR*, Aug. 27, 1960, 101–2: "What the black savages are doing to each other in scores of villages and smaller cities is beyond the imagination of civilized man. Poison, hideous torture, obscene mutilation, cannibalism, are routine." On communism in the Congo, see, for example, editorial, "Myth over the Congo," *NR*, Sept. 24, 1960, 167–68.

141. Philippa Schuyler, "Behind the Congo Crisis," *NR*, Aug. 13, 1960, 76–77.

142. Carrefour (pseud.), "The Mistake of Moise Tshombe," *NR*, Aug. 27, 1960, 102.

143. Anthony Lejeune, "Letter from the Congo," *NR*, March 25, 1961, 182.

gationist, but discriminatory and truly oppressive."[144] He contrasted it to the situation in Portuguese Mozambique, where there was a degree of racial intermarriage, which permitted "those of mixed blood to move with perfect ease in Portuguese society." It was more than a coincidence that "the only part of Africa devoid of racial tension lies in the area controlled by a power which does *not* believe in formal democracy." He admitted that Antonio Salazar's Portuguese government was not without its faults but saw it, on balance, as a champion of Christendom. "The Lisbon government is convinced that Western civilization, due to its Christian, personalist, and scientific character, will gradually conquer the entire globe," and it was accordingly eager to "implant a number of Christian principles in its own territories."[145] William Buckley, visiting the Mozambique capital, Lourenço Marques, in 1962, also found much to admire there.[146]

As with southern Africa, so with Algeria: Catholic conservatives were horrified to discover that de Gaulle was withdrawing from the colony, and they praised Maurice Challe and the other army conspirators who reacted by trying to assassinate the president in 1960: "All normal and legal means having been exhausted, these soldiers . . . placed their duty to their country, their civilization, and their God above their duty to their commander in chief . . . [and] made a desperate and supreme attempt to block the enemy's advance, and thus save France and Europe and the Free World from a mortal danger."[147] This sentiment, expressed side by side with condemnations of Martin Luther King's *non*violent resistance, bespoke more than a little logical inconsistency. Arthur Koestler once commented to George Orwell that truth had disappeared completely in the Spanish Civil War and would not return in this ideological age, since every contender regarded it as an instrument of its own propaganda. Reading such utterly opposed versions of Africa in the early 1960s from within just the Catholic press in the United States confirms this vertiginous sense that truth has disappeared, not because either side was mendacious but rather because each was capable of finding in the vast diversity of African affairs evidence to support its own view of the situation.[148] This bitter public

---

144. Erik von Kuehnelt-Leddihn, "The South African Imbroglio," *NR*, Feb. 13, 1960, 106. *National Review* agreed at the time of the Sharpeville Massacre that apartheid was an untenable and indefensible practice. Editorial, "Dead-end in South Africa?" *NR*, April 23, 1960, 254–55.
145. Erik von Kuehnelt-Leddihn, "The Mocambique Story," *NR*, April 9, 1960, 232.
146. William F. Buckley, Jr., "Must We Hate Portugal?" *NR*, Dec. 18, 1962, 468.
147. Editorial, "Charles de Gaulle, Prisoner," *NR*, May 6, 1961, 270–71.
148. In an uncharacteristic act of soul-searching, *National Review* published a mea culpa on the issue of white French terrorism in Algeria. "For our own part we confess with deep and troubled humility our failure to comprehend this dreadful problem of terror that has more

dispute over imperialism, which continued to intensify for another decade and which, in the Latin American context, still rages today, emphasized the fragmentation of the Catholic outlook in the early 1960s.

The Kennedy presidency, school prayer, the civil rights movement, Africa, and other issues all occasioned growing political animosities among Catholic commentators. Following the death of President Kennedy and the passage of the Civil Rights and Voting Rights acts in Congress, a more volatile era began in United States history. Similarly, with the closing of the Second Vatican Council in the fall of 1965, its edicts and its example precipitated a stormy era in Catholic history. Suddenly, almost none of the old granitic certainties of Catholicism was immune from challenge, and in the following five years the sight of Catholic priests marching in demonstrations, violating the law, denouncing their bishops and the church itself, leaving the priesthood, marrying, even in one case trying to set up a priests' trade union, marked a new epoch. As their clergy broke ranks, laypeople searched for points of certainty and order, finding them no longer in the comprehensive embrace of the church but, more often, in the opinions of Americans from other faiths. Catholic conservatives were forced to make choices. For Buckley and the majority, the conservative political program seemed the most important issue; for others, religious purity in the face of ever-more-threatening contaminants had to take precedence.

---

and more become a pervasive quality of our epoch. Before the problem of terror the mind plunges into a metaphysical despair, as before those other dark dilemmas that have so long weighed on man's spirit: man's free will and God's foreknowledge, God's goodness and the suffering of His creatures. We who are citizens of the civilization that devised saturation bombing, of the nation that hurled the first nuclear bombs on just and unjust alike, should be slow, surely, to judge—if judgment in such matters is, indeed, ours to make." Editorial, "The Secret Army Terror," *NR*, June 5, 1962, 395–96.

4

Crises of the Late 1960s

Before 1960, the American Catholic church was particularly proud of its eminent converts, who brought intellectual dignity, social celebrity, and impeccable patriotic credentials to an organization still burdened by the stigma of foreignness and despotism. Converts were highly influential in advancing Catholic scholarship; eight of the first twenty presidents of the American Catholic Historical Association, for example, were converts, and the figures were comparable in other disciplines. The church worked hard at its proselytizing mission through the first two-thirds of the twentieth century; when, for example, the Trappist abbot of Gethsemane monastery discovered Thomas Merton's literary gifts, he ordered this convert and monk to write the story of his spiritual odyssey. Published in 1948 as *The Seven Storey Mountain*, it became a spectacular best seller and high-quality propaganda for the church, inspiring further conversions in the following years.[1] Father John O'Brien was a popular writer who had been put to work as a specialist in conversions. His best-selling anthology *The Road to Damascus* (1949) contained the conversion narratives of a dozen American and British men and women who had entered the embrace of the church. All told of the joy they felt at final reconciliation with this great anchor of certainty and religious truth after restless lives of searching. The book's success prompted a string of sequels.[2]

1. Thomas Merton, *The Seven Storey Mountain* (New York: Harcourt, Brace, 1948). On the impact of this book, see Monica Furlong, *Merton: A Biography* (New York: Harper and Row, 1980).

2. John O'Brien, ed., *The Road to Damascus* (Garden City, N.Y.: Doubleday, 1949). O'Brien's sequels included *Where I Found Christ* (Garden City, N.Y.: Doubleday, 1950); *The Way to Emmaus* (New York: McGraw-Hill, 1953); and *Roads to Rome* (New York: Macmillan, 1954).

By the early 1960s, however, the stream of converts was beginning to dry up, and the church itself was soft-pedaling proselytism. Russell Kirk, a seminal figure in the new conservative movement, converted at the time of his marriage in 1964, after years of encouragement from his fellow conservatives and Burke scholars.[3] *National Review* editor Jeffrey Hart, another scholar of eighteenth-century political writers, after a long period of intellectual attraction to Catholicism, converted four years later.[4] But the rocklike solidity of the Catholicism to which they had turned was dissolving around them even as they arrived; Father O'Brien was lamenting the decline of conversions while a new generation of ecumenical Catholics was denying that the church should even try to gain more souls.[5] This was one of the many dramatic indications of changed times in American Catholicism, part of the fallout from the Second Vatican Council.

The Council had brought nearly all the world's cardinals and bishops together in Rome. Pope John XXIII had been dissatisfied with certain aspects of the church—its intellectual defensiveness, its administrative rigidity, and its slowness to adapt to a revolutionized demographic structure. For example, it was growing faster in Africa than anywhere else in the world, but there were no black cardinals in 1958 when John became pope. His intention, and the hope of most participants at Rome, was that the church would be strengthened by being brought up to date, enabled to deal with the modern world more effectively and convincingly.[6] Pope Paul VI, who succeeded John in 1963, fully endorsed this mission. During the four long sessions in succeeding autumns, however, unforeseen conflicts developed. The representatives of the Vatican bureaucracy, generally referred to by journalists as the Curial party or simply as the conservatives, tried to minimize proposed modifications of the church. Meanwhile, a group of reformers, relatively weak in numbers of bishops but powerful in the quality of their theological advisers (known as *periti*) and their command of the print media, opposed the Curialists with bold projects for reform. A council that had been designed to hold all sessions in secret, with all speeches in Latin, soon gained the attention of hundreds of journalists, who pestered participating prelates for press conferences. Cardi-

3. Letter of Ross Hoffman to Russell Kirk, Oct. 26, 1964, in the author's possession, courtesy of Mr. Kirk.

4. Personal interview with Jeffrey Hart, Dartmouth, N.H., April 26, 1988.

5. Significantly, O'Brien was reduced to describing *exits* from the priestly vocation, if not the church. See his *Why Priests Leave: The Intimate Stories of Twelve Who Did* (New York: Hawthorne, 1969).

6. On John XXIII, see Paul Johnson, *Pope John XXIII* (Boston: Little, Brown, 1974); Peter Hebblethwaite, *John XXIII* (Garden City, N.Y.: Doubleday, 1985).

nal Richard Cushing of Boston offered to pay for a simultaneous translation system similar to that in use at the United Nations, but he was rebuffed by the Latinists, who feared excessively public debate. Soon, nevertheless, the reformers, cultivating the secular press and Catholic journals throughout the world, found ways of making their point and circumventing the Curia. Procedure was changed under their pressure, and several of the working documents drawn up by Curialists beforehand were laid aside in favor of bolder alternatives.[7]

As a result of these conflicts, the several declarations promulgated at the council's end in 1965 marked new emphases for world Catholicism. Perhaps the most dramatic in the eyes of Americans, and the issue to which the American *periti* present (led by Jesuit John Courtney Murray) had paid special attention, was *Dignitatis Humanae,* the declaration on religious liberty. Abandoning long tradition, the document spoke of Protestants not as heretics but as "separated brethren" and treated the Reformation as a tragic and regrettable rift rather than a massive outbreak of heresy. A second declaration, *Gaudium et Spes,* on the condition of the church in the modern world, emphasized that Catholicism should be conceptualized less as a hierarchical organization than as "the people of God" moving together through history. Coupled with a declaration on the vocation of the laity, *Gaudium et Spes* marked a shift in emphasis, granting laypeople greater dignity within the church and subsequently giving them rhetorical leverage in conflicts with their priests.[8]

Reformers succeeded also in instituting the vernacular liturgy. After centuries of Latin worship, English-language priests began to speak English as they celebrated Mass, not always with entirely satisfactory results. Garry Wills, though he favored the reform, described the ungainly language of the new vernacular mass as "a corpse galvanized into spurts of strange dancing, or a living thing blanched and paralyzed by periodic fits of death."[9] William Buckley said that it was impossible to read the new translations "without the same sense of outrage one would feel on entering the Cathedral of Chartres and finding that the windows had been replaced with pop-art figures of Christ 'sitting-in' against the slum-lords of Milwaukee."[10] Meanwhile the sacrament of Penance (confession) was deemphasized, especially

---

7. On the mood of the debate and the problem of Latin, see Michael Novak, *The Open Church: Vatican II, Act II* (New York: Macmillan, 1964), 42. See also Vincent Yzermans, *American Participation in the Second Vatican Council* (New York: Sheed and Ward, 1967).

8. For a historical explanation of the Vatican II reforms, see Thomas Bokenkotter, *A Concise History of the Catholic Church* (Garden City, N.Y.: Doubleday/Image, 1979), 411–46.

9. Garry Wills, "Cloak and Crozier: Another Anomaly," *NCR*, March 31, 1965, 8.

10. William F. Buckley, Jr., *The Jeweler's Eye* (New York: Putnam, 1968), 324.

for children, and some priests experimented by "making up new formulas for the consecration." Michael Lawrence, a disgruntled conservative layman, recalled the late 1960s as a period of "flagrant idiocies" in Catholic liturgy, which Pope Paul VI, while never approving, was slow to condemn.[11]

Other novelties of the council were a new emphasis on collegiality, or the collective supremacy of the council, rather than the absolute authority of the pope, which had been emphasized since the First Vatican Council of 1870–1871. There were also efforts to heal long-standing rifts in Christianity; Pope Paul VI held discussions with the primate of the Greek Orthodox church, permitted Protestant observers to witness some sessions of the council, and even agreed to consider the question of an *apertura a sinistra*, the possibility of finding a way of getting along with the Communist Left rather than persisting in the century-long policy of dogged anticommunism.[12] Lastly, Paul VI decided to review the question of artificial contraception. In the long run this decision was to have mighty repercussions, as we shall see.

In the middle and late 1960s the phrase "the spirit of the council" was bruited endlessly in Catholic forums, an illuminating clue to the council's overall significance, which far exceeded the particulars of its decrees. In announcing that Catholicism needed to be changed to suit a rapidly developing world, Garry Wills said, "*it let out the dirty little secret. It forced upon Catholics, in the most startling symbolic way, the fact that the church changes.*"[13] From 1965 onward, many Catholics took this lesson to heart and cited the spirit of the council in proposing their particular projects for change, even if the bishops assembled in Rome had had nothing to say on the matter in question. The new definition of the church not as an institution but as the people of God also gave challengers to the status quo a new rhetorical weapon by permitting them to argue that they were loyal to the true spirit of the church at a time when its leaders had deviated.

The council had in effect set off a revolution of rising expectations. To use a political analogy, it is not when repression is at its height but when it is relaxed a little that it seems particularly intolerable to its victims. It is then, once the possibility of change has been demonstrated, that they begin to push for further reforms. The analogy is suggestive but imperfect here because Catholics who appealed for further changes soon discovered that the church had no powers of repres-

11. Telephone interview with Michael Lawrence, Feb. 27, 1991.

12. Bokenkotter, *Concise History*, 425–30.

13. Garry Wills, *Bare Ruined Choirs: Doubt, Prophecy, and Radical Religion* (Garden City, N.Y.: Doubleday, 1972), 21.

sion at all. Membership and obedience, at least for laypeople in the United States, had always been by consent rather than by coercion, and no civil penalty awaited men and women who ignored church teaching on certain issues or stopped attending Mass and Confession altogether. Once the possibility of criticism arose, growing numbers of Catholics found themselves dissatisfied with their church; some resolved their displeasure by leaving, others by lobbying for reform from within. Suddenly, it occurred to unhappy Catholics that they could conceive of themselves as "victims" of their church, psychologically if not physically.

A rush of defections from the priesthood and from convents also began. After decades of sustained growth and the opening of new seminaries and houses of formation, one order after another found, in the late 1960s and through the 1970s, that newcomers to vows of Holy Orders were falling off precipitously.[14] There was trouble even among those priests who stayed in the ranks, especially among junior clergy who had been educated in the changed atmosphere of the conciliar church. In 1965 Father William DuBay, a thirty-one-year-old California priest with a largely black parish on the edge of the volatile Watts district, became indignant when Cardinal James Francis MacIntyre of Los Angeles refused to play an active role in the civil rights movement. First he organized pickets outside the cardinal's chancery, then he wrote to the pope, urging that MacIntyre be deprived of his see for "abuse of authority" and "gross malfeasance." The pope declined to reply, but the cardinal transferred the priest to a white parish.[15] A few months later DuBay held a press conference to announce that he was going to form the American Federation of Priests and was going to affiliate this new trade union with the AFL-CIO.[16] Cries of alarm went up from most of the Catholic media, which had never before witnessed this kind of turbulence.[17] They were hardly mollified by DuBay's book, *The Human Church* (1966), which threw tradition aside as irrelevant and castigated the hierarchy for authoritarianism and psychological repression.[18] DuBay was suspended in 1967; soon afterward Father Brendan

---

14. Andrew Greeley, *The American Catholic: A Social Portrait* (New York: Basic, 1977), 152–63. For the impact of the 1960s on one order of nuns, see V. V. Harrison, *Changing Habits: A Memoir of the Society of the Sacred Heart* (New York: Doubleday, 1988).

15. "Los Angeles Priest Transferred Again," *New York Times*, Feb. 4, 1965, 26.

16. Peter Bart, "Catholic Priest Organizing a Union," *New York Times*, Feb. 23, 1966, 25.

17. Even *Commonweal*, which had sympathized with DuBay over the racial incident, was affronted. See "Father DuBay's Union," *C*, March 11, 1966, 654.

18. William H. DuBay, *The Human Church* (Garden City, N.Y.: Doubleday, 1966). A *Commonweal* reviewer said that "DuBay's approach is simply to throw the past overboard in favor of a purely personal vision of the Church" and that "he goes after the whole theological tradition

Nagle, one of his collaborators in the American Federation of Priests, founded Adelphos, an organization for former priests.[19] The union never got off the ground, but local associations of priests did begin to organize to consider common problems in a way not previously seen.[20] Father James Kavanaugh, already the author of "I Am a Priest and I Want to Get Married" for the *Saturday Evening Post*, wrote an even more impassioned polemic against the church, *A Modern Priest Looks at His Outdated Church* (1967), whose title says it all.[21] He left the priesthood and married soon thereafter. What was notable about these attacks on the church, apart from their temerity, was that DuBay and Kavanaugh no longer worked, as had their priestly predecessors, from natural law or intra-Catholic philosophical premises. Instead, they took the language of secular disciplines—psychoanalysis, sociology, and political science—and turned it critically upon their church from inside, making even harsher indictments than Paul Blanshard and other anti-Catholics had made in the 1940s and 1950s. Their critiques marked the beginning of a new era in Catholic intellectual life.

Marriage was a common sequel to departure from the priesthood. Charles Meconis discovered that "of the approximately fifty celibates in the core of the Catholic Left, slightly more than half of them left their institutional religious roles during their involvement and at least fourteen, twenty-eight percent of the total, promptly got married."[22] What is more, marriage did not always await departure from the priesthood. Philip Berrigan, charismatic leader of the antiwar Catholic Left, secretly married Sister Elizabeth McAlister of the Order of the Sacred Heart of Mary in 1969, even while telling interviewers that celibacy was an advantage for militant antiwar activists. Their love letters, turned over to the FBI by a prison go-between and informer, Boyd Douglas, horrified many of Berrigan's admirers when they were read aloud in court during the trial of the "Harrisburg Seven" in early 1972.[23] Nor was marriage confined to militants: the auxiliary bishop of

---

with a sledgehammer." Robert Johann, "Vanguard and 'Outsider' Theology," C, May 6, 1966, 202–3.

19. Untitled editorial, C, March 24, 1967, 2.

20. See, for example, editorial, "A New Witness," C, May 26, 1967, 277; and John Hill (first chairman of the Association of Chicago Priests), "Priests' Associations Go Regional," C, Oct. 20, 1967, 69–70.

21. James Kavanaugh, *A Modern Priest Looks at His Outdated Church* (New York: Trident, 1967).

22. Charles Meconis, *With Clumsy Grace: The American Catholic Left, 1961–1975* (New York: Seabury, 1979), 95.

23. Ibid., 93.

St. Paul, Minnesota, James Shannon, announced in 1969 that he too was quitting his post to wed.[24]

William DuBay finally left the priesthood, married a divorcée, and went to live in a commune.[25] He and Kavanaugh, like the Vatican II reformers, had found that the American media were attracted to cases such as their own. By portraying the church as a granitic, insensitive monolith, against which they posed as clear-sighted loners who had nonetheless dared to protest, they won coveted "outsider" status and favorable notices in the newspapers, while Cardinal MacIntyre and other authority figures were pictured as "heavy" and reactionary instruments of repression. It became an axiomatic conservative reproach over the next two decades that the press favored Catholic dissidents and portrayed them as Davids taking on an orthodox Goliath, although in fact, they said, the media wielded far greater power than the church ever could, so that the poor bishop was the real David of the case.[26]

By 1965 vigorous reform media were developing inside the Catholic church. Throughout the 1960s the *National Catholic Reporter,* a weekly newspaper from Kansas City edited by Robert Hoyt and receptive to the ideas of reform-minded Catholics such as Michael Novak, John Leo, and Rosemary Ruether, advocated democratic modification of traditional clerical authority, greater activism to end racism, poverty, and war, and a more "open" church. *Ramparts* magazine, founded by Catholic convert and millionaire Edward Keating in 1962, went through a spectacular transformation in the following years. Its purpose, said Keating in the first issue, was to be a "showcase for the creative writer and a forum for the mature American Catholic," and he proposed to publish items "reflecting those positive principles of the Hellenic-Christian tradition, which have shaped and sustained our civilization for the past two thousand years and which are still needed to guide us in an age grown increasingly secular, bewildered, and afraid."[27] The first issue, with articles on the philosopher Gabriel Marcel and the writer J. D. Salinger, was staid enough. Soon, however, Keating became impatient at the pace of Catholic reform and the continued clerical dominance in the U.S. church. In *The Scandal of Silence* (1965) he harshly criticized church politics from non-Catholic premises—an adumbration

24. Charles Rice, *Authority and Rebellion: The Case for Orthodoxy in the Catholic Church* (Garden City, N.Y.: Doubleday, 1971), 2.

25. Ibid., 1–2.

26. See, for example, George A. Kelly, *The Battle for the American Church* (Garden City, N.Y.: Doubleday, 1979), 10. On the paradoxical benefits of outsider status in American religious history, see R. Laurence Moore, *Religious Outsiders and the Making of Americans* (New York: Oxford University Press, 1986), esp. 48–71.

27. "Ramparts," *R* 1 (May 1962): 3.

of the DuBay-Kavanaugh approach.[28] Before the end of Vatican II *Ramparts* took on board non-Catholic associate editors William Stringfellow, Leslie Fiedler, Louis Lomax, and others and began to specialize in investigative journalism, making spectacular revelations about the CIA and the FBI and publishing "grassy knoll" stories about the assassination of President Kennedy. In 1965 and 1966 it still carried an occasional article of special interest to Catholics, usually criticizing the hierarchy's position on birth control, but after that, under a new editor, Robert Scheer, it completely lost its Catholic identity and became part of the countercultural Left, a leading antiwar journal.[29] Six years after its founding this journal for "the mature American Catholic" who was "bewildered" by secularism was featuring the diary of Che Guevara with an introduction by Fidel Castro.[30]

The wind of change began to blow through Catholic universities as well as Catholic media when Vatican II came to an end. Proudly separate from mainstream universities since their foundation, many of them now faced crisis. More professionalized faculty members, priests and laypeople alike, began to ask for academic freedom and security of tenure to match those of professors at non-Catholic universities, as well as parity in pay and working conditions. After years of growing tensions a dramatic and unprecedented faculty strike broke out at St. John's University in New York at the start of 1966. St. John's, with its two campuses in Queens and Brooklyn, was by then the world's biggest Catholic university, but it was still run on paternalistic lines by the Vincentian order, whose priests were outnumbered by laypeople on the faculty but who dominated the administration and the board of trustees. Faculty members were poorly paid and had little discretion in choosing teaching materials; their academic freedom was closely circumscribed; and they were burdened with irksome parietal duties, such as ensuring that students were dressed with fitting modesty.[31] The strike came in response to the arbitrary dismissal of thirty-one faculty members who had criticized these and other aspects of university policy.[32] The dismissals violated even the university's own procedures and raised an outcry among educators and trade unionists

28. Edward Keating, *The Scandal of Silence* (New York: Random House, 1965). See also "Catholic Editor Chides Hierarchy," *New York Times*, April 13, 1965, 2.
29. On contraception, see, for example, editorial, "LBJ and the Politics of Theology," *R* 4 (May 1965): 3–4.
30. "The Diary of Che Guevara," *R*, July 27, 1968, 4–69 (entire issue).
31. On the background to the strike, see "St. John's," *New York Times*, March 7, 1965, 1; John Leo, "Family Planning at St. John's," *C*, April 30, 1965, 184–88.
32. "Strike at St. John's," *New York Times*, Jan. 3, 1966, 21; John Leo, "Strike at St. John's," *C*, Jan. 28, 1966, 500, 502, 504–6.

throughout New York.[33] Strike leaders Rosemary Lauer and Father Peter O'Reilly revolutionized Catholic university protocols by calling press conferences, winning favorable media attention, and generating appeals on their behalf from such sympathetic outsiders as the social activist Michael Harrington, the historian Richard Hofstadter, and the literary critic Irving Howe. They declared that "any organization that exists to maintain and propagate a doctrine simply cannot control a university" and proposed that the Vincentians be removed entirely.[34] Conservative Catholics denounced the strikers for bringing shame to a Catholic college, treating it like any university instead of cherishing its distinctiveness.[35]

The American Association of University Professors censured St. John's.[36] The church responded by summoning a group of Catholic educators, led by Notre Dame president Theodore Hesburgh, C.S.C., to consider the strike and related issues in 1967. They drew up the "Land O'Lakes Declaration," which said that "institutional autonomy and academic freedom are essential conditions of life and growth and indeed of survival for Catholic universities, as for all universities."[37] This large concession to Catholic academics did not entirely head off further controversy, as the cases of Charles Curran and Mary Daly soon demonstrated. Curran, a popular teacher and prolific author, was denied tenure by Catholic University of America, the nation's one pontifical university, despite the unanimous tenure recommendation of the theology department and the academic senate. The trustees gave no reason for denying Curran's tenure, but his colleagues believed that he had been penalized for favoring changes in church teaching on contraception; Curran was no flaming radical. In response, students and professors in overwhelming numbers, loyal to Curran, boycotted classes and forced Catholic University to back down and rehire him.[38] St. John's had remained divided and its strike partial, but in the Curran case protest was all but unanimous. Soon thereafter the university's board of trustees was restructured to give it a lay majority and, within a year, a lay president, Clarence Walton.[39]

33. See, for example, letter from Francis Griffith, C, March 4, 1966, 647.

34. Leo, "Strike at St. John's," 502; "Strike Continues," *New York Times*, Jan. 10, 1966, 27.

35. "In the Vulgate," NR, Jan. 25, 1966, 58–60; Russell Kirk, "Academic Disorder at St. John's," NR, Feb. 8, 1966, 116.

36. Editorial, "Victory' for St. John's," C, June 24, 1966, 382–83.

37. Quoted in Jay P. Dolan, *The American Catholic Experience: A History from Colonial Times to the Present* (Garden City, N.Y.: Doubleday, 1985), 444.

38. Editorial, "This Time Catholic University," C, May 5, 1967, 187–88; Norma Krause Herzfeld, "Blow Up at Catholic U," ibid., 189–91.

39. James Hitchcock, "Repeat Performance," C, Jan. 31, 1969, 556–59.

Mary Daly, an assistant professor of theology at the Jesuits' Boston College, wrote *The Church and the Second Sex* (1968), an early feminist indictment of Catholic gender relations. She too was denied tenure, whereupon a similar sequence of a strike, petitions, demonstrations, television cameras on campus, and bitter controversy over academic freedom ensued, until at last she was granted tenure. Subsequently, her feminist critique of Christianity accelerated, taking her out of the church completely and, so far as she could legally arrange it, out of the company of men altogether, but not out of Boston College's theology department.[40]

At the other extreme, the transformation of Catholicism sparked an antireform, ultratraditionalist movement of Catholics who wanted to preserve everything as it had been before the council, only more so. Father Gommar DePauw, a Belgian-born priest and professor at Mount St. Mary's Seminary in Emmitsburg, Maryland, founded the Catholic traditionalist movement in 1965, urging retention of the Latin Mass and criticizing the Vatican II documents as evidence of a "protestantizing" of the Catholic church.[41] Under threat of suspension from his own superior, Cardinal Lawrence Shehan of Baltimore, DePauw enlisted the aid of the Vatican secretary of the holy office, Cardinal Alfredo Ottaviani, a leader of the Vatican "old guard" who disliked the direction of events in the United States. With Ottaviani's aid, DePauw got himself transferred to the authority of an Italian diocese, which then at once assigned him to work for the U.S. traditionalists. He too, despite his traditionalist principles, soon learned the value of press conferences.[42] In 1968 a Lou Harris poll found that 71 percent of Catholics favored the new vernacular liturgy. DePauw denounced Harris's sample as biased and said that his survey showed only 25 percent in favor of the new Mass.[43]

DePauw was not alone. Walter Matt of St. Paul, Minnesota, left his job as editor of the *Wanderer*, already the nation's most religiously conservative Catholic newspaper, to found a biweekly newsletter the *Remnant*, which he described as "an attempt . . . draw recruits to the cause of Christ and His Church and, whilst avoiding contentious factionalism, rally what is left of the truly devoted 'people of God'—or loyal remnant of little people—to stand firm on the side of Christ and His

40. Mary Daly, "Autobiographical Introduction to the 1975 Edition," *The Church and the Second Sex* (Boston: Beacon Press, 1985), 11–13. See her later "post-Christian" work *Beyond God the Father* (Boston: Beacon, 1973).

41. John Cogley, "Cases of Thirteen Silenced Priests," *New York Times*, Jan. 4, 1966, 2.

42. John Cogley, "Catholic Group Renews Fight," *New York Times*, Jan. 6, 1966, 1, 25; Cogley, "Shehan Bars DePauw from Priestly Functions," *New York Times*, Jan. 29, 1966, 56.

43. John Leo, "News and Views," *C*, March 31, 1967, 36.

Holy church." They would, said Matt, live lives of Christian penance and prayer "and total commitment to Jesus through Mary, to help turn back the tide of an all-engulfing materialism, secularism, and practical atheism," which had all but eliminated "the last vestiges of what was once Christendom from the face of the earth."[44] Traditionalists worldwide soon found a ranking leader in the Swiss archbishop Marcel Lefebvre who teetered on the brink of excommunication for more than a decade before going over it by sticking to the old Tridentine observances in defiance of Rome. The Catholic conservative counterattack against reformers also found consolation in Jacques Maritain's *Peasant of the Garonne*, a caution against radicalism from the church's most renowned living philosopher, and in Dietrich von Hildebrand's *Trojan Horse in the City of God*, which recommended the sturdy good sense of tradition-minded laypeople as an antidote to the current intellectual chaos.[45] Everyone involved in the intra-Catholic dispute after 1965 assumed the support of "the laity," and as usual in disputes of this complexity, everyone had sets of statistics that, rightly construed, seemed to bear out his or her particular point of view.

Few lay conservative intellectuals in the United States followed Lefebvre's traditionalists, though as the years went by they sometimes cast longing glances in his direction and treated his schism gently. Several were drawn to Matt's vision; indeed, the idea of the "remnant," was familiar to them from the Spanish philosopher Ortega y Gasset, about whom Buckley once planned a major study, and from Albert Jay Nock, another influential precursor of the conservative movement; both thinkers believed that only a faithful "remnant" of Christian civilization could hold out against the hurricane forces of modernity.[46]

The creation of Catholics United for the Faith, meanwhile, suggested that conservative intellectuals' claims to the support of the laity were not entirely ungrounded. From its founding in 1968 by another convert, Lyman Stebbins, CUF pledged itself to strict orthodoxy. Stebbins "conceived of an association which would serve as an echo of the magisterium, endeavoring to bring Christ into the world. This great positive task enjoined on the laity by the Council was threatened, not only by secular currents outside the Church but by the imminent dan-

---

44. Robert Campbell, *Spectrum of Catholic Attitudes* (Milwaukee: Bruce, 1969), xv.

45. Jacques Maritain, *The Peasant of the Garonne: An Old Layman Questions Himself about the Present Time* (New York: Holt, Rinehart, and Winston, 1968); Dietrich von Hildebrand, *Trojan Horse in the City of God* (Chicago: Franciscan Herald Press, 1967).

46. On the influence of Ortega and Nock, see John Judis, *William F. Buckley, Jr., Patron Saint of the Conservatives* (New York: Simon and Schuster, 1988), 44–48, 213–18; Garry Wills, *Confessions of a Conservative* (Garden City, N.Y.: Doubleday, 1979), 26–37.

ger of apostasy within."[47] Stebbins, taking a lay initiative with council approval, was an unlikely candidate for orthodox activism. Born in 1911, he was the son of an Episcopal Wall Street stockbroker who, by preternatural good fortune, had got out of the stock market in 1929 just before the crash, and thus enjoyed his fortune thoughout the 1930s while dabbling as a producer of Broadway musicals. The son enjoyed an athletic career at Yale, became in turn a Wall Street broker, and converted to Catholicism in 1945 in the same Jesuit church in London which had earlier received Evelyn Waugh and would later welcome Edith Sitwell into the faith. CUF, founded in the midst of the furore over Pope Paul VI's anticontraception encyclical, *Humanae Vitae*, concentrated on strict observance of Vatican decrees, many of them published in its *Newsletter*, aware that it "could end up by being a cult of its own, of ultra-conservatives," but confident that defense of the faith made the risk worth taking.[48]

By 1968 American Catholicism was in uproar. When the council opened, conservatives had been cautiously optimistic about its prospects for strengthening the church. By the time the council ended in a virtual explosion of reforms and challenges, however, conservatives were horrified. One 1965 issue of *National Review* bore on its cover the anguished question "What in the Name of God is Going on in the Catholic Church?" and the entire issue was given over to trying to answer it. Speaking with his usual pro-Catholic ardor, Will Herberg surveyed new books such as Daniel Callahan's *Honesty in the Church* (whose title implied that honesty was something new there) and new journals such as *Ramparts* ("anticlerical snarling and leftist incitement constitute the bulk of the offerings of this sensation-mongering Liberal magazine") before declaring that the vocation of the church was "not to be forever adapting itself to the changing times" but rather to "stand firm and resolute for the eternal truth about God, man and the world."[49] Thomas Molnar grieved to see a trend away from "the renunciation and sacrifice-seeking part of our being," which is ever "thirsty for distinctness and, yes, the outward marks of such sacrifice as celibacy, chastity, poverty."[50] And Brent Bozell warned that this crisis was worse than many in the past because this time Catholic malcontents

47. James A. Sullivan, "The Planting of a Seed," *Catholic Free Press*, March 17, 1989, 2–3. See also "Ten Years of CUF," *CUF Newsletter* (Oct. 1978): 1–2.

48. Lyman Stebbins, "From Our Founder," *Lay Witness* 9 (Feb. 1988): 15—reprint of Stebbins's editorial of May 11, 1970; telephone interview with James Sullivan, Oct. 8, 1991.

49. Will Herberg, "Open Season on the Church?" *NR*, May 4, 1965, 363–64.

50. Thomas Molnar, "The Ideology of Aggiornamento," ibid., 365–66.

took their norms not from the church but from "mirrors arranged by Christianity's enemies."[51]

Among these gloomy voices Garry Wills struck a more optimistic note. "The thing conservatives should remember," said the former seminarian, "is that the present renewal is not a dissolution of the unchanging original Church but the breakup of a temporal crust over the ancient vitality of the Faith." Undaunted by exaggerated press reports of chaos, Wills concluded that Vatican II had in fact instituted "conservative" reforms that nicely fitted Samuel Johnson's definition of conservation: "The act of preserving; care to keep from perishing: continuance, protection."[52] This positive evaluation was an early augury of Wills's split from *National Review*, which became irrevocable two years later.

Ever since the school prayer decisions, *National Review*, while still primarily Catholic in religious orientation, had been showing a sympathetic attention to the dilemmas facing Protestant and Jewish conservatives. The journal's postmortem on Vatican II was followed a month later by an article, "The Protestant Deformation," by Harold O. J. Brown, editor of the evangelical journal *Christianity Today*. Brown lamented the decline of Protestant vitality in the area of moral reform and the "me-too-ism" shown by white Protestants who had belatedly joined the civil rights movement. Influential liberal Protestant theologians such as Paul Tillich, he added, scarcely mentioned the Bible any more, but without it Protestantism becomes "completely shapeless and purposeless and inevitably takes its direction not from the teachings of the Fathers (as Catholicism could still do in a similar extremity) but from the temper of the times."[53]

In the following years *National Review* also attacked the Protestant "radical" or "death of God" theology, included sympathetic tributes to Jews and Protestants they considered integral to Western civilization, Martin Buber and Reinhold Niebuhr, and invited Max Geltman to write on Jewish issues and cover the court cases of Catholic protesters against the Vietnam War.[54] Echoing Catholic conservatives who feared secularized versions of Christian eschatology such as Marxism, Geltman remarked that Jewish optimism was marvelous when spiritual

51. L. Brent Bozell, "Who Is Accommodating to What?" ibid., 374.

52. Garry Wills, "On the Present Positions of Catholics," ibid., 375–77.

53. Harold O. J. Brown, "The Protestant Deformation," NR, June 1, 1965, 464–66.

54. On the death of God theology, see Will Herberg, "The Death of God Theology, I," NR, Aug. 9, 1966, 771, 799. On Buber, see Herberg "Martin Buber RIP," NR, June 29, 1965, 539–40. On Niebuhr, see Herberg, "Reinhold Niebuhr, RIP," NR, June 29, 1971, 690. On Catholic war resisters, see Max Geltman, "The Berrigans vs. the United States," NR, May 4, 1971, 470–74.

but disastrous when secularized.[55] It is clear that in the face of growing political and social turmoil in these years, many Catholic conservatives had little hesitation in putting aside their religious differences with conservative Protestants and Jews. They were not, for the most part, advocates of ecumenism, in the sense of trying to minimize religious differences (Buckley told an interviewer that he felt "a kind of visceral impatience" with the ecumenical movement),[56] but they saw the advantages of an alliance of practical interests and persisted in that alliance through the 1970s and 1980s. As Robert Wuthnow has pointed out, neither secularization nor abandonment of religion was so significant as realignments of this kind in the 1960s. Protestant, Catholic, and Jewish radicals lined up together against the Vietnam War while Protestant, Catholic, and Jewish conservatives lined up together against abortion. Old interreligious divisions weakened as these alignments took hold and the churches fragmented internally.[57]

As many of the old Protestant denominations split between fundamentalism and liberalism, evidence to support Wuthnow's restructuring theory could be seen clearly in Catholicism as well. A 1969 symposium, *Spectrum of Catholic Attitudes*, for example, canvassed Catholics from the most traditionalist (represented by Walter Matt) to the most avant-garde (represented by the theologian Leslie Dewart, then strongly influenced by the Protestant death of God movement). A project of that kind, dedicated to demonstrating vast differences of opinion within Catholicism, though it implicitly countenanced them with a rhetoric of pluralism, showed the advanced fragmentation of the Catholic community. Buckley, one contributor to the symposium, provided conventionally orthodox views on religious and moral matters in his own answers (though he was careful to stake out a roomy political and economic area which he considered no business of the hierarchy). He was dismayed at the latitude taken by many of his fellow contributors, Dewart, Daniel Callahan, and Marshall McLuhan (another convert), in defining their views of the church and commented in a subsequent newspaper column that only by an act of charity could they be considered Catholics at all.[58]

In light of this fragmentation, it is worth noting that Jeffrey Hart, who converted to Catholicism in 1968 in the midst of this period of

55. Max Geltman, "The Jewish Affirmation," *NR*, Oct. 4, 1966, 977–83.

56. Campbell, *Spectrum*, 134.

57. Robert Wuthnow, *The Restructuring of American Religion: Society and Faith since World War II* (Princeton: Princeton University Press, 1988), 71–99.

58. William F. Buckley, Jr., "The Agony of Pope Paul VI, April 10, 1969," in Buckley, *The Governor Listeth* (New York: Putnam/Medallion, 1971), 296.

conflict and transformation, experienced his new spiritual home very differently from converts of earlier times. That he did was partly, to be sure, a matter of his idiosyncratic personality, but it also reflected dramatically changed historical circumstances. Conversion did not set Hart into a sharply defined population category, as it had earlier twentieth-century converts, nor did it make of him, as it had generations of earlier converts, a meticulous practitioner of orthodoxy.[59] On the contrary, Hart was then considering the radical skepticism of David Hume as germane for conservatives, was dismissive of the papal encyclical tradition on social and economic affairs, and thought church teaching on contraception and abortion "nonsensical."[60] Hart said that his conversion had been a largely cerebral affair, based on prolonged study of Newman, Chesterton, and Catholic intellectual tradition, rather than a mystical event. Whereas Buckley said faith was a gift, Hart described it as something earned. He cherished the intellectual tradition of Catholicism and admired the role the church had played in American history but had no patience with the Catholic Left or with reform-minded bishops of his own day, most of whom, he said, were "half-educated fashionable thinkers," who would "sell their souls for a good piece in the *New York Times* about them."[61]

In 1968, shortly after his conversion, Hart was invited to write a conservative column in the *National Catholic Reporter,* which the editors of this earnestly pro-reform paper wanted to include in the name of Catholic pluralism. "I hated their editorials about Liberation Theology and Saint Che Guevara," he recalled later, but he was willing to participate as long as his columns were run uncut. His first column warned "relevance-minded" Catholics that what seems most relevant one day seems most old-fashioned and irrelevant the next ("like teaching phlogiston theory at M.I.T.") and told them that they would be better advised to "tune out the spirit of the age" than to try chasing after its ephemera.[62] After a few months of regular contributions, however, in which he laid into the Catholic Left with sledgehammer blows, Hart was fired. His valedictory column was a slashing attack on the *National Catholic Reporter* itself: "The American Church has evoked the *National Catholic Reporter* in all its intellectual flaccidity, its fundamental lack of seriousness, its solemn, cliché-ridden moralism. The style of the thing is unmistakably low. The moralism is that of the resentful but impotent

59. This passage is based in part on my interviews with Hart, Feb. 29 and April 26, 1988.
60. On Hume, see Jeffrey Hart, "David Hume and Skeptical Conservatism," *NR*, Feb. 13, 1968, 129–32. On abortion and contraception, Hart interview, Feb. 29, 1988.
61. Hart interview, April 26, 1988.
62. Jeffrey Hart, "On Tuning Out the Spirit of the Age," *NCR*, Aug. 28, 1968, 8.

underdog. . . . That this wretched sheet should receive any acceptance at all . . . is a pathetic testimony to the condition of American Catholic culture."[63] By then, early 1969, intrareligious fires were blazing hotter than interreligious ones. Hart, a professor of English at Dartmouth, senior editor of *National Review*, and a Nixon speech writer, was convinced that the entire nation was on the brink of a revolution, and he was casting about frantically for possible allies against imminent collapse.[64]

In the following years a huge literature on the crisis of Catholicism appeared in the United States, much of it by Catholic conservatives. Notre Dame law professor Charles Rice in *Authority and Rebellion* tried to hold onto the old verities in the face of sweeping intellectual challenges; denying the validity of Catholic pleas for approval of contraceptives, he defiantly dedicated the book to his eight children, all of whom had saints' names. Rice also defended the principles of religious self-discipline and submission to authority, reminding readers that religion was not an earthly movement for self-realization but a guide to eternal truth and salvation.[65] On comparable lines, James Hitchcock, a history professor at St. Louis University, presented a concerted attack on the radicals' position in *The Decline and Fall of Radical Catholicism*. Like Garry Wills and some other conservatives, Hitchcock admitted that the church had needed reform before Vatican II, but he hotly denied that the shattering transformation had been justified. "Responsibility for the failure of aggiornamento must be about evenly apportioned between rigid reactionaries, especially in the hierarchy . . . and radical innovators with little commitment to historic Catholicism." Hitchcock stressed that the source of change was not primarily the laity but a small intellectual elite, both lay and clerical, who used "a democratic rhetoric to mask an elitist conception of religious reform." Whereas the old Catholic clergy had worked conscientiously with and on behalf of ordinary working-class Catholics, the reformers despised both the everyday priests and the "ignorant masses" below them. This era of upheaval "follows a classic revolutionary pattern, including the fact that the revolt masquerades as a spontaneous popular uprising while concealing the fact that special groups will be its primary beneficiaries."[66] In the 1970s the stack of Vatican II postmortems by Catholic conservatives continued to grow.

63. Jeffrey Hart, "A Relief to Sever with 'Wretched Hate Sheet,'" *NCR*, April 23, 1969, 10.

64. On the perceived imminence of revolution, see Jeffrey Hart, "The Coming Revolution in America," *NR*, July 2, 1968, 646–48.

65. Rice, *Authority and Rebellion*, esp. 83–100.

66. James Hitchcock, *The Decline and Fall of Radical Catholicism* (New York: Herder and Herder, 1971), 32, 55, 107.

Several issues, it should be clear, were coinciding to make the mid-1960s a particularly stormy period for American Catholicism. One was certainly the impetus of the Vatican Council and its teachings. A second was the Vietnam War, which made deep cleavages of opinion in the Catholic community as in most other religious groups. In the world wars Catholics had been, in the overwhelming majority of cases, "superpatriots," volunteering to fight in disproportionately large numbers, often with strong prodding from priests and bishops eager to confirm Catholics' complete loyalty to the nation. Vietnam was different. Through the middle years of the century Dorothy Day's Catholic Worker movement; the occasional pacifist, such as Gordon Zahn; and the Catholic anarchist Ammon Hennacy had remained obstinately antiwar, refusing to serve against the Kaiser, Hitler, or Japan, refusing to serve in Korea, and refusing to cooperate in the nuclear civil defense drills held in New York City during the 1950s.[67] In the short term these protestors' influence on rank-and-file Catholics was negligible, but by the early 1960s the Catholic Worker was widely regarded as a "prophetic" movement by intellectual Catholic liberals, and its antiwar principles worthy of emulation. Some interpreted John XXIII's encyclical *Pacem in Terris* (1963) as a blueprint for pacifism and nonviolent civil disobedience.[68] As the American presence in Vietnam began to escalate a young man claiming affiliation with the Catholic Worker movement, Roger LaPorte, set fire to himself on November 9, 1965, and died outside the United Nations building in New York, sacrificing his life in an antiwar protest that imitated those of self-immolating Vietnamese Buddhist monks. Other Catholic Workers burned their draft cards and formed the nucleus of the emerging Catholic Left, a group lacking some of the deference and courtliness of the liberal Catholicism from which it grew, more enthusiastic about direct-action protests, both religious and political, and much more gifted at manipulating the media to gain publicity and (before too long) celebrity.[69] Robert Scheer wrote in *Ramparts* that American Catholics must get rid of the idea of Vietnam Dr. Tom Dooley had given them and learn that the Catholic Vietnamese were an unpopular, parasitic minority, bearing

67. On Day, see William Miller, *Dorothy Day: A Biography* (San Francisco: Harper and Row, 1982). On Hennacy, see James T. Fisher, *The Catholic Counterculture in America, 1933–1962* (Chapel Hill: University of North Carolina Press, 1989), 251–52. On Zahn, see William Au, *The Cross, the Flag, and the Bomb: American Catholics Debate War and Peace, 1960–1983* (Westport, Conn.: Greenwood, 1985), 107–35.
68. Meconis, *With Clumsy Grace*, 6.
69. Ibid., 6–14.

the taint of French imperialism. The United States, said Scheer, was fighting on the wrong side.[70]

The leading figures on the Catholic Left were the Berrigans, Daniel, a Jesuit priest, and his brother Philip, a Josephite priest. Daniel Berrigan, a poet and editor of the Jesuit missions magazine, was one of the first U.S. Jesuits to argue that the great world confrontation lay between the rich North and the impoverished South rather than between the free West and the Communist East. This realignment of the geopolitical compass his order later took to heart, but it had a subversive resonance for many Catholics when first proposed in the mid-1960s. On a visit to Prague and Budapest, Berrigan deepened these suspicions of subversion by dismissing Cardinal Mindszenty, hero of the anti-communist Catholic conservatives, as an anachronism.[71] Strongly influenced by time spent with the "worker-priests" of France in the 1950s, Daniel Berrigan interpreted the U.S. role in Vietnam not as succoring the Catholic victims of Communist persecutors but rather as one more case of imperialist white America lording it over the wretched of the earth.[72] With Lutheran minister Richard John Neuhaus and Rabbi Abraham Heschel, Berrigan was a cofounder of Clergy Concerned about Vietnam, the first ecumenical antiwar group.[73] Berrigan's outspokenness against the war in 1965 alarmed his superiors and they abruptly sent him to Cuervnavaca, Mexico; his many friends and sympathizers interpreted the transfer as a punishment.[74] As an early sign of how Catholicism was changing, this "exile," though Berrigan obeyed it, was widely denounced in petitions and public protests from disgruntled Catholics, notably with a large advertisement in the *New York Times* on December 12, 1965. His superiors soon ignominiously recanted and brought him back to resume his antiwar work.[75]

Meanwhile, Philip Berrigan, already annealed to confrontation in the civil rights movement (the Josephites were founded in 1871 explicitly to aid black Catholics), and already a victim of red-baiting for his outspoken pacifism, decided to undertake antiwar "liturgies."[76] On one occasion, with a group of nuns, seminarians, and laypeople, he went from

70. Robert Scheer, "Hang Down Your Head, Tom Dooley," *R* 3 (Jan.–Feb. 1965): 23–28.

71. Anthony Bouscaren, "The Catholic Peaceniks," *NR*, March 8, 1966, 202.

72. Francine DuPlessix Gray, *Divine Disobedience: Profiles in Catholic Radicalism* (New York: Knopf, 1970), 67–78.

73. Ibid., 100–101.

74. Editorial, "From Glory to Shame," *C*, Dec. 3, 1965, 261–62.

75. Meconis, *With Clumsy Grace*, 14.

76. He was removed from his job as professor at Epiphany Apostolic College in Newburgh, N.Y., because of his antiwar work. The local population pressured the college to remove him as a subversive. See editorial, "Newburgh Again," *C*, May 14, 1965, 239.

his Baltimore home to Washington, D.C. to kneel in the snow outside Secretary of Defense Robert McNamara's house, praying for an end to the war in Vietnam. On a second occasion, October 27, 1967, his group, the "Baltimore Four," threw several pints of blood (partly their own, partly pig's blood from a nearby butcher shop) over draft registration files in Baltimore.[77] Daniel Berrigan joined them while they awaited trial in that case (they had stayed at the scene of the crime until arresting officers arrived and turned themselves in), and together they used homemade napalm to set fire to another set of draft files in the Baltimore suburb of Catonsville on May 17, 1968.[78]

These richly symbolic protests enraged Catholic patriotic and veterans' associations but won acclaim from antiwar Christians, Catholic and Protestant alike. Daniel Berrigan heightened the controversy by going "underground" in April 1970 rather than submit to federal prison following his conviction in the Catonsville case, and for several months he showed up unannounced at "peace" churches, preached an antiwar message, and then slipped away before police and FBI agents could close in on him. He was arrested in August 1970 after achieving broad celebrity with a feature article in the *New York Times* magazine and appearances on educational television.[79] His undoubted charisma, his widely published antiwar poetry, and his popular play *The Trial of the Catonsville Nine* made him a vivid, larger-than-life figure throughout the late 1960s and early 1970s.[80] Catholic anti-war groups imitated the actions of his East Coast Conspiracy to Save Lives, and there was a rash of similar blood and napalm attacks on draft boards, FBI headquarters, and Dow Chemical Company offices throughout the United States.[81]

In stark contrast to these antiwar actions, Catholic conservatives, like the majority of laypeople, supported the army's role in Vietnam, at least until the Tet Offensive of 1968, after which growing numbers began to express doubts about the ever-receding light at the end of the tunnel. Like Dr. Tom Dooley in the 1950s, they interpreted the conflict not only as an anti-Communist war in the "domino theory" tradition but also as a specifically Catholic affair. In 1963, when Vietnam was first attracting headline attention, the Catholic archbishop of Saigon, Ngo Dinh Thuc, wrote for *National Review* that the Buddhist monks'

77. Meconis, *With Clumsy Grace*, 20–21.
78. Gray, *Divine Disobedience*, 132–33.
79. Meconis, *With Clumsy Grace*, 67.
80. Daniel Berrigan, *To Dwell in Peace: An Autobiography* (San Francisco: Harper and Row, 1987), 241–66.
81. Meconis, *With Clumsy Grace*, 99–108. Dow was the manufacturer of napalm.

antiwar protests, some of which involved suicide by fire, should not be taken seriously because the monasteries were thoroughly infiltrated by Communists who drugged the monks and forced them to burn themselves. He added that U.S. Catholics should support the establishment of martial law, which had providentially rescued Vietnamese Catholics from a massacre.[82] Clare Boothe Luce, wife of the *Time-Life* magnate Henry Luce and herself a Catholic convert, profiled Madame Ngo Dinh Nhu, the "Dragon Lady" of Diem's Vietnam, lauding her piety, and comparing her to "the kind of women who went out of style 100 or more years ago—the pioneer women of America."[83] Even following the assassination of President Diem in 1963 and the fading of the widely hated Madame Nhu from the public scene, when the Catholic issue became more muted, most Catholic conservatives believed that Americans had a duty and a right to prevail in Vietnam. At Christmas 1966 Cardinal Spellman visited combat soldiers there and declared that this was a "war for civilization."[84]

A third issue making for Catholic controversy in the mid-1960s, in addition to Vatican II and Vietnam, was the "sexual revolution," then just gathering force. It will receive detailed attention in the next chapter but a preliminary word has to be said here because disagreements about sex helped precipitate an important intraconservative schism. In the 1960s, environmentalists began to pay close attention to the issue of worldwide overpopulation; they anticipated that unless birth rates fell the world would soon face catastrophic environmental degradation, bringing famine, plague, and war in its wake.[85] At first this population issue did not appear to lend itself to a liberal-conservative difference of opinion. As soon as advocates of compulsory sterilization, contraception, and abortion to correct the problem approached the issue, however, it became highly controversial. Most Catholics spoke forcefully against all these methods as violations of natural law and church teaching.[86]

William Buckley, however, reviewing the overpopulation dilemma in 1966, shocked many of his Catholic readers by seeming to endorse abortion as an option for non-Catholics, who were not bound by church teaching. "Surely the principal meaning of the . . . pronounce-

82. Ngo Dinh Thuc, "What's Really Going on in Vietnam?" *NR*, Nov. 5, 1963, 388–90.

83. Clare Boothe Luce, "The Lady *Is* for Burning: The Seven Deadly Sins of Madame Nhu," *NR*, Nov. 5, 1963, 395–99.

84. Meconis, *With Clumsy Grace*, 15.

85. See in particular Paul Ehrlich, *The Population Bomb* (New York: Ballantine, 1968).

86. For drastic birth-curtailment proposals, see Edgar Chasteen, "The Case for Compulsory Birth Control," and Garrett Hardin, "Multiple Paths to Population Control," in *The American Population Debate*, ed. Daniel Callahan (Garden City, N.Y.: Doubleday, 1971), 274–78, 259–66.

ments of Vatican II," said Buckley, "is that other men must be left free to practice the dictates of their own conscience." If their consciences told them abortion was acceptable, he continued, "it would appear to contradict the burden of the Vatican's position to put pressure on the law to maintain the supremacy of one's own position."[87] Buckley would later join the ranks of die-hard Catholic antiabortionists, but at this time, before the issue had become political dynamite, he took it very casually. L. Brent Bozell, by contrast, was already sternly opposed, and he responded to Buckley's remarks with a letter to *National Review*, insisting that abortion was an objectively horrible crime that all people, Catholic or not, should abhor. "One could predict," he said, "that Vatican II's declaration on religious liberty would generate much mischief. But what it seems to have done to my friend was quite unforeseen—to date, to my knowledge, not even the tipsiest representative of the Catholic New Breed has been driven to this bit of recklessness."[88] Bozell also got into an argument with Garry Wills on the legitimacy of contraception within Catholic teaching. In a vigorous exchange of views, Wills leaned toward revision of Catholic natural law teaching on sex, while Bozell leaned equally strongly away from it.[89] This exchange helped solidify Bozell's decision to abandon *National Review* conservatism and to found *Triumph*, which first appeared in 1966.

Plans for *Triumph* had been in the wind for some time. Neil McCaffrey in 1963 had noted the lack of a journal devoted to Catholic conservatism even though "the times cry out for a Catholic journal of opinion that draws its inspiration from the lessons of the past, the dangers of the present, and the hard reality of original sin."[90] Bozell himself had been engaged in prolonged (though always friendly) disagreement with Frank Meyer about the philosophical plausibility of "fusion" between traditionalists and libertarians within the conservative movement; he, Frederick Wilhelmsen, and others doubted the conservative bona fides of libertarians.[91] Precipitating factors for the creation of *Triumph*, then, were, first, the volatile aftermath of Vatican II, which Bozell believed needed to be brought under control; second, the abortion question and the beginnings of the sexual revolution; and third, dissat-

87. William F. Buckley, Jr., "The Birth Rate," *NR*, March 23, 1965, 231; Buckley, "The Catholic Church and Abortion," *NR*, April 5, 1966, 308.

88. L. Brent Bozell, letter to the editor, *NR*, May 3, 1966, 390.

89. Garry Wills, "Catholics and Population," *NR*, July 27, 1965, 643–48; L. Brent Bozell, "Mater Si, Magistra Si," *NR*, Sept. 7, 1965, 772–86; Garry Wills, "Catholics and Population: A Defense," *NR*, Oct. 19, 1965, 933.

90. Neil McCaffrey, letter to *NR*, Aug. 26, 1963, 134.

91. On the Bozell-Meyer "fusion" debate, see George Nash, *The Conservative Intellectual Movement in America since 1945* (New York: Basic, 1976), 154–85.

isfaction with *National Review's* policy-oriented conservatism, which, despite recent electoral defeats (for their presidential candidate Barry Goldwater in 1964 and for their immediate patron William Buckley in the New York mayoral race of 1965), was increasingly preoccupied with practical issues.

Brent Bozell brought out the first issue of *Triumph* in 1966 after himself failing in his one and only bid for a seat in Congress. For years he had been, and had felt himself to be, in the shadow of his celebrity brother-in-law Buckley, with whom he had written *McCarthy and His Enemies.*[92] As an editor and frequent contributor to *National Review* after its foundation in 1955 Bozell made strong traditionalist arguments consonant with Catholic social teaching, though he was still able to participate in the political mainstream. Indeed, his ear for its idiom, and especially for the rhetoric of anticommunism, was so good that he was able to ghostwrite *The Conscience of a Conservative* for Barry Goldwater before even so much as meeting the Arizona senator.[93] "Goldwater didn't know much about conservatism until he read that book," Bozell said later.[94]

His major work in the years before *Triumph*, however, was a book about the Supreme Court, *The Warren Revolution*, researched mainly in the late 1950s and early 1960s, drafted in Spain, and finally published in 1966. Bozell had graduated from law school just before Earl Warren was appointed chief justice of the Supreme Court. In the decade that followed, the Warren Court scandalized conservatives with its decisions. Bozell was especially angered by four areas of the Court's actions: civil rights, school prayer, electoral reapportionment, and the legal rights of "subversives." Bozell believed that the long, "organic" tradition of U.S. law, based on the written constitution and the "fluid" informal constitution of popular beliefs and principles, had now been shattered by ideological zealots. "During the past twelve years," he argued, "the Supreme Court, with the encouragement of the country's intellectual establishment, has instituted a third kind of constitution making, which is revolutionary both in its method and in its consequences." The Court "sought to transfer the solution of some of the most momentous problems of contemporary public policy from the fluid constitution to the fixed constitution, by judicial decree."[95] These

92. This passage is based in part on telephone interviews with L. Brent Bozell, Feb. 26, 1991, and Patricia Buckley Bozell, March 9, 1991.

93. Barry Goldwater, *The Conscience of a Conservative* (New York: Victor, 1960).

94. Brent Bozell interview.

95. L. Brent Bozell, *The Warren Revolution: Reflections on the Consensus Society* (New Rochelle, New York: Arlington House, 1966), 25.

decrees had been made on issues where a broad public consensus was notably lacking, and the justices had all but stated, Bozell believed, that they did not care about either the case precedents or the framers' intent when making their decisions. "A more explicit repudiation of the underlying assumptions of constitutional government can hardly be imagined"(54).

The Warren Revolution was an angry book, nowhere more so than in dealing with the school prayer cases. The Court's claim of state "neutrality" in religious matters, by which it had justified the *Schempp, Murray,* and *Engel* decisions, seemed spurious to Bozell, and he noted that Christ Himself had said that those who were not with Him were perforce against Him (79). If a public school teacher were now asked by a student whether human rights come from a creator God, as asserted by the Declaration of Independence, the teacher would be forced to answer, "I don't know," because either yes or no would constitute taking sides on the religion issue. In this way patriotism as well as faith would be undermined (79). Bozell admired Charles Rice's *Supreme Court and Public Prayer* and quoted at length from it in this chapter of *The Warren Revolution.* He had also reviewed it for *National Review,* where his views of it illuminate his own outlook:

> Are not prayers said—I don't know why I should be embarrassed to write about this but I am—in the hope of being *answered*? And may we not properly assume that unsaid prayers go *unanswered*? And thus that God may not be moved to care much about the fate of a nation that does not pray, that *officially* whores after false gods? The Jewish and Christian traditions are full of reminders that God replies to such nations by taking it out on their hides.[96]

Ostensibly about constitutional law, *The Warren Revolution* was enlivened by periodic excursions into apocalyptic speculation about the end of civilization. Bozell, having recognized the "sickness" that was overtaking the West, now "devote[d] a good part of his waking hours to agonizing over [it] and to searching for the keys (which are probably theological) to recuperation and health"(15). In an early edition of *Triumph* he declared that he had decided to abandon a proposed sequel to *The Warren Revolution,* because he had lost his old faith in the Constitution itself. The Supreme Court justices, he now believed, had "cut themselves off from the divinely ordained restraint on civil power"

96. L. Brent Bozell, "The Court Enjoins God," *NR*, Sept. 8, 1964, 775–76.

and had "built a house in which secular liberalism could live," making the failure of their experiment, sooner or later, inevitable.[97]

The other founders of *Triumph* also felt profoundly estranged from their society. What they could not find in the United States they searched for in Spain instead, and *Triumph* became a bulwark of Hispanophile Catholics in the nine years of its regular publication (1966–1975). The Society for a Christian Commonwealth, *Triumph's* parent organization, arranged summer seminars for college students at the Escorial, which they regarded as one of the symbolic centers of traditional Christendom. Though the *Triumph* Catholics accepted Franco as the rescuer of Spain from communism in the civil war of 1936–1939, they were chiefly enthusiastic about the Carlists, a group of Spanish monarchists. Indeed, at one point they caused trouble for themselves in Spain by declaring publicly that Franco was not Catholic enough and that his decision not to be succeeded by the Carlist claimant, Don Javier, was a tragic blunder.[98] When, at the end of the 1960s, *Triumph* devotees began direct actions of their own, some of which were conservative mirror images of the Berrigans' radical demonstrations, they named themselves Los Hijos de Tormenta (the Sons of Thunder), dressed in the red berets of the Spanish Carlist militia, bore wooden crosses and rosary beads, and chanted, "Viva Christo Rey!" as police arrested and led them away.[99]

Bozell and his wife had spent two years in Spain (1961–1963) for the benefit of their children's education, eagerly encouraged to migrate there by Bozell's old professor, Willmoore Kendall (yet another convert), by Patricia Bozell's brother Reid Buckley, "who sent back glowing reports," and by Frederick Wilhelmsen, then teaching in Pamplona. The Bozells were sorely tempted to stay on in Spain. "In Spain the Churches were full," Patricia Bozell recalled. "The streets were all named after saints; you saw nuns on the street; there were crosses everywhere. You breathed the Catholic thing there; it was rich and full. It didn't chop things off, partitioning religion into an hour on Sun-

---

97. L. Brent Bozell, "The Death of the Constitution," *T* 3 (Feb. 1968): 10–14.

98. Hart interview, Feb. 29, 1988; Editorial, "The Reign in Spain," *T* 4 (Feb. 1969): 8.

99. *Triumph* Catholics, to be sure, never admitted any similarity between themselves and the Left. Neither did they accept the argument that parts of the counterculture, which showed an eclectic enthusiasm for mysticism and a contempt for liberalism, might be seen as a possible ally. Indeed, calling for a "redeeming generation" on America's campuses, Thomas Molnar argued in *Triumph* that until the old Catholic virtues of silence, patience, charity, asceticism, and faith replaced what he regarded as the hedonism and belligerency of the new Left, there was no hope of Christian recovery. "The new left," he added, "is the cutting edge of the neo-sinistrist, Unesco-manipulated, McLuhanite movement of verbal nihilism that would literally outlaw such virtues." Molnar, "Needed, a Redeeming Generation," *T* 4 (Feb. 1969): 25.

days." But they returned to the United States in 1963 "for the sake of the cause," because "our fight was here in America."[100]

Frederick Wilhelmsen, Bozell's coeditor at *Triumph,* was even more enthusiastic about Spain, had earned his Ph.D. in Madrid and worked for seven years (1960–67) at the University of Navarre, all the while praising Spain to the skies and casting aspersions on the United States as the nadir of Godlessness, materialism, and alienation. Always living with at least one foot in Spain, Wilhelmsen was a dedicated monarchist (a "Knight Grand Cross of the Order of the Outlawed Legitimacy"),[101] a deeply traditionalist conservative, militantly anti-Communist, and no less fervently anticapitalist. The strength of monarchy, he believed, was that it harnessed the family, the basic unit of society; the exigencies of government were met with ties of blood, deeper and more primal than any contractual or constitutional system could muster.[102] He despised cultural relativism and was totally uninterested in ecumenism, believing that the glory of Spain was that it alone had defeated in contests of arms the two greatest challengers Christendom had ever encountered, Islam (in the fifteenth-century *reconquista*) and communism (in the civil war): "The crescent and the hammer and sickle: ultimately they have but one common enemy, the cross of Christ and that civilization that took root and flourished from the wood of Golgotha."[103] Despite his brilliantly acute intellect and internally consistent vision, there was not much support for a man such as Wilhelmsen in contemporary America. He was left with the dilemma of wishing to conserve not the society in which he lived but an imaginary society composed of medieval elements, with no history of its own and no possibility of achievement. He recognized as much; as early as 1955 he remarked wryly, "We conservatives have lost our kings and our chivalry. . . . We have nothing to offer the world but our vision.[104]

When the uprising against the Soviet-inspired government of Hungary began in 1956, Wilhelmsen was a thirty-three-year-old professor of philosophy at the University of Santa Clara in California. He interpreted the revolt as a demonstration of Catholic faith overcoming seemingly impossible odds to challenge Soviet atheism, and he set about

100. Patricia Bozell interview.
101. "Frederick Wilhelmsen," *Contemporary Authors,* new revised series, 3 (Detroit: Gale, 1981), 599.
102. See, for example, Frederick Wilhelmsen, "Sir John Fortescue and the English Tradition," in his *Christianity and Political Philosophy* (Athens: University of Georgia Press, 1978), 112–38; Wilhelmsen, "Royalist Revival in Central Europe," *NR,* Jan. 18, 1958, 61–63; Wilhelmsen, "Charlie and Legitimacy," *T* 9 (July 1974): 13–15.
103. Frederick Wilhelmsen, "The Future of Catholic Spain," *T* 10 (June 1975): 11.
104. Frederick Wilhelmsen, "The Conservative Vision," *C,* June 24, 1955, 295–99.

gathering volunteers from the student body to accompany him to Hungary, where they proposed to join the rebels in their battle against Soviet tanks. Wilhelmsen's volunteers were ready to set off when the State Department, anxious to avoid escalation, prohibited their quixotic mission, warning them that any who got as far as Hungary and lived to tell the tale would lose their U.S. citizenship. As a result Wilhelmsen was unabale to meet the Catholic hero of the rebellion, Cardinal Mindszenty, until 1974.[105] Meanwhile he joined other Catholic conservatives in regarding Christians behind the Iron Curtain as martyrs, seeing it as a "monstrous scandal" that "a third of the members of the Church" should be "lying in chains, lifting Christ again to the Cross in Eastern Europe, a Cross formed by the lacerated flesh of millions, who suffer slavery for His sake" under Communist thralldom.[106] Like Bozell in pre-*Triumph* days, Wilhelmsen was willing to countenance nuclear war for the defeat of communism and held to the belief that "the business of beating Communism or getting beaten at the try" was "the only political end which can really interest any decent man" in the late twentieth century.[107] More than any Catholic contemporary, indeed, he adopted a grandiose rhetoric of war and martyrdom which reveled in suffering. "Catholicism is . . . the American Jesuit Father Pro blessing his Marxist and Masonic firing squad in Mexico with the stumps of his arms after the barbarians had finished cutting them off. It is Spanish soldiers charging Communist trenches with fixed bayonets and rosaries. . . . Catholicism is about an army marching through history chanting the Te Deum. Catholicism is about swords."[108]

While successive American presidents delayed launching the apocalyptic war against communism, Wilhelmsen was also trying to establish himself as a Catholic writer, first with an appreciative meditation on Hilaire Belloc (whose economic theories he fully endorsed); next with an elegiac tribute to the last generation of working tall ships, on one of which, a phosphate freighter, he sailed along the Chilean coastline in 1954; and then with an exacting study in neo-Thomistic philosophy of being.[109] Under the influence of Eric Voegelin, a political philosopher widely admired by conservatives, who traced the intellectual lineage

105. Frederick Wilhelmsen, "With Mindszenty," *T* 9 (July 1974): 11.

106. Frederick Wilhelmsen, "Who Wants a Third Eye Anyway?" review of Daniel Callahan, ed., *The Generation of the Third Eye*, in *NR*, May 4, 1965, 380, 382.

107. Wilhelmsen, *Christianity and Political Philosophy*, 107. On Nuclear weapons, see Wilhelmsen, "Toward a Theology of Survival," *NR*, Jan. 12, 1965, 17–19.

108. Frederick Wilhelmsen, "A New Religion," *T* 3 (April 1968): 21.

109. Frederick Wilhelmsen, *Hilaire Belloc: No Alienated Man* (New York: Sheed and Ward, 1953); Wilhelmsen, *Omega, Last of the Barques* (Westminster, Md.: Newman, 1956); Wilhelmsen, *The Metaphysics of Love* (New York: Sheed and Ward, 1962).

of liberalism and communism back to the gnostic heresy, Wilhelmsen developed a critique of contemporary epistemology by denying the legitimacy of the idea of objective knowledge, which had so besotted devotees of Newtonian science and Enlightenment philosophy.[110] The idea was a self-defeating proposition because it implied removal of the human knower. "Not only is such objectivity impossible theoretically, but it is not even an ideal to be desired if ever it were reached. The achievement of historical 'objectivity,' would destroy man's participation in existence because it would require man to empty himself of the substance of his being."[111] Intellectual detachment, in Wilhelmsen's eyes, was a sham, and he had a sharp eye for the ideological bias of ostensibly neutral scientific knowledge.

Like many Catholic intellectuals of the early twentieth century, Wilhelmsen believed that the Middle Ages had been an era of luminous clarity and intellectual brilliance under the benign governance of the universal Catholic church. The Reformation, the Renaissance, the Enlightenment, the French Revolution, and the industrial revolution he saw as successive disasters that had carried the world into ever-greater perils, annihilating the sense of mystery, the reverence for "being," and the contemplation of God. Industrialization had been facilitated by a sort of "epistemological trick, a theoretical suppression of the organic, of the qualitative, in favor of the mind's concentration upon the quantitative, those aspects of the real that can be manipulated, projected, repeated.[112] In other words, he believed that human beings now lived in an impoverished "reality," brutally imposed on us by Promethean technologists. Twentieth-century human beings were interested not in being or the richness of the world as it is but only in the world as it can be transformed by a "mathematicized science." Today, "things are understood exclusively inasmuch as they are quantified. From this follows the procrustean method of imposing rationality on the world, rather than disengaging intelligibility from the world."[113] He noted with pleasure that Werner Heisenberg, the theoretical physicist, had come by a different route to an analogous conclusion, explaining with his uncertainty principle that engaging in a scientific experiment itself influences and modifies the result from the outset,

110. Eric Voegelin, *The New Science of Politics* (Chicago: University of Chicago Press, 1952).

111. Frederick Wilhelmsen, "Israel and Revelation," review of Eric Voegelin, *Israel and Revelation*, in *MA* 3 (Spring 1959), 182–89.

112. Frederick Wilhelmsen, "The Death of the Age of Analysis," *T* 4 (Oct. 1969): 24.

113. Frederick Wilhelmsen, "The Philosopher and the Myth," *Modern Schoolman* 23 (Nov. 1954): 53.

so that science is something scientists *make* rather than a codification of external realities.[114]

Wilhelmsen carried into the mid-1960s militant convictions that had been commonplace among Catholic intellectuals twenty or thirty years earlier but had been muted since World War II and especially since the Second Vatican Council. As the council finished, he wrote an article for the *Saturday Evening Post* bluntly titled "Catholicism Is Right, So Why Change it?" in which he brushed aside all the substantive and rhetorical reasons commonly advanced for reform and transformation of the church. He considered clerical celibacy a benefical self-mortification and favored church authority rather than academic freedom in Catholic universities.[115] Wilhelmsen staunchly opposed any change in church teaching on contraception. When Jeffrey Hart told Wilhelmsen in 1970 that he was going to discuss reelection strategies with President Nixon, for whom he was a speech writer, Wilhelmsen responded excitedly: "I've got the way for him to win the next election; Nixon has to come out against birth control." He had convinced himself that the swing vote was Hispanic and that Hispanic Catholics would support an anti-birth-control candidate. In an interview Hart remarked to me: "That's one piece of strategy I didn't pass along to Nixon."

Wilhelmsen, Bozell, and their principal *Triumph* collaborators, Gary Potter, John Wisner, and Michael Lawrence, faced what was for them an agonizing dilemma, evident on many pages of their old journal. They spoke out for a traditional Catholicism, in which no principle was more sacred than loyalty to the pope. For the last century or more, such loyalty had generally implied social and political conservatism and a dogged preservation of the religious status quo. But in Paul VI they had a leader who was doing little to prevent radical experiments and was sometimes even encouraging them. At home they had priests and bishops eager to involve themselves in the political crises of the 1960s, racial, urban, and military, to the point, as *Triumph* saw it, that "in April 1968 the bishops of the United States [to judge from their most recent conference statement] could think of nothing distinctively Christian to say to their fellow Catholics or to their fellow-countrymen."[116] They also foresaw, quite accurately as it turned out, that the church was more likely to compromise than strengthen its reputation by becoming involved in everyday political matters. "In secular

---

114. Ibid. For an extended comparison of Wilhelmsen and Heisenberg, see Michael Schwartz, "Four Post Moderns, Four Catholics," *T* 9 (March and April 1974): 8–12.

115. Frederick Wilhelmsen, "Catholicism Is Right, so Why Change It?" *Saturday Evening Post*, July 15, 1967, 10, 12.

116. Editorial, "The Autumn of the Church," *T* 3 (June 1968): 10.

matters," they reasoned, "the Church is and can be no more than a shamefaced neophyte, like an immigrant, no longer able to speak its own tongue, Latin, and unable to speak English without exciting the derision of the natives."[117] To accept episcopal and papal directives that seemed to them horribly misguided caused them great anguish. Nevertheless, in their devotion to the principle of obedience, they did so.

The hierarchy overseas offered little comfort. Thomas Molnar, an inexhaustible world traveler, sent in reports to *Triumph* from Brazil, Argentina, Vietnam, Ireland, and France, full of baleful news about recent Catholic innovations. In Latin America, for example, a bishops' meeting at Medellin, Colombia, in 1968 gave ecclesiastical blessing to several themes of the emerging "liberation theology," which placed the church behind the aspirations of the poor even when, as frequently happened, their champions voiced variants of Marxist ideology. The Jesuit order, formerly bulwark of conservatism in Latin America, began to be radicalized in the 1960s and lined up behind some of the area's revolutionary movements in the following decades. The pope, in the opinion of a dismayed *Triumph* staff, made too little effort to restrain these changes.[118]

At home the transformation of the church was particularly poignant because it seemed to *Triumph* a defeat snatched from the jaws of victory. In 1967 Wilhelmsen wrote that the church, strong, assertive, authoritative, had been leading a winning battle against "Communism and modern barbarism," but then, "just when traditionalist Catholics like myself thought that the enemy was about to surrender, our own defenders opened the gates and invited the forces of secularism to occupy the City of God."[119] John Wisner elaborated; Catholics, he said, were simply heading belatedly down a road that had proved catastrophic to Protestantism. The idea of a Protestant United States, he believed, had finally been vanquished at the Scopes Monkey Trial of 1925. After that, "when the upstart scientism found such a vulnerable victim in debilitated Puritanism, Holy Mother Church was behaving admirably" and had drawn many weary spiritual travelers into her embrace. But then, tragically, "at the Second Vatican Council . . . the American bishops chose to follow the Protestants in defeat. . . . Like the Protestants before them they sought to embrace the surrounding secular-liberal culture, itself a degenerate vision of Christian culture, at a cost to eternal truth which has not yet been estimated." It was not

117. Untitled editorial, *T* 1 (Dec. 1966): 10.
118. Thomas Molnar, "Iglesia y Revolucion," *T* 3 (June 1968): 15–18.
119. Wilhelmsen, "Catholicism Is Right," 10.

the Americans' fault alone, Wisner added, for, in his view, the most decisive act of the council was "the decision to abandon Christian civilization," a decision symbolized in the abandonment of that civilization's language, Latin. The end of Christian civilization certainly did not mean the end of Christian truth, but the loss of all its supports made the preservation of that truth more difficult and imperiled the salvation of the weak.[120]

Dismayed by the political reorientation of the church and feeling that "updating" represented a terrible defeat rather than a rejuvenation, *Triumph* Catholics also greeted a new era in interfaith relations with gloom. After centuries of struggling to convert Jews to Christianity, the Catholic church now decided to abandon the task, suppress the long-standing accusation of deicide for killing Jesus, and learn to live in harmony with this partner in the Judeo-Christian tradition. Cardinal Lawrence Shehan of Baltimore was instrumental in arranging this change at the end of Vatican II.[121] Many American Catholics welcomed Shehan's work as a timely ecumenical gesture, but *Triumph* described it as an act of "bigotry" rather than enlightenment. By failing to proselytize, they argued, "Christians would deny to Jews the fulfillment of the promises made to Israel and awaited anxiously throughout the centuries." Catholics would show contempt or negligence rather than respect, for without conversion to the one true faith, Jews faced eternal damnation.[122] *Triumph* also viewed through jaundiced eyes the development of a pentecostal movement within the Catholic church. They regarded it not as an emotional affirmation of faith to be profitably learned from Protestants, as its defenders claimed, but as "a chaotic negation of rationality" and quite possibly as traffic with unholy spirits.[123]

Triumph's estrangement from contemporary assumptions was also apparent in response to Pope Paul VI's decision in 1969 to modify the calendar of saints by removing those whose historical existence— according to archaeological or text-critical methods—seemed dubious. *Triumph* bewailed the decision: "Any pious Christian knows that the fact of an active and long-standing cult around St. Januarius, for example, is far more pertinent proof of the existence of Januarius than any scraping of fossils can provide." Taking a line developed in Wilhelm-

---

120. John Wisner, "What Happened to the Church?" *T* 3 (Feb. 1968): 22. On Latin, see also Dietrich von Hildebrand, "The Case for the Latin Mass," *T* 1 (Oct. 1966): 10.

121. Thomas W. Spalding, *The Premier See: A History of the Catholic Archdiocese of Baltimore, 1789–1989* (Baltimore: Johns Hopkins University Press, 1989), 422.

122. Editorial, "Anti-Semitism in the Vatican?" *T* 5 (Feb. 1970): 42.

123. Thomas Barbarie, "Tongues Si, Latin No," *T* 4 (April 1969): 20–22.

sen's theory of knowledge, the editors said the "demotion" of Januarius from the calendar of saints was a lamentable "concession to rationalist epistemology" which would "mischievously disturb the belief of the faithful," and they added that when the archbishop of Naples, in response to this threat, had taken out his vial of Januarius's blood, it had, as so often before in moments of danger, liquefied! The cult of this saint, in other words, and his miracles were surer proof of his existence than any scientific evidence could provide.[124] Francis Canavan, S.J., a Burke scholar and *Triumph* contributor, noted many other gains of "Enlightenment" thinking within the church and feared that the old philosophes' cry, "Ecrasez l'infame," would be carried out at last not by the church's enemies but from within.[125]

Meanwhile, through the late 1960s and early 1970s the war in Vietnam dragged on. *National Review* conservatives, in most cases, continued to support it. Garry Wills, on the other hand, severed his connection with the journal when the editors refused to publish a conservative justification for opposition to the war, which Wills later worked into the text of *Nixon Agonistes*. *Triumph* Catholics, too, grew skeptical after the assassination of General Diem in 1963 because the war no longer appeared to be in defense of the Catholic Vietnamese.[126] "We support the war provided it is a war worthy of a Christian's sacrifice," the editors asserted in the first issue of *Triumph*, but "it is not such a war if our soldiers are asked to die merely to help install a South East Asian branch of H.E.W." Only a war "to extirpate Communism and advance the Christian order" could win their assent.[127] Under the right circumstances they were still willing to fight. One contributor wrote, "Undoubtedly it is better for a Red to be alive than dead. But God has given men the high vocation not merely of choosing how to live but also of choosing how to die."[128]

Alienation deepened when rumors began to circulate in the mainstream press that the United States was using chemical and biological weapons and had not disavowed the use of nuclear weapons. *Triumph* judged these weapons to be contrary to Catholic just-war theory—a sharp change of opinion for Bozell and Wilhelmsen, who had advocated even preemptive nuclear strikes against the Soviet Union a few

124. Editorial, "Christopher et al.—Saecula Seculorum," *T* 4 (July 1969): 7.
125. Francis Canavan, S.J., "The Catholic Enlightenment," *T* 3 (Feb. 1968): 18–20, 34.
126. John Wisner, "Vietnam Imbroglio," *T* 1 (Oct. 1966): 3, 27. *Triumph* nevertheless condemned the utopian aspect of pacifism: see, for example, Willmoore Kendall, "The Reason for Wars," *T* 1 (Oct. 1966): 30–32.
127. Editorial, "The War," *T* 1 (Sept. 1966): 37. H.E.W. is a reference to the U.S. Department of Health, Education, and Welfare.
128. J. F. Costanzo, S. J., "Pacifism Is Not Peace," *T* 1 (Nov. 1966): 17–19.

years earlier, confident of divine blessing.[129] According to the principles of just-war theory, noncombatant immunity must be observed, the good achieved by fighting must outweigh the damage incurred on both sides, and there must be reasonable hope of success before combat is joined. These and other principles seemed increasingly inapplicable to the conflict in Vietnam, and *Triumph*'s support for the war cooled accordingly. Moreover, believing that American liberal democracy was as morally bankrupt as communism ("a revolt against God"), the editors came to deny the legitimacy of the U.S. mission in Southeast Asia.[130] By 1970 some *Triumph* Catholics could even look favorably on the Berrigans' uncompromising stand against the war.

One editor, John Wisner, spoke with special authority on the issue of the war because he was a decorated combat veteran of World War II. Wisner was born in China and a member of the Harvard class of 1931; he had parachuted into Normandy the night before D-Day in 1944, fighting there, then in the Ardennes snow that winter, and making another combat jump in the Battle for the Rhine of March 1945. Surviving the war, he had "assumed the sweet and easy yoke of Christ" by converting to Catholicism in 1954 in Tennessee. Wisner admired Bozell's writing in *National Review* and joined *Triumph* at its inception, grieving to witness the impact of the Second Vatican Council.[131] By 1970 he was opposed to the U.S. role in Vietnam and sought to detach *Triumph* from its initially nationalist posture in favor of a Catholicism that stood in judgment over conservatives and liberals alike.

Triumph had been launched on a shoestring in 1966, and throughout its existence the editors made regular urgent appeals for funds. The small staff, working from cramped premises in Washington, D.C., and trying in addition to turn out the newsletter *Catholic Currents*, was perpetually overworked. But Bozell had unbounded intellectual and physical energy. He wanted to practice what he preached, and he convinced the editors of *Triumph* that they would have to save Christendom by direct action as well as by writing. When they learned that a radical Catholic group, the Center for Christian Renewal, was going to hold a "teach-in" on Catholics and contraception in St. Matthew's Cathedral, Washington, D.C. on Good Friday 1969 they went in a group to the cathedral and tried to drown out the "harangue" of CCR spokesman James Gibbons by reciting the Good Friday passion narrative.

129. Editorial, "Stop CBW," *T* 4 (Feb. 1969): 7. See also Gary Potter, "Counter Value: America's Pact with Hell," *T* 4 (July 1969): 11–14.
130. Editorial, "The Autumn of the Country," *T* 3 (June 1968): 8–9.
131. Letter to the author from John Wisner, March 3, 1991.

They won a pyrrhic victory. Gibbons left the cathedral, but on the steps he encountered television news cameras and was able to deliver his message to the much wider audience they offered.[132]

Another explosive issue came to popular attention at the end of the 1960s. The new feminism, with its rhetoric of "women's liberation," held little appeal for traditionalist Catholics, especially when it took an antireligious turn and treated Saint Paul as a misogynist and churches in general as instruments of patriarchal oppression. *Triumph* condemned women's liberation when it first drew headlines in 1969 as "a perversion aimed directly at the apogee of creation." Any talk of sexual equality, "besides being phenomenologically absurd, is an insult to women. . . . Woman is obviously the favored sex, the vessel on which God has principally relied to unfold the mystery of human freedom and redemption, and the analogous mystery of love and life."[133] Patricia Bozell, herself a frequent contributor to *Triumph,* agreed with this view and was an outspoken opponent of feminism. In 1971 she witnessed an inflammatory address by feminist Ti-Grace Atkinson at Catholic University in Washington, D.C., who speculated out loud about the Blessed Virgin Mary's sex life, arguing that it would be better if she had been "knocked up" by a man than by Almighty God. Enraged by this blasphemy, Patricia Bozell ran to the front of the auditorium and slapped Atkinson before being forcibly restrained and arrested.[134]

The most divisive gender-related issue of all, however, was abortion. Although the crucial Supreme Court decision *Roe* v. *Wade* still lay several years in the future, *Triumph* Catholics were becoming increasingly concerned about the piecemeal liberalization of state abortion laws in the later 1960s. In 1970 the Sons of Thunder demonstrated at a Planned Parenthood clinic in Dallas (Wilhelmsen since his return to the United States had worked as a professor of philosophy at the University of Dallas). Kneeling on the clinic floor they prayed the rosary and brandished placards that read "The Pill Kills," "Stop Fascist Genocide," and "Viva il Papa," until they were evicted by the police.[135]

On learning that abortions sometimes took place in the clinic of George Washington University hospital, *Triumph's* editors decided on direct action. They invited people throughout the nation to an "Action for Life" to be staged on June 6. It was the first antiabortion drama of

132. Editorial, "Practically Schismatic," *T* 4 (May 1969): 8.
133. Editorial, "Men's Lib," *T* 5 (Oct. 1970): 42.
134. Patricia Bozell interview. See also editorial, "God and Woman at Catholic U," *T* 6 (April 1971): 21.
135. Editorial, "Sons of Thunder," *T* 5 (March 1970): 8.

a type made familiar two decades later by Operation Rescue. Before approaching the clinic itself the demonstrators, all Catholics, went to mass at St. Stephen Martyr church, celebrated by

> four priests; the principal celebrant is the Newman chaplain. . . . concelebrating are a black priest, a Mexican and a Chinese. There is a flock of altar boys. A contingent of the Sons of Thunder, young men in khaki, wearing red berets, rosaries around their necks, carrying papal flags. All take their places in the sanctuary. There is a blast of trumpets and the Mass of the Holy Innocents begins. "Out of the mouth of babes and sucklings, O God, you have fashioned praise because of your foes. . . . A cry was heard in Rama, wailing and loud laments. It was Rachel, weeping for her children and refusing all consolation because they were no more."[136]

Leaving church the demonstrators marched the long block to George Washington Circle. "Many have processional crosses borrowed from local parishes. Other carry crudely fashioned wooden crosses, and this wave of crosses, of red berets, of placards and banners and flags, rolls down the sidewalk." Speeches by Michael Schwartz, a Dallas student, by a visibly pregnant Mary Jo Lawrence, and then by Frederick Wilhelmsen urged the crowd to action. "Wilhelmsen, 47, shakes, burns, his body and face contort with rage as he calls up the horrible vision of the reality euphemistically styled abortion: 'America . . . you are daggering to death your unborn tomorrow. The very cleanliness of your sterilized murder factories gives off the stench of death.'" After swearing to stop the killing, Wilhelmsen began the chant of "Viva Cristo Rey!" and Bozell made the final appeal for action. Then the protestors, about three hundred of them, moved on the clinic itself. Seven protesters, including Bozell and his son Christopher, got inside, scuffled with security guards, and inadvertently smashed a plate-glass window. The police arrived, beat up those already in the building, and arrested them for trespass and malicious damage.[137] Denying all wrongdoing, the demonstrators justified their action at length in *Triumph*, but all were found guilty and given suspended prison sentences.[138]

That Catholic conservatives should be arrested for direct street actions, as if in mimicry of the Catholic Left, was a source of dismay for

---

136. Editorial, "Present Imperfect," *T* 5 (July 1970): 8–9.
137. Ibid., 9–10, Brent Bozell interview; Michael Lawrence interview; Gary Potter, telephone interview, March 4, 1991.
138. Michael Lawrence, "The Trial," *T* 5 (Oct. 1970): 11–14.

National Review conservatives, to whom the preservation of law and order was itself a great good and religiously defensible. At first *National Review* had greeted *Triumph* and its language of the church militant warmly, commenting that its editors were "eloquent and learned men" whose spirit was "a refreshing contrast to some of the fanatical and devitalizing ecumenism of recent years."[139] Jeffrey Hart said that it was "exactly what was needed," as an antidote to the left-liberal outlook of *Commonweal* and *America*.[140] By 1970, however, this esteem was beginning to cool. In a comment on the abortion clinic fracas, *National Review* editorialized, "Viewed politically, it was probably worse than useless. Spanish Carlism, whatever its virtues in its local habitat, is surely exotic in the District of Columbia, and the Sons of Thunder can have moved precious few of the unconvinced over to their side." Even the quite justified claim of police brutality sounded to *National Review* like an overworked leftist cliché.[141] And although Buckley wrote an editorial supporting his sister's attack on Ti-Grace Atkinson, he privately considered it very regrettable.[142] Hart asked that his name be taken off the *Triumph* masthead when Bozell argued that black riots in the major cities were protests against capitalism and materialism. Hart, mindful of photographs of looters carrying off televisions and liquor, saw this behavior, to the contrary, as evidence of the rioters' ad hoc *endorsement* of materialism and considered Bozell overly susceptible to wishful thinking.[143]

Bozell no longer cared about the estrangement from *National Review*; he told an interviewer shortly thereafter that *Triumph* had little in common with Buckley's style of conservatism.[144] Increasingly that was true. Whereas six years earlier Bozell had regarded the United States as God's chosen instrument for the preservation of Christendom and the West, he now declared war on his nation as an enemy of religion. "If she is to protect herself and if she is to abide by her divine mandate to teach all peoples, the Catholic Church in America must break the articles of peace, she must forthrightly acknowledge that a state of war exists between herself and the American political order."[145] In a long and passionate rebuke to conservatives Bozell claimed that even when American liberal democracy was "writhing in the agonies of its death," few citizens had reached out to conservatism for salvation. The reason,

139. Editorial, "At Last: A Conservative Catholic Magazine," *NR*, Sept. 6, 1966, 870–71.
140. Hart interview, April 26, 1988.
141. Editorial, "Abortion," *NR*, June 30, 1970, 658–59.
142. Interview with William F. Buckley, Jr., New York City, Jan. 9, 1986.
143. Hart interview, April 26, 1988.
144. Judis, *William F. Buckley, Jr.*, 321.
145. Editorial, "The Silent Church," *T* 5 (Jan. 1970): 42.

he said, was that conservatives had appealed too much to economic, instead of moral and religious, interests, had been too ready to agree with secularists that society could be ordered without God.[146]

Instead of seeing themselves as guides to a floundering nation and preservers of conservative wisdom, most of the editors of *Triumph* now claimed to represent only the "Christian tribe," one of the many semi-autonomous "tribes" loose in a no-longer-Christian culture, which had lost all its old anchors and was drifting in anarchic seas.[147] Wilhelmsen collaborated with Jane Bret on two books, based on Marshall McLuhan's theory of television, about the end of modernity, the "retribalization" of the world, and the breakdown of nations, literacy, and all the old conventions, out of which this "Christian tribe" would have to find its own way.[148]

Catholic conservatives had denounced George Dunne, S.J., for suggesting in the early 1960s that Western civilization was no longer the incarnational form of Christianity. By 1970 the "Christian tribe" was insisting upon the same point itself and looking to the peripheries rather than the old civilizational center for new inspiration. Michael Lawrence, *Triumph* editor, recalled that his pilgrimage from conservatism to the Christian tribe was a wrenching transition. Raised Catholic in an Irish-American family from Queens, New York, he had been a superpatriot and member of the conservative students' association Young Americans for Freedom. He had graduated from Fairfield University, a Jesuit school, and was studying law at Catholic University when he heard about Bozell's congressional election bid in 1964. He volunteered for the campaign, became fast friends with Bozell, and stayed with him as a *Triumph* editor after the election defeat. By 1970 Lawrence too was convinced of a far-reaching moral corruption in the nation which the conservative movement seemed to be too compromised to correct.[149]

Despite broad agreement on the political and moral situation, stresses were developing within the tribe itself. A bitter editorial meeting had preceded the Sons of Thunder march against the George

146. L. Brent Bozell, "Letter to Yourselves," *T* 4 (March 1969): 11–14; Bozell, "Politics of the Poor: Letter to Yourselves, Part II," *T* 4 (April 1969): 11–13.

147. On the breakdown of the national faith, see John Wisner, "What Happened to the Church?" *T* 3 (Feb. 1968): 21–24.

148. Frederick Wilhelmsen and Jane Bret, *The War in Man: Media and Machines* (Athens: University of Georgia Press, 1970); Wilhelmsen and Bret, *Telepolitics* (Montreal: Tundra, 1972). See also Wilhelmsen, "The Good Earth," *T* 4 (Feb. 1969): 14: "Calvinism, hating the world, married the rationalist spirit; and both of them, pumped up by French lucidity and the greed of Dutch and English capitalism, engendered that Modern Age which today passes out of history."

149. Lawrence interview.

Washington University clinic, with Gary Potter arguing that it was an ill-planned and necessarily forlorn gesture, destined to lead nowhere. "I remember saying that we weren't going to shake down the Anglo-Saxon state by chanting 'Viva Christo Rey!'" He was as opposed to abortion as Bozell but could see no purpose in an action of this kind. The "gung-ho" Carlists, he later recalled, regarded him as a "wet blanket" for this attitude and for his oft-voiced conviction that *Triumph* should be reaching out to young activists with Catholic-based ideas on variety of social and political issues rather than painting itself into a corner with Hispanic esoterica. The demonstration, in which he declined to participate, was the precipitating event for his decision to leave *Triumph* and set up another small journal.[150]

John Wisner joined Potter, and in 1971 they brought out the first issue of *Rough Beast*, named for the creature that stalks through W. B. Yeats's poem "The Second Coming." Less church-related than *Triumph* but no less Catholic in outlook, the first *Rough Beast* bore on its back cover a photograph of an aborted fetus in a hospital disposal can and the legend, "Editorial without words." Potter and Wisner, both gifted writers, developed an antiwar, antitechnology, antiabortion critique of contemporary society in a style that drew considerable attention. Norman Mailer, in the unusual position of being a literary celebrity of the sexual revolution and yet an opponent of abortion, wrote that *Rough Beast* was the only journal then in publication that showed "guts and fiber." Sociologist Robert Nisbet, whose *Quest for Community* was a conservative classic, said it was the most original journal of ideas on the American scene in recent years. Such puffs by themselves were not enough to assure *Rough Beast*'s future. When, in a subscription drive, copies were sent out to every state director of the Young Americans for Freedom, the editors received in return mail nothing but two used condoms. This flippant response confirmed Potter's view that "most conservatism in the United States is nothing but an expression of the right wing of the national liberalism" and that anticontraception politics were of little interest to most young American conservatives.[151]

Potter himself was a colorful character and one of the many Catholic converts who gave the conservatism of that era its distinctive flavor. Born in 1939 in California to parents who had newly migrated out of the depressed agricultural Midwest, Potter grew up in the Assemblies of God faith in Albany, on San Francisco Bay. "My family were fundamentalist evangelicals," he recalled; "I even knew people who were

---

150. Potter interview.
151. Ibid.

turtle-ponders and snake handlers." After public high school and college at San Francisco State University, he joined the Merchant Marine and traveled the world, reading voraciously during long voyages on an oil tanker. Ashore in Hawaii one day in 1961 he decided to follow the advice of Henry James that every young man's education should be completed by a stay in Paris, and he traveled thither at the end of his next voyage. He stayed in Paris from 1961 to 1965, taking classes at the Sorbonne and working as a rewrite man at the *New York Herald Tribune*. He also developed a love for the aesthetic grandeurs of Catholic architecture and took instruction in Catholicism to learn more about its religious meaning. But only on his return to the United States did he finally take the plunge. "I was appalled and hated New York City, and regretted leaving the life I had been living. I came into the Church for the wrong reason really, through the cultural back door. It [conversion] was an act of solidarity with European culture. But Hilaire Belloc says somewhere that he who sticks his finger in Holy Water for whatever reason will end by believing." Although Potter soon developed into a zealously orthodox traditionalist Catholic, he never thought that the Catholic "good old days" in the United States had been particularly good and doubted he would ever have converted into the Irish-American clergy-dominated church before Vatican II without the stimulus of French culture.[152]

Rough Beast's title puzzled so many potential sympathizers that Potter and Wisner soon relented and changed it to *Truth and Justice*. Under this title it staggered on through successive financial crises but finally closed in 1974. The rift with *Triumph* had not been too deep, and Potter returned there to preside over *Triumph*'s last years, before moving on to the *Wanderer* and still later the *Remnant*, while Wisner, in retirement, wrote and circulated among friends a succession of intellectually provocative typewritten letters on the *Truth and Justice* letterhead.

At the height of its popularity, *Triumph* attracted about thirty thousand readers, but for most Catholic conservatives defense of and loyalty to the nation were paramount, and the nation-denying language of the Christian tribe alienated these potential supporters. Anguished exchanges in the letters and editorial columns ensued as *Triumph* tried to work out a modus vivendi with the United States. One reader, John Davenport, sympathized with Bozell's analysis of the breakdown of order but could not imagine how Americans were going to take a "step forward into the Middle Ages." Gerhart Niemeyer, another religious anti-communist and political science professor at Notre Dame, also

152. Ibid.

sympathized with Bozell's view that "a purely man-centered political order" was "untenable" but shied away from the anti-Americanism that followed from that premise. Jeffrey Hart agreed that "in its paradigmatic essence, Conservatism is Christian and Catholic," but he pointed out that here on earth it could not always be quite so pure.[153] One reader, James Fitzpatrick, in refreshingly down-to-earth language, described the problem he was having: "When my face is stuck between the covers of *Triumph*, I'm all yours. You hypnotize me. An aroma of incense from my altar boy days gives me a high. But then I go to work, and stop off for a beer, and paddle around a stream chasing trout with my kids, and, well, I'm not sure things are as un-Christian as you think." Granting that "the stumbling American giant is confused and purposeless at this moment in history," Fitzpatrick nevertheless shied away from declaring war against a country he loved, thick with memories of Douglas MacArthur, Whittaker Chambers, and "the Brent Bozell of old."[154]

The Brent Bozell of old was much changed, however, and from 1970 was beginning to suffer from the manic-depressive syndrome that was to sap his vitality and cast a pall over *Triumph's* early exuberance. Several contributors—Russell Kirk, John Lukacs, Jeffrey Hart, and Thomas Molnar—continued to write reviews and articles for *Triumph* while harboring deepening reservations about its editorial direction. They anticipated, correctly, that its days were numbered and were not surprised by its demise in 1975, by which time its readership had fallen catastrophically. Buckley commented later: "They lost all sense of proportion, and . . . fanned themselves into a kind of angelism, which simply could not cope with the situation," especially once their outlook became "very anti-American."[155] Thomas Molnar, though a sympathizer and contributor, could not help observing that the infatuation with Spain was one of the shortcomings of *Triumph* as a claimant to American Catholics' sympathetic attention. As a European exile Molnar was far less inclined than Bozell and Wilhelmsen to romanticize Spain: "Look at the sorry state of Spain today; under its playboy King it is certainly the least romantic country in the world, a caricature of the consumer societies of the West. . . . it's grotesque." Wilhelmsen, nonetheless, was "a hopeless romantic" on the question of Spain, believing

153. Letters in response to Bozell, "Letter to Yourselves," from John Davenport, Gerhart Niemeyer, and Jeffrey Hart, *T* 4 (June 1969): 17–18.
154. James Fitzpatrick, "Dear *Triumph*: Do You Really Mean it?" *T* 7 (Jan. 1972): 14–16.
155. Buckley interview, Jan. 6, 1986.

quite wrongly that "it was still in the Middle Ages" and then "fantasiz-
ing about this construct."[156]

The entire history of the *Triumph* movement demonstrates strange
parallels between Catholic traditionalists and Catholic radicals in the
late 1960s. Both groups were dismayed by the church after Vatican II:
radicals because the rate of change was too slow, traditionalists because
it was far too rapid. Both were horrified by the U.S. role in the Vietnam
War: radicals because they saw a possible congruence of interests between indigenous revolutionaries in the Vietnamese countryside
fighting for freedom from imperialism with the Christian message of
liberation and hope, traditionalists because they regarded communism
and liberal democracy as twin forms of demonic, anti-Christian power.
Both groups understood the importance of vocal and written protest
and undertook vigorous polemical wars against the church establishment and against one another, taking full advantage of American press
freedoms and scanting the old intra-Catholic restraint. Both had become so estranged from the nation and the church by 1968 that they
resorted to direct protests, using the symbols and rites of their faith
as testaments to their conviction of righteousness. Both groups com-
prised men and women willing to suffer arrest and imprisonment for
their convictions; the Berrigans and Bozell both pointedly violated the
secular law in the interest of a higher law, drawing on the vigorous
precedent laid down by the civil rights movement in the foregoing
years. Both turned against and were condemned by the Catholic and
conservative mainstream.

These were chaotic years, to be sure, for many religious and political
groups. The once nonviolent and racially integrated Student Nonviolent Coordinating Committee had opted for a policy of racial exclusion
and direct action; the Students for a Democratic Society, a leftist group,
was splitting into several factions, including the militaristic Weather
Underground; the Young Americans for Freedom were divided between their own traditionalist wing and an "anarchocapitalist" group
that found it had more in common with the libertarian Left than with
its former Goldwater constituency. Faced with turbulent protests from
many sides, first President Johnson and then President Nixon became,
almost by default, "conservative" leaders to the degree that they struggled to uphold the rule of law and due process, while trying to shore
up their frail and much-challenged legitimacy by appeals to the millions who were not protesting and not making news, "the silent majority," as Nixon called them. William Buckley spent these years moving

<hr />

156. Telephone interview with Thomas Molnar, Jan. 15, 1991.

toward an alliance on policy questions with disillusioned former liberals—Irving Kristol, Nathan Glazer, Norman Podhoretz, Daniel Patrick Moynihan, and many others—whose experience with student rebellion, urban riots, antiwar protest, and a general deterioration of civility had edged them away from their old assurances and toward a view that would crystallize in the 1970s as neoconservatism.[157]

Apocalyptic speculation abounded at the end of the 1960s, giving rise to a vast literature of catastrophe. a genre in which Catholic conservatives excelled. In addition to *Triumph*, which was almost wholly written in that idiom, John Lukacs contributed *The Passing of the Modern Age*, Thomas Molnar explained in *The Counter-Revolution* why people of his type were doomed to irrevocable defeat, and Frederick Wilhelmsen produced *Seeds of Anarchy* (1969), a conservative anthology on the student revolution then in progress at the nation's premier campuses. Contributors to *Seeds of Anarchy* included Molnar, Russell Kirk, Jeffrey Hart, Michael Lawrence, and Wilhelmsen's collaborator Jane Bret, but the most noteworthy name on the list of contributors was that of Ronald Reagan, then enjoying his third year in office as governor of California. The chapter appearing under Reagan's name explained that if only citizens understood more fully the nihilistic and criminal intent of student rebels they would be all the more willing to help the forces of civilization to combat them. After listing instances of campus fire bombings and window smashings this author asked: "Is it conceivable that the perpetrators of these outrages are idealists and reformers, people who intend to do good? I say that it is just not conceivable."[158] In his preface to the collection Wilhelmsen reminded readers that civilization depends on its intellectual heritage and, accordingly, an attack on the university is an attack upon civilization itself. "The flames of revolution threaten to make a holocaust of our intellectual inheritance. Unless that inheritance can be rescued from the burning faggots of anarchy, America—and with her the West—will go down in a Twilight of the Gods from which there will be no recourse." The articles collected in *Seeds of Anarchy* had been written in the hope of "avoiding this late and irrevocable eveningtide" and bringing the nation back from the brink of catastrophe. Wilhelmsen was almost but not yet quite ready to join Bozell in declaring that all was lost for America.[159]

In the 1970s the situation got both better and worse. Those from all

157. On this development, see Peter Steinfels, *The Neoconservatives: The Men Who Are Changing America's Politics* (New York: Simon and Schuster/Touchstone, 1979).

158. Ronald Reagan, "The Key Is Understanding," in *Seeds of Anarchy*, ed. Frederick Wilhelmsen (New York: Argus Academic, 1969), 15.

159. Wilhelmsen, Preface, ibid., v.

points of the political compass who had promised or dreaded imminent revolution discovered that the nation's institutions were more durable than they had anticipated and that what they had taken to be a national volcano was no more than a cluster of energetic mud springs surrounded by a comparatively inert terra firma. Disengagement from Vietnam and political survival through the Watergate scandal vindicated the constitutional system, albeit at high cost. Many took comfort from the nation's ability to survive, but the heritage of the 1960s was huge. Issues raised then have burdened the nation ever since, and of them all, perhaps none proved so baffling and complex as those generated by the "sexual revolution."

5

Sex, Law, and Nature

That a devout Catholic doctor should have played the key role in inventing the birth control pill is one of the painful ironies of recent Catholic history. Dr. John Rock, a Massachusetts gynecologist, at first thought he had simply found a way to smooth out irregularities in women's menstrual cycles, but he soon discovered that the pill was a highly reliable way of forestalling conception. Catholic moral teaching was explicitly hostile to obstructing the free passage of sperm to egg in sexual intercourse, which ruled out condoms and diaphragms for Catholics, but here was a device that did not impede the act of intercourse itself. In *The Time Has Come* (1963), Rock argued that married Catholics could, accordingly, use the pill without violating church teaching. After all, the church permitted them to use the "rhythm method," in which intercourse is restricted to the least fertile times of a woman's menstrual cycle in the hope of avoiding pregnancy. His invention, said Rock, simply created a "pill-established safe period" for married couples. Children were a great good, said Rock on another occasion, but when "love fused by coitus" brought "more children than can properly be cared for, it is dangerously strained, even distorted." Here was a way, he believed, of maintaining Catholic law without playing the notoriously unreliable game of "Vatican roulette."[1]

Rock's subtitle, *A Catholic Doctor's Proposal to End the Battle over Birth*

1. John Rock, quoted in Loretta McLaughlin, *The Pill, John Rock, and the Church* (Boston: Little, Brown, 1982), 161; Rock, *The Time Has Come: A Catholic Doctor's Proposal to End the Battle over Birth Control* (New York: Knopf, 1963). On Rock's work and the development of oral contraceptives, see James Reed, *From Private Vice to Public Virtue: The Birth Control Movement and American Society since 1830* (New York: Basic, 1978), esp. 351–64.

Control, turned out to be a fine piece of wishful thinking. The battle was only just heating up in 1963. When the 1960s began U.S. Catholics agreed, with few exceptions, that artificial contraception was illicit. Liberal and "countercultural" Catholics such as Dorothy Day were just as decided on the point as traditionalists.[2] In this belief Catholics were at odds with nearly all other Americans, for whom the use of contraceptives, especially by married couples, seemed morally permissible and sometimes even laudable. With the all but unanimous Catholic view of abortion as a horrible sin and crime, however, most non-Catholic Americans agreed. The 1960s and 1970s witnessed a dramatic shift in these views. By 1980 many Americans believed that both contraception and abortion were morally permissible, and beginning in 1973, their view was upheld by the Supreme Court. Most Catholics, by contrast, continued to hold out against abortion but split on the question of contraception. After the mid-1960s many continued to oppose it, but many others used contraceptives in violation of papal teaching. This shift had unsettling consequences for the whole Catholic population, particularly the conservatives, among whom it was a serious cause of further fragmentation.

Trends in American sexual conduct and discourse already discernible earlier in the century began to accelerate in the 1960s. A major precipitating factor was the ability reliably to separate sexual intercourse from reproduction for the first time in history. By midcentury developments in birth control technology had made it possible for married couples to plan how many children to bear and at what intervals. Under the advocacy of Margaret Sanger and other "neo-Malthusians," who linked restricted family size to improved health and higher standards of living for working families, the spread of birth control devices had gone on through the first half of the twentieth century despite the fierce opposition of the Catholic church and the inhospitable laws of many states.[3]

Another of the many ironies surrounding the history of sex and religion in recent American history is that these scattered laws against contraception and the laws against abortion then on the books of every state had nearly all been passed by militant Protestants, yet now found their most ardent defenders among the Catholics. Protestant abortion law reformers in the nineteenth century, some of them militantly anti-Catholic, had feared that without such laws Catholics would soon swamp the Protestant population because the Catholic birth rate was

2. James T. Fisher, *The Catholic Counterculture in America, 1933–1962* (Chapel Hill: University of North Carolina Press, 1989), 122.
3. Reed, *From Private Vice*, 67–139, 281–316.

so much greater.[4] U.S. law and Catholic teaching on sex, indeed, largely coincided through the early part of the twentieth century, and the church fought to keep it that way, opposing efforts in the 1940s and 1950s to overturn the Massachusetts and Connecticut statutes prohibiting the dissemination and use of contraceptives. Like abortion, homosexual intercourse was a criminal offense in every state, and the family—which Catholic social theorists regarded as the basic unit of society—enjoyed special privileges and protections in law.

The sexual revolution, part of which was a challenge to all such laws, transformed this situation. The Kinsey Institute brought actual sexual practices to public attention, phrasing its reports on male and female sexuality (1948/1953) in value-neutral language and presenting them as scientific studies of human behavior. Parts of the literate middle class took the reports as scandalous revelations of moral corruption. Kinsey reported high levels of premarital and extramarital sexual intercourse among both men and women and documented the frequency with which, at differing times of their lives, individuals of both sexes were homosexually active.[5] During the 1950s and 1960s, popular Freudianism encouraged the view that sexual repression was potentially a source of mental illness; books of advice about sexual fulfillment enjoyed booming sales. Alfred Kinsey, William Masters, Virginia Johnson, and their cohorts studied the mechanical, affective, and expressive aspects of sex more than its reproductive function.[6] *Playboy* magazine, founded in 1953, challenged American sexual conventions by positing as its ideal the modern, sexually liberated man, and Helen Gurley Brown gave a measure of respectability to previously shocking notions with *Sex and the Single Girl*.[7] Many American women, by the early 1960s, regarded premarital sexual experience as no impediment to their dignity or marriageability, and non-Catholics widely used the forms of contraception then available. The development of reliable contraceptives did not *cause* the sexual revolution; deeper cultural forces were at work to create far-reaching social changes in this aspect of

4. James Mohr, *Abortion in America: The Origins and Evolution of National Policy, 1800–1900* (New York: Oxford University Press, 1978), 90–91.

5. Alfred Kinsey et al., *Sexual Behavior in the Human Male* (Philadelphia: W. B. Saunders, 1948); Kinsey et al., *Sexual Behavior in the Human Female* (Philadelphia: W. B. Saunders, 1953). On the reception of the Kinsey reports, see Barbara Ehrenreich et al., *Remaking Love: The Feminization of Sex* (Garden City, N.Y.: Anchor Doubleday, 1987), 43–45.

6. William H. Masters and Virginia Johnson, *Human Sexual Response* (Boston: Little, Brown, 1966).

7. On *Playboy*, see Barbara Ehrenreich, *The Hearts of Men: American Dreams and the Flight from Commitment* (Garden City, N.Y.: Anchor/Doubleday, 1983), 42–51; Helen Gurley Brown, *Sex and the Single Girl* (New York: B. Geis Associates/Random House, 1962).

human conduct.[8] While avoiding any technological determinism, however, it is at least worth noting a commonly voiced perception of the times, expressed by Midge Decter, that "without birth control the very idea of a married woman's entitlement to full sexual pleasure, not to mention that of a young woman's freedom to pursue sex outside of marriage, would be an idle and rather bitter joke."[9]

Catholic teaching on sex, contrary to widely circulating myths, had not been unchanged for centuries but was also in a state of development. The first modern statement on the question was Pope Pius XI's encyclical *Casti Conubii* of 1930. It described contraception as "an offense against the law of God and of nature" and those who employed it as "covered with the guilt of a grave sin." Abstinence from sexual intercourse was the only method of birth prevention the church would countenance; each sexual act had to be "open" to the transmission of new life.[10] In the 1920s, however, studies of the female menstrual cycle had established the existence of fertile and infertile periods each month, on the basis of which various systems of "natural family planning" were developed.[11] Logically speaking, the Catholic position would have denied the legitimacy of these methods if they were used in the hope of forestalling conception. But Pope Pius XII, in an allocution to Italian midwives in 1951, signaled his approval of the "rhythm method."[12] This concession would later prove to be a foot in the door for Catholic advocates of contraception. If human ingenuity could be used to prevent conception with the aid of thermometers, charts, and mucus tests (all of which were tools of "rhythm" devotees), why not with the pill?

In the early 1960s, however, such advocates were few and far between; Dr. Rock was uncharacteristically outspoken for his times, and most Catholic journals did not greet his work warmly. *America* found Rock's use of moral theology seriously flawed and criticized him for not seeking his bishop's imprimatur before publishing so controversial a book.[13] Even *Commonweal*, the principal liberal Catholic journal, accused him of "chronic ambiguity" in his exposition and shameful oversimplification of complex matters, adding that Rock's experiments on human embryos over the previous two decades constituted, in the

8. Ehrenreich, *Remaking Love,* 41.

9. Midge Decter, *The New Chastity and Other Arguments against Women's Liberation* (New York: Coward, McCann, and Geohegan, 1972), 145.

10. John T. Noonan, Jr., *Contraception: A History of Its Treatment by the Catholic Theologians and Canonists* (Cambridge: Belknap Press of Harvard University Press, 1965), 424–28.

11. Ibid., 443.

12. Ibid., 445.

13. Joseph S. Duhamel, "The Time Has Come," *A,* April 27, 1963, 608–11.

church's eyes, "lethal human experimentation" and served as strong testimony against his reliability on any subject.[14] Protestant and secularist reviewers, by contrast, saw it as a healthy sign that a Catholic doctor was willing to speak out plainly against his church's teaching, and anti-Catholic polemicists who had opposed the Kennedy presidency three years earlier rejoiced to see Kennedy praising Rock and agreeing to study overpopulation and other sex-related questions.[15]

Most Catholic writing on sex in the early 1960s was stylized and stilted, based on the church teaching that the purpose of sex and marriage was procreation. "Mutual service and allaying of concupiscence," said a characteristic formulation of the time, were of strictly secondary importance.[16] To be named Catholic family of the year by the Christian Family Movement, twelve or more children counted strongly in a couple's favor. At the same time, Catholic history displayed many examples of abhorrence for sex and glorified the self-mortification and asceticism of the monastic tradition. Priests often assumed that their celibacy was spiritually elevating, whereas the "carnality" of married laypeople dragged them down to an earthier status. Some theologians still had to struggle, even in 1960, to admit to themselves the natural law principle that sex, as part of nature, is itself good. The Jesuit theologian John Thomas, who was to become an advocate of change in the 1960s, could not yet tear himself away from the view that abstinence was morally superior. "The argument that periodic continence deprives marital love of its freedom and spontaneity," he wrote, "is based on two false premises. It supposes that the sexual impulse must not be subjected to rational control like all other human impulses, and it assumes that marital love cannot be expressed in other ways. Indeed it is frequently forgotten that the virtue of chastity . . . applies to married couples as well as to others." This celibate's yearning for celibacy in marriage was almost palpable.[17]

There was, nevertheless, a groundswell of pro-reform sentiment among Catholics. One of the "New Breed" theologians, Michael Novak, gathered the testimony of Catholic couples with large families in *The Experience of Marriage* (1964) and described the problems that resulted from an overabundant fertility; without ever coming right out and saying it, Novak indicated the need for a change in the teaching,

14. Herbert Ratner, "The Rock Book: A Catholic Viewpoint," *C*, July 5, 1963, 392–95.

15. See, for example, editorial, "Catholic Physician Favors Birth Control," *Christian Century*, May 29, 1963, 699–700; editorial, "Catholics Support Planned Parenthood," *Christian Century*, Aug. 21, 1963, 1021.

16. John L. Thomas, S.J., "Sex, Love, and Self-Mastery," *CW* 191 (Sept. 1960): 336.

17. Ibid., 337.

and in the next five years, he wrote more directly in its favor.[18] Daniel Callahan, in *Honesty in the Church*, declared that the falsely mechanical-biological approach theologians took in discussing sex amounted to dishonesty about a vital question.[19] *Commonweal* admitted that, whatever the shortcomings of his book, John Rock was "one of the few Catholics in America who has had the nerve to say what is on his mind." He had helped to overcome "a pervasive atmosphere of fear" surrounding sexual questions.[20] Emboldened, *Commonweal* ran a symposium on "responsible parenthood" in 1964, with nearly all participants pointing to faults in the current natural law prohibition on contraceptives and proposing significant changes in the teaching.[21]

The most important single book on the subject of Catholics and contraception, however, which outshone the suddenly mushrooming Catholic literature on the issue during Vatican II, was John Noonan's *Contraception: A History of Its Treatment by the Catholic Theologians and Canonists* (1965). Following the positive reception of his first book, *The Scholastic Analysis of Usury*, Noonan had left his Boston law practice in 1959 and accepted a professorship at Notre Dame Law School.[22] In his new book on contraception, researched and written in the early 1960s while the debate gathered force, Noonan attempted to do for the history of Catholic teaching on contraception what he had previously accomplished for usury: to show that it had been involved in constant change and development and to imply, without actually saying as much, that further development in the teaching, which would enable Catholics to use contraceptives, would do no violence to tradition. "The key terms in this history," he began, "are tension, reaction, option and development. All these metaphors imply that a human process is going on, that what is happening is not the unilateral action of God making His will increasingly evident." Noonan showed in painstaking detail that developments in basic scientific understanding in classical times, then the grafting of Aristotelian science onto Christianity by Albertus Magnus and Aquinas, then the development of gynecology and obstetrics, had prompted repeated modifications and refinements of church teaching. He showed that scholasticism, after dealing with

18. Michael Novak, *The Experience of Marriage: The Testimony of Catholic Laymen* (New York: Macmillan, 1964).

19. Daniel Callahan, *Honesty in the Church* (New York: Scribner's, 1965).

20. Editorial, "Dr. Rock's Book," *C*, May 17, 1963, 213–14.

21. Symposium, "Responsible Parenthood," by Bernard Haring, Richard McCormick, Thomas Burch, George Casey, Daniel Callahan, Louis Dupre, Edward Schillebeeckx, Louis Janssens, and Michael Novak, *C*, June 5, 1964, 311–47.

22. This passage is based in part on personal interviews with John T. Noonan, Jr., Berkeley, Calif., June 10, 20, 24, 1985.

the question imaginatively and creatively in the twelth and thirteenth centuries, had rigidified against its own best traditions, losing touch with scientific and philosophical developments. Noonan was glad to note that "the phenomenology of Edmund Husserl and the existential personalism of Gabriel Marcel" had exerted "fecund influences on Catholic thought" in the twentieth century and that, "as biological regularity came to be less emphasized than the freedom of the spiritual person . . . so it became more difficult to insist that biological norms should completely govern human acts."[23]

Temperamentally as well as intellectual conservative, Noonan was not the man to demand or even suggest new papal directives on the question, but his book provided ample ammunition to those who did begin to make such demands. Reviewing it for *National Review*, Garry Wills noted that at a stroke Noonan's book upstaged every other statement on the question and laid solid ground for a development of church teaching on the issue.[24] Along with Rock's and Novak's books, Noonan's bore witness to a new openness about sexual issues in the previously sexually repressive church. Soon thereafter priests and theologians would begin to debate the merits of celibacy, and influential voices would be raised in favor of voluntary rather than compulsory priestly celibacy.[25]

The Second Vatican Council freed up debate on sex as on all other matters of Catholic teaching, and Noonan's book was in many ways a classic product of the council years. "Whatever the final decision of Pope Paul on the birth control problem," *Commonweal* noted as the council drew to a close, "it is difficult to see how the Church can ever again be as certain as it once was," and the editors now came right out in the open with a plea to the pope that "in serious circumstances, a couple be free to choose those methods of family limitation which are medically sound."[26] Without writing a decree on contraception, the council itself took an important step by speaking of the *two* ends of marriage as communion between two persons in love and procreation of children. For the first time the church made no effort to subordinate the former to the latter and wrote of marriage in personalistic rather than biologistic terms.[27]

As the council ended, Pope Paul VI convened the Pontifical Commis-

23. Noonan, *Contraception*, 5, 231–57, 483.

24. Garry Wills, "Contraception," review of Noonan, *Contraception*, in *NR*, Oct. 19, 1965, 944.

25. On optional celibacy, see, for example, James Hitchcock (against), "The Utility of Celibacy," *CW* 207 (Aug. 1968): 211–13; Rev. James Doherty (in favor), "The Celibacy of the Secular Priest: An Open Letter to Karl Rahner," *CW* 208 (Dec. 1968): 103–6.

26. Editorial, "Birth Control Decision," *C*, Dec. 10, 1965, 296–97.

27. Gregory Baum, "Birth Control: What Happened?" *C*, Dec. 24, 1965, 369–71.

sion on the Family, Population, and Natality to review the birth control question. Many U.S. Catholic commentators believed that the commission was sure to recommend changes in the teaching on contraception and to find in favor of John Rock's pill and possibly even other contraceptive methods.[28] Noonan, whose study of the history of contraception marked him out as the world's most knowledgeable man on the issue, was made a lay adviser to the commission. At the meetings, his historical-contextual approach impressed many of the participants and influenced them in favor of change. "No one was familiar with the history except me," Noonan recalled later. "The theologians had thought the history was built into the theology and didn't realize there were so many steps you could see, but I was able to give them a parallel with the usury development." As Noonan soon discovered, however, both sides in the controversy, pro- and anticontraception, could use his book as a compendium of declarations to support their contentions. The very thoroughness of his research gave traditionalists ammunition of which they had previously been unaware; they, of course, scanted the developmental framework in which he had placed it.[29]

In the United States, meanwhile, in the perfervid mood of the mid-1960s, Catholics debated the question of sexuality with growing urgency and in a progressively more explicit and outspoken way. They had had to overcome a long tradition of reticence on the subject even to raise it, but as the volume of sex-related articles in all media rose dramatically, and as evidence accumulated that a sexual revolution was under way, they were inevitably drawn in. Three discernible positions emerged. The first and least traditional position was that Catholics had a right to use contraceptives, and to deny them this right would be atavistic. Those asserting this position—including the nascent Catholic Left at *Ramparts,* the theologian Charles Curran, the *Commonweal* editor Daniel Callahan, and his wife Sydney Callahan (author of *Beyond Birth Control*)—supported their claims by drawing attention to the "population explosion," the growing conviction that world overpopulation was reaching the dimensions of a crisis.[30] Small families, said Daniel Callahan, would not only be more manageable emotionally and

28. On the work of the commission, see Robert Kaiser, *The Politics of Sex and Religion: A Case History in the Development of Doctrine* (Kansas City, Mo.: Leaven, 1985).

29. Noonan interview, June 20, 1985.

30. See editorial, "Lyndon Johnson and the Politics of Theology," *R* 4 (May 1965): 3–4, 6; Sydney Callahan, *Beyond Birth Control: The Christian Experience of Sex* (New York: Sheed and Ward, 1968); Daniel Callahan, ed., *The American Population Debate* (Garden City, N.Y.: Doubleday, 1971), xi–xv; Charles Curran, "Personal Reflections on Birth Control," in *The Catholic Case for Contraception,* ed. Daniel Callahan (New York: Macmillan, 1969), 19–29.

economically, they would be environmentally sound.[31] These advocates of change pointed out that new historical circumstances required new teachings. In former ages, so long as wars, epidemics, and famines had kept the human population at a low equilibrium point, maximizing childbirths had some justification. But now that life expectancy was rising dramatically and infant mortality was at a historic low, over-population was presenting the opposite problem; Catholics should react accordingly.[32] This view had massive support outside the church in the mid-1960s; in *The Population Bomb*, the greatest best seller of the decade on this issue, Paul Ehrlich treated Catholics with large families as hardly better than environmental criminals.[33]

The second Catholic view, probably held by the majority, favored a change in the contraception teaching but only with the permission of the pope. Gary Wills and William Buckley represented this view among Catholic conservatives; Buckley told an interviewer in 1969: "I tend to the conclusion that it is not an obvious violation of the marital ideal to permit contraception. . . . I would consent, subject to prior consent by the Church, in any collective endeavor to suggest means by which the size of a family can be regulated by couples who desire to do so."[34] Wills and Buckley were aware of the population dilemma, aware of the economic burden of big families in contemporary America, and convinced by Noonan's work that the teaching could be changed without doing violence to tradition or natural law. In a characteristically scholastic argument on this theme, Wills pointed out that by "procreation" the church had traditionally meant not simply the physical production of new children but their education and nurture. If a married couple had more children than they could manage to raise adequately, they would deviate from their procreative duty more severely than if they had restricted family size with the aid of contraceptives. "We are not here to run quantitative fertility races."[35] *National Review* had no objections in 1965 when the last anticontraception statutes were swept away by the Supreme Court in *Griswold* v. *Connecticut*.

The third position, taken by most of the uncompromising traditionalists at *Triumph*, the *Remnant*, and the *Wanderer*, was that there should be no change in the teaching. The insistence on linking sexuality directly to procreation rather than praising its intrinsic physical delights

31. Callahan, cited in Robert Campbell, *Spectrum of Catholic Attitudes* (Milwaukee: Bruce, 1969), 102–3.
32. See, for example, "Johnson and the Politics of Theology," 3–4.
33. Paul Ehrlich, *The Population Bomb* (New York: Ballantine, 1968).
34. Buckley, quoted in Campbell, *Spectrum*, 101.
35. Garry Wills, "Catholics and Population," *NR*, July 27, 1965, 643–48.

was one of the church's glories in standing against a hedonistic world.[36] They practiced what they preached. Charles Rice and his wife had ten children, as did Brent and Patricia Bozell; Michael Lawrence and his wife had six. They deplored John Rock, Daniel Callahan, and other advocates of change; were among the first groups to publicize evidence that contraceptive pills could have adverse health consequences for longtime users; and supported black leaders who denounced proposals that "welfare mothers" should be compelled to use contraceptives.[37]

In 1965 the editors of National Review ran a special edition on the population explosion, in which they took the issue seriously and discussed the various methods then under consideration for its alleviation. One contributor was Alan Guttmacher, president of the Planned Parenthood Federation.[38] In the 1970s Guttmacher was to become an arch-villain for Catholic conservatives when he reversed the traditional antiabortion position of Planned Parenthood. In 1952 in his book on childbirth, Guttmacher had written that as soon as conception took place, the life of a new baby had begun, but this section was deleted for the 1973 edition, after Planned Parenthood had become prochoice. Antiabortion conservatives accused him of acting in bad faith, trying to veil the fact that he was knowingly advocating the killing of children. It would have been unthinkable to welcome Guttmacher to National Review after 1973, but in 1965 he was introduced respectfully as an expert on population.[39]

After lengthy secret deliberations the pontifical commission's working papers were "leaked" to the National Catholic Reporter in April 1967. The leak showed that sixty of sixty-four theological experts on the commission favored changes, as did nine of the fifteen cardinals; some seem to have been willing to include not only the pill but even the recently developed intra-uterine device, whose abortifacient properties were not yet fully understood. Their report argued that so long as a marriage was "open to fecundity" it was not necessary for each distinct sexual act to be so open.[40] The commission's minority, led by John Ford, S.J., author of a weighty textbook on the traditional teaching, advocated a preservation of the status quo and pointed out that to change now would be to imply that for the last half century God had

---

36. Editorial, "Chaos in the Church: A Reassurance," *T* 4 (Jan. 1969): 42.
37. Michael Lawrence, "The Pill: An Epidemic for the Healthy," *T* 4 (May 1969): 11; Charles Rice, *The Vanishing Right to Live* (Garden City, N.Y.: Doubleday, 1969), 118, 134.
38. Alan Guttmacher, "How Births Can Be Controlled," *NR*, July 27, 1965, 641–42.
39. For later conservative criticisms of Guttmacher, see John T. Noonan, Jr., *A Private Choice: Abortion in America in the 1970s* (New York: Free Press, 1979), 37; Germain Grisez, *Abortion: The Myths, the Realities, and the Arguments* (New York: Corpus, 1970), 58.
40. Editorial, "Reveal Papal Birth Control Texts," *NCR*, April 19, 1967, 1, 8–12.

been on the side of the procontraceptive Protestants. "It would be tantamount to seriously suggesting that the assistance of the Holy Spirit was lacking to [the church]."[41] The pope meanwhile had issued a decree retaining the old teaching, for the moment at least, and announcing that he would soon make a major statement on the issue.[42]

This interim papal declaration caused grumbling among Catholics who had believed a change was imminent. One prominent English theologian, Charles Davis, whose work was influential in U.S. theological circles, denounced the pope as a liar and used the occasion to separate himself from the church altogether.[43] By contrast, John Noonan, though he had invested at least as much time and energy in the issue as anyone else, took the declaration calmly, saying that "this is a decision not of a callous but of a conscientious man. Its honesty requires respect."[44] He had not intended to set off controversy, and like other Catholic conservatives, he was careful to insist that contraception, like all church teachings, had to be considered in light of the entire "economy of revelation" and entered into subjectively by the believer rather than with an outsider's cold objectivity. Indeed, his book had begun with the reminder: "The meaning of doctrine is grounded in a charity which escapes analysis. The propositions live, acquire force, make sense, only for the man animated by a love of God and his neighbor."[45] Non-Catholics, in other words, would be ipso facto bewildered by teachings that began in nature but ultimately transcended it in the realm of grace. Nevertheless, a hint of irritability is detectable in Noonan's reactions. "The law of the life of the Church" he said, in a pamphlet on the issue from 1967, "is the law of organic growth, not a mechanical repetition of molds. Only he who fails to grasp this secret of the Church's vitality will suppose that a norm once made is made to be repeated for ever, however inappropriate it may become."[46] This remark was aimed against such diehards as John Ford, but Noonan sounded quite like Ford in his reminder that "argument about the desirability of change cannot be turned into doubt about the existence of the norm."[47]

It was not until Paul VI issued the encyclical *Humanae Vitae* in 1968

41. John Ford, S.J., quoted in McLaughlin, *The Pill*, 186–87.
42. Editorial, "The Pope and Birth Control," *C*, Nov. 11, 1966, 157.
43. On his departure from the church, see editorial, "Charles Davis, Christian," *C*, Jan. 6, 1967, 359–60.
44. John T. Noonan, Jr., "The Pope's Conscience," *C*, Feb. 17, 1967, 559–60.
45. Noonan, *Contraception*, 3.
46. John T. Noonan, Jr., *The Church and Contraception: The Issues at Stake* (New York: Paulist/Deus Books, 1967), 7.
47. Ibid., 9.

that a dam of accumulated tensions broke. *Humanae Vitae* reasserted the old teaching, prohibited Catholics from using any artificial contraceptives, approved the rhythm method only for "grave reasons," and praised the benefits of abstinence as a sign of "honest love." It all but ignored the commission's findings and implicitly turned aside Noonan's case for a developmental approach to the question. "The moment has not come," declared Pope Paul, "for man to entrust to his reason and his will, rather than to the biological rhythms of his organism, the task of regulating birth." Moreover, the proliferation of contraceptives might cause men to "lose respect for the woman and . . . come to the point of considering her as a mere instrument of selfish enjoyment."[48] The U.S. bishops at once acclaimed the new encyclical.[49] *Triumph*, too, was delighted to see the pope, after years of hesitation, make what it saw as a forceful reassertion of orthodoxy.[50] *National Review's* editors, on the other hand, were a great deal less impressed, maintaining that "this is one of those many papal statements the Church will come— fairly universally—to regret" and that it was unwise of the pope to have gone against "a reported eighty percent" of his own commission members. They saw the outcry that greeted *Humanae Vitae* as part of the general crisis of authority whose signs were everywhere in 1968 and noted that "if one of the most ancient and revered chairs of authority cannot maintain its power among its own, then what pillars will remain unshaken?"[51]

But if conservatives had mixed feelings, liberal and radical Catholics were dismayed. "To say that this is a bitter disappointment is an understatement," wrote *Commonweal*. "It will plunge whole sections of the Church into gloom."[52] The day after the publication of *Humanae Vitae* forty priests signed a protest to Cardinal Patrick O'Boyle of Washington, D.C. notifying him (and the national press) that they would not try to enforce conformity to the encyclical among their parishioners. Seventy-eight teachers of theology joined Charles Curran at Catholic University of American in declaring that the encyclical was invalid in its ecclesiology and "incompatible with the Church's authentic self-awareness as expressed at Vatican II." It showed an "inadequate awareness of the natural law" and an "overemphasis on the biological aspects of conjugal relations as ethically normative." Finally, it exhibited "an

48. Text of *Humanae Vitae, CM 66* (Sept. 1968): 35–48.
49. This ready assent itself annoyed liberal Catholics. See editorial, "Loyalty: To Whom?" *C,* Aug. 23, 1968, 548–49.
50. L. Brent Bozell, "*Humanae Vitae:* A Two-Part Assent to Its Law and Its Mystery," *T* 3 (Sept. 1968): 19–27.
51. Editorial, "The Encyclical," *NR,* Aug. 13, 1968, 786.
52. Editorial, "The Birth Control Encyclical," *C,* Aug. 9, 1968, 515–16.

almost total disregard for the dignity of millions of human beings brought into the world without the slightest possibility of being fed and educated decently." They added that it was not an infallible statement of the magisterium (taking exactly the line against *Humanae Vitae* for which many of them had criticized *National Review* conservatives in the *Mater et Magistra* affair seven years before) and that thoughtful Catholic couples should feel free to disregard it.[53] Over six hundred Catholic theology teachers from around the country signed this protest in the following weeks.

One curious sequel to this story is that prior to 1968, despite all their anguish over the issue, many (though by no means all) observant American Catholics appear to have obeyed the traditional restrictions on use of contraceptives. Once the encyclical was published, however, Catholics began to abandon the rhythm method in large numbers and to take advantage of more reliable systems of contraception, as if accepting the advice of the dissident theologians.[54] Uncertain confessors did little to enforce adherence to *Humanae Vitae*; neither did many of the bishops try to "hold the line" on the issue. Unlike Cardinal O'Boyle of Washington—one of the few who disciplined his recalcitrant priests, ultimately defrocking twenty-five of them—Cardinal Lawrence Shehan in the neighboring Baltimore diocese took only circumspect consensual action against complaining priests in his flock, and this was the more usual course.[55] U.S. Catholics after 1968, in other words, acted almost as though the pope had said what they had *hoped* he would say rather than what he had said in fact. "For the first time in Catholic history," noted one commentator, "the rank-and-file of the laity simply ignored one of their Church's pronouncements. They concluded that the pope and celibate clergy didn't know what they were talking about when it came to sex."[56] By the late 1970s, they used contraceptives with the same frequency as the general population; this was one more way in which they became assimilated, one more point of differentiation lost.

53. "The Theologians' Retort," *C*, Aug. 23, 1968, 553.

54. Andrew Greeley, *The American Catholic: A Social Portrait* (New York: Basic, 1977), 141–43. Greeley suggests that the widespread belief in an imminent change of teaching during the mid-1960s had encouraged some Catholic women who already used contraceptives to resume Communion, from which they had earlier lapsed. After 1968, he believes, "the partial alienation of Catholics from the institutional church seems to be almost entirely the result of the unresponsiveness of the church's sexual teaching, particularly as demonstrated by the encyclical letter *Humanae Vitae*" (143).

55. On the priests' conflict with O'Boyle, see Jay P. Dolan, *The American Catholic Experience: A History from Colonial Times to the Present* (Garden City, N.Y.: Doubleday, 1985), 435. On Shehan's conciliation, see Thomas W. Spalding, *The Premier See: A History of the Catholic Archdiocese of Baltimore, 1789–1989* (Baltimore: Johns Hopkins University Press, 1989), 463.

56. McLaughlin, *The Pill*, 191.

The question was closed neither by the encyclical nor by the mass disobedience to it. Innumerable articles, editorials, and "forums" in the Catholic press debated the issue in the following years, with defenders of *Humanae Vitae* generally forced onto the defensive by the overwhelming weight of procontraceptive popular opinion.[57] True to form, John Noonan broke the general mold of debate on the encyclical by making the astonishing claim that *Humanae Vitae,* properly understood, actually gave papal *approval* to contraception, appearances to the contrary notwithstanding. While liberal Catholics impatiently denounced the pope, Noonan, after a restrained expression of dismay, conservatively contradicted the pope with expressions of enthusiastic assent to his decree.[58] He noted that Paul VI, at the council and again in the encyclical, had specified two functions for conjugal intercourse, procreation and the strengthening of the marriage bond. They were not placed hierarchically, as they had been in earlier papal declarations, but rather stood coequal. Noonan reasoned that since we now knew about the safe period and since intercourse during it to strengthen the marriage bond was not sinful, there could be no violation of the teaching by Catholics who fortified the safety of the safe period with contraceptive pills. Contraception during the fertile period would indeed be sinful, he said, but from his study of recent obstetrical research Noonan concluded that the fertile period was limited to only three or four days every month. "It is clear," he said, that "not every act need be open to the transmission of life; and it is inferable that to preserve the sterility of times which are intrinsically sterile is unobjectionable. To secure such sterility is not to act against the divine design but to cooperate with it."[59]

There is plenty of evidence that the pope had had nothing of the kind in mind, and Noonan was rebutted by critics, notably Joseph

57. See, for example, the anti–*Humanae Vitae* symposium including Gregory Baum, J. C. Gerber, Daniel Callahan, and William Clancy, *C,* Aug. 23, 1968, 553–62; editorial (equivocating), "An Editorial Statement on Human Life," *A,* Aug. 17, 1968, 94–95; Bishop John R. Quinn "Birth Control and the Irrelevant Church," *A,* Sept. 7, 1968, 159–62; John Sheerin (also equivocal), "The Birth Control Encyclical," *CW* 208 (Oct. 1968): 2–3; Peter Riga (against), "Pope Paul's Encyclical on Birth Control," *CW* 208 (Dec. 1968): 107–11; and Anthony Padovano (for), "In Defense of the Encyclical," ibid., 112–16; Rev. Robert Kirtland (for), "Just One Minute, Father Curran," *CW* 208 (Jan. 1969): 151–54; Norbert J. Rigali, "Right, Duty, Dissent," *CW* 208 (Feb. 1969): 214–18.

58. Noonan's first published response to *Humanae Vitae* was "Historical Precedents for Fallible Statements," *NCR,* Aug. 7, 1968, 9: "With full reverence and allegiance to the teaching office it is not amiss to point out that the present encyclical suffers from both internal inconsistency and from inadequate preparation." Noonan here also complains about the "military secrecy" with which the document was prepared and issued.

59. John T. Noonan, Jr. "Natural Law, the Teaching of the Church, and the Regulation of the Rhythm of Human Fecundity," *American Journal of Jurisprudence* 25 (1980): 33.

Boyle, who accepted the plain intent of the encyclical, and Noonan's former Notre Dame colleague Charles Rice. Rice, who admired much of Noonan's other work, especially his opposition to abortion, was annoyed. "Instead of whining about the Church's stand on contraception and trying to weasel out of it, he ought to say, 'Serviam!'—I will serve—and devote his considerable talents to advancing the teachings of the Vicar of Christ."[60] Noonan's method of showing how to change while declaring no change seemed to Rice more dangerous than frank denunciations of *Humanae Vitae*. Noonan had become, in Rice's eyes, a "contraceptive" fifth columnist in the citadel of "life."[61]

Noonan's ingenious reinterpretation of *Humanae Vitae* can be compared to Garry Wills's *Politics and Catholic Freedom* (1964). Each was designed as a conservative attempt to reconcile the needs of American Catholics with papal encyclicals when the two appeared to be in conflict. Wills's approach was to study the history of the encyclical letters and to show that historically they had had none of the binding power of ex-cathedra definitions. His conclusion that encyclicals were advisory rather than mandatory exonerated Catholic conservatives who had dissented from the tenor of John XXIII's *Mater et Magistra*. Noonan's technique was to gain leverage not against the encyclical itself but against the ambiguities of history and language it offered. Both men, however, aimed to preserve the forms, avoid antagonizing the church, and yet adapt its teachings to contemporary conditions.

Noonan's work at the beginning of the 1970s was undergoing a shift. Still sympathetic to the basic natural law position, he was increasingly aware of how it could be shaped and distorted in differing hands, aware too that in the last resort it has to be decided rather than simply discovered. He began to place a new emphasis on legal personalism as a complementary principle to natural law, following a marked trend in twentieth-century Catholic intellectual life of shifting attention away from argument by syllogism and abstraction and toward the exigencies of historical, personal life.[62] In this move he was strongly influenced

60. Joseph Boyle, "Human Actions, Natural Rhythms, and Contraception: A Response to Noonan," *American Journal of Jurisprudence* 26 (1981): 32–46; Charles Rice, "Reducing *Humanae Vitae* to a Symbolic Gesture," *Wanderer*, May 21, 1981, 1–6.

61. Telephone interview with Charles Rice, March 3, 1991.

62. "I saw the term [natural law] was fluid and misleading for many people. What was meant as an ecumenical bridge often turned out to be a barrier. Instead of Christians and Jews being brought together by the natural law, they were divided by it; so on the whole I've gotten away from using the term in later writing and found thought focused on the person much more attractive and more likely to be persuasive. While I accept as reality certain things given in nature including human beings and their orientation towards God, I don't like to reason so much from other natural-law assumptions any more." Noonan interview, June 10, 1985.

by the work of neo-Thomist philosophers Etienne Gilson, Gabriel Marcel, and Jacques Maritain, for whom "person" connoted the spiritual qualities that distinguish human beings from animals. Noonan's series of Oliver Wendell Holmes memorial lectures, given at Harvard in 1972 and published as *Persons and Masks of the Law* (1976), urged lawyers to abandon positivistic and pseudoscientific models of jurisprudence, to get rid of all evolutionary metaphors in thinking about legal change, and to remember that their function was to aid flesh-and-blood persons to resolve their conflicts humanely and with an eye to future harmony. Law schools, he believed, should "contribute to the moral education essential to the professional preparation of lawyers, who are to be formed less as social engineers than as the charitable creators of values." Lawyers must respond to persons, not the "masks of the law," and must do so through a reverence for historical and religious experience.[63] The historical scholarship that underlay all Noonan's legal and religious judgments bore witness to this faith; most Christian reviewers received *Persons and Masks* warmly, but secular law journal reviewers were baffled and dismayed by his spiritual incursions into their science.[64]

One aspect of Noonan's personalism was a continuing insistence, in the face of what he saw as the advancing secularization of society, that the entire civil and legal tradition of the United States presupposed God's providence. "The authority of the courts as oracles of justice, the sovereignty of government as a power ordained by God, the sanctity of the human person as created in the image of God—all these vital presuppositions of our system of law—have religious roots; all express mythic-moral perceptions."[65] If these religious underpinnings were swept away, he believed, the legal system would become an arena of self-advancement for litigants rather than—as he preferred to regard it—a zone of human reconciliation in the light of divine truth. What the law should do, he added, endorsing the views of his Notre Dame colleague Robert Rodes, was "to put man in a posture conducive to a deeper encounter with God."[66]

63. John T. Noonan, *Persons and Masks of the Law* (New York: Farrar, Straus, and Giroux, 1976), xi, 160.

64. See, for example, John T. Banon (in favor), untitled review, *American Journal of Jurisprudence* 22 (1977): 199–202; and Ronald Nehring (against), untitled review, *Journal of Contemporary Law* 4 (1977): 14–18; and (against) unsigned, untitled review, *Harvard Law Review* 91 (1978): 1114–16.

65. John T. Noonan, Jr., "The Family and the Supreme Court," *Catholic University Law Review* 23 (1973): 255.

66. John T. Noonan, Jr., untitled review of Robert Rodes, *The Legal Enterprise*, in *American Journal of Jurisprudence* 22 (1977): 190–91.

Noonan's twin fascinations with law and Christian love—themes long joined in the institution of marriage—came together in another encyclopedic historical study, *Power to Dissolve: Lawyers and Marriages in the Courts of the Roman Curia* (1970). In retrospect it can be seen as part of Noonan's intellectual defense of a family-based legal system at a time when, to his dismay, it was rapidly being supplanted by an individual-rights approach.[67] He accorded the Vatican annulment court a measure of praise for its treatment of many nettlesome marriage cases, but after a lengthy analysis illustrated by six case histories, he faulted it for gradually taking on a legalistic rather than personalistic view of its task. "Setting out to defend a symbol of love," he concluded, the Vatican marriage lawyers "made the commonest of human mistakes, to have forgotten the purposes of their endeavor."[68] The court's nit-picking legalism was responsible for the growing cynicism with which it had been viewed, until in the twentieth century it became almost a byword for the corruptibility of Vatican bureaucracy. The story illustrated the need, in church and civil law, for an ethos that kept personal realities in clear sight, not the abstractions of "blind justice."[69]

As Noonan's work in these years showed, sex, like law, was for Catholic conservatives an encounter with God as well as between persons. It is important to keep in mind that Catholics who took seriously the traditional church teaching on these questions had a distinctive view of what sex itself really is. The particular circumstances in which an act of sexual intercourse took place, they believed, had a profound bearing upon its meaning, depending on whether it strengthened or violated the familial bond. Intercourse between a husband and wife they conceived of as different from intercourse between any other two persons. The physical actions might the same same, but the natural law context was quite different. Catholic conservatives saw marital intercourse as an affirmation of the sacrament of marriage. Michael Novak, who during the early 1970s was retreating from radicalism, described this sacramental character of sex: "The human body is the dwelling place of God, and the joining of a man's and a woman's body in matrimony is a privileged form of union with God. The relationship is *not* merely that of a mechanical linking, putting genitals here or there. It is a metaphor for (and an enactment of) God's union with mankind. Marital intercourse thus re-enacts the basic act of creation.

---

67. John T. Noonan, Jr. *Power to Dissolve: Lawyers and Marriages in the Courts of the Roman Curia* (Cambridge: Belknap Press of Harvard University Press, 1972). See also, from this period, Noonan, "Family and Supreme Court."

68. Noonan, *Persons and Masks*, 398.

69. On the history of the Curia's bad reputation, see Noonan, Preface to *Power to Dissolve*, xii.

It celebrates the future."[70] Sex for pleasure outside of marriage, by contrast, violated this sacramental union and so perverted a divine gift. It violated both the natural law orientation of sex toward procreation and the natural law ordinance of marriage itself.

The Catholic contraceptive controversy of the 1960s was prelude to a larger storm over abortion, which became in many ways the most contested and divisive U.S. political issue of the 1970s. During the early 1960s, as contraceptives became commonplace and as the last legal obstacles to their dissemination were swept away, a handful of doctors and politicians began to raise questions about ambiguities in antiabortion laws. Most states permitted abortion if the mother's life would be threatened by allowing her pregnancy to continue. Dramatic improvements in obstetrics, such as the perfection of delivery by Caesarian section, in the first half of the twentieth century had greatly reduced the number of such cases. As a result some doctors, construing the statutes strictly, believed abortions were becoming less necessary and would soon be a thing of the past. Others, broad constructionists, took into consideration economic and emotional questions as well as immediate threats to life and remained willing to grant abortions to petitioners with such claims. In response to this interpretive ambiguity in the early 1960s the American Law Institute wrote a model statute whose aim was to forestall possible prosecution of "broad constructionist" doctors who performed abortions. Meanwhile, pregnant women who did not want to bring their pregnancies to term but could not claim life-threatening circumstances, turned to illegal abortionists. The number of illegal abortions and abortionists is a source of controversy; reliable statistical evidence is, inevitably, hard to procure. It is noteworthy, however, that the issue of traumatic illegal abortions began to appear in novels of the 1960s, such as John Updike's *Couples* and Joan Didion's *Play It as It Lays*.[71]

Several new circumstances in the 1960s turned abortion from an obscure medical and legal issue into one with pressing public repercussions. The first incident was the Sherri Finkbine case. Finkbine, an Arizona housewife and mother of four, was pregnant with a fifth child when her husband, a national guardsman, went to Germany as part of the Cuban missile crisis mobilization in 1962. He brought back some sleeping pills for his wife. After taking them for a time she learned that

---

70. Michael Novak, "Men without Women," *HLR* 5 (Winter 1979): 64.

71. On the historical background to abortion reform, see Kristin Luker, *Abortion and the Politics of Motherhood* (Berkeley: University of California Press, 1984), 54–91. For fictional portrayals of illegal abortion in the 1960s, see John Updike, *Couples* (New York: Knopf, 1968); Joan Didion, *Play It as It Lays* (New York: Farrar, Straus, and Giroux, 1970).

they contained the drug Thalidomide, which was then being linked to severe birth defects in European children. Her doctor, in consultation with the local board that reviewed possible abortion cases, agreed that birth defects were likely and arranged for her to have an abortion in a local hospital a few days later. Awaiting the abortion, she told a sympathetic friend who worked for the local newspaper what had happened. The paper published the story, and a storm of protest broke over Finkbine's head. She received death threats; her house was picketed; and she was accused of murder. Finkbine received police protection, but the hospital backed off in alarm, and she was finally able to get an abortion only by flying to Sweden.[72] The case demonstrated the existence of a large, latent, but vigorous antiabortion conviction among the population. Two years later an epidemic of rubella, which was then (wrongly) believed to cause fetal deformities, again raised the issue of whether abortions should be licit in such cases and helped catalyze further discussion and controversy.[73]

A second factor that turned the issue into a public controversy was the rise of the feminist movement. At first concerned principally with jobs, equal protection of the law, and personal fulfillment, American feminists soon came to focus on questions of "sexual politics." It seemed to many of them unjust that boards of doctors, generally men, should sit in judgment over women seeking abortions and some feminists now made the previously unheard claim that they had a right to abortions without regard to the circumstances by which they had become pregnant. To advance their case they produced stories and statistics to illustrate their belief that there was a huge traffic in illegal abortions and that maltreatment at the hands of abortionists led to a high death rate among reluctantly pregnant women. Since women would have abortions one way or another, said these advocates, let them have safe abortions. At early proabortion demonstrations, some women parodied the Catholic antiabortion position by carrying posters with the assertion: "If men could get pregnant, abortion would be a sacrament."[74]

The Finkbine case and the new feminism combined with widespread fears of overpopulation to bring abortion into political debate from the mid-1960s. When Daniel Callahan edited *The American Population Debate* (1971) most of his contributors assumed that both contraception and abortion were necessary instruments of population control, dif-

72. Luker, *Abortion*, 62–65.

73. Ibid., 80–81.

74. Ibid., 96–97. See also John D'Emilio and Estelle Freedman, *Intimate Matters: A History of Sexuality in America* (New York: Harper and Row, 1988), 314–15.

fering with one another chiefly on the question of whether governments should require these measures of fertility restriction or simply permit them.[75]

In response to these new circumstances, several states in the late 1960s began to reform their abortion laws, clarifying and sometimes broadening the circumstances under which abortions could be performed. None went so far as to grant the radical feminist position of abortion on demand, however, and in the two states that held referendums on the question, Michigan and North Dakota, abortion law liberalization was defeated.[76] Even the circumscribed new state laws were sufficient to draw howls of protest from Catholic traditionalists; this was the chief issue that led *Triumph* to "declare war" on America and brought the Sons of Thunder out into the streets for the first antiabortion "action," at the George Washington University clinic in 1970.

In 1970 John Noonan edited and contributed to a collection of essays on the emerging abortion controversy. Again using the historical-developmental approach, he described protection against abortion as "an almost absolute value in history." Noonan began with the assertion that life begins at the moment of conception and that, accordingly, abortion kills a person. This view was strongly rooted in Catholic teaching, but Noonan argued that it could and should be made on purely secular and scientific grounds. Neither the sperm nor the egg alone can become a human being, he said, but once they have joined, a new and unique human being is fully genetically encoded. No further genetic input is required for this individual to grow to human adulthood. Conception, therefore, provides the one clear moment of objective discontinuity between mere biological tissue, on the one hand, and a human life, on the other. It also represents an immense jump in probabilities. It would be difficult to describe as human life any one of the thousands of a woman's eggs, or any one of the billions of a man's sperm, whose chances of fertility were infinitesimally small, but a fertilized egg stands about four chances in five of developing successfully to a live birth. Noonan observed that none of the other suggested dividing lines for defining life (birth, viability, etc.) had the same scientifically verifiable distinctiveness.[77] Not surprisingly, he denied that when life begins is simply a metaphysical question about which indi-

75. Edgar Chasteen, "The Case for Compulsory Birth Control," in *American Population Debate*, ed. Callahan, 274–78. On voluntary methods, see Arthur Dyck, "Population Policies and Ethical Acceptability," ibid., 351–77.

76. Luker, *Abortion*, 66–91. On Michigan and North Dakota referendums, see Noonan, *Private Choice*, 34.

77. John T. Noonan, "An Almost Absolute Value in History," in *The Morality of Abortion*, ed. Noonan (Cambridge: Harvard University Press, 1970), 55–57.

viduals must make personal chocies.[78] He regarded prochoice claims that government confirmation of his view would establish a religious principle in law and so breach the First Amendment "wall of separation" as an anti-Catholic canard.[79]

In another essay, written with his colleague David Louisell, Noonan showed that in the preceding decades the legal protections afforded the fetus had been getting steadily stronger in the United States. Courts had found that a fetus could be awarded damages, even in the event of a subsequent miscarriage, could be the beneficiary of a trust fund before birth, and had standing as a litigant in court on its own account. In a 1965 case from Washington, D.C., a court had ordered a pregnant Jehovah's Witness to permit an intrauterine blood transfusion to her unborn baby, whose life was threatened, even though the mother's religion forbade transfusions. In that case, Noonan and Louisell noted, the life and rights of the baby had been taken to override even the mother's prized First Amendment right to the free exercise of her religion, suggestive testimony to the court's conviction that the fetus was a person deserving the protection of the law.[80] Other scholars, such as the three Catholic members of the New York State Commission on Abortion, noticed that the United Nations General Assembly, in its "Declaration on the Rights of the Child" (1959) had specified "legal protection before as well as after birth" and that the state of Wisconsin in 1960 had defined an unborn child as "a human being from the time of conception until it is born alive."[81] All the precedents, these Catholic scholars concluded, pointed toward strengthening fetal rights rather than broadening abortion rights.

As the issue heated up, *National Review* conservatives began to work out a more consistent position on the issue than they had hitherto espoused. They were finding it difficult under a Republican president to preserve the same intensity with which they had opposed the Democratic administrations of Kennedy and Johnson. As James McFadden, one of the *National Review* editors, recalled later: "They didn't want to hate Nixon (although eventually a lot of them did)." Nevertheless, they did find other issues on which to take a stand, and abortion

---

78. Ibid., 53.

79. Noonan interview, June 20, 1985.

80. David Louisell and John T. Noonan, "Constitutional Balance," in *Morality of Abortion*, ed. Noonan, 220–44.

81. Quoted in Robert Drinan, S.J., "Reflections on the New York Commission on Abortion," *CW* 207 (Sep. 1968): 261–63. Drinan, then dean of Boston College Law School, subsequently became a Democratic congressman from Massachusetts, the only Jesuit to serve in Congress, where he favored liberal policies on most questions but remained doggedly antiabortion.

was one freighted with intense passion.[82] They had looked solemnly at the population question in 1965 and taken it very seriously; now they decided that they had been misled, that claims of an overpopulation crisis were spurious, at least in the United States, and that the issue was being manipulated to justify relaxing abortion laws. "More nonsense is currently being talked on the subject of population than on any other subject," they declared in 1967. The U.S. birth rate in 1966 had been the lowest on record, and "in the developed countries there is no case to be made for enforced contraception."[83] John Noonan argued at a conference on reproductive freedom that population theorists' notion of an "optimal population" for a nation was a myth and that their "apocalyptic threats bear the familiar marks of religious parody."[84] Charles Rice, author of *The Vanishing Right to Live* (1969), said that the overpopulation issue was "a fraud from beginning to end," noted with staisfaction that one by one all of Paul Ehrlich's doom-laden prophecies were being proved false, and pointed out that the case of Europe showed no correlation between high population density and imminent starvation.[85] Never to be outdone on such a question, *Triumph* echoed that the population explosion had been mythical from the start: "So many millions have been spent over the last decade to advance the myth that most men seem convinced of its truth, and seek rescue in a veritable sea of estrogen and vaginal foam."[86]

Unlike the many Catholic converts in the conservative movement, Rice was a "cradle" Catholic, proud of his lifelong orthodoxy. He had been raised in Queens, New York, in a middle-class Catholic environment, which he remembered as a "very cohesive" community where "the parish was the center of all activities," a source of pride and identity rather than a constricting "ghetto." He enjoyed his education in parochial schools, at Holy Cross College in Worcester, Massachusetts, and at Boston College Law School. Like many midcentury Catholic patriots he did military service, two years of active duty in the Marine Corps (1956–1958) followed by twenty-four years in the Marine Reserves, rising to the rank of lieutenant colonel. After gaining a doctorate at New York University (his first and only non-Catholic school)

---

82. Interview with James McFadden, New York City, Oct. 12, 1987.

83. Editorial, "The Population Firecracker," *NR*, Oct. 7, 1967, 999. See also Colin Clark, "World Power and Population," *NR*, May 20, 1969, 481; editorial, "The Politics of Population," *NR*, Oct. 6, 1970, 1040.

84. John T. Noonan, "Freedom to Reproduce: Cautionary History, Present Invasions, Future Assurance," New York University Conference, 1970, unpublished typed transcript in Boalt Hall Library, University of California, Berkeley.

85. Rice, *Vanishing Right*, 112–15; Rice interview.

86. Editorial, "The Myth Exploded," *T* 6 (Feb. 1971): 45.

with a dissertation on the First Amendment, Rice accepted a law professorship at Fordham University, "where," as he later recalled, "the priests took the vow of poverty and the laity lived it."[87] He assisted Bert Daiker, one of the principal lawyers in the *Engel v. Vitale* school prayer case and, when his side lost, wrote *The Supreme Court and Public Prayer*, a scathing attack on the court's method and a brief against secularization and moral relativism.[88] He said of his own first book, *Freedom of Association*, that it put even him, the author, to sleep.[89] Thereafter all his books were to be enlivened by polemical anger and fervent support for traditional Catholic morality. Meanwhile he served as vice-chairman of the New York State Conservative party throughout the 1960s, years in which it ran William Buckley in a colorful but unsuccessful bid for New York City's mayoralty and then his brother James Buckley in a successful campaign for the U.S. Senate.[90]

At Fordham, in the office adjoining his own, Rice met Robert Byrn, one of the first Catholic scholars to oppose changes in U.S. abortion laws, and under Byrn's influence Rice gradually became more preoccupied with the rising issues of contraception and abortion. In *The Vanishing Right to Live* (1969) he argued that the right to life is threatened by artificial insemination, abortion, contraception, euthanasia, homosexuality, and the abolition of the death penalty for murder.[91] All these trends eroded the moral and legal status of the family as basic unit of society. Whereas many commentators favored abortion in cases of fetal deformity, as in the Sherri Finkbine case, these seemed to Rice especially evil reasons for an abortion: "To kill defective children in the womb . . . is no different on principle from the Nazi 'final solution to the Jewish problem.'"[92] Only when people recovered their knowledge of God's authority would they once again govern themselves according to natural law rather than according to hedonistic principles that violated nature itself. Rice was one of few Catholic conservatives to argue that contraception should be illicit not merely for his coreligionists but

87. This passage is based on Rice interview.
88. Charles Rice, *The Supreme Court and Public Prayer* (New York: Fordham University Press, 1964).
89. Rice interview. The book is *Freedom of Association* (New York: New York University Press, 1962).
90. On William Buckley's campaign for mayor of New York, see his *Unmaking of a Mayor* (1966; New York: Bantam, 1967). On James Buckley's Senate campaign (1970), see John Judis, *William F. Buckley, Jr., Patron Saint of the Conservatives* (New York: Simon and Schuster, 1988), 312–16.
91. Each is the subject of a chapter in Rice, *Vanishing Right*.
92. Rice, *Vanishing Right*, 8.

for all Americans; in 1969 he wanted the anticontraception laws restored in the name of family integrity.[93]

From Fordham, Rice moved in 1969 to Notre Dame Law School and became coeditor, with Robert Rodes, of the law journal. This publication, the *Natural Law Forum*, had hitherto been the almost exclusive preserve of Catholic scholars. John Noonan and others on the editorial board wanted to broaden its appeal to non-Catholics interested in theoretical aspects of the law, and soon after Rice arrived, against his own vote, the board changed its name to the *American Journal of Jurisprudence*.[94] This was an era in which the explicitly Catholic provenance of some other journals was being muted with comparable name changes, one aspect of the "melting" of Catholic scholars into the general academic environment.[95] As the abortion law reform movement began to gain prominence, Rice emerged as a die-hard, no-compromise prolifer and joined the editors of *Triumph* in trying to prevent liberalization of the laws. Their love of dramatic gestures and their sense of burning urgency soon clashed with the Catholic church's more methodical antiabortion bureaucracy, leading Rice and Bozell into direct conflict with the church when they tried to organize a National Right to Life Congress in 1971 without ecclesiastical backing.[96] Rice, despite this and other disappointments over the direction of the nation and the church, retained his patriotic devotion to God and country, and he never endorsed Bozell and Lawrence when they abandoned patriotism altogether.

In March 1971 Rice, together with *Triumph*'s Society for a Christian Commonwealth, created an ecumenical antiabortion organization, Americans United for Life, a "non-sectarian, educational organization of persons who affirm the sacredness of all human life from conception to natural death." The group planned "to gather and disseminate evidence of the calamitous effects of abortion, not only on the unborn child, but on the mother, the father, the family, the community, and society at large."[97] Prominent Protestant professors George Huntston Williams and Arthur Dyck from Harvard Divinity School and Jewish

93. Ibid., 134.

94. Noonan interview, June 24, 1985; Rice interview.

95. The phenomenon is explored in Philip Gleason, "The Crisis of Americanization," in *Catholicism in America*, ed. Gleason (New York: Harper and Row, 1970), 133–53. For the parallel example of the *American Catholic Sociological Review*'s changing its name to *Sociological Analysis*, see 141.

96. Bozell, circular letter, March 12, 1971, Private papers of Charles Rice, Notre Dame, copies in author's possession by courtesy of Rice. See also "A Catholic Abortion," an exchange of letters between Bozell and Father James McHugh of the Family Life Division of the U.S. Catholic Conference, *T* 6 (April 1971): 7–12.

97. Americans United for Life, "Declaration of Purpose," Aug. 15, 1971, Rice papers.

law professor Victor Rosenblum (from Northwestern University) joined, but the critical mass was Catholic. The movie star Loretta Young served as honorary chair. Almost at once AUL ran into trouble because the *Triumph* Catholics who had brought it into being wanted to take a maximalist position against contraception, zero-population growth, and abortion in all circumstances, whereas many of the other members favored confining their opposition to the one issue of abortion on demand.[98] Indeed, George Williams, elected chairman of AUL in 1971, favored abortion in cases of rape and incest, statutory rape, and fetal deformity; Rice and Bozell were totally opposed in all these cases.[99]

Within a year, therefore, AUL had severed its ties with the Society for a Christian Commonwealth and Rice had resigned from the board, observing that although Americans United for Life could "attract wide support by limiting itself primarily to the abortion issue," it was not rigorous enough for his convictions. It would work better and do much good, he added, without "the burden of having to pacify continually those on its board, such as myself," who wanted to attack on a broader front and who beleived that there should be no exceptions whatsoever to the antiabortion position.[100] Rice however told Bozell, who had angered many of the AUL founders with a hectoring four-page letter against what he saw as their halfheartedness, that "there should be absolutely no rock-throwing" between conservative Catholics such as themselves, and others who opposed abortion.[101]

Catholic lay conservatives were split down the middle on how to respond to the issues of contraception and abortion. Some, including John Noonan, Michael Novak, and William Buckley, believed contraceptives should be made easily available to married couples, especially non-Catholics, and should be legitimated by the Catholic church. With reliable contraceptives sufficiently widespread, they believed, unexpected pregnancies would become less common, and women's temptation to avail themselves of abortions would diminish.[102] By contrast, James McFadden, Brent and Patricia Bozell, Charles Rice, Michael Lawrence, and others believed that the only logical position was to oppose both abortion and contraception. McFadden explained that a couple having sex, if they decided to use a contraceptive, were already turning their backs on God's gift of life. If, nevertheless, the woman

98. Arthur Dyck to Board Members of AUL, Jan. 26, 1972, Rice papers.

99. Rice to George Williams, Feb. 10, 1972, Rice papers.

100. Rice to Germain Grisez, March 27, 1972, Rice papers.

101. Rice to Bozell, March 15, 1972, Rice papers.

102. Interviews with William F. Buckley, Jr., New York City, Jan. 9, 1986; Michael Novak, Washington, D.C., April 9, 1985; and Noonan, June 10, 1985.

became pregnant, she would feel inclined to have an abortion because she had wanted sex while wanting not to have a child: she had already made the crucial choice to separate sex from procreation. "Contraception," said McFadden, "is the John the Baptist to the Antichrist of abortion."[103]

Despite this disagreement, Catholic conservatives from both sides of it dedicated themselves to opposing abortion in the first years of the 1970s. William Buckley, from the procontraception side, noted with dismay that liberalized abortion laws were passing with little concerted Catholic opposition, though ten years previously even the threat of opposition would have been sufficient to prevent their enactment. This change was symbolic, Buckley believed, of the ruinous costs of aggiornamento: "The Catholic Church threw away fish on Friday, liturgical Latin, tough rules for the priests and nuns, and for its pains got emptier and emptier churches. When the time came to rally protests against permissive abortion laws, the troops were simply not there. . . . Whereas ten years ago the furor against abortion would have imperiled the political life of almost any state legislator, now they go mostly unscathed."[104] Germain Grisez, Catholic professor of philosohy at Georgetown University, from the anticontraception side, published the most comprehensive study of abortion to date, *Abortion: The Myths, the Realities, and the Arguments* (1970), as a response to the legal, ethical, and medical changes taking place around him and as a plea to stop the legal trend toward permissiveness. Among his findings were that those most likely to have abortions were white, college-educated, unreligious women who used contraceptives.[105] Thus, Grisez initiated a tactic that was to become commonplace among antiabortion activists in the coming years, narrowing down the sociological profile of persons who advocated and availed themselves of abortions. It was a way of insisting that the prochoice position—though heavily overrepresented in the middle-class media and the government "new class"—was a special interest at variance with the public interest. Grisez endorsed natural law absolutes on "life" questions and tackled even the thorny issue of pregnancy resulting from rape, seeing it as an opportunity for creative self-sacrifice:

> A woman who has been raped can simply reject any possible child by viewing it as the extension of the attacker and his brutal deed. But she might also consider the child as an opportunity to extend

103. McFadden interview.
104. William F. Buckley, Jr., "Catholics and Abortion," *NR*, Dec. 15, 1970, 1366–67.
105. Grisez, *Abortion*, 52–53.

her own selfhood in a unique way. By forgiveness, generosity, and gentleness she can overcome violence, whereas abortion would only compound the violence done to her by violence to another who has also sprung—although unwillingly—from herself.[106]

Triumph, Grisez, Buckley, and the Americans United for Life, were squabbling on a cliff edge, but when they finally went over it, the chasm was even deeper than they had expected.

The really bad news on abortion, from their point of view, came in 1973 when the Supreme Court amazed all parties to the controversy with its decisions in *Roe v. Wade* and *Doe v. Bolton*. Abortion during the first trimester of a pregnancy, said the Court, was a right, an aspect of the constitutional right to privacy which it had enunciated the previous year in *Eisenstadt v. Baird* (1972). Justice William Brennan had written in that decision: "if the right of privacy means anything it is the right of the *individual*, married or single, to be free from unwarranted governmental intrusion into matters so fundamentally affecting a person as the decision whether to bear or beget a child." Antiabortion advocates were horrified both by the decision itself and by the increasing salience it gave to individual rather than familial rights. Even prochoice advocates were surprised at the sweeping scope of *Roe v. Wade*, which, in effect, endorsed much of the radical feminist position.[107] Equally surprising, in the aftermath of *Roe* the number of legal abortions performed each year in the United States rose rapidly, soon approaching one million.[108] To those, Catholic conservatives included, who believed that an abortion is the killing of a child it now seemed that the United States was legally sanctioning the extermination of a million or more children every year. No wonder they were quick to make comparisons with Hitler's extermination of the Jews. Hitler's criterion had been race: America's criterion was age.[109]

For a moment it seemed that the abortion decision might restore a measure of unity to a fragmented U.S. Catholicism, if only the unity of opposition. The editors of *America* deplored the decision, which put them in mind of the *Dred Scott* case of 1857, by which legal personhood had been denied to a large group of Americans because of their race.

106. Ibid., 295.
107. Marian Faux, *Roe v. Wade: The Untold Story of the Landmark Supreme Court Decision That Made Abortion Legal* (New York: Macmillan, 1988). On its citation of *Eisenstadt*, see 152.
108. The Centers for Disease Control reported 988,267 abortions in 1976, or 312 abortions for every 1,000 live births, an 18 percent increase over 1975. See *Catholic Almanac, 1980* (Huntington, Ind.: Our Sunday Visitor, 1980), 93.
109. Noonan, *Private Choice*, 14, 18; Charles Rice, *Beyond Abortion: The Theory and Practice of the Secular State* (Chicago: Franciscan Herald Press, 1979), 10–13.

The Civil War and the Fourteenth Amendment had been needed to reverse it, they noted. Now, ironically, a privacy doctrine derived from the Fourteenth Amendment had been used to deny personhood to another category of Americans, the unborn.[110] Robert Byrn, Charles Rice's former colleague, argued that with this decision the Supreme Court had severed the long-standing U.S. support for the traditional Judeo-Christian reverence for life.[111] *Commonweal* condemned the Court's decision as unconscionable, violative of precedent, and inhumane, as did the overwhelming majority of the diocesan press and other journals.[112]

By 1973, however, intra-Catholic tensions were too deeply rooted to permit lasting unity even against abortion. Some Catholic intellectuals, even though they did not favor abortion, reproached Catholic newspapers for what seemed to them an excessively shrill response—"sheer sensationalism"—to the *Roe* decision: "Catholics must have a better answer than a simple, unrealistic 'never,'" cautioned Charles Whelan, and he poured cold water over the idea of constitutional amendments to reverse the Court.[113] *America's* editors, despite their opposition, also said they planned to "respect the court's decision," while others, such as Jeffrey Hart, were simply unable to work up much interest in the issue, not feeling any certainty that life begins at the moment of conception.[114] *Triumph* applied the epithet "collaborators" to Catholics who did not at once protest the Court decision, among them Charles Curran, Congressman Robert Drinan, S.J., and Mary Daly. These were "hard core remnants of the 'Catholic Liberals,' the men and women who will stop at nothing to maintain solidarity with the American dream of two cars in every garage and an emptiness in every womb."[115]

Triumph acknowledged *Roe* v. *Wade* with a black-covered edition (March 1973), inside pages edged in black, and a sixteen-page insert, "America's War on Life" printed on gray paper with a fetus and crossbones logo atop each page. The United States, it said, had now declared itself a murderous nation, and Catholics should have "no hesitation about conforming their conduct to the norms of a higher

110. Editorial, "Supreme Court on Abortion," *A*, Feb. 3, 1973, 81.
111. Robert Byrn, "Goodbye to the Judeo-Christian Era in Law," *A*, June 2, 1973, 511–14.
112. Editorial, "The Abortion Decision," *C*, Feb. 16, 1973, 435–36.
113. Charles Whelan, "Of Many Things," *A*, Feb. 10, 1973, ii. Even more caustic against the tone of most Catholic media was S. J. Adamo. See his "Hot Rhetoric," *A*, April 21, 1973, 375–77 and letters denouncing his approach from Joseph Brieg and Kathleen Maher in *A*, April 21, 1973, 505.
114. Editorial, "Supreme Court on Abortion," *A*, Feb. 3, 1973, 81; letter from Keneth O'Loane, critical of this "respect," *A*, March 10, 1973, 201; Interview with Jeffrey Hart, Feb. 29, 1988, Dartmouth, N.H.
115. Editorial, "The Collaborators," *T* 8 (April 1973): 6–7.

law than the civil law. . . . law and order can no longer be a slogan for Catholics."[116] In the mid-1960s, as we saw earlier, William Buckley had equably accepted that some non-Catholics favored abortion. No longer. He too was horrified by *Roe v. Wade* and began to polemicize bitterly against it. *National Review* said that the decision marked "the death of pluralism," that John Courtney Murray's faith in collectively held American "truths" was now destroyed, and that "the abortion decision cannot but have a fragmenting and weakening effect on American society" since it was bound to alienate Catholics, orthodox Jews, and many others opposed to abortion.[117]

John Noonan too was dismayed. His careful drawing of distinctions, which he favored in the question of contraception, made way for a sweeping condemnation of abortion. From being an almost cloistered academic before 1973 Noonan now became an antiabortion polemicist and activist, writing biting legal, religious, and medical critiques of abortion and its consequences and giving speeches on the issue throughout the land. Noonan was one of many Catholic conservatives to become engrossed in the opposition to abortion. Robert Byrn, Robert Destro, Charles Rice, and Basile Uddo—all lawyers—complemented Noonan by elaborating arguments against the jurisprudential basis of *Roe v. Wade* and working out the possibilities of constitutional amendments and legislative strategies to reverse or vitiate the decision.[118] For these purposes, alliance with evangelical Protestants was essential, and readily embraced. Protestants who had led the anti-Catholic charge against the Kennedy candidacy in 1960 were eagerly cooperating with Catholic prolifers by the mid-1970s.[119]

The growing volume of antiabortion literature needed a clearinghouse and found it in 1975 with the *Human Life Review*, the brainchild of James P. McFadden.[120] Son of a Catholic farmer and a Lutheran mother, McFadden was the youngest of seven children, all raised within the church by parental agreement at the time of the marriage. He had served in military intelligence after World War II, and wit-

116. Editorial, "The Catholic Obligation," *T* 8 (March 1973): 31.

117. Editorial, "The Death of Pluralism," *NR*, Feb. 16, 1973, 193–94.

118. Destro was a professor of law at Marquette Law School. See his "Abortion and the Constitution: The Need for a Life-Protective Amendment," *HLR* 2 (Fall 1976): 30–108; and "Religion: Establishment, Free Exercise, and Abortion," in *New Perspectives on Human Abortion,* ed. Dennis J. Horan and David Mall (Frederick, Md.: University Publications of America, 1981), 237–48; Basile Uddo (professor of law at Loyola of New Orleans), "When Judges Wink, Congress Must Not Blink," *HLR* 5 (Summer 1979): 42–60.

119. On Protestant-Catholic collaboration, see J. Gordon Melton, "The Historical Context of the Contemporary Abortion Debate," in *The Churches Speak on Abortion* (Detroit: Gale, 1989), xxv.

120. The following section is based in part on McFadden interview.

nessing the division of Europe and the Soviet grip on the eastern side had made him an ardent anti-Communist. In 1956 after a chance meeting with William Buckley, McFadden became business manager of *National Review,* where he worked for the next nineteen years, lukewarm about capitalism but passionate about the Catholicism and the tradition the journal represented to him. A dedicated admirer of Buckley, McFadden called him *"the* Catholic layman in America" and credited him with reversing the massive trend toward welfare liberalism which, McFadden said, had characterized American history between the beginning of the New Deal and the election of Ronald Reagan. McFadden had never been impressed by the "population explosion" scare. "My wife was pregnant eight times in the nine years [between 1960 and 1969]" he said in an interview; "so I wasn't really busy opposing the population revolution at that period!"

McFadden combined the old Catholic passion for God and country which the 1960s had done so much to wear away, and although he sympathized with Brent Bozell and *Triumph* as a venture, he, like Charles Rice, deplored the antipatriotic turn it took at the end of the 1960s. "Brent's a saint . . . a Don Quixote type . . . a leader with the Sons of Thunder and the Carlists. It's delightful if it's not serious, but if it's serious it's disastrous." McFadden's feet stayed firmly on the ground of traditional loyalties. "The Church isn't perfect, but if Christendom is going to go down, the only thing I can do is dig my trench in front of Saint Peter's and fight, and be overwhelmed. God brings good out of evil, but I can't. The same is true of America; I have to fight for my country. If I'm wrong and it's going down the tubes, that doesn't make any difference."

Many Americans still remember the exact circumstances in which they learned of the death of John Kennedy. For McFadden, learning of the abortion decision on January 23, 1973, had a comparable impact. He was vacationing on Buckley's boat on the Florida coast when he read of the *Roe* v. *Wade* decision in the *New York Times.* It was, he told me fifteen years later, his "road to Damascus," the moment of realization that this was *his* issue, and he must become completely devoted to it. Leaving Florida at once, he headed back to New York to create the first of many antiabortion committees to rise in the wake of *Roe* v. *Wade,* the Ad Hoc Committee in Defense of Life. Two years later, after extensive canvassing and organizational work in which from long experience he had become very adept, he launched the first issue of the *Human Life Review,* which, along with *Lifeletter* and *Catholic Eye* (other McFadden productions) has since become the literary center of the antiabortion movement. Published quarterly by the Human Life Foundation in the format of a scholarly journal, it emanated from the same New York office building as *National Review* and retained intimate links with this parent journal. Heavily Catholic in flavor, it nevertheless featured new articles by Jewish and Protestant antiabortionists and specialized in reprinting materials from ephemeral media (newspaper columns, speeches, etc.) for preservation in this permanent record. It also reprinted relevant articles from diverse journals, bringing them together in a concentrated prolife setting.[121]

Its interests, after the first few issues, were not solely confined to the question of abortion. The *Human Life Review* also worried about the beginnings of advocacy for legalized euthanasia and about gains made in recognition of and legal protection for homosexuals since the dawn of gay militancy in the 1969 Stonewall Riot.[122] McFadden, with a broad base of financial contributors, sent out hundreds of copies of each issue to members of Congress, state governors and legislators, Catholic bishops, the pope, and other influential people in government, media, and church. "Hundreds of copies are bound in leather and they are in President Reagan's library, they're in many congressional libraries, they're in the Pope's library, and so on," said McFadden, adding, "The idea of the *HLR* is to make it look important. That's the idea of the stodgy appearance. . . . I am competing not just for people's time but to get them interested in something that's distasteful, that is deep, difficult."[123]

Unlike John Noonan and many other antiabortion activists, McFadden did not really favor a constitutional amendment prohibiting abortion because he anticipated that it would be unworkable and would bring the enforcement agencies into disrepute, as had Prohibition in the 1920s. "I'm certainly not unrealistic or dumb enough to argue that there *is* a consensus or that if you pass a prohibition of abortion amendment that it would work. That's heresy to the hard line right-to-lifers and when I say that they go bananas." In the meantime, however, he was willing to offer provisional support to amendment proposals because "anything that enlarges the warfare tends towards [the] goal" of making the status quo unworkable, forcing the political system to "cough the issue up." His preferred solution was to hand the issue

121. Representative non-Catholic views were Harold O. J. Brown, "Protestants and the Abortion Issue," *HLR* 2 (Fall 1976): 131–39; Rabbi Seymour Siegal, "A Jewish View," ibid., 140–43.

122. On euthanasia, see Joseph Sobran "The Right to Die, I" *HLR* 2 (Spring 1976): 27–32; and Everett Koop, "The Right to Die, II," ibid., 33–58. On gay rights, see Joseph Sobran, "Bogus Sex: Reflections on Homosexual Claims," *HLR* 3 (Fall 1977): 97–105; and Novak, "Men without Women," 61–67.

123. McFadden interview.

back to the states for individual adjudication, even if it "gets back to the way gambling used to be, [that] you'll be able to go to Las Vegas and have [an abortion]."[124]

McFadden had no illusions about the difficulty of the task he confronted, noting that abortion would not stop until American attitudes toward sexuality were radically transformed (he saw no immediate prospect that they would) and until women who had not planned to become pregnant nevertheless learned to cherish the babies they would have. Meanwhile, he thought, "you can't wipe [abortion] out, but make it hard!" Just as he believed pornography should be illegal, shaming as well as endangering those who trafficked in it, so should abortion be illegal once again. "Some people would suffer, yes, but some people always suffer," whatever the legal arrangements, and in this instance the suffering would have positive consequences for the public morality. A self-confessed defender of chivalry toward women, he saw feminism as an attempt to deny deep-seated differences for ideological reasons and had no patience with the proposed Equal Rights Amendment ("I would qualify as a pretty good exmaple of what [feminists] would call a 'male chauvinist pig'"). "No society that is going to survive is going to have women in combat positions in its army, fire department, police department. . . . Feminism is part of the symbolic decline of our civilization."[125]

One of the most regular contributors to the *Human Life Review* was Joseph Sobran, part of a new generation of Catholic conservative intellectuals. Born in 1946 and a convert to Catholicism during his teens, Sobran became an editor of *National Review* in 1973, then started a newspaper column for the *Los Angeles Times* syndicate, contributing meanwhile to almost every issue of McFadden's journal. Sobran's bruising polemical talents made him valuable to the antiabortion movement. He took up Germain Grisez's tactic of narrowing the opposition, depicting those who favored abortion rights as a callous, sinister minority with undue influence in media and government, hoodwinkers of the general public, enemies of civilization and Christianity. In a time-honored rhetorical move, echoing Buckley's claim twenty years previously that he would rather be governed by the first two thousand names in the Boston telephone directory than by the faculty of Harvard University, because the ordinary folk respect common sense and God's law, Sobran depicted the prolife movement as representative of ordinary

124. Ibid.
125. Ibid.

American opinion, over against an unpatriotic, irreligious, cynical, liberal elite.[126]

Sobran reasoned from natural law premises and, like Michael Novak, regarded sex in light of its relational significance. "The use of the word 'sex' to refer to an activity rather than to a gender," he wrote in one instance, is "fairly novel. It is even used to refer to genital activities between members of the same gender. This implies the conception of such activities as ends in themselves with procreation a mere possible by-product." In other words homosexual acts might not warrant the name of sex at all. The relational aspect rather than the act itself was what mattered; sex was as much a spiritual as a physical activity.[127] Sobran and fellow Catholic conservatives differed on whether criminal sanctions should be imposed on homosexuals, but they agreed that such acts should be made socially odious.[128] Sobran, arguing against gay rights, continued to believe what by the 1970s was the largely discarded theory that homosexuality was a psychological disorder, a form of infantile regression. He said he was willing to treat homosexuals sympathetically to the extent that their condition was involuntary, but he wanted them to be counseled against succumbing to temptation and acting upon their inclinations. It would, he believed, be "a victory of humanity to undo the damage of the gay rights movement by persuading its members, without humiliating them, that they need not pretend their vice is a virtue in order to belong to the moral community. To put it another way, homosexuals should be encouraged to realize that homosexuality is unworthy of them."[129] As in the struggle against abortion, Sobran found himself powerless to stem the tide, and gay rights gained increasing recognition and legal protection.

Sobran recognized the importance of seizing the high moral ground on the abortion issue and related "human life questions," and like all participants in the abortion debate, he angled his rhetoric in such a

126. Joseph Sobran, "Abortion, Rhetoric, and Cultural War," *HLR* 1 (Winter 1975): 88–98; Sobran, "The Abortion Sect," *HLR* 1 (Fall 1975): 101–8; Sobran, "The Abortion Ethos," *HLR* 3 (Winter 1977): 14–21. On the telephone directory, see Buckley, "A Reply to Robert Hutchins," in Buckley, *Rumbles Left and Right* (New York: Putnam, 1963), 134–35.

127. Joseph Sobran, "In Loco Parentis," *HLR* 5 (Fall 1979): 14.

128. When the New York legislature debated a gay rights bill in 1974, *National Review* editorialized against it as an attack on the moral integrity of the Western tradition. It noted that the language of the New York bill, "reflecting the avowed goals of various gay liberation organizations, would make homosexuality merely another life-style in the eyes of the law, and would break down social resistance to it and stigmatize such resistance as 'bigotry.'" Editorial, "Gay Rights," *NR*, July 19, 1974, 635–36.

129. Sobran, "Bogus Sex," 105. On the changing medical/psychological definition of homosexuality, see John D'Emilio, *Sexual Politics, Sexual Communities: The Making of a Homosexual Minority in the United States, 1940–1970* (Chicago: University of Chicago Press, 1983), 140–44.

way as to elevate his own side and abase the opposition. Opponents of *Roe* v. *Wade* described themselves as "prolife" and their opponents as "proabortion," whereas those who favored the *Roe* precedent called themselves "prochoice" and their opponents "antichoice." Prolifers spoke of "the mother," "the baby," and "killing children," while prochoicers spoke of "the woman," "the fetus," and "terminating a pregnancy." There is no need to doubt the sincerity of either group or to be surprised at their manipulation of language to boost their own position; like many of the great conflicts in history, this was a clash less between an obvious right and a dire wrong (though the contestants all saw it that way) than a conflict between two sets of rights, differently perceived and applied. It could be resolved perhaps only with agreement on the question of when life begins and how it should be valued—metaphysical problems on which a nationwide consensus was lacking.

Women as well as men worked for the *Human Life Review*, and they introduced a distinctive approach to the abortion question. Clare Boothe Luce, a convert to Catholicism in 1946, was one. She had supported the Equal Rights Amendment since its first introduction to Congress in 1923. Now, she brought a note of feminist asperity to the abortion issue, about which she was undecided when it first began to win wide media attention in the early 1970s. "Like so many of the books which learned men have written about 'women's problems,'" she wrote of Noonan's first antiabortion anthology, "this is really a book about the problem men are having with other men who refuse to see the 'woman's problem' as they do. . . . not a single woman lawyer or moralist is quoted on a subject which is a uniquely female experience."[130] In the early 1970s she resolved her uncertainties in favor of a clear prolife position, and after *Roe* v. *Wade*, she decided that making a united stand against abortion was more important than criticizing gender bias within the debate. In 1978 she withdrew her support for the Equal Rights Amendment (after more than half a century of advocating it), remarking that it was now likely to fail and that "a large part of the blame must fall on those misguided feminists who have tried to make the extraneous issue of unrestricted and federally-funded abortions the centerpiece of the equal rights struggle."[131] The amendment did indeed fail; after meteoric successes in the early 1970s, it was brought to a halt partly by the lobbying efforts of women in StopERA,

130. Clare Boothe Luce, "Two Books on Abortion and the Questions They Raise," *NR*, Jan. 12, 1971, 27.
131. Clare Boothe Luce, "A Letter to the Women's Lobby," *HLR* 4 (Spring 1978): 5.

Phyllis Schlafly's traditionalist alliance of Protestant and Catholic religious women.[132]

Clare Boothe Luce was convinced that the purpose of feminism was to fulfill women's nature, not to contradict it, and yet abortion, she believed, would do exactly that. Natural law and divine law were the foundations on which the American constitution had been built, and an amendment that violated those laws was doomed. "Nature made man to be the inseminator, woman to be the childbearer. . . . It is natural—and normal—for the woman who conceives to carry her child in her womb to term, to give birth to her, and her mate's, baby. . . . It is not the nature of women to abort their progeny. . . . Induced abortions are against the nature of women."[133] Another antiabortion activist, Janet Smith, agreed that it was against nature itself for women to seek abortions. "Behind women's demands for unlimited access to abortion lies a profound displeasure with the way in which a woman's body works and hence a rejection of the value of being a woman." Childbirth, she pointed out, had never been safer, the demand for children to adopt was growing all the time, and only a pernicious ideological aversion to the vocation of motherhood could have motivated the feminist advocates of abortion.[134]

Among Catholic women Ellen Wilson was one of the most prolific writers against abortion.[135] Wilson, born in 1956, had grown up in a Catholic family in Yonkers, New York. Halfway through her Sisters of Charity grade school the impact of Vatican II reached Catholic schools, and Wilson recalled the "staggering speed" with which, from being in a "completely pre-Vatican II environment," she found herself in a "completely post-Vatican II environment," with "mini-skirted nuns, liturgies in which we read the work of radicals instead of the gospels," guitar music at mass, and a sudden reluctance among religion teachers to advance dogmatic positions. "My parish had a couple of associate priests while I was in my teens, who would go down . . . to mass with the Berrigan brothers, then come back and be 'inspired.' I remember vividly one sermon in which the associate called the congregation racists for sending their children to parochial schools, because they were doing so in order to avoid having their children mingle with blacks and Puerto Ricans in the public schools. I simply couldn't imagine why

132. On Schlafly and StopERA, see Carol Felsenthal, *Phyllis Schlafly: The Sweetheart of the Silent Majority* (Garden City, N.Y.: Doubleday, 1981).

133. Luce, "Letter to the Women's Lobby," 7.

134. Janet Smith, "Abortion as a Feminist Concern," *HLR* 4 (Summer 1978): 62–76.

135. The following passage is based in part on a telephone interview with Ellen Wilson, March 11, 1991.

they were running the school if they thought it was simply a dumping ground for the children of racists." At age thirteen Ellen Wilson discovered the work of William Buckley, read it extensively, followed up his allusions to such writers as G. K. Chesterton and C. S. Lewis, subscribed to *National Review*, and grew up as part of the second generation of new conservatives. She decided against Catholic college not because it promised to be too strict and repressive, as of old, but because she foresaw a weak and feeble religious education there. Her teenage rebellion took the form of a sharp move toward orthodoxy and conservatism. As Peter Berger has observed, in the pluralistic America of the 1970s orthodoxy itself had become just one more of the dozens of choices one could make, rather than a broad and certain way from which it took an act of daring to deviate.[136] Ellen Wilson, in effect, deviated into orthodoxy.

Wilson, a talented polemicist with a populist touch, fired her first salvos against abortion and against the fallout of the sexual revolution before graduating from Bryn Mawr in 1977, and she carried on through early adulthood, working first for the *Human Life Review* and then rising as a journalist to the position of book reviews editor at the *Wall Street Journal* before the age of thirty.[137] "Ellen," said James McFadden, "combines feminism with a very sharp intelligence. She managed to meld modernity into traditionalism and Catholicism. She's not a tough dame but a nice girl."[138] Wilson herself denied these claims by her old boss that she was in any way a feminist, arguing that in "all those areas where feminism has had the most influence we see the most severe problems facing society." She had in mind divorce, the suffering of children in broken homes, and liberalized abortion laws. Like Sobran, Wilson criticized prochoice advocates for refusing to face up to the fact of killing children, and like Patricia Bozell and the other women who wrote for the antiabortion cause she emphasized that having an abortion was an act not of self-assertion but of self-hatred or self-repudiation. Indeed, after marrying in the mid-1980s she gave up her career in journalism to devote herself to motherhood. The experience of marriage intensified her conviction that the issues of abortion and contraception were linked, that the only logically tenable position was to oppose both, and that natural family-planning methods were as reli-

---

136. Peter Berger, *The Heretical Imperative: Contemporary Possibilities of Religious Affirmation* (Garden City, N.Y.: Doubleday, 1979).

137. Her first appearance in McFadden's journal was Ellen Wilson, "Young and Gay in Academe," *HLR* 3 (Fall 1977): 90–96.

138. McFadden interview.

able, if used conscientiously, as artificial contraceptives, while exhibiting none of the medical and moral dangers.[139]

Wilson, like Sobran, was equally opposed to the developing gay rights movement, which she criticized in the language of natural law, and in one characteristic passage she explained why homosexuals, deviants from natural law, were prone to radicalism in other respects:

> Homosexuals cannot propagate by means of homosexual liaisons; since homosexual unions are barren, in the literal sense, they are antithetical to family life. Thus militant homosexuals are spared the strong, sentimental attachment toward the family which poses a hurdle of greater or lesser proportions to many social revolutionaries. In other words, homosexuals who campaign for universal acknowledgment of their normality are likely to be social revolutionaries in all areas, since their definition of normality dethrones the family from its sovereign position as the foundation of society.[140]

Wilson was also aware that feminist pressure for women's careers and equality tended to weaken the bonds of monogamous marriage, turning it from a sacramental bond into something more like an association and steadily degrading the status and self-esteem of women who were "only" housewives. By 1980 she was depicting a society at war with itself in the most fundamental area of gender relations and reproduction.[141]

Antiabortion Catholic intellectuals worked mightily at their assigned task between the *Roe v. Wade* decision in 1973 and the election of President Reagan in 1980 but were able to make little headway. *Triumph* went out of business in 1975 after nine years of limping along on a shoestring. After 1976 Congressman Henry Hyde and others were able to challenge federal funding of abortion-related programs, but legalized abortion remained intact; no congressional laws, state laws, or constitutional amendment had managed to limit it.[142] Many pro-choice women felt so certain of having won a once-and-for-all victory that (to the alarm of feminist organizers) they began to neglect further advocacy to protect their newly acquired right.[143]

In 1979, as what for conservative Catholics had been a disheartening

---

139. Wilson interview.

140. Wilson, "Young and Gay in Academe," 95.

141. See in particular Ellen Wilson, "The Ineluctable Happy Ending," *HLR* 4 (Spring 1978): 33–39; Wilson, "Mother Didn't Know," *HLR* 4 (Fall 1978): 25–33.

142. On the unsuccessful Hyde amendment to the Constitution, see Basile Uddo, "Victory, at a Snail's Pace," *HLR* 6 (Fall 1980): 27–38; Faux, *Roe v. Wade,* 319–20.

143. Faux, *Roe v. Wade,* 323–24.

decade drew to a close, John Noonan published the single most powerful and concentrated antiabortion statement to date, *A Private Choice:
Abortion in America in the 1970s*. Fruit of a decade's thought and activism, it made the strongest possible arguments, legal, medical, historical, and philosophical, against abortion, and it remains the best guide
to the antiabortion armamentarium. The title was meant ironically, for
as Noonan pointed out, the ostensibly private choice of an abortion
had large public consequences. It involved doctors, nurses, congressmen, and taxpayers; it split political parties, led to Orwellian perver-
sions of language, turned doctors from caring for two patients to caring
for only one, making them killers as well as healers; and it threw the
tradition of constitutional law into jeopardy by abandoning venerated
legal traditions of defending human life. In a daring rhetorical move,
Noonan surrendered a favorite term from the American lexicon, "liberty," by using it pejoratively. The extension of the "abortion liberty,"
as he used it, brought to mind negative visions of libertinism and
libertarianism rather than Patrick Henry's "Give me liberty or give me
death." Indeed, this was a case where, as Noonan saw it, one person's
liberty was another person's death. He cited cases, notably the grue-
some *Edelin* case of 1975, when an aborted fetus of seven months was
born alive but permitted to die, exposing the doctor in the case to a
conviction for manslaughter but exonerating him on appeal. "In ideological terms the case was a great victory for the pro-abortion party.
The frontier of the liberty—liberty to commit infanticide—had almost
been reached."[144]

Noonan explained and amplified the analogy with slavery, which,
along with nazism, was a favorite of prolifers. In 1857 in *Dred Scott* v.
Sanford, he noted, the Supreme Court had seized the right to declare
who in the eyes of the law was a person and who was not. Now, in
Roe v. *Wade*, the Court had done it again, and these two cases became
the most shameful in U.S. legal history, arbitrarily hacking away the
legal personhood of entire categories of people (13–14). Sympathetic
to the proposed Hyde amendment to the budget to prevent federal
funding of abortions, Noonan compared opposition to abortion funding with opposition to the notorious Fugitive Slave Act of 1850, by
which even opponents of slavery in the North had been forced to
cooperate in it by recapturing runaways and sending them back to the
South. To pay taxes the government then used to fund abortions, said
Noonan, would be to ask citizens who believed abortion was the killing
of children nevertheless to pay for it (84).

144. Noonan, *Private Choice*, 136.

Noonan closed by advocating a constitutional amendment, and he helped to draft such an amendment during the late 1970s and another in the early 1980s, despite his awareness of the technical and political difficulties involved in enacting them (178–86). Of all his arguments, the most sustained was that he was not arguing from a religious position and that one did not have to be a Catholic to share his views. Like all the Catholic conservatives he had to show reasons beyond his religion why ideas derived from it should be enacted into law. "Christian opposition to genocide, urban air raids, and the Vietnam war," he pointed out, were not inadmissible in American public debate merely because Christians happened to hold them. Wherever the ideas came from, American citizens held them and, as citizens, were equally entitled to voice them (53).

In trying to establish the objective, scientific personhood of a fertilized egg, however, it is possible to see how Noonan's philosophical personalism was rebounding against him. In his arguments against Catholic teaching on contraception he had urged a diminution of the biological and a privileging of the existential and personalistic approach to life. He was now faced with a situation in which large numbers of Americans, nearly all those who favored "choice" in the abortion debate, did not believe that a fertilized egg was a person. For him to tell them that they were simply flat wrong and to fall back on a genetic definition represented a backward step according to his own earlier development.

Noonan's colleague and rival Charles Rice published *Beyond Abortion: The Theory and Practice of the Secular State* in the same year as *A Private Choice*. Rice, though he admired *Persons and Masks of the Law*, had not followed Noonan's reasoning on *Humanae Vitae* and had not made the move to philosophical personalism.[145] Therefore he was able to argue on classic Catholic natural law lines against abortion and the "contraceptive mentality" from which it grew. Like Noonan, however, Rice was a fierce critic of legal positivism, the philosophy that the positive law is not backed by any natural law, that "the principle of utility is the sole rationale for legislation." Positivism, said Rice, using the overworked argument *ad hitlerum*, "was totally dominant during the Hitler years from 1933 to 1945" and was becoming dominant in contemporary America. By contrast, claimed Rice, in terms strongly reminiscent of Ross Hoffman and John Courtney Murray, the Constitution was based on natural law, with clear roots in the Aristotelian-Thomist tradition. The natural law embodied in U.S. law, he believed, had

145. Rice interview.

flourished well into the twentieth century but then had come under attack. "In *Roe* v. *Wade* probably the clearest example of triumphal positivism in American law, the Supreme Court said it need not decide whether the unborn child is a human being" because it had decided that the fetus was a legal nonperson. Although Rice had always believed the antiabortion case could be made on purely secular grounds, he now thought the deterioration of public morality had reached a point from which only national rededication to God would save it. He proposed a constitutional amendment declaring that "this nation is in fact under God who has created all human beings and endowed them with unalienable rights" and that "nothing in this constitution shall prevent the United States or any state from affirming this fact."[146]

The election of 1980 seemed a propitious moment to Rice, even though he never expected his God amendment to be adopted. Catholic conservatives hoped for a sexual counterrevolution when Ronald Reagan won the election that year. They anticipated a pattern of profamily legislation, an antiabortion constitutional amendment, and a stronger traditionalist representation on the federal bench. Evangelical Protestants, who entered conservative electoral politics in a coordinated way for the election of 1980, shared many of these proreligion and profamily interests. In the event, both groups were disappointed. The American conservative movement championed not only traditional values but also free-market capitalism, and the "Reagan Revolution," such as it was, dealt chiefly in economic issues. Workable "family" policies would have necessitated new bureaucracies—one of the targets of the Reagan campaign—and seemed likely to prove costly and unworkable, while prochoice advocates had made plain that they would violate antiabortion laws, if it came to the point, in large numbers.

Catholic conservative intellectuals made an energetic case against the sexual license of their age—against homosexuality, against abortion, and against the diminishing legal privileges of the family vis-à-vis the individual—but were unable to translate their ideas, even on this narrow range of subjects, into policy. The tensions within the conservative movement account for some of their disappointments; tensions within the Catholic church account for others. The case against homosexuality and abortion rested on arguments from natural law, but Buckley, Noonan, Novak, and other Catholic conservatives argued against the traditional natural law teaching as it applied to contraception. In doing so, they gave further evidence of the protean

146. Rice, *Beyond Abortion*, 9–13, 49, 71.

rather than rocklike character of natural law, that natural law has to be decided rather than discovered. They showed none of the traditional Catholic deference to church guidance in deciding it. U.S. Catholic unity had been shattered in the 1960s over Vatican II, contraception, the vernacular, the Vietnam War, and questions of discipline. The church showed itself unable to repair the damage and regain its old unity in the 1970s even when most Catholics agreed that abortion was a terrible wrong. The church had lost the veto power it formerly possessed over such matters as film censorship and access to contraceptives. By the time U.S. Catholic bishops decided, at the opening of the 1980s, to investigate a major public policy issue, nuclear weapons, they had lost the ability to wield any appreciable political clout.

6

A Tale of Two Exiles: John Lukacs and Thomas Molnar

This chapter and the next deviate from the chronological development observed up to this point to take a closer look at two pairs of Catholic lay intellectuals: first John Lukacs and Thomas Molnar, second Garry Wills and Michael Novak. My aim in these two chapters is to show how the convictions of four prolific and independent-minded conservatives diverged in the post–World War II era. The events of the mercurial 1960s in particular had a decisive effect on all four men, but all, despite their differences, remained detached from and critical of American liberalism, its faith in science, and its secularization, which they held responsible for the nation's social and political woes.

John Lukacs and Thomas Molnar, as we have seen, grew up in Hungary and came of age during World War II, experiencing acute hardship. Lukacs endured aerial bombardment and life as a deserter and fugitive in the smoldering ruins of Budapest. Molnar spent several years as a slave laborer and was imprisoned at Dachau, the Nazi concentration camp, as the war neared its end. They emigrated to the United States from an Eastern Europe in which Nazi repression had been exchanged for Soviet repression.[1] Devotees of Western Christendom, they hoped that the United States and the Catholic church could be its new guardians. Thus, they lamented many trends in an

---

1. On Lukacs's war experiences and expatriation, see his *Confessions of an Original Sinner* (New York: Ticknor and Fields, 1990), 43–110. For Molnar's war experiences, see his "Last Days at Dachau," C, March 1, 1957, 169–72. This chapter is based in part on interviews with Lukacs, Nov. 8, 1990, Phoenixville, Pa., and Molnar by telephone, Jan. 15, 1991.

increasingly secular nation in the 1950s and 1960s and the diminishing spiritual contrast between the United States and its Soviet rival. They treated their adopted country as culturally provincial, an outpost of Europe. Spared the harrowing "education" of two world wars, Americans seemed to them at times optimistic to the point of utopianism, insufficiently aware of the world's grim realities.[2] Neither held his students in high esteem, seeing them rather as passive, deferential, and devoid of learning. "They are ignorant about the world at large and about the history of their entire culture," said Lukacs, in a remark either of them might have made.[3] Both men held the professoriat, to which they belonged, in even lower esteem and rarely had a kind word for American intellectual life. Lukacs saw in most American professors an "uneasy compound of optimism and pessimism, of naivete and despair," and a pervasive "lack of responsibility"; Molnar found in them a chronic "intellectual insecurity and poverty of imagination."[4]

Life in the United States did not fulfill the hopes with which Molnar and Lukacs had arrived. They gained little popularity and few disciples, remaining largely unknown beyond Catholic and conservative circles. Even among conservatives they ran into difficulties. Molnar's frank rejection of democracy after 1970 made him anathema to many indigenous conservatives, and he finally gave up the title of conservative altogether, declaring that he was, rather, an adherent of the European political Right or that politically he should be termed simply a Catholic.[5] Lukacs's annoyance with most American conservatives' willingness to defend libertarian capitalism also kept him at arm's length from the movement, and he distanced himself from "movement" conservatives by adopting the label of "reactionary," transforming an epithet into a badge of honor.[6]

Their unusual approaches to history, philosophy, politics, and the meaning of conservatism make Lukacs and Molnar important to this history even though they have not been widely influential. Despite their eccentricities they shared several of the principal convictions of the indigenous Catholic conservatives. First, they despised contemporary American liberalism, treating it as a thin and enervated outlook devoid of the transcendent principles that had succored Christian civi-

2. On the dangers of utopianism, see in particular Thomas Molnar, *The Two Faces of American Foreign Policy* (Indianapolis: Bobbs-Merrill, 1962), 10–11; and Molnar, *Utopia, the Perennial Heresy* (New York: Sheed and Ward, 1967). See also John Lukacs, *A History of the Cold War* (Garden City, N.Y.: Doubleday, 1961), 51–54.

3. Lukacs, *Confessions*, 213.

4. Ibid., 217; Thomas Molnar, *The Decline of the Intellectual* (Cleveland: Meridian, 1961), 261.

5. Molnar interview.

6. Lukacs, *Confessions*, 3–42.

lization through two millennia. Second, they hated communism, regarding Marxism as old-fashioned and mechanical in theory and
mendacious in practice. Third, they shared the elitist bent of the new
conservative movement, defended the principle of social and intellectual hierarchy, and criticized egalitarianism. Both saw great dangers to
society in the misuse of the instruments of publicity and mass communication around which American political life and elections were organized. Lukacs spoke for both when he said, "The cult of popularity is
the cult of cowardice. It reeks of the decay of the spirit."[7] Fourth,
American progressive education seemed to them both poorly organized and intellectually anemic. Raised under rigorous discipline and
exacting curricula in Hungary, they found U.S. postwar educational
orthodoxy weightless and trivial, incapable of preparing the next generation of leaders either intellectually or morally for the task of defending a venerable civilization.[8] And fifth, both believed that the U.S.
Catholic church, while potentially a rallying point for the West in the
great confrontations of the age, was in practice too willing to compromise and to accommodate to its secular surroundings. They thought
it was much too eager in the age of Vatican II to surrender its distinctiveness, forgetting the hard lessons of experience which it had learned
over the centuries.

Sharing these views with indigenous Catholic conservatives, Lukacs
and Molnar were involved in the conservative political and journalistic
revival of the 1950s and early 1960s. Both hoped that the United States
could preside over a rebirth and revivification of Europe.[9] Both saw
Alexis de Tocqueville as a prophet, a European aristocrat who had
found strengths as well as weaknesses in American democracy.[10] Both,
at first, had a guarded faith in democracy, despite their severe judgments of its character in the United States. Even when Molnar was
near despair in the late 1960s, he had to exempt the U.S. democracy,
"whose legitimacy the citizens take for granted," from his general denigration, for in few other nations was democracy "not a divisive but a

7. John Lukacs, "Light from the East," *NR*, Oct. 26, 1979, 1352.
8. For the critique of progressive education, see Molnar, *Decline of the Intellectual*, 117–56;
John Lukacs, *Outgrowing Democracy* (Garden City, N.Y.: Doubleday, 1984), 290–312.
9. See in particular John Lukacs, *The Decline and Rise of Europe: A Study in Recent History,
with Particular Emphasis on the Development of a European Consciousness* (Garden City, N.Y.: Doubleday, 1965); Lukacs, *1945: Year Zero* (Garden City, N.Y.: Doubleday, 1978); Thomas Molnar,
"Return to Europe," *C*, May 1, 1959, 126–28; Molnar, "Europe and Unity," *C*, Jan. 6, 1961,
384–87.
10. On Tocqueville, see Thomas Molnar, "Free in History," *NR*, March 28, 1959, 623–24;
John Lukacs, *Tocqueville: The European Revolution and Correspondence with Gobineau* (Garden City,
N.Y.: Doubleday, 1959); Lukacs, "De Tocqueville's Message for America," *American Heritage* 10
(June 1959): 99–102.

unifying principle." Along with the Catholic church, the United States seemed to him one of the last remaining ordered societies. "Our civilization will no doubt come to an end," he warned, "the day the Catholic Church and the US join the revolution."[11]

As time went on, however, it seemed Molnar's worst fears had been realized; he and Lukacs had become pessimistic about the United States by 1970, dismayed by what seemed to them its rubbishy popular culture, its militant secularism, its vulgar materialism, and its unwillingness to accept the simple realities of life. They were dismayed too by what they took to be the insubstantiality of political conservatives' responses to the crises of the age. In 1973 Molnar wrote despairingly that both the American and the Russian public ideals had become manifest falsehoods but that at least most Russians knew their official ideology was a lie. "The monstrous thing about the American lie is that it is believed. Washington, more than the Kremlin, rapes the *logos* of history by actually suggesting that the constitution of being was left on the 'other shore' and has lost its validity."[12] He now believed the nation, swept by urban riots, student uprisings, and a cynical politics of popularity, had fallen into the hands of a permanent revolutionary terror. Lukacs agreed that the American "New Man" had not been able to abolish the human condition or the reality of original sin, adding that the endemic violence of American life was undergirded by a moral degeneration that had become a form of "savagery," a legitimated savagery embodied in multilevel parking lots, the cult of motor vehicles, football, and rock and roll music.[13]

Lukacs and Molnar certainly did not speak with one voice despite these shared views and a common march toward disillusionment. They disagreed on key issues as each developed a distinctive, indeed idiosyncratic, view of the world in the 1960s and 1970s. Lukacs, first of all, was an Anglophile. Despite his strictures on democratic politics he found much to admire in the British and American political systems. He had praise for many secular politicians, among them Winston Churchill, Harold Nicolson, and George Kennan.[14] Molnar, by con-

---

11. Thomas Molnar, *The Counter-Revolution* (New York: Funk and Wagnall's, 1969), 200, 202.
12. Molnar, "America in History," *T* 8 (Jan. 1973): 23.
13. John Lukacs, "America's Malady Is Not Violence but Savagery," *C*, Nov. 15, 1968, 241–44.
14. On Anglophilia, see Lukacs, *Decline and Rise of Europe*, 236–39. On Kennan, see Lukacs, "The Making of a Geopolitician," *New Republic*, Oct. 28, 1967, 28–31. On Churchill, see Lukacs, "The Lingering Agony of a World in Dissolution," *C*, Jan. 1, 1954, 335–36. Of his friend Nicolson, Lukacs said: "For a while a man who influenced me, who was my idol in that he wrote English the way I *wanted* to write it, was Harold Nicolson" (Lukacs interview). By contrast Molnar saw George Kennan as the typical American liberal: "As a Western liberal brought up in the humanistic tradition, Kennan is really *annoyed* that in his own lifetime such subterranean forces as quasi-religious convictions and destructive ideologies [i.e., commu-

trast, was a Francophile and never got much purchase on the Anglo-Saxon political tradition, treating it with growing disdain as he aged. He revered such prophetic French Catholic intellectuals as Georges Bernanos and François Mauriac and found his political home among French right-wingers rather than any American party.[15]

Molnar was more dedicated than Lukacs to the defense of Catholic religion itself. Resisting the centrifugal pressures of U.S. Catholicism in the 1960s and 1970s and the new pluralism it championed, he tried to preserve the old principle of orthodoxy. In a series of philosophical and political studies in the years following Vatican II, Molnar defended church teaching on the nature of God, the theory of the state, and the history of heresy and wrote a book-length condemnation of the ecumenical movement. He traced society's contemporary woes back to the nominalist-realist dispute of the scholastic theologians and in the 1970s and 1980s could still work up genuine ire against William of Occam and Marsilius of Padua, influential nominalists who, he said, had initiated a still-unfolding civilizational catastrophe.[16] Lukacs rarely addressed theological issues directly, though he, like Molnar, lamented the excessive "Americanization" of his church in the 1950s and most of the changes wrought by Vatican II. "Many of Vatican II's outcomes," he wrote in 1970, "reflected an astonishing extent of psychological ineptitude on the part of its churchmen. They did not realize that by opening the windows they were letting in neon light rather than sunlight, gasoline fumes rather than fresh air, the din of publicity rather than the harmonies of nature."[17] His own works of history and historical theory never hinted at apologetics or defenses of the church, however. They showed more existentialist traces than natural law influences. Lukacs's Catholicism, like John Noonan's, demonstrated a basic natural law position greatly enriched by twentieth-century philosophical insights. He sometimes illustrated his writing with discussion of religous experiences but rarely raised the question of orthodoxy. When he did address Catholicism directly, it was often with political issues in mind. For example, he declared in 1979 that the Polish pope John Paul II, like Alexander Solzhenitsyn, had "come to America from

---

nism] have reappeared when the universal humanistic values ought to have extirpated them long ago." Thomas Molnar, "All Too Hasty Wisdom," *NR*, July 15, 1961, 20–21.

15. Molnar's first English-language book was *Bernanos: His Political Thought and Prophecy* (New York: Sheed and Ward, 1960). On Mauriac, see Molnar, "The American Experiment Through French Eyes," *C*, March 23, 1956, 635–38.

16. See, for example, Thomas Molnar, *Ecumenism or New Reformation?* (New York: Funk and Wagnall, 1968); Molnar, *God and the Knowledge of Reality* (New York: Basic, 1973), 19–22, 162; Molnar, *Politics and the State: The Catholic View* (Chicago: Franciscan Herald Press, 1980).

17. Lukacs, *The Passing of the Modern Age* (New York: Harper and Row, 1970), 159.

the East as a witness to certain truths" that the West had long neglected. This new pope, said Lukacs, was a fine antidote to the poisons
of bureaucracy and routinization which in the United States had "in-
fected, penetrated, and enveloped the Church."[18] He used the pope,
in other words, as a stick with which to beat the American church. In
his personal life, meanwhile, Lukacs was prepared to deviate from
church teaching to the extent of marrying a divorcée.

Molnar found the highest wisdom in the "moderate realism" of Saint
Thomas Aquinas.[19] Lukacs, however, had little to say about scholasticism; he preferred Saint Augustine and modeled the title of his own
autobiographical history after Augustine's *Confessions*. The contrast between Augustine and Aquinas mirrors the contrast between Lukacs
and Molnar. Lukacs, like Augustine, had a vivid, anecdotal, affective
style and wrote colorful tales of his misspent youth, sexual adventures
included; like Augustine, he believed his age was coming to an end,
and he tried to create a new way of understanding to fit new circumstances.[20] Molnar, like Aquinas, had a stiffer, didactic, style with fewer
rhetorical effects, and a rigorously analytical approach to issues. Far
from sharing Lukacs's view that the age was coming to an end, Molnar
saw such claims as characteristic fallacies of the contemporary intellect,
polemicized against them, and claimed that adherence to the old verities was as vital now as always. Revolutions could follow one after another but the nature of reality, the "constitution of being," remained
unchanged.[21]

Whereas both men were sharp-witted historians of ideas, Lukacs
believed that human beings play with, twist, and appropriate ideas to
suit their needs, but Molnar saw ideas as dense and forceful things
that seize human beings and change them. This difference sharply
distinguished them in the cold-war days: Molnar was a theoretical anti-
Communist who dreaded the ideology itself, while Lukacs was primarily anti-Russian, contemptuous of Communist ideology but dismayed
much more by what he thought of as the barbarian horde that had
overrun his homeland. Reviewing and praising Lukacs's *History of the
Cold War*, Molnar wrote that its comparative neglect of ideological communism "comes as a painful surprise to the author's friends, who
would never expect Mr. Lukacs, a disciple of Tocqueville, to underrate

18. Lukacs, "Light from the East," 1352.

19. See, for example, Molnar, *God and Knowledge*, 62, 156; Molnar, *Politics and the State*,
6–9, 24–31.

20. Lukacs describes his book about his own life, *Confessions of an Original Sinner*, as an
"auto-history," emphasizing external events and disdaining psychological self-scrutiny. On the
"end of an era" theme, recurrent in his work, see especially Lukacs, *Passing of the Modern Age*.

21. The durable constitution of being is the theme of Molnar's *God and Knowledge*.

the significance and power of ideologies, of Marxism." True, said Molnar, it was exasperating to deal with Americans who found "Communist conspirators under every bush," but this was no cause to belittle the Communist ideology, springing as it did from the dark side of the human spirit: "Let us agree that Marxism is a variant of the age old temptation of the mind to destroy the individual—free, incalculable, spontaneous—and erect the scientific anthill; that it is a heresy coeval with Adam."[22]

Lukacs never took Molnar's warning to heart. When he wrote of communism he treated it as an exhausted ideology that lacked the "radiance" U.S. democracy still possessed. He therefore lamented what seemed to him the rigid dogmatism of American anti-Communists during the 1950s; their inflexibility hindered compromise with the Soviet Union and thus postponed the de-Russification of Hungary.[23] To make matters worse, American Catholics were some of the worst offenders, and he upbraided them for it: "For an American Catholic to bask in the respectable knowledge of his anti-Communism in 1954 requires neither audacity, nor determination, sacrifice, noble charity, inner fortitude, courage, nor wisdom. It connotes rather a temper of easy self-satisfaction." Lukacs urged them to remember that falling in with the majority opinion, as most of them were more than willing to do at the height of the cold war, was no guarantee of righteousness. Often, in the twentieth century "majority principle and liberty" had been "mortal enemies," and the United States now showed ominous signs of establishing its own countertotalitarianism. Salvation would come from the Catholics who opposed it with the same fervor they opposed communism.[24]

Molnar and Lukacs remained on the fringes of the conservative movement, even while bringing a conservative and Catholic vision of human nature to their journalism and works of history and philosophy. They abhorred many aspects of the maturing political conservatism in the 1960s and 1970s, above all when it came to power with the election of President Reagan in 1980. Lukacs labeled himself a "reactionary" as a way of distancing himself from it, worked in local politics as a conservation-minded conservative (in his own words a "conservative Green"),[25] and despised the philistine capitalism of shopping malls

22. Thomas Molnar, "The Cold War without Communism," *NR*, April 22, 1961, 255–57.
23. Lukacs, *History of the Cold War*, 195–220, 275, 100–109.
24. John Lukacs, "The Totalitarian Temptation," *C*, Jan. 22, 1954, 397.
25. Lukacs interview.

and sprawling suburbs around his Pennsylvania home.[26] Molnar withdrew into concentration on theoretical issues in politics, religion, and philosophy, playing no further role in the practical political issues of the day.

JOHN LUKACS AND THE IDEA OF HISTORY

Lukacs was a notable stylist. His European education and fearsome wartime experiences lent an existential edge to his work as a historian, and although he was a college professor (at Chestnut Hill College, Philadelphia) he ignored many of the conventions of American academic history. His books were not monographs; they contained few reference or source notes but were dense with anecdotal footnotes, often drawing from incidents in his own life to illustrate general historical themes and shifting confidently from world political events to homely domestic analogies. Disdaining a sharp separation between the styles appropriate for history and fiction, he would use vivid, even poetic effects to substantiate an analytical point. Thus, haunting passages on his life in the rubble of Budapest set the mood and usher in the analytical sections of his books *Decline and Rise of Europe* and *1945: Year Zero*. The latter begins with a vignette of himself walking through the air-raid debris:

> In May 1945 the cities and towns of Central Europe stank with their corpses. One day this writer, thin as a rail and famished, was going up to the hills above his native city with a beautiful woman, to lie on a green meadow spangled with wildflowers. Like the landscape, she, too, was recovering; she had been violated by Russians but a few weeks before. Wending his way through the ruined streets, he bought a handful of apricots from a peasant woman for a handful of paper money. He had to wend his way between the enormous heaps of collapsed houses under some of which lay hundreds of bodies freshly dead. Their smell swam in his nostrils, as did the scent of the apricots and the flowers.[27]

Lukacs's religious sensibility, usually subordinate to the mundane, broke through in places, even in his most rigorously theoretical work,

---

26. On local politics, see Lukacs, *Confessions*, 286–91; on Reagan, see Lukacs, *Outgrowing Democracy*, 282–85; on shopping malls, see Lukacs, "It's Half-Way to 1984," *New York Times Magazine*, Jan. 2, 1966, 32.

27. Lukacs, *1945: Year Zero*, 8.

Historical Consciousness, as when he was illustrating his idea of the developing Western sense of historical self-awareness:

> One day in May 1963, driving down the country road not far from our house, I experienced a moment of great happiness. It was a glittering cool morning, full of green and gold, dappled with sunlight and the shimmering richness of fresh, wet, leafy trees. A moment later it occurred to me that while in another century someone touched by such a sense of happiness may have felt the need to exclaim his utter thankfulness to God for having created these leaves, these trees, this sun, I felt a deep gratitude to Him for having created *me,* that is, *my capacity* for perceiving and appreciating these trees, this sun: of allowing me to participate in this world, in this universe, in this way.[28]

This stylistic range was theoretically justified in Lukacs's frequent refrain that a historian's basic tool is words, that he or she must deploy them as artfully as possible, eschewing all claims to "scientific objectivity," that the historian's standpoint is subjective and participatory.[29]

It may well be that these assertions and his anomalous style kept Lukacs relatively uninfluential among American historians, who enjoyed a prolonged romance with the methods of the social sciences throughout the postwar decades.[30] Like Frederick Wilhelmsen in philosophy, Lukacs accepted little of the conventional wisdom of his discipline. *Historical Consciousness,* his most important book, denigrated the objective and scientific pose of many contemporary historians while advancing the idea that a unique historical awareness was the most distinctive attribute of the modern world. It became a cardinal point in Lukacs's historical method that "laws" of history could not be discovered, that any form of "scientific" schematization falsified the nature of history, its nonrepetitiveness and its quirky originality.[31] He elabo-

28. John Lukacs, *Historical Consciousness; or, The Remembered Past* (New York: Harper and Row, 1968), 233–34n.

29. See, for example, Lukacs, *History of the Cold War,* 11.

30. Lukacs was not entirely neglected. See, for example, the appreciative article by Philip Gleason, "John Lukacs on History and Twentieth-Century America," *CHR* 72 (Oct. 1986): 639–47; and Eugene Genovese, "Outgrowing Democracy," *Salmagundi* 67 (Summer 1985): 198–205. Genovese deplored the fact that Lukacs, because of his unorthodox convictions, had been turned into a "non-person" by historians and declared that Lukacs's *Historical Consciousness* should be assigned to all history graduate students. Lukacs recounts that he was overcome by a "black cloud of rage" when the journal *History and Theory* omitted *Historical Consciousness* from a comprehensive bibliography on historical theory in 1969. *Confessions,* 272.

31. "The brutal power of Spengler's imagination appealed to me; his suggestive capacity to make those astonishing connections of all kinds of matters or, rather, of symptoms; in sum, the achievement of a historian of cultures. Yet I found the Germanness of his categories,

rated on this conviction by criticizing the Cartesian and Newtonian scientists whose methods scientific history tried to emulate. In addition he tried to hedge in science, to nullify some of the larger claims made on its behalf, placing it within the more comprehensive embrace of history itself. Science, after all, he said, is a man-made affair, a series of experiments and statements desgined to explain connections between certain things in nature from a human vantage point. Science, properly understood, is inseparable from the history of science, and though such scientific approaches to the world as Newton's and Darwin's have been widely influential, each in turn has been shown to be the fruit of its time, limited rather than universal in application. What is more, he argued, the scientific master schemes have contributed little or nothing to human self-understanding, the proper object of learning; those who try to obscure the anthropocentrism of science have even discouraged self-knowledge.

Lukacs liked to say, contra scientific orthodoxy, that the sun really does rise in the morning and set in the evening, that it is *truer* for a person to say the sun moves round the earth than the converse, that is, to accept a subjective or existential standpoint and avoid the "objective" standpoint by which the earth can be said to move around the sun.[32] Or, contra Darwin, he would say that Lamarck had it right in the most significant case of evolution, that of human beings, when he argued that acquired characteristics can be inherited, as the example of accumulated historical knowledge passed down from one generation to the next demonstrates.[33] These examples raised the question of the meaning of truth, which Lukacs was willing to meet, again by treating science as a limited subset of history. He certainly did not mean to sink into the swamps of relativism in which truth was held to be purely contingent; indeed, he was a stickler for historical accuracy even while doubting that "facts" were the instruments by which truth is conveyed.[34] Facts connoted for Lukacs discrete pieces of information which scientific historians thought could be bolted together in the manufacture of truth.[35] Historical experience, he believed to the contrary, did not lend itself to such mechanical analogies; pieces of knowledge were no substitute for "understanding"—a term that possessed affective or even spiritual connotations in his conception.

of his schematic tables, his rapid dedication to systematizing, a kind of German idealistic determinism, repellent." Lukacs, *Confessions*, 302.

32. Lukacs interview.

33. Lukacs, *Outgrowing Democracy*, 137.

34. On accuracy, see Lukacs, "Tom Wolfe's Novel and Its Reception as a Significant Historical Event," *NOR* 55 (Sept. 1988): 6–12.

35. Lukacs, *Confessions*, 225.

Lukacs was influenced in these reflections by Werner Heisenberg's indeterminacy principle; indeed, he befriended Heisenberg, a fellow Catholic, and ensured that he had correctly construed the epistemological significance of indeterminacy theory.[36] Many theoretical scientists since Heisenberg, he observed, had recognized that there is no apodictic scientific certitude; its illusion had been generated only by imperfect experimental and conceptual approaches. They had also accepted that the ideal of objectivity is illusory; the experiment modifies the behavior of matter even in physics, and the observer is a crucial contributor to, and determinant of, the observations made.[37] Olympian science was in retreat; even mathematics, once thought to be incontrovertible in its absolute truthfulness, had been relativized by a master mathematician, Kurt Godel, in the 1930s, thus catching up with the much older insight of a nonscientist, Goethe, who asked, "What is there exact in mathematics except its own exactitude?"[38] In the same way, Lukacs argued, crystalline theories and an Olympian standpoint are of only limited usefulness in history and soon break down under detailed scrutiny. This was a point on which Thomas Molnar, also eager to trim back scientists' and social scientists' pretensions, concurred with Lukacs. Citing Thomas Kuhn's momentous *Structure of Scientific Revolutions*, whose shadow overhung all debates of this nature in the 1960s and 1970s, Molnar observed: "We now know enough of the history of science to declare that scientific world-views for the most part cannot claim 'truth-value'; they are new perspectives obtained by a shift of various factors, previously regarded as incontrovertible expressions of the *real*."[39]

In view of Heisenberg's work, Lukacs argued, physics and the other sciences had to face "the breakdown of the mechanical concept of causality." Physicists, in other words, were now realizing in their discipline what at least a handful of historians already knew in theirs, that "the necessarily narrow logic of mechanical causality harmed our understanding."[40] Causation in history inevitably involved several levels simultaneously, not only material circumstances (these sometimes least of all) but the operation of human memory and such vital influences as tradition, morale, anticipation, desire, faith, true and false beliefs. Lukacs compared the situation of history to the awareness imparted by Heisenberg to physics:

36. Ibid., 241.
37. Lukacs, *Historical Consciousness*, 276–78.
38. Ibid., 281n.
39. Molnar, *Politics and the State*, 32. See Thomas Kuhn, *The Structure of Scientific Revolutions* (Chicago: University of Chicago Press, 1970).
40. Lukacs, *Historical Consciousness*, 283.

We cannot avoid the condition of our participation. [There are] personal and moral and historical implications of this recognition, that instead of the cold and falsely aseptic remoteness of observation we need the warmth and the penetration of personal interest: but this is no longer the solitary longing of a humanist, a poetic exhortation. For "even in science," as Heisenberg says . . . , "the object of research is no longer nature itself, but man's investigation of nature. Here, again, man confronts himself alone."[41]

Science, in other words, had caught up with the older Christian and historical conviction of the centrality of the thinking, believing person. Only the glacial slowness of thought in this age and the mental opacity of a science-obsessed people, said Lukacs, had prevented the newly refined anthropocentric message from winning wide and easy assent.

An application of these insights can be found in Lukacs's treatment of the rise of publicity and public opinion in the United States during the middle and later twentieth century. Since World War II, it seemed to him, the growing importance of public relations experts, pollsters, and image makers had marginalized many of the political issues once central to a president's work. Pollsters, thinking of themselves as social scientists running objective tests, imagined that there was such a thing as "the people" and that "the people" had opinions that could be gathered and quantified. They thus committed a fallacy of misplaced concreteness, insufficiently understanding that it was often their own predigested questions that *created* the very thing they purported to study. This activity reached the point under President Reagan that policy decisions were made for the sake of public approval rather than their intrinsic political wisdom, even though the public opinion in question was largely manufactured, ephemeral, and insubstantial.[42] By the twentieth century, said Lukacs, "popularity could be manufactured by publicity. . . . This was the political and social phenomenon corresponding to the so-called Heisenberg principle . . . that the observation of a certain matter may influence and change the matter itself. By repeating and repeating that someone is popular he may become popular."[43] A civilization given over to systematic self-delusion of this kind, he feared, could not long endure. Attachment to a spurious science was negating rather than clarifying truth.

Lukacs saw in history an avenue of salvation from the banalities of an age of science. The central theme of *Historical Consciousness* was that

41. Ibid., 286–87.
42. Lukacs, *Outgrowing Democracy*, 283–84.
43. Ibid., 272.

humankind had become more historical in its outlook. The enormous popular interest in history, witnessed in the celebration of anniversaries and centenaries, the establishment of historical parks and preservation projects, and the growing fascination with all aspects of the national past, was unparalleled in world history.[44] Whereas other ages had come to an end without the participants' self-conscious awareness of the fact, the modern age was ending under intense self-scrutiny. He pursued this point in *The Passing of the Modern Age* (1970), a book similar in its mood of apocalyptic gloom to Garry Wills's *Nixon Agonistes* and dozens more produced in America between 1967 and 1973 to pronounce the death of an era. Its distinctiveness came from the author's faith that historical awareness was one of the greatest achievements of the modern age, a bourgeois-Christian achievement and a fund of wisdom for guidance in the coming dark age.[45]

As historical consciousness had increased along with mass education and literacy, Lukacs believed, the technical problems faced by historians had increased; there were fewer and fewer people and issues they could afford to ignore. Whatever their doubts about democracy historians had to practice their craft more democratically.[46] The historical self-consciousness of democratic peoples made them the subjects of history in a way their more unselfconscious ancestors had not been. In the great events of the twentieth century, preeminently the world wars, tens of thousands of men and women were acutely self-aware participants, whose actions and beliefs themselves conditioned the outcome of events.[47]

Historians, said Lukacs, had to come to terms with this new historical self-awareness and the proliferation of material (written, visual, artistic, and bureaucratic) which came with it. His own histories were crammed with remarks and speculations about all conceivable matters; the shape of cars, fashions, films, popular fads, and such vital but intangible matters as European Americophilia (Goebbels admired Hollywood, German air ace Adolf Galland named his Messerschmidt 109 "Mickey Mouse")[48] and Anglophilia in the nineteenth and twentieth centuries ("an attitude that included a respect for tradition, a disdain for demagoguery, a kind of liberal elitism of the spirit").[49] Lukacs's *Last European War*, an effort to fulfill his own theoretical require-

---

44. Lukacs, *Historical Consciousness*, 4.
45. Lukacs, *Passing of the Modern Age*, esp. 195–207.
46. Lukacs, *Confessions*, 226.
47. This conviction is one of the central themes of John Lukacs, *The Last European War, September 1939–December 1941* (Garden City, N.Y.: Anchor Doubleday, 1976).
48. Ibid., 509.
49. Ibid., 403.

ments, was an encyclopedic 550-page book about a two-year period, jammed with information about black markets, eating and sexual habits, journalism, refugees, radios and music, national character, and hope; it was a demonstration of his belief that "what 'really happened' . . . includes not only what happened but also what could have happened: actuality mixed up with potentiality."[50] It was all presided over by the participants' awareness that they themselves constituted history. As in all his empirical histories, Lukacs dealt briskly with material, military, and economic aspects of the war, then moved with growing assiduity to the mental construction of the realities he addressed.

For example, Lukacs argued that Hitler's Judeophobia must be conceived as a mental, not a material, phenomenon, with some unexpected cerebral consequences.[51] Hitler, he believed, was more dedicated to exterminating the Jews and to universalizing his hatred of them than to any other objective, but the widespread revulsion against his "final solution" led to the rapid *decline* of anti-Semitism in Europe and the United States, undermining the very objective he had pursued so single-mindedly.[52] No economic or materialist explanation of the Holocaust could do justice to this chain of events; they were questions of consciousness, and made all the more so by the increasing "cerebralization" of history in the twentieth century, nourished by mass-communications media, wherein vast abstractions took the place of local concrete realities, and the growing historical consciousness of entire populations made the perception of earlier historical events a continuing influence on current conduct. Hitler could carry out the Holocaust but could not engage its mental outcomes. As Lukacs remarked somewhere, "The pen is mightier than the sword but philosophy cannot stop a bullet."

More difficult than the history of events and ideas and yet more significant was religious history. Lukacs viewed religion as the deepest and, in his sense, the most "real" of all human concerns because it addressed questions of ultimate meaning. Paradoxically, however, religious history was the hardest nut for historians to crack because what people believed was not always clear even to themselves, was harder to detect than what they thought or did, and usually had to be deduced

---

50. Lukacs, *Confessions*, 225.
51. *The Last European War*, like most of Lukacs's histories, is divided into a shorter first section, "The Main Events," and a longer second section, "The Main Movements," on these less tangible issues.
52. Ibid., 427–53.

from their statements and outward behavior.[53] Historical consciousness, Lukacs emphasized, was intimately linked with Christianity and its abiding concern with history as the unfolding of events imbued with a divine significance. Lukacs treated Jesus himself as preeminently a historical figure, whose example taught moral and methodological lessons:

> The fact that Jesus, unlike other mythical founders of religions, was generally reluctant to perform miracles is evident from His own words. The fact that He was tempted by the devil suggests, too, that His historical life was not automatically predestined, that He had free will, that He had choices, that He was responsible for His acts: He was a potential savior who became an actual one. . . . The Christian heritage of Western civilization derives, therefore, not only from our recognition of the virtues of His teachings but from our capacity to emulate His human acts. This belief in His historical existence is a higher task than the belief in Him in His capacity as a miraclemaker.[54]

Christianity sharply delineates the problematical nature of what is important or significant in history. Religious history must contend with a "double hierarchy of events . . . temporal and transcendental ones." Although historians can attend only to earthly events or to the earthly consequences of divine events, such as the appearance of the Blessed Virgin Mary to Bernadette at Lourdes, they must reserve judgment on the question of what kind of event is most significant in the long run. Sometimes the point could be grasped readily from an example: "The earthly consequences as well as the very existence of Christ have been historical events. The earthly consequences of His life turned out to be more important than those of his contemporary Augustus Caesar. On this point historians and Christians are in accord."[55] Elsewhere, to be sure, the question of significance could not be granted so readily, becoming, rather, another area where historians must exercise discretion and judgment rather than apply a formula.

From his cogitation on historical method, Lukacs concluded that there was an inescapable tension between religious orthodoxy and historical analysis. For a historian to be orthodox, he said, was virtually a contradiction in terms. If one confined oneself beforehand to preor-

---

53. Lukacs, *Historical Consciousness*, 216. See also his presidential address to the American Catholic Historical Association, "The Historiographical Problem of Belief and Believers: Religious History in the Democratic Age," *CHR* 64 (April 1978): 153–67.
54. Lukacs, *Historical Consciousness*, 221.
55. Ibid., 222.

dained conclusions in the interest of upholding dogmatic propositions, one was not really a historian at all. To the contrary, one must have complete freedom of interpretive choice. The word *heresy* is derived from the Greek word for "choosing" and thus, as Lukacs noted, "there was a time when the Church, even in the West, was hostile to historical thinking," sensing that it could sow discord.[56] Lord Acton, an eminent Catholic historian of the nineteenth century, had recognized this problem; in 1861 he wrote in a letter to John Henry Newman that science and religion must be reconciled through "the encouragement of the true *scientific* spirit and *disinterested* love of truth." For Lukacs, this sentence was a virtual distillation of nineteenth-century fallacies, many of them still regrettably widespread. His update of Acton's answer to the dilemma was a condensed version of his own historical philosophy: "What we need is the encouragement of the true *historical* spirit, together with the *interested* love of truth: it is not so much science or philosophy but the study of history which must be reconciled with religion."[57] Lukacs's 1977 presidential address to the American Catholic Historial Association elaborated on this theme. Endorsing an earlier association president's view that "Catholic historian" is itself a sanctified vocation, Lukacs went on to note that historians must accept their creative as well as their preservative role; they were not only "guardians of a tradition" but also "its constant procreators." The Catholic historian should be "a philosopher teaching by his own existential example," enriching and deepening the faith by his learning.[58] The idea of the Catholic historian as scourge of the Protestants and defender of orthodoxy could win no assent from Lukacs, though he did offer a common platform to Christian interpreters of the past against their secular and scientific counterparts.

Despite the often unconventional theoretical frame on which it rested, Lukacs's work exhibited many of the characteristics of traditional historiography. A reader unversed in theory would not find his histories unapproachable and would soon gain a vivid sense of the author's outlook and ideals from the frequent obiter dicta (antireductionist and antimaterialist declarations) scattered through his texts. Lukacs scrupulously avoided jargon, sought out trade publishers in the hope of gaining a wider audience than he could expect from university presses, and remarked, "Most historians are not interested in history: they are interested in historianship," and, in another place, "Historians

56. Ibid., 219.
57. Ibid.
58. Lukacs, "Historiographical Problem," 167.

should not write only for other historians."[59] Flashes of demonstrative, unacademic passion, an almost childish relish for coincidences and anniversaries, cryptic remarks about the Garden of Eden, tirades against this or that scholar—all jostled in texts dense with learning and analysis, made approachable and reassuring to the reader by the use of logic, implicit appeal to definitions, and a recognizable sense of causation. Despite his hopes for the creation of a new history, he perceived a shortfall in innovativeness and joked that he was no more than the John the Baptist of this new history, which still "awaited its genius."[60]

In another way Lukacs seemed more old-fashioned than innovative in his method. He was convinced of the importance of concepts many of his professional contemporaries had come to doubt, in particular national character and the power of a genius to change the course of history. In the 1960s and 1970s a generation of social historians devoted themselves to breaking down generalizations about the "American character" which had been historiographical staples of the 1950s; many of the new social historians, using social-scientific methods, scrutinized small groups whose conduct gave the lie to the old generalizations, and emphasized differences more than similarities. Lukacs's Hungarian background and his experiences as an exile had forced upon him the idea that there *is* an American national character, of which American historians, studying their own nation without the perspective of distance, were unaware. As the United States had become the world's most powerful nation in the twentieth century, he believed that the strengths and weaknesses of this national character would have a powerful bearing upon events. Denial of its very existence, especially when its habitual weaknesses seemed to him so glaring, was regrettable.[61] Lukacs's attentiveness to the history of ordinary people, their thoughts, beliefs, hopes, and everyday activities, might seem to place him among the new social historians, but he eschewed their company. Reconstructing the lives of past ages, he said, "must be achieved through the *esprit de finesse* rather than through that of *geometrie;* through a sympathetic and evocative attempt of comprehension and not through a kind of retrospective sociology, cobbled together with fragmentary (and sometimes fraudulent) statistics—and through the recognition of the intrusion of mind in the structure of events, indeed of matter itself." He believed that sympathetic re-crea-

59. Lukacs interview; Lukacs, *Confessions,* 250.
60. Lukacs, *Confessions,* 251.
61. On national character, see especially Lukacs, *Historical Consciousness,* 199–210; and Lukacs, *Last European War,* 414–26.

tion of this kind had been achieved by a few historical geniuses in the past, notably Jakob Burckhardt, Tocqueville, and Johan Huizinga.[62]

Lukacs loved to repeat Pascal's dictum that men are both beasts and angels. He once juxtaposed it to Arthur Schlesinger, Jr.'s remark (in *The Age of Jackson*) that men are neither beasts nor angels, as a way of criticizing the "gray liberal egalitarianism" of Schlesinger's idea of human nature, which he took to be representative of American liberal thinking in general.[63] This sense that contemporary American liberals were naive about the range of human nature partly explains Lukacs's severe judgment of Woodrow Wilson and his legacy.[64] Wilson had made what Lukacs considered the most momentous decision of the twentieth century, the decision to commit troops to World War I and so end the long era of U.S. isolation. "If we judge events by their consequences we ought to realize that the great world-revolutionary was Wilson rather than Lenin," he said, because Wilson's idea of national self-determination proved far more influential and widespread in the long run than Lenin's idea of coordinated international workers' uprisings.[65] Wilson in 1919 had had an opportunity never previously seen and never to be enjoyed again of settling the future of Europe without needing to mollify or conciliate the Russians, weakened as they were by defeat, revolution, and civil war. Neither the Congress of Vienna nor the post–World War II allies had had a comparable opportunity; yet each managed a more durable peace than Wilson. The Wilsonian principle of national self-determination, he argued, was a self-defeating proposition based on pious abstractions about human reasonableness rather than the chastening lessons of European history. The breakup of the Austro-Hungarian Empire had made the whole area of Eastern Europe ruinously vulnerable, as subsequent events soon proved. Wilson's exaggerated hopes for the League of Nations, meanwhile, had inaugurated a tenacious belief among American foreign policy liberals, still not overcome, that discussion could ultimately replace war and the balance of power.[66]

To make matters worse, Lukacs added, Wilson had not forgone force completely, as his conduct in the Mexican Revolutionary Wars and World War I demonstrated. "He possessed, indeed, he took unusual pride in possession of, two sets of ideas that were contradictory." He

62. Lukacs, *Confessions*, 230.

63. Ibid., 313.

64. See, for example, the interpretation of Wilson in Lukacs, *Outgrowing Democracy*, 29–33, 223–26.

65. John Lukacs, "A Dissenting View on the Day That Shook the World," *New York Times Magazine*, Oct. 22, 1967, 32–33, 70–89.

66. Lukacs, *Outgrowing Democracy*, 223–24.

displayed "a school-masterish compound of idealism and venge-fulness, of a narrowmindedness that could be rigid beyond belief and a broadmindedness that was so broad as to be flat." And alas he was not an exception: "He was a peculiar, but not untypical, representative of American progressivism with its mixture of idealism and scientism." The weaknesses of Franklin Roosevelt's foreign policies were traceable to persistent Wilsonian delusions; throughout World War II, Lukacs believed, Winston Churchill's appreciation of events had been far keener than Roosevelt's, and they continued to be so after the war when the baleful Wilsonian legacy took shape in the U.S.-inspired United Nations.[67]

As we shall see, Garry Wills also singled out Woodrow Wilson, the solemn Presbyterian, as the mastermind of twentieth-century American liberalism, the man at whose door responsibility for many of the woes of our age could be laid. Like Wills, Lukacs managed, in his historical work, to comment ceaselessly on contemporary affairs through the medium of interpreting the past. Although at first glance he might seem removed from the central issue of this book, the trans-formation of Catholicism and conservatism, Lukacs was moving along the same path as the other figures considered here, opening up a space for the lay Catholic scholar, disdaining what he saw as the secular and liberal pieties of his age, and finding in the resources of his faith, rightly construed, the materials to rebuild a disoriented church and nation.

Thomas Molnar and the Disenchantment of Intellectual Life

Thomas Molnar migrated to the United States and studied for a Ph.D. in French literature at Columbia University because he believed that "in the post war desolation of Europe there wasn't much of a chance for an apatride to find a position, certainly not in teaching."[68] A series of temporary jobs at Catholic colleges in California was fol-lowed by appointment to a permanent faculty position at Brooklyn College, City University of New York, where he taught French and world literature throughout the 1960s and 1970s. He traveled exten-sively in Africa, South America, and Asia during the 1960s and contin-ued to live intellectually at least as much in Europe as in America,

67. Ibid., 224, 234–38.
68. Letter to the author from Molnar, Jan. 24, 1991.

published several books in French and Italian, and wrote for French, Spanish, Italian, and German journals.[69]

Molnar's style is forbidding, highly cerebralized. Although he criticized the tendency of philosophers to use abstractions that obscured "the constitution of being," his own philosophical work is dense with scholastic terminology, and his defense of Thomistic "moderate realism" seems at times neither moderate nor realistic. Molnar believed he had explained or understood an idea only when he had traced it back to its earliest historical antecedents. He found the source of many recent intellectual difficulties in a place to which few contemporary Americans have traveled, the scholastic nominalism of William of Occam and the conciliar theory of Marsilius of Padua.[70] History, to judge from Molnar's approach, is the story of how ideas have played themselves out across the centuries. He stressed the thoughts and the writings of small elites, taking the view that neither in the past nor in the present are the conduct or beliefs of the masses significant except as amplifications of these elite ideas. "In today's world the masses have no influence, regardless of what the prevailing orthodoxy says. It is the elite at all times in history which has influence."[71] In this respect the antithesis of Lukacs, who saw a growing complexity for historians in the rise of widespread historical consciousness and tried to encompass the history of events, fashions, cars, books, sex, and popular culture as well as ideas, Molnar had an austerely idea-centered outlook. This tendency became more marked as his life progressed; early ventures in reportage gave way after the mid-1960s almost entirely to contemplative intellectual history abstracted from its social context.

Molnar's first book was a study of the political ideas of the French Catholic novelist Georges Bernanos. It was a tribute to the man he found most sympathetic in recent Catholic history, and it played a role in Molnar's intellectual development comparable to Frederick Wilhelmsen's celebration of Hilaire Belloc, or Garry Wills's hymn to G. K. Chesterton, blending analytical appraisal with lavish praise.[72] In each of these books (all three were published by the Catholic house of Sheed

69. Molnar's non-English books include *La izquierda en la encrucijada* (Madrid: Union Editorial, 1970); *L'animal politique* (Paris: La Table Ronde, 1974); *Le socialism sans visage* (Paris: Presses Universitaires de France, 1976); *Le modèle défigure* (Paris: Presses Universitaires de France, 1978); *Lo stato debole* (Palermo: Thule, 1978).

70. See, for example, Thomas Molnar, "The Medieval Beginnings of Political Secularization," in *Essays on Christianity and Political Philosophy*, ed. George Carey and James Schall, S.J. (Washington, D.C.: University Press of America, 1984), 41–54.

71. Molnar interview.

72. Thomas Molnar, *Bernanos: His Political Thought and Prophecy* (New York: Sheed and Ward, 1960). Cf. Frederick Wilhelmsen, *Hilaire Belloc: No Alienated Man* (New York: Sheed and Ward, 1953); Garry Wills, *Chesterton, Man and Mask* (New York: Sheed and Ward, 1961).

and Ward) so closely did author and subject sympathize that their voices blended.[73] Garry Wills reviewed Molnar's *Bernanos* enthusiastically, concurring in Molnar's view that Bernanos was "a prophet, a man come to indict the age."[74] Bernanos (1888–1948) had struggled with successive ideological temptations. He belonged first to Charles Maurras's nationalist movement Action Française before and during World War I but broke with it in 1920 because of its willingness to manipulate the church for political ends. Despising communism and tempted briefly by fascism as an antidote, Bernanos turned against Franco in the Spanish Civil War when he witnessed Francoist soldiers' atrocities in the Balearic Islands. Repelled by Hitler's brutality and vexed by French conservatives' inability to see the danger Hitler represented in the late 1930s, Bernanos moved to Brazil and spent the war years there, returning to France only in 1946. By then he had become disillusioned with all the political ideologies of the mid-twentieth century. Only in the traditional teaching of the Catholic church could he find defensible principles. During the Spanish Civil War the poet and mystic Simone Weil had experienced a disillusionment about the Left comparable to Bernanos's experience with the Right. After reading Bernanos's *Grands cimetières sous la lune* (1937) Weil had written Bernanos that although they had taken opposite sides in the great ideological war of the century she felt closer to him than to any other contemporary. Molnar found it "moving to see how these two human beings whom everything separated—age, faith, intellectual background, world outlook—were absolutely of one mind in their denunciation of injustice"; he admired their ability to rise above political labels into the sublimities of the spirit.[75]

A generation younger than Bernanos, Molnar had experienced comparable struggles, encountering political disillusionments one by one and seeking refuge in a profounder Catholic orthodoxy. As a young man he had, he recalled, "run with public opinion," had called himself "a democrat, a liberal, a socialist, etc., which means I was far from understanding the philosophical roots and concrete consequences of these notions." His experiences in the United States prompted him in the mid-1950s to take a much more conservative posture on political questions, "largely in reaction against American democracy, pluralism, capitalism." These were also the years in which a mild inherited Ca-

73. One critic observed that "all too often" Molnar made "no clear distinction between his own views and those of Bernanos." Robert Henault, untitled review of *Bernanos*, in *CHR* 46 (Jan. 1961): 515.

74. Garry Wills, "Fear of the Flesh," *NR*, June 18, 1960, 401–2.

75. Molnar, *Bernanos*, 111.

tholicism matured into a fervently held faith. Catholicism "had to conquer me intellectually," he recalled, and in San Francisco, under the religious influence and example of Mother Helen Casey, a teaching sister with whom he worked, it did so. "From that moment on for the next few years I revamped my whole conceptual world in harmony with the Catholic faith."[76] Molnar, like Lukacs, was never procapitalist and scorned the libertarian side of the new conservatism, but he stayed close at first to the conservative movement's interests (especially anticommunism) and regularly contributed to its journals through the 1960s. But by the 1970s he, like Bernanos, could no longer call himself a conservative, only a Catholic.[77]

Before disillusionment set in, Molnar had a high regard for the intellectual vocation he had chosen. In "The Plight of the Intellectual" (1955), he wrote that an intellectual should be "an ambassador from the Realm of Truth," free from the compromising pressures that beset more practical people, and willing to suffer for his or her ideas. "A quality of gratuity, mysticism, and esoterism is inseparable from true intellectual life."[78] In the United States, however, the intellectuals he encountered seemed to him prosperous but uprooted, hardly more than the servants of ideologies or institutions, their work justified by utilitarian criteria. He added that both American and European intellectuals must take the blame for their current lowly status because they had led the way in deposing the church, within which intellectual life had once been nurtured, from its central place in society and in offering themselves as state servants or ideologues. "They battered the walls of spiritual values for so long that when the edifice finally collapsed the flying stones hit them first."[79] This article, written toward the end of the McCarthy era, when academic freedom and campus loyalty oaths had aroused heated controversy over the intellectual's position in society, led to a sympathetic *Time* magazine article on Molnar which suggested that, for the moment, he sat comfortably in the mainstream of academic self-criticism.[80]

76. Molnar interview.
77. Molnar adds: "It appeared to me that conservatives merely protect the status quo because it is favorable to them. Anglo-Saxon cautiousness would always prevent them from philosophically, even politically, exploring further, because they know that both . . . Catholicism and the political right-reactionary views would edge them toward renouncing democracy and capitalism." Letter to the author, May 14, 1991.
78. Thomas Molnar, "The Plight of the Intellectual," *C*, Aug. 19, 1955, 488.
79. Molnar, "Plight of the Intellectual," 488.
80. "The Siren Song," *Time*, Sept. 5, 1955, 45–46. Among the intellectuals he held up as exemplars of his time in this article, Molnar included Edmund Wilson, Walter Lippmann, Russell Kirk, Arthur Schlesinger, Jr., Peter Viereck, and Thornton Wilder. Few or (more likely) none of these names would have been included in 1970 or thereafter.

He was not to enjoy future patronage from *Time* as his criticism of the "ideological" bent of American intellectual life became more searching. By ideology, Molnar meant a pattern of thinking based on a desired and hypothesized end point of history; to be the servant of an ideology invalidated one's claim to be an intellectual, in his view, because it truncated the range of ideas open to speculation and fore-closed on the freedom of the will.[81] Each of the principal contemporary ideologies could be traced to one of the great heresies, all of which had prospered to the degree that they grasped (albeit in distorted form) part of the Christian truth. Communism was a prime example; its aspiration for the "end of history" was a secularized version of the Christian millennium; its scientific pretensions were a degraded form of scholastic nominalism; and its vision of social classes locked in strug-gle was an earthly replay of the Christian vision of God's war against the Devil and his angels. Even Marx's sense of outrage over the unjust sufferings of the proletariat could best be understood as a seculariza-tion of Christ's sympathy for the afflicted.[82]

Molnar's major early work on intellectuals and ideology, *The Decline of the Intellectual* (1961), was greeted warmly by Garry Wills, who wrote that "in a saner age" this book would have "become a political classic overnight"; it was the testimony of a "prophet," written so that "even when no one hears, the truth be spoken."[83] *The Decline of the Intellectual* traced the history of the Western intellectual tradition and the causes of what Molnar saw as its deterioration into tendentious ideology. The supreme medieval intellects were those of Saint Bernard, Saint Thomas Aquinas, and Saint Dominic. But contemporaneous with them, regret-tably in Molnar's view, a succession of intellectual virtuosos, such as William of Occam, Peter Abelard, and Roger Bacon, "men of powerful mind, [had] set out by themselves, seeking not only new approaches to the truths held by the Church but also roads that led in directions not approved by her."[84] Occam's nominalism and its political offshoot, the conciliar theory of Marsilius, were fruits of this new intellectual exploration, and in time they came to underlie the works of Machia-velli, Hobbes, and subsequent secular political philosophers. The mo-mentous and almost wholly baleful consequences of nominalism dominated Molnar's work after 1960:

81. Molnar, *Decline of the Intellectual*, 207–8.
82. Molnar, *Utopia*, 35–42. See also Molnar, "Paradox of the Marxist Philosopher," *NR*, Dec. 15, 1964, 1107–10.
83. Garry Wills, "Harvard Commutes to Washington," *NR*, May 22, 1962, 371–72.
84. Molnar, *Decline of the Intellectual*, 8. Richard Weaver, another prominent figure in the new conservative movement, also traced the decay of the West to Occam. See George Nash, *The Conservative Intellectual Movement in America since 1945* (New York: Basic, 1976), 39, 49.

Nominalism rejects the real existence of so-called universals; it proposes, in other words, that there is no such thing as mankind, only individual men and women; no such thing as friendship, only friendly attitudes between two or more persons. If that is so, then State, Church, corporations, institutions, etc. are not *real* either; politics is reduced to empirically observable acts that the weakness of our minds tends to group under names which remain empty of content. Thus the proper actors of the political sphere are concrete individuals with here-and-now interests, not corporate wholes. It follows that the area of politics is exclusively that of the secular power—whose motions and motives can be empirically ascertained—and that the spiritual authority has no place in it.[85]

Nominalism, then, was the philosophical precursor of Western secularism and scientific empiricism. It had, in Molnar's view, narrowed the range of issues accessible to reason by turning too much attention to observation of discrete entities, too little to deduction and intuition. Worse, it underlay two false claims: first, that reasonable knowledge of God is impossible and, second, that the universals of natural law are fictitious. As nominalism matured into secularization, he believed, God had become ever more distant from philosophy until, by the nineteenth and twentieth centuries, His very existence was widely denied by Marx, Freud, and the other principal shapers of contemporary thought. Christianity, the fountainhead of Western civilization, then became an object of ridicule to the people it had fathered.

Molnar, though he found this crippling flaw in the intellectual tradition of recent centuries, did not condemn Western philosophy completely. In the 1950s and early 1960s, he still believed that intellectuals were the most important of all social groups, whose ideas gave others in the population a courage and integrity they could not match on their own. He noted of the last desperate days in Dachau, when he and his fellows had feared they might still be exterminated even though rescue was only a few miles away, that those who had had strong intellectual convictions were best able to keep up their hopes and sense of purpose, rather than fall into the listless resignation that for many others preceded death: "There were those whom the moral force that an ideal had generated and kept alive made active to the point of restlessness." This was the good side of ideological passion.[86] Similarly,

85. Molnar, "The Medieval Beginnings," 48.
86. Molnar, "Last Days at Dachau," 170–71. Elsewhere he remarked: "Ideologies, however emotion-laden, succeeded in articulating the needs and desires of large numbers of people; they also showed the indissoluble relationship between material conditions, intellectual concepts, moral climate, and spiritual drives. No matter how destructive our ideological commit-

meetings in the 1950s and 1960s with escapees from behind the Iron Curtain encouraged him with the realization that Eastern Europe and Russia still had a vigorous, albeit largely underground, intellectual life that had not been suborned by official Communist dogma.[87] Likewise in Hungary in 1956, "very few intellectuals have sold their souls to the Stalinist devil without reprieve. The immense majority, the professors in the universities, the poets . . . the journalists . . . continued to think and even act, and became—after a very short honeymoon with the regime—the unassimilable splinter in the despot's flesh."[88]

Only when the free-minded intellectual was degraded into an ideologue and the ideologue in turn gave way to the still more circumscribed social engineer, was the thinking person to be feared.[89] Molnar grieved to see evidence in the 1950s and 1960s that a "convergence" of the U.S. and Soviet systems was taking place as each became dominated by its technologists and managers; like other Catholic new conservatives, he wanted the spiritual and philosophical differences between the two systems to be emphasized as much as possible.[90] The direction of American policy in the 1950s and 1960s, to his regret, seemed to be occluding the spiritual dimensions of the cold war, replacing them with a mere competition over production and weaponry. In his fear of the emergent social engineer Molnar echoed a theme common in the new conservative movement, one voiced earlier by James Burnham in *The Managerial Revolution*, echoed from behind the Iron Curtain by Milovan Djilas in *The New Class*, and subsequently an important theme in the neoconservative analysis of liberalism made by Michael Novak and others.[91]

In other ways too Molnar's work on intellectual problems in the late

---

ments proved to be at times, they sharpened our wits, demanded our efforts, fed our enthusiams. They were no substitute for religion, but they pointed, at least, to an ideal." Molnar, "Ideology and Politics," *C*, June 12, 1959, 271–73.

87. Thomas Molnar, "Dinner with Valery Tarsis," *NR*, July 12, 1966, 684.

88. Molnar, "Lessons of Hungary," *C*, March 1, 1957, 564–66. In 1990, with the decay of the Iron Curtain, Molnar was appointed professor of the philosophy of religion at the University of Budapest, where he planned to teach each fall semester. After his first semester there, he reported, "I was amazed at the students' intellectual and moral maturity, which I simply no longer find anywhere in the West. I was immensely impressed and I attribute it to the suffering under the Communist regime, to the maturation forced by historical pressures, and to the resistance of the soul to its robotization and to its destruction." Molnar interview.

89. Molnar, *Decline of the Intellectual*, 199–222.

90. See, for example, Molnar, "The American Experiment," 635–38; Molnar, "Imperial America," *NR*, May 3, 1966, 409–11.

91. James Burnham, *The Managerial Revolution* (New York: John Day, 1941); Milovan Djilas, *The New Class: An Analysis of the Communist System* (New York: Praeger, 1957); Michael Novak, *The Spirit of Democratic Capitalism* (New York: Simon and Schuster/Touchstone, 1982); Irving Kristol, *Two Cheers for Capitalism* (New York: Basic, 1978).

1950s and early 1960s echoed topical themes of the time. He was one of many conservatives to decry progressive educational theory as espoused by John Dewey. In *The Future of Education* (1961) he explained the boredom of schoolchildren as a reaction to the thin intellectual diet they were fed in contemporary schools, whose standards were so low they discouraged excellence. "All the great saints, prophets, philosophers, artists and teachers have understood," he declared in one characteristic passage, "that unless man tries to overcome not only his animality but even his humanity, he does not fulfill his destiny."[92] Transcendent objectives, not such dreary goals as social adaptation, were needed if schools were to instill Western values in new generations. No wonder some students rebelled, albeit in a distorted way, against their bland regimen. Paul Goodman in *Growing Up Absurd* and Norman Mailer in "The White Negro" each offered analogous explanations for juvenile delinquency—that there is nobility in nonconformity when the ideal for conformists is so drab. In one of the great intellectual thunderclaps of the 1950s, likewise, David Riesman and his colleagues had lamented the social conformity that blanketed an America packed with joyless "other-directed" personalities.[93] All agreed that children were being stifled, treated as interchangeable units, rather than being nourished as unique individuals who could transcend, rather than fit into, their society. Whereas Goodman, Mailer, and Riesman suggested temporal solutions, Molnar linked the problem directly to the decline of a religious vision and purpose in education.

There was a personal element in this dissatisfaction with U.S. education. Molnar had found his life as an American college teacher bitterly disappointing. From the beginning, Brooklyn College did not live up to his expectations, and in the 1960s conditions there went, in his view, from bad to worse as academic standards were relaxed in the name of an egalitarian open-enrollment system. His vision of a university as an impartial arena for dedicated study came up against the more prosaic reality of an institution buffeted by political pressures and cultural fashions, beset by financial crises and tempted to yield to business offers of funding in exchange for influence.[94] Most of the students he met seemed uninterested in scholarship. Finally he distanced himself

92. Thomas Molnar, *The Future of Education* (New York: Fleet Education, 1961), 120. See also Molnar, "Ideology and Politics," 271–73.

93. Paul Goodman, *Growing Up Absurd* (New York: Vintage, 1960); Norman Mailer, "The White Negro: Superficial Reflections on the Hipster," in Mailer, *Advertisements for Myself* (New York: Putnam, 1959), 337-58; David Riesman, Nathan Glazer, and Reuel Denney, *The Lonely Crowd: A Study of the Changing American Character* (New Haven: Yale University Press, 1950).

94. Thomas Molnar, "The Dogheads of the West," *NR*, Nov. 14, 1967, 1287–88; Molnar, "D-Day at Brooklyn College: The Day the Liberals Caved in," *NR*, Jan. 30, 1968, 86–87.

from the entire process, claiming a cold indifference to university life as something almost unconnected with thought.[95] Even among his colleagues, he said, "it is regarded as not nice to speak of intellectual matters." In Hungary "one puts one's heart, one's soul, one's mind in intellectual things," but "there is something in my [American] colleagues which does not permit them this outpouring of the soul."[96] He was disgusted to witness campus uprisings throughout the country in the years following the 1964 Free Speech Movement in Berkeley. When his own campus became the scene of Students for a Democratic Society demonstrations at the end of 1968, he hardly knew which to criticize more fiercely: the students themselves or the administrators, who seemed to Molnar pathetically willing to yield to the students' demands. Even when the demonstrators were not violent, he reviled them as agents of "terror" because their barrage of criticism undermined the reverence for learning upon which a university was supposed to be based.[97]

The direction of contemporary education and contemporary intellectual life, Molnar feared, was to exalt science and diminish the sovereignty of the human conscience, while the dominant American pragmatism nullified natural law and took away any fixed point of aspiration from which to pass moral judgment. Recent history, as he interpreted it, provided warnings of the horrors that could ensue from such a situation. A year or more before Hannah Arendt's *Eichmann in Jerusalem* popularized the idea of the "banality of evil," Molnar reviewed the memoirs of Auschwitz commandant Rudolf Hoess, written as Hoess awaited execution. The tale was dreadful, said Molnar, because Hoess was so ordinary, "an 'average' monster," who had simply applied his managerial mind to exterminating people, just as he had earlier applied it to other mechanical tasks. At that point, spring 1960, Adolf Eichmann had been seized by Israeli agents but not yet brought to trial; nettlesome questions of ex post facto juridical legitimacy surrounded the prospective court case, just as they had at the Nuremberg war-crimes trials. Despite his high regard for the rule of law, Molnar would not be diverted by the procedural issue. "In the eyes of God and man," he wrote, "Eichmann deserves to die, as did Hoess and the other mass murderers. Their fate and their example must serve as a reminder in an age which dilutes and denies individual responsibility

---

95. He judged the situation in Europe to be the same and was equally dismayed by the student uprisings in France. See, for example, Molnar, "Needed: A Redeeming Generation," *T* 4 (Feb. 1969): 25–26.
96. Molnar interview.
97. Molnar, "D-Day at Brooklyn College," 87.

by citing the determinism of psychological and sociological 'factors' or by hiding behind 'orders,' however contrary to conscience."[98]

Molnar's angry studies of the threatened Western intellectual tradition at the end of the 1950s were pitched at a theoretical level, but at the same time he was working hard as a critic and a journalist on issues of immediate concern. He wrote extensively on French literature and theater, much of which he judged to be degraded by the nihilistic influence of Jean-Paul Sartre.[99] In Molnar's works Sartre was the secular arch-ideologue of the age, rivaled in mendacity within the church by the evolutionary and progressive biologist-theologian Jesuit Pierre Teilhard de Chardin, whom Molnar viewed as a dangerous utopian.[100]

Molnar also took a keen interest in the French political crises of the late 1950s and early 1960s. This was a period of jolting reorientation in French politics. Retreat first from Indochina (1954), then from Suez (1956), had angered French right-wingers and imperialists, many of them Molnar's close friends. The end of the Fourth Republic in 1958 and Charles de Gaulle's return to power lifted his spirits at first; he believed the almost mythical de Gaulle could end the Algerian crisis and fulfill the promise of merging France and Algeria into joint parts of a greater France.[101] But when de Gaulle decided to cut his losses in Algeria and withdraw from that colony too, Molnar shared the French Right's sense of betrayal. "To the eternal shame of France, de Gaulle has acted toward the pro-French population of Algeria—of European and Moslem descent—as if it were a criminal element" rather than a stronghold of loyalty to a greater France.[102] Molnar praised the conspirators who attempted to thwart de Gaulle, finding in them the true spirit of militant Christendom, and he predicted only bloodshed, disaster, and repression in an independent Algeria.[103]

From Algeria he moved to a study of the end of colonialism through-

98. Thomas Molnar, "An 'Average' Monster," *NR*, July 16, 1960, 25–26.

99. Thomas Molnar, "The Novel in Crisis," *NR*, Oct. 8, 1960, 214–15; Molnar, "The Spiritual Poverty of the French Theater," *CW* 192 (March 1961): 347–50; Molnar, "The Theater Season in Paris," *R* 2 (May 1963): 16–19.

100. Thomas Molnar, *Sartre: Ideologue of Our Time* (New York: Funk and Wagnall, 1968); Molnar, "Sartre and the Cancellation," *NR*, Sept. 6, 1965, 270; Molnar, "Between Existentialism and Marxism," *T* 9 (June 1975): 24; Molnar, "Teilhard's Collectivist Salvation," *NR*, June 4, 1963, 464–65; Molnar, "To the Anthill, with Love," *NR*, Dec. 1, 1964, 1073–74.

101. Thomas Molnar, "Letter From Paris," *NR*, Aug. 30, 1958, 163–64; Molnar, "Dedication to France," *NR*, July 18, 1959, 215–16.

102. Thomas Molnar, "France: Paternalism or Civil War," *NR*, Sept. 11, 1962, 180. See also Molnar, "Algeria: Integration or Independence?" *CW* 192 (Feb. 1961): 286–95; Molnar, "Retreat in Algeria," *NR*, Feb. 11, 1961, 84–85: Molnar, "The Terrible Meaning of the Algerian Settlement," *NR*, May 8, 1962, 321–23.

103. Thomas Molnar, "The Fury of the Legions," *NR*, March 13, 1962, 168–69; Molnar, "No New Road," *NR*, Feb. 8, 1966, 122, 124.

out the rest of Africa where he traveled extensively in 1963–1965. Just as he condemned de Gaulle for cowardice in "abandoning" Algeria, so he criticized Britain's rapid withdrawal from its remaining colonies there. In dozens of articles and two books Molnar outlined the case against decolonization.[104] Under colonial administrations, he believed, Africa had made great progress. The repulsive cruelty of tribal warfare had stopped. Native peoples had for the first time gained access to Western medicine; they had been provided with good roads, had learned to read, and had converted in large numbers to Christianity. The natives' economic condition had improved, thanks to the selfless work of missionaries (Catholic priests and nuns prominent among them), whose energetic reforms had accompanied the promise of salvation.[105]

That the forces of civilization should now be turning tail and abandoning their charges as though they accepted the accusations of ideological antiimperialists seemed to him disgraceful evidence of spiritual malaise. While the "leftist and liberal press" acted like "a pack of ideological wolves," criticizing all aspects of imperialism, Molnar spoke out in favor of imperial paternalism and paid tribute to the European administrators of Africa as, for the most part, "men of extraordinary devotion to their difficult task."[106] Like Doctor Dooley in Vietnam and Laos, he simply could not find anything to fault in the picture of devoted Western doctors, nurses, priests, and teachers, coming to the aid of plague-ridden natives in their old tribal lands, especially when the Western Christians' departure was likely to be followed in short order by Soviet, Chinese, or Cuban Communist arrivals. Similarly, in Latin America, where he also traveled widely, he regarded the first stirrings of liberation theology as an entering wedge for communism rather than as a hope of salvation for the persecuted peasantry, and he berated the church authorities in South America for their feebleness in combating the liberationists' "revolutionary chatter."[107]

104. The books are *Africa: A Political Travelogue* (New York: Fleet, 1965); *South West Africa: The Last Pioneer Country* (New York: Fleet, 1966).
105. On the humane and economic improvements of African life under colonial regimes, see, for example, Thomas Molnar, "Portugal's Foreign Minister Pleads for Western Firmness," *NR*, Dec. 2, 1961, 374, 378; Molnar, "First Step in the Transkei," *NR*, Feb. 25, 1964, 155–56; Molnar, "The Truth about Angola," *NR*, April 7, 1964, 280; Molnar, "Death of Federation," *NR*, May 5, 1964, 353.
106. Molnar, *South West Africa*, 50–51.
107. Molnar, "South America Updated: The State of the Revolution," *T* 7 (Feb. 1973): 27. See also Molnar, "Letter from Latin America: Christian Socialism's Day," *NR*, April 4, 1967, 348–49; Molnar, "Iglesia y Revolucion," *T* 3 (June 1968): 15–18. His views on Africa, not surprisingly, made Molnar anathema to many reviewers, who showed no interest in his distinctions between benign and mendacious aspects of imperialism (to which, in South Africa, for exam-

Again like Doctor Dooley, Molnar also saw the developing Southeast Asian war in religious terms. Christianity, he said, introduced by French colonizers, had brought to Vietnam "two things which were unknown there . . . dynamism in the social sphere and charity in the spiritual sphere." In his opinion the benefit of the exodus of North Vietnamese Catholics to the South in 1954–1955, following French withdrawal, had been that these Catholics began to establish hospitals and charities throughout South Vietnam, spreading news of their sufferings at northern Communists' hands and hardening the South Vietnamese will to resist. The religions of Asia Molnar judged to be "moribund" and lacking all social dynamism; they were "empty shells, existing more by inertia and habit than by vital contribution to peoples' lives and thoughts." Accordingly the escalating Vietnam War had to be seen as a conflict between Christianity and communism, with these two vehicles of westernization competing for the population's loyalties.[108]

As American involvement in the Vietnam War continued into the mid-1960s Molnar continued to believe it could be won, but only by aggressively taking the battle to the enemy in the North.[109] The quagmire soon deepened and when the United States dispensed with Diem's Catholic elite, Molnar, on a visit to Vietnam, began to doubt his own prognosis, showing in this as in all things a willingness to reconsider (generally along more pessimistic lines).

> I remember one day in Saigon, having breakfast. Three officers walked into the room. Two were huge, towering American colonels, the third a little Vietnamese colonel. The small man looked like a caricature and I said to myself, "Here the war is lost, because these two men will never understand the little man, who in turn will never dare tell them what he wants." That's just a little anecdote but to a

---

ple, he was not blind). One characteristic response to Molnar's *Africa: A Political Travelogue* said that the book was "remarkable for its superficiality, its racism, and its naive credulity" and charged Molnar with gathering up "cliches about 'the African' from non-Africans" in a book that was no more accurate or useful than "medieval travelers' tales." Roland Oliver, "The African Revolution," *New York Review of Books*, July 1, 1965, 23–24. Other reviewers found in his version of events in Africa a breath of fresh air. The English journalist Malcolm Muggeridge, for example, wrote an enthusiastic review of *Africa: A Political Travelogue* for *Esquire*. Molnar, he wrote, "deserves a pat on the back for having kept his head and resisted the temptation to get a pat on the back from the *New York Times*, not to mention the *New Republic*, for having made the white man the bad guy of the story." Untitled review, *Esquire* 64 (July 1965): 24, 26.

108. Thomas Molnar, "Religion in the Far East," *CM* 63 (April 1965): 16–21.

109. Thomas Molnar, "Six Months after the Coup," *NR*, June 16, 1964, 491. He added that the Buddhist protests that preceded the assassination of Diem had been a "phony" issue, engineered by Communists, and that the "strategic hamlet" program had been working well in the year prior to Diem's death.

large extent this huge giant America does not understand how much it falsifies affairs when it appears on the scene. It is part of the puritanic, messianic myth, which ever since the early Puritans . . . has been so much in evidence that one should almost write a comedy about it.[110]

Molnar was increasingly convinced that this liberal "messianism," which he had first diagnosed in *The Two Faces of American Foreign Policy* (1962), was a stumbling block to national self-knowledge.

In the mid-1960s Molnar came to believe that liberal messianism was affecting not just Vietnam and other aspects of foreign policy but Roman Catholicism itself, which ought to have been a bastion against it. "Rome too," he concluded, "swallows large doses of American-type liberalism."[111] The Second Vatican Council filled him with dismay; the "ideology of aggiornamento," he said, was the work of utopian liberal intellectuals within the church who had scant regard for the religion of rank-and-file Catholics and who seemed blind to elementary psychological aspects of their faith. "Those who, in the name of 'modernism,' wish to put priests and nuns in worldly garb forget that the renunciation and sacrifice-seeking part of our being is thirsty for distinctness and yes, the outward marks of such sacrifice as celibacy, chastity, and poverty."[112] Elimination of Latin in the liturgy seemed to him a backward step; Latin had been part of the "rich ceremony" of traditional Catholicism which had always provided "esthetic uplift and joy" and enabled worshipers "to celebrate [their] meeting with God in beautiful surroundings."[113]

After the council, as experiments in liturgy and theology grew bolder, justified by the "spirit of the council," Molnar began writing defenses of orthodoxy. The first was *Utopia: The Perennial Heresy* (1967). In this history and typology of utopian theories, Molnar found a heresy to match every utopia in Western history, including liberalism and Marxism. "Utopia is to the political realm what heresy is to the theological," he argued, noting the proliferation of utopian thinking since the great heretical outbreaks of the Reformation.[114] Utopians were motivated, he believed, by a common unwillingness to accept the permanent presence of evil or imperfection in the world. In other words, they rejected basic worldly reality and the human condition. Surely,

110. Molnar interview. On the same theme, see Molnar's *Triumph* article "America in History," 22.
111. Molnar letter to the author, May 14, 1991.
112. Thomas Molnar, "The Ideology of Aggiornamento," *NR*, May 4, 1965, 365–66.
113. Ibid., 366. See also Molnar, "Catechism v. the Child," *T* 3 (April 1968): 17–20.
114. Molnar, *Utopia*, 4n.

many asked, the goodwill and good intentions of those who plan for a better future should not be resisted? At times they should be, Molnar answered, because their acts can bring greater consequential evil than the good they do, contradicting nature itself: "Utopian thinking is itself evil . . . and it leads people to commit evil. The one intolerable fact to the utopian is the scandal that evil exists in an otherwise perfect or potentially perfect world." Utopian regimes, preeminently the Communist regimes, were forced to make war against remaining vestiges of evil around them, but since an unchangeable human reality resists perfection, the regime's war against its enemies usually became perpetual, and the regime itself a tyrannical secular theocracy at war against its own people.[115]

Molnar followed *Utopia* with a fierce polemic against recent changes in the church, *Ecumenism or New Reformation?* (1968). Like Lukacs's *Passing of the Modern Age*, it bore the hallmarks of that tempestuous period in American history: apocalyptic gloom, and warnings that with enemies inside the gates as well as swarming through the outside world, a new retreat to the catacombs might well be close at hand. At a time when William Buckley was welcoming Jews and Protestants into the conservative movement and minimizing religious tensions, Molnar was still scourging Protestants as fiercely as he scourged atheists and Marxists. The Reformation, he said, "was a unique impoverishment of the religious domain when all over the northern half of Europe churches, statues, missals, woodcarvings, were whitewashed, broken, crushed, and burned, but the spirit in whose name it was done was more devastating still. Protestantism generally denied the rights of the body and of the senses, and its puritanic variety inflicted horrible punishments on the most innocent expressions of earthly joy." In four centuries, he added, Protestantism had given birth "to only one religious genius, Soren Kierkegaard, who ended up in despair, absurdity, and irrationality"; yet it was to Protestant models that the post–Vatican II church seemed to be looking.[116] Reflecting on the events of the 1960s, Molnar argued that the church had fallen into a "trap prepared by puritanism and its child, the industrial society," and that Pope Paul VI had betrayed his origins in the Milanese bourgeoisie by permitting the old glories of the faith to be replaced by a "streamlined religion" shorn of its ceremonial beauty.[117] Like Frederick Wilhelmsen, Molnar remained dedicated to the sole and exclusive truth of Catholicism, which meant, whatever tactical embarrassment it might cause his fellow con-

115. Ibid., 5, 191–98.
116. Molnar, *Ecumenism*, 76, 77.
117. Molnar interview.

servatives, that all other religions were false and could not bring salvation.[118] He also challenged the claim, often made after 1970, that a
reorientation of religious affiliations was taking place; he contended
that Protestant anti-Catholicism still survived and that "the papists are
still the devil for a large number of Protestants." Anti-Catholicism,
after all, was a foundational myth for the United States, which had
been a puritanical nation from the outset. He himself had almost been
"lynched" when, in a speech at Lynchburg, Virginia, before a largely
evangelical Protestant crowd, he condemned John Calvin.[119]

Molnar's aversion to liberal democracy and his antiecumenism made
him a ready friend of the *Triumph* Catholics after 1966. Although he
did not share their sentimental idealization of Catholic Spain, he did
share their increasing detachment from the conservative movement in
the age of President Nixon, and he became convinced that the United
States was in the throes of a full-scale revolution: "Political science has
not yet coined the terms, so we are hard put to name the revolution
constituted by the series of events which has swept through the West
this past decade. . . . But there is no doubt that they do amount to a
revolution, and that this country is its model as well as its central
stage."[120] In *The Counter-Revolution* (1969) he argued that revolutionaries in France (1789), Russia (1917), and now the United States (1968)
had in each case learned how to manipulate the print and popular
media of the day to make their ideas appear respectable, chic even, so
that counterrevolutionaries like himself—seeming to defend disgraced
and outmoded principles—had already lost the battle of ideas before
they even took to the field (71). There was an irony in this situation:
"It may sound paradoxical but it is true that counter-revolutionary
authors are generally rejected because what they describe is reality
whereas revolutionary writers, from Saint Just and Hegel to Sartre and
Marcuse, are popular *because* they are speculative" (73). The counterrevolutionaries' assertions often seem boring because of the familiarity
and homeliness of what they have to say in defense of reality, whereas
revolutionary literature "intrigues because it represents the luxury and
gratuity of speculation, the instability of movement, the temptation to
follow fancy" (73). Hence, educated, prosperous elites are attracted to
revolution and tend to disdain "the wisdom of the ages and ancestors,
mankind's distilled experience" (73). Molnar's anguish was of course
intensified because of his belief that the revolution of his times afflicted
the church as well as civil society. He interpreted the clamor of criticism

118. Molnar, *Ecumenism*, 162.
119. Molnar interview.
120. Molnar, "Nihilism, Phase II," *T* 6 (Jan. 1972): 37–38.

from laity and priests against bishops and the pope as revolutionary manifestations. By comparison, he said, "the murder of the Pope would be . . . a lesser act of terror, because bullet or bomb would hit the *man;* the defiance of his moral and teaching authority has the *Pope* as target" (188). Here was a vivid demonstration of Molnar's adherence to the scholastic realist principle that the "pope" is something quite distinct from the man occupying the office, and that the office deserves reverence even when its occupant might not (the occupant in question, Paul VI, seemed to Molnar a very weak reed).

The Counter-Revolution cited counterrevolutionaries from whom embattled Americans might learn: Miklós Horthy, Franco, Salazar, even Mussolini (131). Few critics, even from the conservative camp, were impressed by this list or by Molnar's argument. Stephen Tonsor said that "the remedy he offers is as wasting and corrupting as the disease itself." Tonsor, American born and bred, favored a "fusionist" conservatism that could bring together traditionalist and libertarian elements of the philosophically diverse conservative movement; he foresaw nothing but trouble from Molnar's schemes. "In his detestation of this revolution," said Tonsor, "Molnar is correct. . . . But it is difficult to imagine a program, short of Maoism, less in touch with the realities of the seventh decade of the twentieth century. Not even George Wallace talks such rubbish."[121]

Ironically, Tonsor, a down-to-earth critic, had missed a crucial part of Molnar's message. Although Molnar dedicated himself to working for the counterrevolution, and although he specified that only the counterrevolutionary parts of the Catholic church and the United States now stood between reality and disaster, he also spelled out, in passages most critics neglected to mention, that the counterrevolutionaries were destined to continue losing.[122] Molnar was not so much making a call to action as diagnosing defeat from the losing side; the book was a lament for an already irrevocable loss. He attributed this defeat to the revolutionaries' use of publicity, which he, like Lukacs, analyzed extensively. Publicity and the stirring of emotions through recitation of grandiose abstractions, he believed, were crucial if an idea was to spread, take hold, and influence events. But the opponents of the "revolutionaries" disdained publicity.[123] Molnar seemed almost to relish painting himself into a corner: if counterrevolutionaries used mass publicity techniques and held out messianic promises of social transformation (without which they could expect no following), they

121. Stephen Tonsor, "Athena's Bat," *NR*, Feb. 10, 1970, 160–61.
122. See, for example, Molnar, *Counter-Revolution*, 113–14.
123. Ibid., 76–83.

would no longer be counterrevolutionaries but become instead, like the betrayer de Gaulle, a part of the revolutionary enemy.[124] There was an odd grandeur in Molnar here, reminiscent of Joseph Schumpeter's anticipation (albeit in a quite different context) that the civilization he prized and by which he lived contained the seeds of its own destruction, against which no amount of rigorous analysis could prevail.[125]

Many prophets of doom had something to feel slightly ashamed of by the mid-1970s. Most, without any explicit repudiation of harsh words spoken in the heat of the sixties' worst controversies, cooled down and went about their work without a backward glance, except for purposes of retrospective self-justification; Michael Novak, as we shall see, is a case in point. Molnar, however, though his rhetoric had also cooled, demonstrated in 1973 that he was determined neither to yield any philosophical ground in the light of recent experiences nor to offer himself an escape route from his gloomy prognostications. Instead, he moved to a higher level of abstraction. *God and the Knowledge of Reality* (1973), indeed, went farther than earlier work by denying not only the truth of postscholastic Western philosophy but even its right to the name of philosophy. Intellectuals, even if non-Christian, had won Molnar's praise before 1960 for their vigor and independence. No more. The major schools of thought since the Enlightenment, he now argued, had abandoned the first premise of true philosophy, to know human beings and the world as they really are (the "constitution of being") and to reason about the human condition in light of that knowledge. Instead, Western philosophers had become ever more determined to *transform* human beings and turn the world into a perfect place where history, strife, and sin would cease. This perfect place, moreover, was to be achieved by "philosophers" who claimed unlimited access to the knowledge of reality. G. W. F. Hegel, a principal exponent of this false philosophy, had made what Molnar regarded as "a philosophically unauthorized *transposition* of the speculative order onto the historical sequence: what the philosopher discovers as the processes of reason he applies to the structure of the world" (xi). It seemed axiomatic to Molnar, by contrast, that our knowledge of reality is incomplete and imperfect: even though we can know the natural law, we can neither fully comprehend reality nor transform it at will. Historical experience since Hegel should have shown us that history

124. Molnar reserved particular scorn in this book for de Gaulle and other counterrevolutionary "heroes" who rose to power by their mystique only to betray their friends' and supporters' loyalty by switching allegiances when their power was secure. Ibid., 157–66.

125. Joseph Schumpeter, *Capitalism, Socialism, and Democracy* (New York: Harper and Brothers, 1942).

will not submit to any philosophical master plan: "History 'uses' only temporary catalysts, and uses them only in a limited fashion; history is not the conflict of the universal and the individual, and the first is not the victor, nor the second the vanquished; there are always new motive forces, for history does not coagulate and serve as a form of expression to a philosophical doctrine" (xii). To admit as much, Molnar believed, was to humbly accept the reality of "the extramental world," the human self as something more than "inventions or projections of the mind," and humankind as something created. And what is created, he added, presents itself as evidence of the existence of a creator (xv).

The problem of God, seemingly marginal in Western philosophy for several centuries, was, in Molnar's view, still as central as it had ever been. Some philosophers, without actually denying the existence of God had made Him so remote from life that He could take no part in it; human beings were left with a clear field for their desires (3–31). Others, pantheists, had made God immanent in all things but with similar consequences; once God was part of each person, pantheists could undertake their transforming projects with Promethean, or Faustian, self-confidence (32–51). Only a third position, in which God was held to be both transcendent and personal, near enough to affect events, yet distinct from human beings as their creator and judge, was compatible with true philosophy. This was the God of Aquinas and scholastic orthodoxy (52–69). Denigrating the major philosophers of the last four centuries, Molnar traced their lineage back to the astrologers, alchemists, and magi of bygone ages. Their impatience to override natural laws and transform the world through manipulation of perfect knowledge had led them into what he saw as worse follies than the effort to make gold from lead (73–124). This was an audacious charge to make against all Western philosophy since Descartes; the indictment included materialism, idealism, and existentialism, flattening out their differences and categorizing their work as a branch of the history of heresy. It was of course grossly unfair to the many philosophical positions, including skepticism and pragmatism, which acknowledged, and indeed were based upon, the incompleteness of knowledge, but Molnar considered such systems deficient because of the *nature* of their modesty; they turned their eyes away from the knowledge of God, in which Molnar could be confident.

In his extensive work on utopianism and heresy, Molnar acknowledged a debt to Eric Voegelin.[126] Like Frederick Wilhelmsen, Molnar

---

126. See, for example, Thomas Molnar, "Perennial Gnosticism," *MA* 14 (Summer–Fall 1970): 334–37; Molnar, "Voegelin as Historian," *MA* 19 (Fall 1975): 427–29; Molnar, *God and Knowledge*, 60–61.

was impressed by Voegelin's *New Science of Politics* and *Order and History*, which emphasized the strong continuities from Greek to contemporary philosophy and identified gnosticism as the besetting sin of all who hoped to "immanentize the eschaton."[127] Molnar's own search for ancient and medieval ancestors to contemporary problems was reminiscent of the Voegelinian method of deep intellectual genealogy. Voegelin presented Molnar with a dilemma, however, because he never claimed to be a conservative, was not a Catholic, and preferred Greek philosophers, Plato above all, to their Christian successors. Molnar, of course, thought Voegelin's elevation of Plato a misstep. He saw Plato's search for the ideal, albeit one he considered unattainable, as a forerunner of utopianism.[128] Voegelin, not defending a Christian position, could find high virtue in Hellenic philosophy, Judaism, and Christianity alike as guardians of civilization and as ethical teachers. For Molnar, by contrast, the Incarnation was the decisive moment of history, which transformed the world irrevocably, shining a new light on all things. Warning conservatives that even the revered Voegelin should not be beyond criticism, Molnar remarked: "Voegelin remains a 'Greek,' placing us in the *metaxy*, the field of force between man and God, but in such a manner that the upward pull remains the *experience* of a force, not more," rather than "the Unknown God, whom Paul met at Athens." Although pre-Christian sources, especially the Greek, could be called upon, they were never more than ancillary to the supreme wisdom of Christ and the tradition of the church fathers.[129] This quarrel with Voegelin was strictly an intraconservative tempest, of course; on the need to preserve a complex and spiritually based civilization they were in close accord.

The weakness in much of Molnar's work after the mid-1960s was a tendency to exaggerate the hopelessness of the situation and to scant its paradoxes and ambiguities. For polemical purposes he diminished the distinctions among recent philosophical schools, simplifying and draining each one of its content to such an extent that readers could get no sense of their function, context, or intrinsic merits. One critic, not unsympathetic to his general counterrevolutionary outlook, lamented in 1970 that "all change seems to Molnar to be 'revolutionary,'" and for this reason, "it is difficult for him to determine just what 'revo-

127. "Immanentize the eschaton" is Nash's phrase in *Conservative Intellectual Movement,* 49–50. See Eric Voegelin, *The New Science of Politics* (Chicago: University of Chicago Press, 1952); Voegelin, *Order and History,* 4 vols. (Baton Rouge: Louisiana State University Press, 1956–74).
128. Molnar, "Perennial Gnosticism," 336.
129. Molnar, "Voegelin as Historian," 429.

lution' is."[130] Frederick Wilhelmsen, another self-confessed loser in the great struggles of recent history, felt that Molnar's antiutopianism had reached the dimensions of an obsession when even Plato's ideals won his opprobrium: "Failure to make . . . crucial philosophical distinctions opens [Molnar] to the charge of condemning as utopian any lifting of the human mind above the pragmatically given. Yet if man, Western man, cannot raise his heart beyond the miserably mediocre moment in which he lives . . . he will risk nothing and he will gain nothing."[131] Dietrich von Hildebrand, a conservative Catholic theologian at Fordham, echoed Wilhelmsen's caveat and pointed out that the fathers of the church had named Plato a teacher who prepared the way for Christianity.[132] How could the irony be keener than this? Wilhelmsen and von Hildebrand were pointing out that Molnar, in his discontent, seemed determined to stifle Christian or conservative aspirations just when they were the only remaining solace to those the zeitgeist had abandoned.

Neither John Lukacs nor Thomas Molnar led an altogether successful or satisfactory intellectual life in the United States, even though here they had the freedom to voice discontents that would have brought them to prison and silence in Hungary. In each man's work there was a tendency to grand exaggeration and frequently an imbalance between dramatic philosophical rumination and easily assimilated practical conclusions. Lukacs could be seen quite simply as a conservative historian of recent European and American history and Molnar as a crotchety foe of Catholic renewal and American liberalism. But to neglect the way they thought about these issues would be to overlook what is distinctive about these two Hungarian exiles, as well as some of the ironies of recent conservative and Catholic history. Each man conscientiously refused to conform to certain conventions of his time, and each paid a price for his unfashionableness, though it is well to remember how much lower a price than would have been exacted in Hungary. Lukacs would not adhere to the approved career path of contemporary academic historians or conform to the cherished historiographical principles of his day, and he was repaid with neglect. Molnar would not deviate from an intellectual, racial, and cultural elitism and a reli-

130. Tonsor, "Athena's Bat," 161.

131. Frederick Wilhelmsen, "The Perpetual Itch," *NR*, Aug. 22, 1967, 916–17.

132. Dietrich von Hildebrand, "The Utopian Mirage," *MA* 11 (Fall 1967): 421–26. Von Hildebrand added (425) that Molnar's sweeping dismissal of post-Thomist philosophy was likewise unfair to Descartes: "Descartes is above all the champion of objective truth against skepticism. And as a faithful Catholic he neither arrogated to man divine attributes nor replaced the Christian emphasis on the individual soul with a collectivist bias. . . . In no way was he the father of subjectivists."

gious orthodoxy that had become highly unpalatable to most of his contemporaries—some of whom questioned even the existence of a single Catholic orthodoxy—and he too was marginalized. Each was left with a comparatively small circle of admirers and followers but negligible influence on the intellectual life of his times, not because his work was unimportant but because it failed the tests currently imposed both by the arbiters of taste and by the market. In this respect the two Hungarians lacked the acuity and business sense of their homegrown contemporaries William Buckley, Michael Novak, Garry Wills, and others, who mastered the arts of self-promotion, identified and pleased large potential markets, and made themselves important public figures.

Lukacs and Molnar are worthy of consideration, nevertheless, because they enriched American conservatism with their European training and insight and because the hard scrutiny they applied to their adopted land shone new light on its intellectual and political habits. In particular their critique of the "publicity" apparatus as self-deceiving and morally degrading, their steady resistance to philosophical materialism, capitalism, and the popular materialism of U.S. culture (where they echoed themes from the Left and the environmentalist critique), their skepticism and caution about current interpretations of democracy, and their deflation of exaggerated claims for science, were serious challenges even to those who lacked the Catholic standpoint from which their attacks were launched. Their fate, that of being only *slightly* influential, illustrates in acute form the fate of Catholic conservatism in recent decades; unable alone to mount a political challenge, especially when it lost its solid footing in a unified church, it could either join forces with a more pragmatic conservatism, thus losing much of its distinctiveness, or else become the cerebral preserve of intellectuals hoping in the long term for a vindication their own age seemed unwilling to provide.

7

Redrawing the Boundaries of Conservatism: Garry Wills and Michael Novak

John Lukacs and Thomas Molnar never adapted fully to the American environment and each endured personal and professional disappointments. In marked contrast stand Garry Wills and Michael Novak, two of the most successful and influential Catholic conservative writers of the 1960s and since. Wills and Novak, a decade younger than the two Hungarians, grew up in the United States and came to maturity in the shelter of Catholic seminaries. Each set out as a young man to be a priest, and though both left the seminary before ordination, they bore witness to serious lay vocations in subsequent writings on Catholicism. They helped shape the public image of "the emerging Catholic layman" in the early 1960s, and participated in debates on the effects of the Second Vatican Council. Both men married and had children; both joined in the stormy debates on Catholics and contraception, on the Vietnam War, and on the rise of the new Left. Their experience in the 1960s transformed both, but in contradictory ways.

Wills began his public career in 1957 as an ardently antiliberal and anti-Communist writer at *National Review,* but in the 1960s he reconsidered many of his political judgments, partly in light of the civil rights movement, the Vietnam War, and the Nixon presidency, partly as his way of life changed from the sedentary routine of college professor to the risky confrontations of a "new journalist" at demonstrations, sit-ins, and briefly in jail.[1] Though he retained the conservative label and philosophical outlook throughout the storms of the 1960s, by the early 1970s he had adopted political views more congenial to some of his former adversaries. Novak, by contrast, first came to public notice in the early 1960s as a Catholic liberal, fervently enthusiastic about the Kennedy presidency and reform in the Catholic church. As a champion of the laity, Novak raised controversy by challenging theological orthodoxy and by deviating from Catholic anti-Communist orthodoxy when he took an outspoken position against the American role in Vietnam. After 1968, however, Novak began a steady retreat from radicalism, alarmed by the excesses of the student movement and dismayed by some of the changes in the church, which were much more sweeping than he had foreseen. By the mid-1970s he was emerging as a Catholic neoconservative, constructing theological justifications for capitalism and working as *National Review's* religious affairs editor.

Considering the two men solely as political writers, one could argue that Wills's public career showed a steady trend to the left while Novak's displayed an equally inexorable march to the right, with the two men "passing" each other in about the year 1968. They were, however, both men of complex intellect, whose political and religious views were closely intermingled. The metaphor of a linear right-left spectrum cannot do justice to their motives, interests, and actions or to their evolving understanding of the world. By 1980 Wills, still calling himself a conservative, was far less right-wing than Novak, who by then designated himself a neoliberal. Both should be understood as members of the generation that transformed U.S. Catholicism and participated in its pluralization, or fragmentation. For each in his own way, religiously based principles guided political understanding, even though the old Catholic consensus about how to apply them had disappeared.

In an age when political passions were so heated, changing one's mind in public was not easy; it meant leaving behind old comrades, who often felt as though they had been betrayed, and taking up with new ones, who were sometimes suspicious of a man so recently their rival. Garry Wills, a brilliantly gifted intellectual virtuoso, wrote some of the cleverest pages of *National Review* before 1968; after that his former colleagues and his successors at the journal, notably Joseph Sobran, hounded him with contemptuous disdain.[2] Novak, likewise, described being "cut" publicly by former friends in the antiwar move-

1. See Garry Wills, "War Protest: Jail," in his *Lead Time: A Journalist's Education* (Garden City, N.Y.: Doubleday, 1983), 11–28.
2. See, for example, Joseph Sobran, "The Newborn Garry Wills," *NR*, June 22, 1973, 676–81; Sobran, "No Growth," *NR*, March 5, 1982, 236–37.

ment and reacted by trying to justify each of his changes of mind, sometimes in a painfully self-conscious way.[3] Each was accused of acting in bad faith, of making opportunistic rather than principled changes of view. Conservatives accused Wills of succumbing to the blandishments of the "liberal establishment," against which they portrayed themselves as a dignified and embattled minority.[4] Liberals accused Novak of "selling out" to big business and the "power structure," forsaking the courageous minority that represents the nation's conscience.[5] Whichever of these groups, conservatives or liberals, had better claim to the coveted outsider status, their accusations seem to me unjust. Wills and Novak, though far from faultless, were both conscientious men responding to the logic of events as they saw them and willing to follow their convictions rather than remain locked into the niches where they had first become well known.

They angered contemporaries in part because they were risk takers. Wills and Novak were both capable of breaking academic ties at a time when universities dominated American intellectual life. Wills was a professor of classics at Johns Hopkins University in the early 1960s; Novak held professorships for a time at Stanford, Old Westbury (State University of New York), and Syracuse. But neither man was primarily academic in orientation. Each worked extensively in journalism, writing works aimed at a wider readership than just their disciplinary colleagues. Each fell foul of academic orthodoxy. Wills's extensive and polemical journalism angered his Johns Hopkins department head, and he was denied tenure in 1966, after which he lived by writing alone for almost a decade before accepting professorships once more, first at Johns Hopkins, later at Northwestern University.[6] Novak's distractions from professional development prevented him from even completing his doctoral degree; therefore, he was always on the margins of university life rather than squarely on the academic ladder. His "professorship" at the American Enterprise Institute after 1978 was actually the position of a foundation resident, with no teaching duties. But whereas academic marginalization led to obscurity for Lukacs and Molnar, it gave Wills and Novak the opportunity to prosper. Topical, closely attuned to current fashions and cultural changes, they were always able to attract readers and to replace lost allies with new ones;

3. Personal interview with Michael Novak, Washington, D.C., April 9, 1985.

4. Joseph Sobran again provides the best example; see his review of Wills's *Confessions of a Conservative*, "Up to Liberalism," *NR*, May 25, 1979, 684–87.

5. See, for example, Peter Steinfels, "Michael Novak and His Ultrasuper Democraticapitalism," *C*, Jan. 14, 1983, 11–16.

6. On Wills's tenure dispute, see his *Confessions of a Conservative* (Garden City, N.Y.: Doubleday, 1979), 68.

they were always in demand as writers and speakers. Russell Jacoby has argued, in *The Last Intellectuals,* that universities have gobbled up all the men and women who might in another age have become talented, independent writers and have driven them down the baleful road of cramped specialization. Free spirits to compare with Edmund Wilson and Lewis Mumford, he says, have vanished. Jacoby makes a partial exception for conservatives, however, and notes that William Buckley escaped the academic trap; he could have added that Wills and Novak too carved out places for themselves as contemporary "public intellectuals," who published in a diversity of widely circulating journals, appeared often on television and radio as "experts," and wrote their own syndicated newspaper columns.[7]

Garry Wills and Michael Novak were born within a year of each other. Novak began life in Johnstown, Pennsylvania, in 1933, the son of an insurance salesman, and Wills in Atlanta, Georgia, in 1934, the son of a traveling appliance salesman. These were far humbler origins than those of Buckley, the oil millionaire, or the Budapest bourgeois Lukacs and Molnar. As teenagers both responded to vocations to the priesthood. Wills majored in philosophy at St. Louis University as a Jesuit seminarian and took a master's degree in philosophy at Xavier University in Cincinnati, Ohio. Novak attended Stonehill College, the Gregorian University in Rome, and then the Catholic University of America. This rigorous training inside the preconciliar church left lasting marks on their intellectual style, their skill in syllogistic reasoning, and their phenomenal productivity and powers of concentration.[8]

For Wills the break in his plans to become a priest came in 1957. Wills remembered later that *Time* and *National Review,* though officially prohibited, had circulated surreptitiously at his Jesuit seminary and that his dislike of the former and admiration of the latter had prompted him to write a parody, "Timestyle." He sent it to William Buckley, who liked it so well that he not only ran the article in *National Review* but offered Wills a summer internship with the two-year-old journal.[9] Wills, then only twenty-three, wrote a succession of articles and reviews that summer and remained a regular contributor until the mid-1960s. Meanwhile, he studied for a Ph.D. in classics at Yale, writing a doctoral dissertation on Aeschylus's *Oresteia.* He married in 1959, after

7. Russell Jacoby, *The Last Intellectuals: American Culture in the Age of Academe* (New York: Basic, 1987), 193–94, 167–68, 203–7.

8. The details of Novak's early life are from my interview. On Wills, whom I was unable to interview, see his entry in *Current Biography,* 1982 (Detroit: Gale, 1983), 441–45; and Wills, *Confessions,* 3–90.

9. Garry Wills, "Timestyle," *NR,* Aug. 3, 1957, 129–30, 149; Wills, *Confessions,* 3–7.

which, of course, a return to the priesthood would have been impossible.

Graduate school was not for Wills, as it is for many young men and women, a period of profound immurement in a discipline for the single-minded pursuit of a dissertation. Instead, it was a time of vigorous creativity. As a graduate student, in addition to the frequent articles for *National Review,* he also wrote anti-Communist editorials for the *Richmond News-Leader,* Bible stories for children, and an admiring biography of G. K. Chesterton. Just after graduate school he wrote *Politics and Catholic Freedom* to vindicate William Buckley's position in the *Mater et Magistra* dispute of 1961.[10] Already several themes that were to persist in his work through the coming decades were apparent. First was his contempt for liberalism, which he considered the regnant intellectual and political style of his times. Lacking any transcendent principles, he argued, it could not provide the basis for resistance to communism and the preservation of our beautiful but "intricate and fragile" civilization.[11] By positing the isolated individual as the basic unit of society, liberalism fragmented the social organism and weakened its defenses against messianic communism. It is impossible to understand Wills's later work, when his retention of the "conservative" label seemed paradoxical, without recognizing that he never lost this fierce aversion to individualistic liberalism.

A second persistent theme was Wills's sharply critical view of some forms of conservatism. Wills did not believe libertarians and defenders of economic laissez-faire should be allowed the label conservative, because their views were premised upon a society made up of isolated human atoms and the belief (clearly utopian, in Wills's view) that without external restraint it could work like an almost frictionless mechanism. Wills, to the contrary, took the family as the basic unit of society and saw society as an organism rather than a contractual or mechanical arrangement between independent agents. Complementarity through difference rather than stark equality of all seemed to him the underlying reality of society, and any political system that ignored this reality deviated from natural law.[12] No wonder Wills was an admirer of Thomas Molnar; at this stage their views were in close accord.[13] Wills mocked Murray Rothbard and the theorists of radical libertarianism and wrote a smashing indictment of Ayn Rand's *Atlas Shrugged* (1957),

10. See Wills, *Confessions,* 3–79.

11. Garry Wills, "The Liberals Convert a Cardinal," *NR,* Jan. 16, 1960, 37–40.

12. Garry Wills, "Vive la Difference," *NR,* Jan. 30, 1960, 82–83.

13. Garry Wills, "Harvard Commutes to Washington," review of Molnar, *The Decline of the Intellectual,* in *NR,* May 22, 1962, 371–72.

then a cult classic for libertarians.[14] The libertarians, like the liberals, he said, defined their "most precious quality," freedom, in a "passive way," as simple absence of external restraint. Wills, to the contrary, had a positive conception of freedom as "dominion over the self, and the origin of all right rule in the state." Freedom and authority, he believed, were complementary rather than antithetical principles.[15]

If the libertarians who abolished the state were fantasts, so too were the totalitarians, who absolutized the state. Wills needed a theoretically defensible alternative to both, and a third continuity throughout his public career was his theory of the "convenient state," first explained in a masterful essay on the great tradition of political philosophy, written when he was still only in his midtwenties.[16] Most political philosophers since Plato, he argued, had justified the state as an instrument for achieving justice through the exercise of reason. Rousseau, for example, had regarded reason and justice as the objectives of the state, but "because man's reason is not of itself free, the state based on 'pure reason' only recognizes the freedom to be right; the state must, in Rousseau's famous phrase, 'force men to be free'" (17). Because in the West "unfettered reason has accomplished so much," the tendency to think of politics as a rationalistic search for a justice-creating mechanism was understandable, but Wills contended that the theoretical richness of this tradition, which he named "the order of justice," was offset by a paucity of historical examples; states based on the "order of justice" usually eventuated in tyranny or totalitarianism, which in the name of a great good did great harm. "The seeds of tyranny were in the ideal from the beginning. Robespierre and the Terror are the logical consequence of Rousseau and the Social Contract" (17–19).

By contrast with this "order of justice," the "order of convenience" could offer plenty of fine practical examples but had a much poorer intellectual pedigree. In fact *The Federalist* was almost the only sustained effort to theorize about its key principles, not justice but compromise and reconciliation (20). In the order of convenience the pursuit of justice was a necessary but subordinate state function. Justice alone was not the end of the state, just as it was not in the family; love and nourishment of the community were its primary goals. The presiding genius of Edmund Burke and the more immediate influence of John Courtney Murray, S.J., were apparent here, and Wills quoted a key

14. Garry Wills, "But Is Ayn Rand Conservative?" *NR*, Feb. 27, 1960, 139.
15. Garry Wills, *Politics and Catholic Freedom* (Chicago: Henry Regnery, 1964), 273.
16. Garry Wills, "The Convenient State," in *Did You Ever See a Dream Walking? American Conservative Thought in the Twentieth Century*, ed. William F. Buckley, Jr. (Indianapolis: Bobbs-Merrill, 1970), 7–37.

passage from Murray in describing U.S. constitutional government as an example of the order of convenience: "Its basis was not the philosophic rationalism that called itself Enlightenment, but only a political pragmatism more enlightened than the Enlightenment ever was, because it looked to the light of experience to illuminate the prudential norms necessary to guide it in handling a concrete social reality that is vastly complicated" (34).

As with Ross Hoffman and the Catholic Burke scholars, so with Wills: he did not mean to argue that politics is entirely a matter of compromise, without any consideration of first principles. Not at all. "This kind of politics can return to the real genius of natural law theory. It will recognize the laws of nature, not as dictates for an ideal life, but as the structure of reality calling at each moment for a real response, individual and social" (33). Although it required no explicit religious sanctions, the order of convenience, first adumbrated, Wills said, in Augustine's *City of God*, had been facilitated by the rise of Christianity. The convenient state offered a provisional order to the saved and the damned alike: "The modern state, in its best manifestations (like the American Constitution), retains the secularization paradoxically created by Christianity's otherworldliness" (36). The convictions Wills expressed in "The Convenient State" guided his whole career in political writing.

Another continuity in Wills's life was his religious faith, which he believed deserving of engaged intellectual scrutiny. He saw in the Catholic intellectual tradition a complete theory of humanity worthy of painstaking study: "Catholic thought involves an endless retracing of different strands in the traditional teaching. These strands unite and intertwine, and their entire force cannot be felt if isolated issues are dealt with. The economy of revelation must be considered as a whole; separate moral insights attain validity only as enunciated within this economy, as emerging out of a large and providential pattern, as interdependent with many other moral truths."[17] Never satisfied with perfunctory observance and dismayed by efforts (such as the pentecostal Cursillo movement) to substitute emotional fervor for intellectual clarity, he treated faith as a momentous challenge to the mind and admired men who, in earlier generations, had grappled intellectually with their faith—notably Saint Augustine, John Henry Newman, and G. K. Chesterton.[18] "The dangers of religion are real," he remarked in

17. Garry Wills, "Catholics and Population," *NR*, July 27, 1965, 644.
18. On the Cursillo movement, see Garry Wills, "Brainwashing for God's Sake?" *NCR*, Feb. 17, 1965, 8; Wills, "In Answer to a Hundred Cursillistas," *NCR*, Dec. 8, 1965, 8. On Augustine, see in particular Wills, *Confessions*, 187–231. On Chesterton, see Wills, *Chesterton, Man and*

one characteristic essay of the early 1960s, "because the object of religion is real. Men perish because they must try to cross the chasm between them and God. . . . All the resources of nature and grace are needed to keep man on the right side of the line that separates sanctity from insanity. And those who are safe from religious lunacy may have to confess that it is because they are far too safe from religion."[19] Catholicism, then, he saw as both spiritually and emotionally demanding but, when properly understood, a thing of great beauty and explanatory power. He never regarded it as closed or oppressive; to the contrary, he said he was impressed by its scrupulosity over intellectual conflicts and by its unparalleled intellectual fertility.[20]

The manifestations of religion in Wills's published work, however, do indicate development and change over time. In the early 1960s he showed a profound respect for the scholastic tradition and at that point was still keeping alive the flame of Catholic medievalism, which had burned so brightly earlier in the century and had doubtless been passed along in the seminary.[21] In response to the usual allegation that the scholastic theologians had wasted their time arguing about angels dancing on the head of a pin, Wills declared that "the entire ignorance of modern man is summed up in that charge; with an unerring instinct for pinning the wrong accusation on the past . . . we have called typical the one debate that no medieval theologian could ever have taken seriously." Medieval theologians, after all, had understood angels to be incorporeal; the modern caricature masked a wonderful effort of the imagination to conceptualize "endless differences of rational essence." This was not narrow-minded hairsplitting but a "large-mindedness to transcend anthropomorphism."[22] Wills raised the possibility that unremitting secularization and the current refusal even to raise such questions was true narrow-mindedness. Secularization had not so much clarified intellectual life as fostered idolatry and brought forth a plethora of religious surrogates. He instanced what seemed to him American liberals' idolization of the United Nations, which we ap-

---

Mask (New York: Sheed and Ward, 1961); Wills, "G.K.C. Organized," *NCR*, Nov. 10, 1965, 8. On Newman, see Wills's articles "Liberals Convert a Cardinal"; "Elusive Matterhorn," *NR*, Feb. 25, 1961, 120–21; "Conservatism and Change," *NCR*, June 30, 1965, 8; "The Most Dangerous Man," *NR*, Oct. 23, 1962, 319–20; "Please Don't Canonize Newman," *NCR*, Oct. 13, 1965, 8.

19. Garry Wills, "A Slip in Definitions," *NR*, Dec. 16, 1961, 423–24.

20. Wills, *Politics and Catholic Freedom*, 36.

21. On American Catholic reverence for the medieval and scholastic, see Philip Gleason, "American Catholics and the Mythic Middle Ages," in Gleason, *Keeping the Faith: American Catholicism Past and Present* (Notre Dame, Ind.: University of Notre Dame Press, 1987), 11–34.

22. Garry Wills, "Finding Someone to Talk to," *NCR*, Feb. 9, 1966, 8.

proach "on our knees, in uncritical reverence," surrounding it with "clouds of secular incense."[23]

As an intellectually engaged layman himself, Wills was confident in the early and mid-1960s that laypeople in the United States were capable, independent men and women who no longer needed the close guidance the church had provided on all matters during the "immigrant era." Catholics had no further need to be an insulated community. On questions of faith and morals, to be sure, the church was every Catholic's guide, but on economic and political questions it spoke simply as one voice among many. It enunciated general principles of conduct, but Catholics who claimed that church teaching indicated a blessing for particular political programs were making an unwarranted transposition from the moral into the realm of prudential judgment. His point, fully developed in *Politics and Catholic Freedom*, was that sometimes there is no one Catholic position on a political question.[24] When the *National Catholic Reporter* began publication in 1963 as an independent lay Catholic voice, sympathetic to reform, its editor, Robert Hoyt, offered Wills a weekly column as conservative commentator, matching him with liberal columnist John Leo in weekly debates across the editorial page.[25] In his column Wills alternated exhortations to vote for Barry Goldwater with praise for the initiatives of the Second Vatican Council, which had dignified the laity.[26] He expressed the hope that this season of reforms would not be followed by rigidification into a new codified orthodoxy but would instead set the scene for constant self-scrutiny and further modifications.[27]

Wills, in endorsing flexibility, was no antinomian, but he believed that church history, properly understood, bore witness to constant development and adaptation.[28] Introduction of the vernacular liturgy, for example, which shocked many Catholics, was in Wills's view a reform in keeping with tradition. After all, Saint Jerome had translated

23. Garry Wills, "Uncritical Reverence for Political Institutions," *NCR*, March 10, 1965, 8.

24. On the maturity of the laity, see Wills, "Cloak and Crozier: Another Anomaly," *NCR*, March 31, 1965, 8, and Wills's contributions to "What Our Columnists Think about Vatican II," with Martin Marty, Arthur Hertzberg, John Leo, and Joseph Nolan, *NCR*, Sept. 15, 1965, 1, 3, 6. See also Wills, "Remembering to Forget," in *The Generation of the Third Eye*, ed. Daniel Callahan (New York: Sheed and Ward, 1965), 234–40.

25. Wills, *Confessions*, 66–67.

26. On Goldwater, see, for example, Wills, "Creeping Papalism," *NCR*, Nov. 25, 1964, 8. On Vatican II, see Wills, "Up from Fanaticism," *NCR*, Dec. 15, 1965, 8.

27. "The true spirit of reform should make it possible to change even the changes that have so far taken place. Otherwise there will be no room for experiment. Each new thing will acquire instant rigidity, making it paradoxically less budgeable than ancient practice." Wills, "Penance Renewal," *NCR*, March 30, 1966, 8.

28. Wills, "Conservatism and Change."

the originally Greek Gospels into Latin, the lingua franca of the Roman Empire, to facilitate conversions. Wills, confidently taking the long view, depicted the centuries-long "freeze" into Latin as only a temporary halt in a process of constant adjustment, which he saw as the basis of orthodoxy.[29] Doctrine, he reasoned, far from being static, develops perpetually, "for doctrine is stable enough to benefit by the worthwhile discoveries of the ages." Doctrine, in other words, is a set of norms for evaluating historical changes, and "it has life because it draws on a complex of thoughts, experiences, stresses, institutions, and inner tensions." Here Wills borrowed from John Henry Newman's conception of doctrinal development, while emulating John Courtney Murray's technique of justifying change as the more traditional Catholic method, no novelty at all.[30]

Wills left the seminary in 1957, aged twenty-three. Michael Novak did not leave until 1960, when he was twenty-six and just a few months from ordination to the priesthood. From two thinly fictionalized accounts of seminary life in his two published novels, *The Tiber Was Silver* (1960) and *Naked I Leave* (1970), it is possible to reconstruct Novak's growing dissatisfaction with the priesthood as it stood in the late 1950s and his anguish over abandoning that way of life despite immense pressures to remain.[31] "The priest, by his ordination, becomes sacred in his very person, dedicated to God and linked mysteriously to the person of Jesus Christ. The conception is awesome and magical. To break from it requires an inner agony that is searing and intense, particularly if one retains one's faith and one's attitude on almost all other matters."[32] Novak, a mercurial temperament, already recognized in himself an impatience with authority and discipline and, not foreseeing the imminent transformation of the church, when the vow of obedience would begin to bear less heavily on many priests, decided to quit.[33] He, like Garry Wills, went to an Ivy League graduate school; he undertook doctoral study at Harvard in philosophy and continued a prolific output of books and articles which never subsequently lagged.

But whereas Wills moved smoothly and rapidly through graduate school, Novak had repeated stops and starts. First he was called back to Rome by an invitation to cover the second session of Vatican II for *Time* magazine (Wills's old nemesis). His reporting, consolidated in *The*

---

29. Wills, "The Latin of the Liturgy," *NCR*, Nov. 18, 1964, 8.

30. Wills, "Liberals Convert a Cardinal," 38.

31. Michael Novak, *The Tiber Was Silver* (Garden City, N.Y.: Doubleday, 1961); Novak, *Naked I Leave* (New York: Macmillan, 1970).

32. Novak, *Naked I Leave*, 22.

33. Novak interview.

Open Church (1964), shows Novak to have been a warm partisan of the reformers at the council. He did not interpret the council as a conflict between liberals and conservatives, the instinctive approach of non-Catholic observers. Instead, he described the opponents of change as advocates of a "nonhistorical orthodoxy" based on the Council of Trent (1545–1563) and the First Vatican Council (1870–1871), against whom the reformers were trying to reinvigorate a much older tradition: "Contemporary theology is strong by reason of its historical sense, its recovery of the concrete, its technical gains in stating the historico-literary meanings of Scripture, its proximity to prayer and life. The reform party . . . draws its strength from the vigorous archaeological, anthropological, and textual advances of the last seventy-five years—advances which have turned it to a sense of time and history."[34] The reformers, in other words, were the true conservatives! Indeed, Catholic liberals of the early 1960s sharply differentiated themselves from secular liberals on matters of general outlook and took their devotion to history and tradition with intense seriousness. Novak remembered later how he had admired John Cogley, the archetypal liberal Catholic of that time, "as a brother, almost as a father figure, a model," because he sensed that Cogley was a "Whig, like Burke or Lord Acton, having a strong sense of community, of prayer, of interiority."[35]

Most of Novak's work from the early 1960s differed markedly from Wills's, partly because Novak was trying to change the idiom of Catholic theology from abstract syllogism toward a more experiential and affective approach. In his early twenties Novak hoped to use fiction as a vehicle for theological reflection (a method now commonplace in divinity schools, then almost unknown). One unpublished novel he wrote in the 1950s analyzed the confrontation of Christianity and atheism through the drama of a war story; another raised the moral and spiritual dilemmas confronting a man who has committed the perfect crime.[36] *The Tiber Was Silver*, his first published novel, worked chiefly as a critique of church bureaucracy's obstructions to passionate faith. Its seminarian hero struggles to retain his integrity as an artist within a philistine and bureaucratized church just as Novak planned to fulfill his gifts in writing fiction.

Novak gradually and sorrowfully realized that he was not going to be a great novelist because of his inability to distance himself ade-

---

34. Michael Novak, *The Open Church: Vatican II, Act II* (New York: Macmillan, 1964), 11.
35. Novak interview.
36. The unpublished novels are "Wind and Sky: A Novel of World War II," typescript, dated 1955, Novak Papers, Stonehill College, Easton, Mass., box 1; "The Restless: A Novel-Poem," typescript, dated 1956, Novak Papers, box 2.

quately from the situations of his fiction; his stories invariably took the form of idealized dialogues between conflicting debaters' positions, too formulaic and lacking in nuance to convince readers of their verisimilitude. Novak's gift was expository prose. He compromised by continuing to write occasional short stories and by developing, over the next fifteen years, a theological method that paid tribute to every person's distinctive "story" and "horizon." Thus, he resisted overschematization and tried to personalize the issues of faith for every Christian.[37]

His first attempt at experiential theology, based on the actual events of everyday life, was *The Experience of Marriage* (1964), a pioneer study based on interviews with thirteen married Catholic couples who had been "blessed" with more children than they could easily manage. Its text showed how they tried to conform to papal teachings against contraception while its subtext surreptitiously argued against the teachings themselves. Novak wrote in his introduction that "an empirical method is . . . fruitful for theology" and that Catholics had too long erred in taking "a merely biological point of view" about sex. In his view, sex had to be understood in its relational context and not simply as an intrinsically procreative act.[38] If so, of course, the testimony of married laypeople was considerably more valuable than that of the celibates who had hitherto dominated moral theology. The book, which never quite advocates the use of artificial contraception, now appears almost blushingly modest and circumspect, but it caused a minor sensation in 1964.[39] For a time Novak was barred from addressing Catholic college and convent audiences, on whose lecture circuit he was gaining the reputation of a young Turk.[40] Garry Wills, whose own religious writing was then firmly bound by the old idiom, condemned this "theology by true confessions" as a breach of religious civilities, even though he agreed with Novak that the moral theology of sexuality was in need of revision.[41] It was not the last time Wills would judge Novak harshly.

37. The "story" and "horizon" themes are elaborated in Michael Novak, *Ascent of the Mountain, Flight of the Dove: An Invitation to Religious Studies* (New York: Harper and Row, 1971); and Michael and Karen Laub-Novak, *A Book of Elements: Reflections on Middle-Class Days* (New York: Herder and Herder, 1972).

38. Michael Novak, *The Experience of Marriage* (New York: Macmillan, 1964), x.

39. "It was . . . a capital event in the development of testimony when in the fall of 1964 there appeared *The Experience of Marriage*, edited by Michael Novak, in which thirteen Catholic couples stated their own experiences in attempting to observe the theological doctrines on contraception and rhythm." John T. Noonan, Jr., *Contraception: A History of Its Treatment by the Catholic Theologians and Canonists* (Cambridge: Belknap Press of Harvard University Press, 1965), 489.

40. See John Leo, "The Campaign against Novak," *NCR*, April 21, 1965, 8.

41. Garry Wills, "True Confessions," *NCR*, Aug. 18, 1965, 8.

Novak's hopes for the Catholic church in the early 1960s were a virtual distillation of the Catholic liberal agenda, much of it delivered in euphoric "New Frontier" rhetoric.[42] The age of the Vatican Council, he believed, presented Catholics with the opportunity to transform their liturgy, adopt the vernacular, and even repair the breach in Christianity which the Reformation had opened. The Reformation, he said, had split away the "prophetic" element of Christianity, leaving Catholicism in the all-too-firm grip of its "priestly" element.[43] Novak believed that elements of "prophetic" Protestant insight could enrich a Catholic education. For example, he said, "there is no better way for a young American Catholic to approach the historical tradition of Aristotle and Aquinas and to avoid the grievous misunderstandings of Latin Scholasticism and a legalistic moral theology than through the concrete, pragmatic, experimental, Biblical wisdom of Reinhold Niebuhr."[44] In sum, Novak believed that a great future awaited this "renewed" Catholicism, but "everything depends on the prophets seizing leadership from the hands of the bureaucrats."[45]

Extensive writing commitments and long absences from Harvard differentiated Novak from most graduate students of his day. He was offered a job in the department of religion at Stanford University in 1965 when his doctoral studies were still not well advanced. Novak loved to teach undergraduates, and he was a gifted and well-loved teacher. Soon he also became involved in Stanford's nascent anti–Vietnam War movement as a faculty adviser.[46] He was, he recalled later, always on "the right wing of the radical movement. . . . The Left regarded me as the most reactionary they would allow into the group. . . . I argued prudence: 'Don't carry Viet Cong flags; this is an American issue, so carry American flags.' "[47] Perhaps because of these and many other distractions he failed his Ph.D. general exams and, despite the counsel of his Harvard professors, failed them again at a second attempt.[48] He had published far more than most contemporaries, including some of those now examining him, but often in a

---

42. See in particular Michael Novak, *A New Generation: American and Catholic* (New York: Herder and Herder, 1964).

43. Novak, *Open Church*, 151–52.

44. Michael Novak, "Niebuhr on Man and Society: Equanimity after Polemics," *NCR*, Feb. 23, 1966, 9.

45. Novak, *New Generation*, 249.

46. Personal interviews with Novak; Max Stackhouse, Andover Newton Seminary, Dec. 11, 1985; Carol Christ, Harvard Divinity School, January 30, 1987. On Stanford, see Novak, "Green Shoots of the Counter-Culture," in his *Politics: Realism and Imagination* (New York: Herder and Herder, 1971), 98–125.

47. Novak interview.

48. Stackhouse interview.

nonacademic idiom and on issues ranging well outside the usual pur-
view of American academic philosophy. From this point on, though he
spent much of his life in universities, his position was always anomalous. From Harvard he took away only his 1965 master's degree.

A shock far worse than failure in exams was the news in 1964 that
his elder brother, a priest and Arabic scholar, had been killed in a
religious riot in East Pakistan (now Bangladesh).[49] This death, interpreted in existentialist terms, precipitated a crisis of faith for Novak,
and in the following years he began to write in a theological style that
would have been inconceivable for any Catholic just five or ten years
earlier. Novak's departure from stylistic orthodoxy between 1960 and
1970 is symbolic of the general fragmentation of American Catholicism
in those years. Borrowing heterogeneously from his former teacher in
Rome, the theologian Bernard Lonergan, from Albert Camus, and from
a new generation of Protestant "radical theologians," Novak challenged more Catholic conventions than in his early work.[50] In *Belief and
Unbelief* (1965), *A Theology for Radical Politics* (1969), and *The Experience of
Nothingness* (1970) he criticized traditional Catholic exclusivist claims
with the abrupt assertion that in the "secular city" of the 1960s the
differences between the believer and the unbeliever, let alone Protestant and Catholic, were negligible.[51] Every lonely, isolated individual,
"thrown" into the world in circumstances beyond his or her own choosing, said Novak, grapples in the "polar night" of the soul for religious
understanding, but "it is not at all certain that it makes any difference
to our identity whether there is a God, a heaven, and all the so-useless
paraphernalia of a Church."[52] All the church's traditional efforts to
guide and educate its flock in faith and to demonstrate the existence
of God now seemed illusory, and Novak declared that "God is equally
hidden from believer and from nonbeliever."[53] He infuriated more traditional theologians at a liturgical conference by proposing that the

49. Michael Novak, *Belief and Unbelief: A Philosophy of Self-Knowledge* (New York: Macmillan, 1965), 11.
50. On Lonergan, see Novak, "Lonergan's Starting Place: The Performance of Asking Questions," in Novak, *A Time to Build* (New York: Macmillan, 1967), 79–96. On Camus, see "The
Christian and the Atheist," ibid., 51–59, and "The Odd Logic of Theism and Non-Theism,"
ibid., 60–69. On Protestant "radical theology" or the death of God movement, see "The Emergence of Hope," ibid., 285–300.
51. Novak, *Belief and Unbelief*; Novak, *A Theology for Radical Politics* (New York: Herder and
Herder, 1969); Novak, *The Experience of Nothingness* (New York: Harper and Row, 1970). The
term "secular city" is a reference to Harvey Cox's influential book *The Secular City: Secularization
and Urbanization in Theological Perspective* (New York: Macmillan, 1965), one of the manifestos
of radical theology in the 1960s.
52. Novak, *Belief and Unbelief*, 11.
53. Ibid., 133.

towering brick and mortar churches (for whose construction generations of poor Catholic working people had made great sacrifices)
should be abandoned, and liturgy now take the form of simple discussion groups in private homes.[54]

Novak's Catholic crisis of faith was analogous to those of the Protestant "radical theologians" Thomas Altizer, Gabriel Vahanian, Paul Van
Buren and William Hamilton, whose work made a press sensation in
1966 under the headline "God Is Dead." To simplify for the sake of
summary, these theologians argued that secularization, far from being
the enemy of Christianity, was its logical outcome, indeed, that Christianity, a radical monotheism, by clearing away the cluttered pantheon
of local and particular gods and separating the secular from the divine,
had taken the most decisive steps in secularization. We had now
reached the stage, they argued, of bidding farewell to the superstitious
remnants of the old religion and the old anthropomorphic father God,
and opening the pathway to full human maturity.[55]

The "death of God" theologians, far from being downhearted over
secularization, believed a brighter and nobler future lay ahead in the
human "coming of age." As they saw it, the truly religious tasks of
their day were secular: to aid in the achievement of civil rights for black
Americans, to prevent war in Southeast Asia, to help in the then newly
minted "war on poverty." They also had the idea that history itself
was, so to speak, speeding up, leaving behind the ponderous age of
books, balances of power, and intellectual systems.[56] Death of God
theology never lacked for critics, and even the radical theologians
themselves, who declared that theology was bringing itself to an end,
weakened their case by remaining in their posts as professors of theology! Nevertheless, several of their ideas were influential during the
middle and late 1960s among both Catholics and Protestants, as was
the split mood of the movement, which swung back and forth between

54. Michael Novak, "The Nonbeliever and the New Liturgical Movement," in *A Time to
Build,* 70–78.
55. The sensation was largely the making of *Time* magazine, with its cover of April 8, 1966,
bearing the slogan "God Is Dead." See also the story, "Theology: Toward a Hidden God,"
ibid., 82–87. The four theologians specified had not previously regarded themselves as a
movement, despite analogous themes in their work. See in particular William Hamilton and
Thomas Altizer, eds., *Radical Theology and the Death of God* (Indianapolis: Bobbs-Merrill, 1966);
Paul Van Buren, *The Secular Meaning of the Gospel* (New York: Macmillan, 1963); Gabriel Vahanian, *The Death of God: The Culture of Our Post-Christian Era* (New York: George Braziller, 1961);
Cox, *Secular City.*
56. See, for example, William Hamilton "Thursday's Child," and "The New Optimism: From
Prufrock to Ringo," in *Radical Theology,* ed. Hamilton and Altizer, 87–94, 157–70.

anguished existential gloom, on the one hand, and exuberant celebration of human freedom, on the other.[57]

Secularization as opportunity rather than threat was a persistent theme in Novak's writing in the middle and later 1960s. "In the Middle Ages" he said, reversing the usual Catholic veneration for medievalism, "men located God in bits of bread; in our day, our Eucharist *is* the poor and the oppressed."[58] This idea echoed radical theologian William Hamilton's formulation that "Jesus is best understood as neither the object nor the ground of faith, neither as person, event nor community, but simply as a place to be, a standpoint." Today's theologian should be working with "the Negro" but definitely "not evangelizing."[59] Neither Novak nor Hamilton feared the sin of pride in giving religious sanction to political work; rather, they criticized modern Christians for excessive political diffidence and treated a secular, politicized Christianity with almost Promethean self-confidence.[60] In another decisive reversal of Catholic tradition, Novak argued that this new outlook offered a bridge between Catholicism and Marxism. Both systems promised effective human action to end suffering and fulfill human potential by overturning "structures of oppression."[61]

Novak seems never to have been entirely comfortable with some of his own effusive formulations; even in these years of personal and religious crisis his traditionalist, anti-Enlightenment background retained some hold on his imagination, reining in his radicalism and hinting at his later swerve to conservatism. Of Harvey Cox, for example, a Harvard contemporary and best known of the radical theologians for his book *The Secular City* (1965), Novak remarked that "he protected himself too little against simple identification with the spirit of our own age; he did not seem to retain enough ground for the launching of prophecy and criticism against the urban, pragmatic, profane style we both admire."[62] Likewise, he was uneasy with Hamilton's dissolution of Jesus into political activism: "Unless Jesus is God, the mystery of his attractiveness reduces to personal whimsy, and there are cer-

57. For critics and interpreters of death of God theology, see (from a much larger literature) Charles N. Bent, S.J., *The Death of God Movement* (Westminster, Md.: Paulist Press, 1967); J. L. Ice and J. J. Carey, eds., *The Death of God Debate* (Philadelphia: Westminster Press, 1967); E. L. Mascall, *The Secularization of Christianity* (London: Darton, Longman, and Todd, 1965); Bernard Murchland, ed., *The Meaning of the Death of God* (New York: Random House, 1967).

58. Novak, "Emergence of Hope," 294.

59. Hamilton, "Thursday's Child," 92.

60. Novak, "Emergence of Hope," 293. Cf. Harvey Cox, *On Not Leaving It to the Snake* (New York: Macmillan, 1967), 3–25, which argued that apathy or sloth, rather than pride, was the deadly sin against which contemporary Christians must strive.

61. Novak, "Emergence of Hope," 294–98.

62. Ibid., 286.

tainly many historical figures closer to us who speak with greater relevance to our time."[63] And Novak was certainly never willing to say that God was dead. "The terrifying thing about the discovery of God is that one comes to see he has been there all the time. He is not dead: we have been dead."[64]

In these extensive theological writings, which received respectful attention from Protestant, Catholic, and even nonreligious critics, Novak tried to show the inescapably personal and experiential dimensions of faith, to emphasize that flashes of insight rather than deductive reasoning lead to understanding and conviction and that religious experience is not amenable to the orderly and systematic idiom of traditional theology.[65] Continuing the prolonged Catholic critique of the materialist and scientific outlook from this unorthodox vantage point, he treated scientists as devotees of an elaborate yet ultimately arbitrary "myth," rather than as discoverers of a rocklike reality, and he insisted that the new young generation, raised on "the experience of nothingness" at this moment of historical "acceleration," would have to construct its ethics neither on Godly certainty nor on scientific granite but on a harrowing awareness of relativism.[66] Ironically, his very way of outlining this new dilemma, thick with quotations from Camus, Sartre, Heidegger, and Lonergan, belied Novak's intentions. As one critic noted, "Novak . . . is duplicating the precise error of that theology, sometimes called . . . traditional, against which he is in revolt; the belief that Christianity requires philosophical foundations, as though what God says to man in Christ requires the Imprimatur of a committee of philosophers before it can be taken to be authentic."[67] And was it not merely rhetorical legerdemain to speak of nothingness as an experience? In the 1970s Novak would resolve his self-invalidating arguments by toning down the relativism and speaking more confidently of a substantial world about which reasoning from shared assumptions to logical conclusions was both possible and necessary.

If Novak had doubts about the nature of religious meaning and authority he had few doubts about the misguided American involvement in the Vietnam War. In the early 1960s, under the powerful influence of Reinhold Niebuhr, Novak had for a time seen himself as a "hard-

63. Ibid., 287.

64. Novak, *Belief and Unbelief,* 156.

65. For critical enthusiasm, see Robert McNally, "Belief and Unbelief," *C,* Nov. 19, 1965, 221–22; Roger Shinn, untitled review, *Journal of Religion* 51 (Oct. 1971), 307–8; Mary Daly, "Michael Novak and Christopher Derrick: A Study in Contrasts," review of Novak, *A Time to Build,* in *C,* Sept. 6, 1968, 601–2.

66. Novak, *Experience of Nothingness,* 34–37, 69–81.

67. J. M. Cameron, "What Is a Christian?" *New York Review of Books,* May 26, 1966, 4.

boiled liberal" and had supported the logic of the domino theory and the need to blend faith with realpolitik, but this conviction soon gave way to repudiation of the war as U.S. troops began to sink into the jungle quagmire of Vietnam.[68] In 1966 Novak joined the liberal Protestant writer Robert McAfee Brown, Lutheran pastor Richard Neuhaus, Rabbi Abraham Heschel, and Daniel Berrigan in establishing the ecumenical group Clergy Concerned about Vietnam (later Clergy and Laity). Brown, Novak, and Heschel collaborated on a manifesto, *Vietnam: Crisis of Conscience* (1967), in which, as the voice of Catholic resistance to the war, Novak hacked away at the tradition of Catholic anticommunism, portrayed the United States as an international outlaw for refusing to abide by the Geneva Accords of 1954, and treated its role in Vietnam as an example of imperialist persecution, which no American could support in good conscience if he or she thought about it "in the light of either the message of the prophets or the gospel of Jesus of Nazareth."[69] Elsewhere, in phrases breathless with exaggeration, he called the war "evil on a mass scale never known in history."[70] He spent a month visiting Vietnam in 1967 and wrote articles contrasting the peaceful, constructive work of a few idealistic U.S. agriculturalists and doctors there to the massive destruction unleashed by the military.[71] He also went with religious support groups to visit draft resisters and deserters who had fled abroad, to France and Sweden, treating them as existential heroes.[72]

Novak knew perfectly well, despite his antiwar fulminations, that plenty of Americans, Christians not excepted, were supporting the war, among them William Buckley. For Buckley and like-minded conservatives, Novak lamented, old ways of thinking, inadequate to the new environment of an accelerating history, had led them to a prowar position; they still believed that "an act is ethical precisely insofar as it falls under a general rule: an ethical action is an exemplification of a universal natural law." Novak, to the contrary, said that this new Vietnam era showed the need for a less formulaic, more personalist ethics: "The criterion for discriminating between acting well and acting poorly is the example of specifiable concrete human beings."[73] This kind of religious reasoning has landed Catholic controversialists in endless

68. Novak interview.

69. Michael Novak, Abraham Heschel, Robert McAfee Brown, *Vietnam: Crisis of Conscience* (New York: Herder and Herder/Association Press, 1967), 25–30, 7.

70. Novak, *Theology for Radical Politics*, 23.

71. Michael Novak, "Voluntary Service in Vietnam," and "Vietnam at Peace," in *Politics: Realism and Imagination*, 32–38, 39–48.

72. Novak, "Desertion," ibid., 25–31.

73. Novak, *Experience of Nothingness*, 67, 69.

trouble in the years since Vatican II. It falsely implies that the truly Christian way is apparent in any controversy, while simultaneously demonstrating just the opposite when Christians line up on both sides of the issue. Novak eventually realized that this posture brought with it the hazards of hubris and self-righteousness and in subsequent rhetoric, while always finding God sympathetic to his general course of action, allowed the Omnipotent a little more distance.

Garry Wills had precious little sympathy for Novak's theological transgressions, but he too found that new experiences in the mid-1960s were forcing him to question long-held convictions. He was less involved than Novak in strictly theological issues during the middle and later 1960s but when he came to make another major statement about Catholicism in 1972, his vision of the church had also been transformed from the "priestly" to the "prophetic." The swing in Wills's outlook, which had political as well as religious resonances, is more obvious in his changing treatment of the civil rights movement, which he interpreted largely through its religious manifestations.

In 1961 Wills spent mornings at the *Richmond News-Leader,* where he wrote anti-Communist editorials. This paper's editor, James J. Kilpatrick, was one of the architects of southern "massive resistance" to desegregation after the 1954 Supreme Court decision in *Brown* v. *Board of Education* and author of *The Southern Case for School Segregation.*[74] To be associated with him was to be close to the hub of segregationist organization. At first, indeed, Wills had little patience with the civil rights movement. He indignantly denied James Baldwin's claim in *The Fire Next Time* that Christianity was no more than an elaborate lie, used to justify white persecution of blacks, and he judged Martin Luther King, Jr.'s "Letter from Birmingham Jail" to be a terrible piece of scholarship.[75] King, he said, had misunderstood Thomas Aquinas, taken Socrates out of context, and manufactured a spurious historical lineage for his civil disobedience. Such a use of history was hardly better than "empty sloganeering," and this supposedly major statement on civil disobedience was "marred by an almost total lack of intellectual rigor."[76] When the riot in the Watts district of Los Angeles broke out in the summer of 1965, Wills shared the horror of his conservative colleagues, calling it a "nihilist rebellion" and attributing it to disrespect for the law. Even the nonviolent civil rights leaders, he believed,

74. James J. Kilpatrick, *The Southern Case for School Segregation* (New York: Crowell Collier Press, 1962); Wills, *Confessions,* 51.

75. Garry Wills, "What Color Is God?" review of Baldwin, *The Fire Next Time,* in *NR,* May 21, 1963, 408, 417; Wills, "Dr. King's Logic," *NCR,* Aug. 4, 1965, 8.

76. Wills, "King's Logic."

must bear part of the blame for this lawlessness. Although demonstrations such as the 1963 March on Washington were defensible and dignified, the sit-ins and freedom rides, which claimed the right to challenge particular laws in the name of a "higher" law, brought the rule of law itself into question, diminishing the salutary sense of civil restraint. "It is the custom," said Wills, "to call James Farmer, Martin Luther King, Bayard Rustin . . . [and even] Adam Clayton Powell the 'responsible Negro leaders.' Yes: responsible for Watts."[77]

At the same time, despite these harsh judgments, Wills was already looking at the racial crisis in a way that set him apart from most other conservative commentators. Explaining the tenacity of racial prejudice as a psychological phenomenon that could yield neither to solutions based on geometric blueprints nor to doses of liberal goodwill, he advocated gradualism and voluntary programs as ways to move toward ending segregation.[78] In 1964 he believed this approach could best be assured by a vote for Barry Goldwater, who favored "the primacy of moral initiative" and would avoid the monolithic bureaucratic approach of Johnson's nascent Great Society.[79] There was nothing radical in this part of his approach, but Wills also believed, unlike many contemporaries, that "conservatives are bound to accept the concept of 'historic guilt' for racial wrongs, since those who glory in inherited values and traditions must admit accountability for historic wrongs."[80] He added that "the wrong done to the Negro" was "so unmanageably large a debt that even those with the best will in the world try to evade the logarithmic ordeal of itemizing these accounts."[81] Wills, never an individualist, was quick to abandon the individual rights approach to race relations which was to prove a stumbling block in the introduction of affirmative action programs and other methods of achieving integration.

Invoking this conservative principle of "historic guilt," Wills also used characteristic "family" language to explain the situation of the black community within the social "organism." "The negroes as a group are at an awkward age," he wrote in another 1964 article, "pressing upon social adulthood yet drawn back by many ties toward their tortured childhood. We [whites, presumably] must acquire the pa-

77. Garry Wills, "Responsibility for the Riots," *NCR*, Aug. 25, 1965, 8. See also Wills, "Civil Disobedience and Civility's Limits," *NCR*, April 7, 1965, 8; and Wills, "Civil Disobedience II," *NCR*, April 14, 1965, 8.

78. Garry Wills, "The Structure of Hate," *NR*, Sept. 21, 1965, 814–16.

79. Garry Wills, "Who Will Overcome?" *NR*, Sept. 22, 1964, 818–20. See also Wills, "Negro Rights, States Rights," *NCR*, March 24, 1965, 8.

80. Wills, *Confessions*, 76–77.

81. Wills, "Structure of Hate," 816.

tience of the bewildered parent who recognizes himself in the odd behavior of his growing son, and not expect invariably adult composure from people only now being allowed to exercise some of their legitimate adult rights."[82] By later standards this sort of rhetoric would be judged insufferably patronizing and paternalistic, but it demonstrates the continuing hold of familial analogies in Wills's thought. The family analogy harks back to the centrality of shared affections in his "convenient state," and shows how Wills, looking at the issue as a familial rather than a jurisprudential matter, could take what many other American conservatives, sticking within an individualist paradigm, regarded as a lurch to the left.

After 1966 Wills's work on the racial crisis lost its measured tone of disengagement and sounded a new note of existential immediacy. These were the years when Wills, leaving academic life under a cloud, was offered a job as staff writer for *Esquire* magazine and at once encountered some of the most jarring confrontations of the 1960s. The impact of raw experience prompted big changes in Wills's rhetoric and provided the basis for his development of a masterful "new journalist" style, in which the author made himself central to the news rather than effacing himself from the story. Reflecting later on this change, Wills admitted: "I had led a very sheltered life until 1967 when I became a full-time journalist. After going from Jesuit seminary to graduate school and from there straight into the classroom, I suddenly found myself in strip joints, police helicopters, black nationalist headquarters."[83] At one point a deranged black revolutionary messiah held him at gunpoint all afternoon, trying to work out a bizarre power deal. Wills commented later, "This was the authentic sixties feeling, of being locked up with a madman whose power made no sense."[84] His experiences, he said, were "an odyssey in reverse, one that made me lose, in some measure, my home, the things I had taken for granted, had thought of as familiar and safe. . . . I was discovering an alien, armed place, not at all the one I thought I had been living in; one I knew continually less about and admired less. My great discovery seemed all a process of erasure."[85]

Wills now began to develop the style he perfected in his 1968 election reports and *Nixon Agonistes*. He would begin with a description of a

82. Wills, "Who Will Overcome?" 820.

83. Wills, *Lead Time*, ix.

84. Garry Wills, "The Sixties," *Esquire* 80 (Oct. 1973): 135–38.

85. Garry Wills, *The Second Civil War: Arming for Armageddon* (New York: New American Library, 1968), 12.

person, incident, or conversation, always engaging, not infrequently malicious, as with his cruel description of Richard Nixon's face:

> The famous nose looks detachable. In pictures its most striking aspect is the ski-jump silhouette . . . but the aspect that awes one when he meets Nixon is its distressing *width,* accentuated by the depth of the ravine running down its center. . . . The nose swings far out; then, underneath, it does not rejoin his face in a straight line, but curves far up again, leaving a large but partially screened space between nose and lip. . . . When he smiles, the space under his nose rolls up (and in) like the old sunshades hung on front porches.[86]

From the grossly physical Wills then moved to high levels of political and philosophical abstraction, meditating on and drawing out the significance of what he had observed, showing how it could be tied to issues that seemed at first glance quite unrelated. Under his piercing gaze a vivid yet convincing picture of a society in crisis, composed of disparate but never unintelligible fragments, came into focus. The larger-than-life situations into which Wills, still in his early thirties, inserted himself, energetic, daring, and yet detached, too shrewd to be swept away in the utopian currents of the moment, provided fine material for this brilliantly creative period of his career. Ironically, Michael Novak, frustrated novelist and devotee of direct unmediated experience, could never quite match Wills's imaginative reconstruction of his adventures. Novak followed other existentialist philosophers by showing, unwittingly, that straight experience can be a highly theoretical matter!

In a book based on his urban discoveries, *The Second Civil War,* and in reporting from the Miami riot of 1968, which took place almost unnoticed against the backdrop of the Republican National Convention in nearby Miami Beach, Wills's attitude to racial politics was transformed. He visited the sordid desolation of the poorest areas in Chicago and Miami, talked with police and community activists about ghetto life, and juxtaposed these scenes to the smugness and self-congratulation of Nixon's ("plastic man's") world.[87] No wonder poor black men and women, alienated from the dominant society, felt desperate:

> Hundreds inside these low, lime-colored houses do not even know how to cry for help. The police who should protect them fear them,

86. Garry Wills, *Nixon Agonistes: The Crisis of the Self-Made Man* (1970; New York: New American Library, 1971), 24–25.
87. Wills, *Second Civil War,* 137–53; *Nixon Agonistes,* 272–82, 368–80.

think each summons may lead to an ambush. Miami's blacks, knowing this, long ago despaired of any visit from police but the hostile or accidental kind—a dash into apartments near those with bombs or bottles, a retaliatory (frightened) canister or club or bullet. This is the system black men live with, and Agnew asks them to praise.[88]

Wills, to be sure, never endorsed direct or militant action in response to the privation and misery he discovered among poor black Americans. His understanding of black radicals' impatience with procedural reform was always attenuated by a faith in conservative and Christian remedies: he wanted to help heal social wounds rather than widen them, as he believed violence must always do.[89] He had, alas, few specifics to offer, being always more effective with criticism than with policy proposals.

Moved by his ardor for reconciliation rather than further estrangement, Wills reconsidered the central figure in the civil rights movement with successive increments of sympathy. When Martin Luther King, Jr., was assassinated in 1968, Wills rode from Memphis with a busload of black mourners traveling to join the funeral procession in Atlanta. His sympathetic account of King's work in the *Esquire* article based on that journey contrasted vividly to his earlier schoolmasterish condemnation of the "Letter from Birmingham Jail." Without relaxing his critical judgment of King's writings, Wills now placed them sympathetically in context, and emphasized that King's mission had been to find Christian sources of resistance to suffering and, after its years of quiescence, "to make southern religion relevant" once again.[90] In subsequent reflections on King, Wills went further, using this religious theme as a way of portraying the black leader as an essentially conservative figure. King, wrote Wills in 1980, "was not 'charismatic' in the sense of replacing traditional and legal power with his will. He relied on the deep traditions of his church, on the preaching power of a Baptist minister; and he appealed to the rational order of the liberal state for peaceful adjustment of claims advanced by the wronged."[91] Once again he saw the innovator as more truly conservative than the conservatives he ousts.

Wills's work for *Esquire* brought him right out of the Catholic and

88. Wills, *Nixon Agonistes*, 281.

89. See, for example, Wills's distinction between rebels and martyrs in "Civil Disobedience II."

90. Garry Wills, "Martin Luther King Is Still on the Case," *Esquire* 70 (Aug. 1968): 94–104, 124–29.

91. Garry Wills, *The Kennedy Imprisonment: A Meditation on Power* (New York: Simon and Schuster/Pocket Books, 1983), 311.

conservative literary ghettos and into the mainstream of American journalism. *Nixon Agonistes* (1970) then won him high repute as one of the most gifted nonfiction writers in the nation, worthy of comparison with Norman Mailer, Tom Wolfe, and Joan Didion, the luminaries of the new journalism.[92] Parts of the book, which Wills clearly designed as a conservative analysis of the United States in 1968 and as an antiliberal compendium, he first offered to *National Review,* but Wills's position on the racial question, his aversion to liberal capitalism, and much more, his growing doubts about the U.S. role in Vietnam led Buckley to reject them; from that time on, despite mutual professions of respect, the two friends were estranged.[93]

Another old conservative friend, the ex-Communist and soon-to-be-Catholic Frank Meyer, reviewed *Nixon Agonistes* bitterly, lamenting that Wills had gone over to the new Left.[94] From this distance it is at first difficult to see why, since the book contains such a comprehensive and damning critique of the new Left, whose "crusade" against U.S. militarism, Wills said, was no more than a mirror image of the very crusade mentality that had taken the country into Vietnam in the first place. Moreover, the student radicals' critique of President Johnson's government exhibited a form of parody McCarthyism, in Wills's view. In the 1950s the radical Right had feared "cool, educated Achesons engaged in clever treason"; the "traitors" identified by the new Left, however, "no longer accomplish our retreat from China but our involvement in Vietnam." In each case, "the point about McCarthyism, old or new, is that whatever has gone wrong was *planned* to go wrong. It was treason conspired at." The student Left had constructed a "demonology" of the "establishment" and declined to "accept the standard of a more prosaic truth" when their "symbolic truth" offered them fantasies of a war between good and evil.[95] He depicted two groups of self-righteous ideologues facing each other across heaped-up barriers of mutual hostility.

A moment's reflection explains many conservatives' hostile reception of the book, its antileftism notwithstanding.[96] In 1968, when Buckley

92. Favorable reviews of *Nixon Agonistes* included Robert Semple, "Nixon Agonistes," *New York Times Book Review,* Nov. 1, 1970, 3, 36–37; Nicholas Von Hoffman, "Nix," *New York Review of Books,* March 25, 1971, 16–18. Von Hoffman remarked: "The only objection you can make to the book is that it's about Nixon. Wills has such a good mind you wish he'd chosen a subject that could keep it occupied" (16).

93. Wills, *Confessions,* 78–79.

94. Frank Meyer, "Attack on Middle America," *NR,* Oct. 20, 1970, 1112.

95. Wills, *Nixon Agonistes,* 66, 63.

96. Conservative reviews as indignant as Meyer's include Francis Graham Wilson, "The Embattled Mr. Nixon," *MA* 15 (Spring 1971): 195–97.

and most other practical conservatives saw Nixon as the standard-bearer of decency, stability, and resolution in the face of a catastrophic social breakdown, Wills lampooned Nixon personally and politically, depicting him as "the last liberal," whose entire raison d'être was to bring about the society real conservatives should want least. Long before Watergate made Nixon an unmissable target, Wills demolished his plausibility not on the basis of his misdeeds but on the basis of what, given every benefit of the doubt, Nixon regarded as political wisdom and right conduct. In the great confrontations of 1968 Wills would not take sides with the procapitalist conservatives or with the "liberal establishment" or with the young rebels. He had no sentimental veneration for "the young" which had become an almost incantatory phrase for Novak by then,[97] and in *Nixon Agonistes* he made a prolonged assault on major liberals of the era: Arthur Schlesinger, Jr. (312–18), Richard Neustadt (208–211), James MacGregor Burns (211–15, 409–12), Richard Goodwin (455–71), John Kennedy (337–40), and Lyndon Johnson (214–17).

The principal sections of *Nixon Agonistes* were devoted to exploding the governing metaphors of U.S. society and politics. Wills's main target was the idea of "markets," central to liberalism since the days of Adam Smith and Jeremy Bentham. "Liberalism clearly was covertly (I shall argue, still is) the philosophy of the marketplace, and America is distinguished by a 'market' mode of thought in all its public (even private) life" (ix). Wills then showed that, despite the cherished beliefs of most writers and politicians, politics, education, the economy, and moral life could not possibly run on free, open, and democratic "market" principles. In fact, they quite failed to do so and *must of necessity* avoid their own ostensible logic and self-justification. Wills treated as equally delusive businesspeople's belief that they were enacting market behavior (181–291) and professors' claims that there is a "free marketplace of ideas" (295–380).

Markets were not the only metaphors under attack. The dominant economic metaphor, for example, was that of a "race" being run by all the citizens, every one of them required from birth to be an economic "athlete." "Every American is told that this land guarantees him 'opportunity'; if he fails it is his own fault—so *he must not fail.* Yet if he succeeds, it must be as a 'common man,' one who moved out from an equal starting place and who is not blocking an 'equally equal start' for all those around him. He must start the race again every day, doubt past achievement, justify his success by repeating it" (531). Wills

97. See especially Novak, *Theology for Radical Politics*, 17–29.

pointed out to a nation just discovering jogging that to spend one's entire life running an endless race is a disheartening prospect, especially if the putative winners are not even allowed to trust in their own victory. With his skillful rhetoric this bright land of universal opportunity takes on the qualities of a hallucinatory nightmare, especially when presiding over it is the quintessential liberal, Richard Nixon himself, "the striver [who] can never stop striving. . . . It is because Nixon is so totally this sweaty, moral, self-doubting, self-made, bustling, brooding type, that he represents the integral liberalism that once animated America" (531–32). A lifetime of racing produces only Richard Nixon and a polity dedicated to adjudicating the race. Under probusiness administrations, said Wills, government takes its role to be the removal of obstacles to the running of the race, whereas more liberal administrations concern themselves with lining up the competitors fairly at the starting gate. Both groups accept the metaphor, but Wills showed that it is hopelessly unsuitable and inaccurate, for the race can neither be started nor stopped (494–504). Besides, he said, "the Adam Smith free market never existed in America" because the institutions of family, community cohesion, and religion closely circumscribed the theoretically independent agents of capitalist theory and because "influential businessmen did not *want* the market to work; they could get much greater rewards from monopoly, protectionism and government contracts than from the ministrations of the invisible hand" (466). The business community, not knowing its own history, attributed to economic liberalism what it had often achieved through state aid and community cooperation. Much of the rest of the population was left struggling, discouraged, and envious, unable to emulate racers whose advantages were overpowering. It was an iniquitous system that spread dismay, jeopardized community, and atomized society.

Abhorrence of perpetual striving was the domestic theme of *Nixon Agonistes*; it was matched by abhorrence of liberal messianism in foreign policy—another way in which Wills strikingly endorsed Thomas Molnar, while drawing quite different conclusions. Unlike critics of the Vietnam War who saw it as evidence of malfunctioning in the political system, Wills treated the descent into war as a logical outcome of American foreign policy principles. Among these principles was the belief that the United States had a mission to spread democracy throughout the world and that the nation, in carrying out this mission, could embody a single "national will." Whereas many in the new Left had come to see U.S. foreign policy as the incarnation of evil by 1968, Wills treated the overseas disaster as the outcome of unrealistic good intentions, a large-scale illustration of original sin in action, so to speak. As he said, "It is when America is in her most altruistic mood that other countries better get behind their bunkers" (397). For Wills, as for John Lukacs, the worst exemplar of this messianism was Woodrow Wilson, who had shown, first in Mexico, then in World War I, his faith in wars for democracy. Wills took Richard Nixon's admiration for Wilson as a danger signal. The old Wilsonianism, he added, was all too evident in Vietnam, where American troops were "preaching democracy with well-meant napalm, instructing (as we obliterate) children with our bombs. We believe we can literally 'kill them with kindness,' moving our guns forward in a seizure of demented charity"(396–97). In fine contrast to Nixon was his former patron Eisenhower, who, tempted to intervene years earlier in Vietnam, had drawn back from the brink, complaining bitterly of how tiny nations can sometimes "pester giants with impunity" but then remarking, "We must put up with it." There was, said Wills "a world of neglected wisdom in that statement," which almost no one seemed to honor in 1968 (131). The United States had now reached what he considered the ludicrous position of charging its average taxpayer $402 per year for armaments but only $2.52 "for food to feed his fellow-citizens" (451).

Wills debunked another widely endorsed aspect of Wilsonian-Nixonian foreign policy, "the doctrine of national selflessness," the claim that the nation is not at war in order to get anything other than a general and abstract "good." This notion encouraged wishful thinking, and again, Vietnam was a vivid case in point: "We limped into that impasse babbling a mishmash of 'universalist,' 'selfless' and self-interested arguments" (445). Moreover, it was really a deeply immoral idea, which permitted the sacrificing of some people's lives in the interest of other people's ideals (434). Wills remarked later that his wife, a complete pacifist, had influenced his thinking strongly in this area; he had certainly drawn far back from his anti-Communist bellicosity of ten years earlier and now disparaged the idea of remorseless Communist expansionism. He still accepted the need for wars of national self-defense, however, and thus he admired Robert E. Lee, who, though opposed to slavery, had fought for the defense of his home in the Civil War, an act Wills found defensible even though the Confederacy's cause was unjust. "For him country *meant* one's friends—the bond of affection that exists among countrymen; and when a rift opened in this union of persons, he had to choose those to whom he was bound by primary rather than secondary ties" (441). Here echoes of the convenient state resounded as Wills lauded the community, a bonded group of families with shared affections, which took precedence over such abstractions as "justice" and "national freedom."

Praise for Lee and his defense of the organic community were matched by Wills's interpretation of the "generation gap." Regarding families as the basic unit of society, he was dismayed at their fragmentation and at the student radicals' slogan: "Don't trust anyone over thirty." To Wills, indeed, the surest sign of social crisis was the generational conflict, so that his own anguish, usually suppressed under an artful rhetoric, burst out when he witnessed street fighting between students and police at the 1968 Democratic convention in Chicago. Sidestepping the issues that had led to fighting, he asked:

> Does it . . . matter which side is wrong? If the society is so good, how did it produce such monstrous progeny? Or if, on the other hand, it is so evil, where did the wisdom of the kids come from (they are the ones most completely formed by this society)? Whichever way you come at it, the problem of the kids is central to America's agony. A nation that forfeits the allegiance of its offspring is a nation that is dying. That was the true menace of Chicago. These *were* our children in the streets, indicting us. (308)

The "us" is significant here. Wills instinctively placed himself on the adult side of the generational divide, though his own children were still much too young to be participants in the demonstration. The message of his book was that liberalism, once a source of pride and an incentive to striving, had now a worn and threadbare look, was indeed so enfeebled that an entire generation had decided to give up striving completely and "drop out" instead. "It is one thing to fail at self-restraint; it is a totally different and terrifying thing not even to try for it, aspire toward it, honor its imperatives" (533–34). Garry Wills's America was in crisis because of its generational fragmentation. The need to outgrow liberalism and restore the organic community were now imperative, though he had few programmatic suggestions to offer.

For Michael Novak as for Garry Wills, it was the encounter with young, disaffected, and radical students, the growing generational rift, and the rising paranoia at the edges of political life which provoked a reassessment of his values and objectives. At Stanford, Novak had enjoyed the company and shared the antiwar indignation of the wealthy and gifted students of that elite school. Even there, "the young" whom he eulogized did not include students indifferent to protest or those who were patriotic about the war and did not clamor for social transformation.[98] But from Stanford and from what he later

<hr />

98. Novak, *Politics: Realism and Imagination*, 108–10, 115–16.

referred to as a West Coast idyll that appealed to his "sybaritic" sensibilities, Novak moved back to the East Coast in 1968. Reputed to be a radical and innovative educator, he was offered the position of professor and dean of students at the experimental campus of the State University of New York, Old Westbury. Still only in his midthirties, Novak now moved into a position of authority, albeit greatly attenuated by the university's dedication to the removal of all traditional constraints. Students were not graded, did not have to fulfill curriculum requirements, and were represented at every level of decision making. Accustomed to protest, they found all the obstacles against which students had rebelled at Berkeley and Columbia already gone. The result, however, was not a calm, consensual place, free of bureaucratic irritants; Old Westbury was soon torn by conflicts over what, to Novak, seemed imaginary problems. As one of the few available authority figures there he became a target. "There was a sort of insanity on that campus," he said later. "We had some psychologists stay with us and they just could not believe the paranoia. There were bomb scares; my children were threatened. People were living out radical fantasies, but since there were only radical students there, there was no one to rebel against. That precipitated a very rapid and strong revulsion and an intellectual rethinking of almost everything."[99] Old Westbury, he wrote later, "showed me conclusively some of the pathologies to which the Left is prey, and taught me that not only the Right has tyrannical and duplicitous tendencies."[100]

Along with the shock of Old Westbury, where he stayed until 1973, came a shock of ethnic self-recognition for Novak, an aspect of identity embodied even in his name but rarely before singled out for scrutiny. He had already frequently mentioned his sense of estrangment from both Protestant and Jewish sensibilities.[101] Until 1969 or 1970 he attributed the difference to his religion, but now he wondered whether it might not be traced to his ethnic background as a Slavic American. As his discontent with Old Westbury intensified, he became a leading spokesman for the "white ethnic" self-assertion movement which came hard on the heels of, and partly in opposition to, black cultural "self-discovery." It was pointedly unfashionable, antiutopian, antiuniversalist, viscerally if not intellectually conservative, and a sure way to dis-

99. Novak interview.

100. Michael Novak, *Confession of a Catholic* (San Francisco: Harper and Row, 1983), 12.

101. "I was constitutionally unable to proceed within the framework of my mentors," says Novak's fictional alter ego in *Naked I Leave*. "I did not have the intellectual roots they did. I was neither Jewish nor Protestant establishment. The world of Marx and Freud, so dear to the radical Jewish tradition, and the more genteel, hard, clear literary sense of the Anglo-Saxons, were foreign to me" (56).

tance Novak from students he increasingly saw as spoiled and arrogant.

The emergence of Novak's ethnic self-awareness can be traced in his earlier writing. The hero of an early unpublished novel, "Wind and Sky," was named Bill Sinclair, an anodyne Anglo-Saxon name. By contrast, the hero of *Naked I Leave*, completed while Novak was at Old Westbury, is the Slavic American Jon Svoboda, whose ruminations unmistakably are fictionalized versions of Novak's own. His writing on Catholicism and Vietnam through the 1960s had made little reference to ethnicity and very little to social class, but, when he began moonlighting as a researcher and speech writer for Democratic candidates in this period, among them Robert Kennedy, Sargent Shriver, Edmund Muskie, and George McGovern, Novak began to take cognizance for the first time of the persistence of ethnic enclaves in many cities. That realization, coupled with his election-related travels between 1968 and 1972, led him to view the new Left through the eyes of lower-middle-class ethnic working people.[102] From that vantage point he could see what he had earlier overlooked in the student radicals: an arrogance, a lack of appreciation for their advantages, and a form of snobbery toward the working people in the army, police force, garage work, and other prosaic jobs. The fate of such people was particularly hard, he now realized. Sprung like himself from immigrant families and subjected to forced Americanization earlier in the twentieth century, they had attained a fragile measure of affluence and stability through self-discipline and hard work, only to be greeted by cries of "fascists!" or "pigs!" from the young radicals for doing what they saw as their patriotic duty and for trying to uphold law and order.[103]

At least for the moment, however, Novak did not mean to surrender his "progressive" identity; instead, he depicted what he called the PIGS (Poles, Italians, Greeks, and Slavs) as mainstream Democrats. These PIGS were the central characters in *The Rise of the Unmeltable Ethnics* (1972), the book that did for Novak what *Nixon Agonistes* had done for Garry Wills, elevating him from the position of "Catholic writer" to that of national controversialist.[104] In *The Rise of the Unmelt-*

---

102. Novak interview; Novak, *Confession*, 12.

103. An illuminating transitional article, first written for *Christianity and Crisis*, is Novak, "The Volatile Counter-Culture," reprinted in *Politics: Realism and Imagination*, 140–51).

104. Michael Novak, *The Rise of the Unmeltable Ethnics* (New York: Macmillan, 1972). Many reviews were critical or suspicious, but all recognized that Novak had struck a resonant note in the politics of the early 1970s. See, for example, Arthur Cooper, "Unmelted Americans," *Newsweek*, April 24, 1972, 95, 97. Cooper joked that "Michael Novak promises to become this season's Charles Reich," that is, fashionable but ephemeral like utopian environmentalist Charles Reich. Peter Ognibene, "A Glass of Dago Red," *New Republic*, Nov. 25, 1972, 27;

able Ethnics he argued that the United States was a set of subcultures, arrayed against and latently hostile to the white Anglo-Saxon Protestant "superculture," whose instruments were television, universities, and the press and whose characteristic tone of voice was "preachment and the manipulation of guilt."[105] Jews, whose style was one of "alienation and dissent," and Catholics, whose style was "dramatic and liturgical," both felt left out in the cold by this "superculture," which humiliated and covertly oppressed them.[106] Just as Wills saw liberalism as bankrupt and unraveling, so did Novak judge the WASP superculture (in a sense, perhaps, the same thing, though seen from a quite different point of view); he claimed that "ethnics" who had crossed over into the mainstream, at least in their working lives, found it so impoverished that they skulked back to their "roots" at weekends to live the lives of "Saturday ethnics."[107] In his anecdotal, inflammatory, yet rambling argument, Novak granted honorary "ethnic" status to white Protestants whom he favored on other grounds, but in general the book posed a polar antagonism between the "good" Catholics and Jews and the "bad" Protestants.[108] At a strange new pitch, the old interreligious battles of the 1950s had come to life again, this time in ethnic guise. Other books of the time, such as Peter Schrag's *Decline of the WASP*, made similar claims.[109]

Novak's contempt for WASP moralism was particularly keen. The moralizing style of the television networks, he said, "imposes a superego more demanding than a Puritan father"(129). Like Frederick Wilhelmsen, Novak now argued that the Faustian transformation and manipulation of the world was a specifically Protestant trait, a war against nature and its laws. "Facing society, the Protestant tends to be 'concerned.' The Catholic tends to be 'reconciled.' Nature and creation the way they are already make the Catholic's heart sing. To the Protestant, creation is apparently 'redeemed' only through being mastered" (191). Their obsession with organization and abstraction enabled WASPs to commit acts of violence without facing their real human costs, both in Vietnam and at home. In a particularly grotesque image, attuned to the most divisive rising social issue of the 1970s, Novak argued that those who supported women's right to abortion (a WASP

Kenneth Clark, "Professor and Student: Moral Inconsistency and Failure of Nerve," *American Scholar* 42 (Winter 1972–73): 156.

105. On the "superculture," see Novak, *Rise of Unmeltable Ethnics*, 123–26.

106. These phrases come from Michael Novak, *All the Catholic People* (New York: Herder and Herder, 1971), 196, a collection of essays on the same themes as *Rise of the Unmeltable Ethnics*.

107. Novak, *Rise of Unmeltable Ethnics*, 31–35.

108. See in particular chapter 7, "Jewish and Catholic," ibid., 167–95.

109. Peter Schrag, *The Decline of the WASP* (New York: Simon and Schuster, 1971).

phenomenon, according to his formula) should "grind an aborted fetus underfoot. . . . Let everybody face physically what they would prefer to accomplish at a distance" (195).

Even though Novak had clearly hit a sensitive nerve in raising the issue of publicly neglected white ethnic groups, his critics, of whom there were many, pointed out the absurdities of this best-selling and widely cited book. One reviewer described it as "containing something to irritate, if not offend, almost every reader" and noted that Novak was more interested in summoning the mood of anger and frustration some white ethnic groups undoubtedly felt than in trying to explain their situation.[110] Another critic noted that ethnicity more often stifled creativity than liberated it, as Novak seemed to imply, that it was "by its very nature a conservative concept," and that *The Rise of the Unmeltable Ethnics*, whatever its author's liberal pretensions, "is indeed a profoundly conservative book."[111] Nathan Glazer, Jewish coauthor (with the Catholic Daniel Patrick Moynihan) of the much superior *Beyond the Melting Pot* (1963), lamented Novak's vagueness about what exactly constituted his own ethnic Slav-ness.[112] No critic, however, had harsher words for Novak than Garry Wills.

In the preceding year or two Novak had begun praising both Wills and William Buckley as Catholic writers who had managed to take on the WASP mainstream on its home turf while retaining their distinctive voices, but this admiration was by no means mutual.[113] Wills, now a regular contributor to the *New York Times Book Review*, declared that Novak, "a very moral man," had written "an immoral book," whose "bright aphorisms and seductive phrases" would soon add to "the rapidly growing literature on the social uses of hatred." Nothing is quite as strange "as a naturally pleasant person who feels it his duty to be unpleasant; to call civility an Anglo-Saxon deceit." Wills described the book as a shameful exercise, which could teach new hatreds even to an Archie Bunker. He took Novak to task for the illogic of the political nostrums with which *The Rise of the Unmeltable Ethnics* concluded. Throughout Novak had emphasized that ethnicity matters most in the United States, but at the last minute, he claimed that the white ethnics and the black population could submerge their differences and together form a new Democratic party, united by their shared economic difficulties. Wills saw Novak here as a Democratic

110. Robert Greene, "Unmeltable Ethnics," *Dissent* 20 (Spring 1973): 235–38.
111. Robert Alter, "A Fever of Ethnicity," *Commentary* 53 (June 1972): 68–73.
112. Nathan Glazer, "Seeking the Tap-Root," *NR*, Aug. 18, 1972, 903–4.
113. See, for example, Novak, *Rise of Unmeltable Ethnics*, 63 (on Buckley); Novak, *All the Catholic People*, 43n (on Wills).

counterpart of Kevin Phillips, mastermind of the Republican party's "southern strategy." Just as Phillips tried to get white southerners into the GOP because of their racism, so Novak was trying to get blacks and ethnic minorities together in the Democratic party "by substituting one hate for another."[114]

In the following years Novak followed up this new departure into ethnic self-consciousness by creating the Ethnic Millions Political Action Committee and by refining his theories of ethnicity as culturally enriching rather than stifling. Defending *The Rise of the Unmeltable Ethnics* when the original storm of criticism had died down, he contended that it had angered some professional academics because they were unwilling to extend the principle of multiculturalism to cultural groups they found (wrongly, in his view) atavistic.[115] Struggling still to maintain his self-image as a man in the vanguard of social change and wary of the title "conservative," even if it was true that his writings were "rooted in the social and earthly sensibility of Catholic experience,"[116] Novak explained that avowals of ethnic diversity would strengthen democracy: "The pluralistic personality counters individualism with self-conscious and disciplined participation in specific cultural traditions, institutions, loyalties and symbol systems. A human being cannot properly pretend to be infinite or universal; he or she necessarily participates in concrete cultural traditions."[117]

The vitriol with which Novak had attacked WASPs in general began to flow in narrower channels in these later works on ethnicity, written during the mid-1970s. His anger was now directed specifically against one element of the WASPs, the "new class" or, as he first called it, "the new adversarial elite," that is, the intellectuals in news media, government, foundations, and universities who celebrated the Enlightenment tradition, who spoke for individualism rather than family and community, and who preferred abstractions such as universal justice to the particularities of family and home.[118] Like many neoconservative intellectuals subsequently, Novak had to face the contradiction of being a member of the very group he labeled pernicious; in 1973–1974 as his anti-new-class rhetoric took shape, he had finally gotten away from Old Westbury and was working in what might well be regarded as one

114. Garry Wills, "New Material for Archie Bunker," *New York Times Book Review,* April 23, 1972, 27–28.
115. Michael Novak, *Further Reflections on Ethnicity* (Middletown, Pa.: EMPAC Books/Jednota Press, 1977), 8–19.
116. Novak, *Rise of Unmeltable Ethnics,* 83.
117. Novak, *Further Reflections,* 74.
118. Ibid., 33.

of the sacred groves of Protestant liberalism, the Rockefeller Foundation.[119]

One of Novak's charges against the new class was that it overrationalistically reduced all issues to questions of mechanics and procedure, draining away the metaphysical dimensions of life to which he had always been attentive. In the 1960s Novak had written a "theology for radical politics," but now he began work on a "theology of American culture," seeking out and implicitly blessing the rituals and assents through which ethnically diverse peoples became bound up with one another in "the symbolic texture of daily religious life." Joining in a historians' and theologians' debate that turned upon Robert Bellah's and Sidney Mead's idea of "civil religion," Novak now depicted presidential elections as liturgical events, emphasizing their suprarational character. "A president is rather more like a shaman than we might wish," he explained in one characteristic passage, for his power over our lives and deaths has "surrounded [him] with a nimbus of magic."[120] President Nixon, he added, had won the election of 1972 because he had, in effect, said the right prayers of the civil religion, while George McGovern had profaned it.[121] Elections were important less because they represented an accurate measure of the popular will than because they played out the familiar and venerated motifs of a "secular liturgy." *Choosing Our King*, a book on these themes, and *The Joy of Sports* (1976), on the religious and liturgical aspects of participatory and spectator sports, elaborated Novak's embryonic "theology of culture."[122]

Despite hints of conservatism in this work, Novak had not become a celebrant of the status quo; the ambiguities of his work in the 1970s reflect those in the work of Reinhold Niebuhr, for whom his admiration, temporarily eclipsed in the late 1960s, was reviving.[123] Just as Novak had set about reforming the church in the 1960s, so now he proposed reforms to the political system in the 1970s. He wanted to

119. On the characteristics and paradoxes of neoconservative thinking, see Peter Steinfels, *The Neoconservatives: The Men Who Are Changing America's Politics* (New York: Simon and Schuster/Touchstone, 1979), On the new class, see esp. 55–65, 285–90.

120. Michael Novak, *Choosing Our King: Powerful Symbols in Presidential Politics* (New York: Macmillan, 1974), 10. The civil religion debate began with Robert Bellah's now famous article "Civil Religion in America," *Daedalus* 96 (Winter 1967): 1–21, reprinted in *Secularization and the Protestant Prospect*, ed. J. F. Childress and D. B. Harned (Philadelphia: Westminster, 1970), 93–116. See also Sidney Mead, *The Nation with the Soul of a Church* (New York: Harper and Row, 1975).

121. Novak, *Choosing Our King*, 38–39, 223, 228, 275.

122. Michael Novak, *The Joy of Sports* (New York: Basic, 1976).

123. See, for example, Novak, *Choosing Our King*, chap. 15, "Beyond Niebuhr: Symbolic Realism."

find a way of breaking up the great concentrations of power invested in the presidency, and he sketched a political system that placed new obstacles in its way; this project became timely and topical when the Watergate scandal broke, and *Choosing Our King* appeared at the height of it.[124] Novak wanted to enrich the sometimes uncritical celebratory theology of civil religion with a Niebuhrian ambiguity as a way to temper exaggerated political hopes: "A mature dream, then, replaces the romantic dream of happiness with an acceptance of evil, the irrational, tragedy, and absurdity. . . . wisdom begins with insight into the tragic quality of human life"(293).

Novak's most striking venture in composing his theology of American culture was *The Guns of Lattimer* (1978), a partially fictionalized account of a famous incident in Slavic-American history, the Lattimer Massacre of 1897, which was the bloodiest encounter in all of U.S. labor history. Thirty-five striking coal miners from Hazleton, Pennsylvania, most of them Slavic immigrants, marching unarmed and carrying the Stars and Stripes, were shot down and killed by a sheriff's posse that panicked as the strikers approached. All the posse members were exculpated by local juries of WASP property holders, even though it was discovered that many of the miners had been shot in the back as they fled from the first volley. Novak, though himself a descendant of these miners, did not use the incident to inveigh against WASP intolerance, as he would have done five or six years earlier. His intention, rather, was to show how, through a "sacrament of blood," bonds of community reconciliation had ultimately formed, teaching a lesson his contemporaries seemed reluctant to learn.

> Before native Americans in the Lattimer region would accept other races as brothers, they first submitted them to ritual bloodshed to "teach them a lesson" and then, in subsequent waves of guilt, those who taught the lesson also learned one. Our nature is a dual one, rational and animal, and both its sides require special tutoring. We are by nature sacramental. More than an enlightened age would like to imagine . . . moral advances cost blood, not metaphorical blood but the blood of individuals. . . . Mere bloodshed is insane, chaotic, meaningless. But reason, glacial under prejudice, is sometimes broken open by the heat of symbolically spilled blood.[125]

124. Ibid., xiv: "I begin with two convictions: that the presidency is the nation's most central religious symbol and that American civilization is best understood as a set of secular religious systems. The drama of the last six months has lent my thesis public demonstration I did not expect."

125. Michael Novak, *The Guns of Lattimer* (New York: Basic, 1978), 245.

This was not at all the sort of interpretation or conclusion to which labor historians were accustomed, and most were irritated by Novak's drift into symbolic theology and metaphysics at the crucial interpretive moment.[126] Novak seemed to regard the bloodshed as ultimately salutary, by direct contrast to Wills, for whom violence more than anything shattered community. Novak had entirely begged the question of why so many other strikes and disputes had been resolved without comparable bloodshed; nor had he adequately investigated, as one critic noted, "whether the structure of the mining industry . . . did not and does not lead to tragedies that are potentially avoidable."[127]

While Novak was elaborating his theology of culture and moving step by step toward a frank celebration of capitalism, which finally flowered in *The Spirit of Democratic Capitalism* (1982), Garry Wills was becoming ever-more estranged from the norms of conventional American conservatism. In the same year that Novak's *Rise of the Unmeltable Ethnics* argued for the durability of ethnic communities and habits, Wills showed in *Bare Ruined Choirs* that one of the main supports of white ethnic community life, the traditional Catholic church, had been shattered beyond recovery. The ecclesiastical counterpart of *Nixon Agonistes,* this book of dazzling insights and wild exaggeration argued that the American church, like the United States itself, had lost the old certitudes in which it once excelled and was newly capable of self-doubt. Could a new and purified faith rise out of these ruins? Wills, once an apologist for the logical, orderly, "priestly" functions of Catholic faith, now made a passionate case for the "prophetic" element in Catholicism. He declared that the moment had come for a return to the Catholic catacombs, trusting to people such as Daniel Berrigan rather than big guns of the establishment such as Cardinal Spellman.[128] Ironically, Thomas Molnar was also casting a wistful glance at the catacombs in those same years, but for the opposite reason; Molnar's catacombs were a place to protect the vanishing orthodoxy, while Wills's catacombs were forcing grounds of "prophetic" Catholic radicalism.[129] As it turned out, both men were able to stay above ground, finding that they had considerably exaggerated the imminence of doom.

At the time of Vatican II, Wills had criticized the routine religious observance of many Catholics, whose faith seemed no more than a

126. See, for example, Richard Kluger, "An Act of Homage," *New York Times Book Review,* Jan. 28, 1979, 12, 29.

127. See the review by Richard W. Fox, *Chronicle of Higher Education,* Feb. 5, 1979, 7.

128. Garry Wills, *Bare Ruined Choirs: Doubt, Prophecy, and Radical Religion* (Garden City, N.Y.: Doubleday, 1972), 250, 230–50.

129. Thomas Molnar, *Ecumenism or New Reformation?* (New York: Funk and Wagnall, 1968).

convention. In the much more open Catholic debating environment of the early 1970s he was more explicit, reflecting that the great benefit of Vatican II and the religious upheavals of recent years had been to sort out the passionately faithful from those to whom religion was merely a way of setting a good example to the children. In *Bare Ruined Choirs*, condemning such conventional Catholics, Wills declared, "The greatest enemy to belief is pretending, especially when you are pretending out of deference to others"(9). For all the trouble it had caused, the Vatican Council had been essential. It had forced Catholics to think for themselves by letting out "the dirty little secret . . . . that the church *changes*"(21).

From Newman, Wills had long been familiar with the concept of doctrinal development, and though he disliked many of the infelicities of the new liturgy and the aesthetic blunders of the new Catholicism, he believed Catholics had to learn how to accommodate themselves to change (64–71). *Bare Ruined Choirs*, all the same, exhibited an elegiac tone, as it evoked Wills's boyhood memories of an entire way of life in a church and a subculture that had now been swept away (15–37). Although the idiom, influenced now by his journalistic style, was vastly changed from his early religious writing, the book itself showed strong thematic continuities. Praising John Courtney Murray (141–58), Wills reiterated his condemnation of Teilhard de Chardin (97–117); scorned what seemed to him the trivialities of death of God theology, which he called and "a clumsy grope of the mind back toward God through his own death" and "religion's way of crying from the tomb" (94); and sorrowed at the deterioration of deference and scholarship in the Jesuit order since his own days as a seminarian (191–213). But along with these continuities came a new willingness to criticize openly the bishops, church teaching against contraception, and Paul VI's encyclical *Humanae Vitae* (174–87), and to defend the antiwar priests Daniel and Philip Berrigan while criticizing Catholic bishops who favored the Vietnam War (230–50).

In 1965, the twilight of his Goldwater days, Wills had criticized the Berrigan brothers for advocating resistance to government policy in Vietnam and for claiming that it was a religious duty to do so. As with Martin Luther King, so with the Berrigans, Wills had feared that they were undermining the rule of law upon which the survival of a fragile civilization rested.[130] Yet in 1966 when Daniel Berrigan was exiled to Mexico by his Jesuit superiors for his role (with Michael Novak) in

130. Wills, "Civil Disobedience, II"; Wills, "The Point Where Martyrs Become Rebels," *NCR*, April 28, 1965, 8; Wills, "Father Berrigan's Ideological Labyrinth," *NCR*, May 5, 1965, 8; Wills, "The Cult of Commitment," *NCR*, May 26, 1965, 8.

founding Clergy Concerned about Vietnam, Wills had signed a protest petition. He did not share Berrigan's political views, he explained then, but he believed the Jesuits had abused their authority, first by permitting Berrigan to make public statements and then by reversing their authorization when his stridency embarrassed them. "Without explanation, without warning, without candor, his superiors severed all these ties, and implicitly claimed an immunity from all criticism not granted to any others who join in public life and debate."[131] If the Jesuits were going to play a direct role in politics, in other words, they would have to expect hard political knocks.

By 1972 Wills had gone a lot farther; he had come to admire the Berrigans' protests against the war, which took the form of symbolic blood and napalm attacks on draft boards in Baltimore and Catonsville. Even when he saw their actions as foolish, he granted them an uncharacteristically charitable indulgence by remarking that "they did dumb things for peace; others have done nothing, dumb or smart."[132] As if to assure that he would not "do nothing" Wills was himself arrested in 1973 on the steps of the Capitol in Washington, D.C., for obstructing access to the building during an antiwar protest and spent an anxious night in a jail cell.[133] His journalistic experiences had convinced Wills, in the years since 1967, that lawful conduct is not in absolutely every case the sole permissible route to reform and that peaceful resistance can be a powerful catalyst for change.

Characteristically, however, Wills attributed his admiration for the Berrigans' transgressions not to what was new in their conduct but rather to how they connected up with Catholic tradition. Comparing the Berrigans to sixteenth-century Catholic martyrs in Elizabethan England, Wills said that "the sense of a large moral heritage, of belonging in the line of Christian witnesses against the world, gives the Berrigans an insouciance that often looks like arrogance" but is really a largeness of spirit not shared by "here and now" Catholics (*Bare Ruined Choirs*, 241). He was careful to explain their doctrinal orthodoxy and their adherence to the priestly vows. When Daniel Berrigan deviated from Martin Luther King's example by refusing to accept his punishment as part of his protest against the law (instead, Berrigan jumped bail and went "underground"), Wills could still praise him as a man who used his faith to bear witness against aggression and militarization.

131. Garry Wills, "The Protest over Berrigan," *NCR*, Feb. 2, 1966, 9. See also Wills, *Confessions*, 67.

132. Garry Wills, "Love on Trial: The Berrigan Case Reconsidered," *Harper's* 245 (July 1972): 63–71.

133. Wills, *Lead Time*, 11–28.

One part of Catholicism is a captive of the state; and the other part is trying to free it. This latter part of the Church not only looks free itself, but has a greater sense of identity, of continuity with the past. By contrast the official church looks lost, out of contact with its own principles—the timorous parish priest prays in a mishmash of styles, all forced and unfelt, while Daniel Berrigan speaks confidently out of what he calls "the ennobling common patrimony."(248)

Once again Wills, like Novak, shied away from the idea that there was something new in the world. The Berrigan protests were certainly behavior unheard of in the annals of U.S. Catholic history, but Wills linked them, perhaps spuriously, to heroic protests in the larger Catholic past. In another marked departure, Wills now praised not only Catholic antiwar workers but also the "prophetic" Protestants and Jews whom he found most admirable: Martin Luther King, Jr., William Stringfellow, William Sloane Coffin, A. J. Muste, Everett Gendler, and Arthur Waskow. "Prophecy," he wrote, "looks simultaneously backward and forward, assigns men fresh tasks with an urgency born of ancient obligation. In this way prophets summon men into history, down to where the deep streams run, fed by the oldest springs" (250).

The superbly evocative early passages of *Bare Ruined Choirs*, on the breakup of the old Catholic ghetto, drew the applause of nearly all critics, but Wills's interpretations of Catholicism in the 1960s fueled more controversies. As usual, he had done nothing to gain the affection of Catholic liberals, and one of their leading lights, the Chicago sociologist Father Andrew Greeley, was incensed by Wills's cutting and sometimes scornful rhetoric. He denounced the book for demolishing, "cleverly, cruelly, and unfairly," everyone "connected with the Catholic 1960s." "Little of what he describes," Greeley added, "has anything to do with the Catholic masses, about whom he knows nothing and cares less."[134] John Lukacs, by contrast, writing in *Triumph* and missing the point of this book just as Frank Meyer had missed the point of *Nixon Agonistes*, said that Wills had simply given in to the temptations of liberalism, becoming a fashionable Catholic leftist as a way of gaining social status.[135] Most stinging of all were Joseph Sobran's withering attack on "the newborn Garry Wills" as a traitor to conservatism and the doctored photograph on the cover of *National Review*, which placed Wills's head on Black Panther Huey Newton's body to express the contempt of mainstream conservatives.[136] By now, as must be clear, Wills,

134. Andrew Greeley, "Catholic Chic," *Commentary* 55 (Feb. 1973): 90–92.
135. John Lukacs, "Bare Ruined Choirs: Ample Parking in Church Yard," *T* 7 (April 1973): 22–24.
136. Sobran, "Newborn Garry Wills," and cover, *NR*, June 22, 1973.

like Novak, had made a lot of enemies who were not willing to give him the benefit of the doubt or to follow the internal logic of his ideas.

By the early 1970s Wills had left *Esquire* and was working as a syndicated columnist for the Universal Press Syndicate. The title of his column, "Outrider," suggested that Wills was still traveling along in support of his country and its conservatives, but as a loner, a fair distance away from the main expeditionary forces. The column reached over fifty newspapers nationwide through the 1970s, though Wills was never able to shine in the compact format so well as Buckley, who remained the more successful columnist. Buckley was never better than with one thousand words; Wills prospered most when he was allotted a hundred thousand, space enough to "load on the evidence like a scholastic philosopher, then nail it down with rhetorically driving analysis."[137]

In 1973, by then a widely renowned controversialist, he returned as an adjunct professor of humanities to Johns Hopkins University, which had denied him tenure seven years previously. A celebrity intellectual, he now had the opportunity to write introductions to other authors' books. His extraordinary introduction to Lillian Hellman's *Scoundrel Time* (1976) indicated just how far he had moved politically in the foregoing years and constituted the high-water mark of his disillusionment with the verities of his youth. Condemning ideological thinking of left and right, Wills praised personal rectitude and declared that in the face of red hunters (Truman Democrats and McCarthyite Republicans alike) Hellman, an "unfriendly" witness, had exhibited commendable courage. He now treated the United States not as the enemy of ideology but as its epitome, especially when politics was based on monolithic anticommunism. "Ours was the first of the modern ideological countries, born of revolutionary doctrine, and it has maintained a belief that return to doctrinal purity is the secret of national strength for us." By contrast, Wills said, most of his radical friends, Hellman included, had resisted ideological thinking in the interest of preserving their personal responsibility: "Most radicals I have met were extraordinarily civil. They oppose the general degradation, not with a programmatic 'solution' but with a personal code that makes pride possible in a shameful social order. They do not wish to be implicated in responsibility for society's crimes, which means that they must take a special kind of responsibility for their own acts. Ideology is, by contrast, an *escape* from personal responsibility."[138] This claim that the Right was a slave

137. John Gardner, "Bare Ruined Choirs," *New York Times Book Review,* Oct. 29, 1972, 1, 10.
138. Garry Wills, Introduction to Lillian Hellman, *Scoundrel Time* (Boston: Little, Brown, 1976), 19, 31.

of ideology and the Left free of it marked a hundred-and-eighty-degree turn from Wills's beliefs in the late 1950s; his contention that the United States was the first ideological nation and a "shameful social order" also flatly contradicted the more common Catholic conservative view, popularized in the 1950s by Ross Hoffman and John Courtney Murray, of the last nonideological nation, standing proudly apart from the infection of Jacobin Europe and preserving the old natural law tradition. The antinationalist tone was never again to be so strident as here; in subsequent work Wills mitigated the ferocity of his attacks on American tradition.

Indeed, as the crises of the late sixties and early seventies began to dissipate Wills turned away from contemporary history (though he continued to cover political campaigns extensively in the 1970s and 1980s) and toward the formal study of remoter times. In doing so, he did not cease to provoke controversy. The fruit of this new period of historical scholarship, *Inventing America*, a study of Thomas Jefferson's draft of the Declaration of Independence, was a work of vertiginous revisionism, and it raised Wills's reputation a few more notches by winning him two major literary prizes.[139] Far from owing its chief philosophical debts to John Locke, as most historians had long assumed, Wills believed that Jefferson's declaration was based on the work of communitarian Scottish Enlightenment philosophers, principally Thomas Hutcheson, Thomas Reid, and David Hume. Wills, always an intellectual swashbuckler, horrified intellectual historians of the eighteenth century by questioning whether Jefferson had even so much as read Locke's *Second Treatise* and by asserting that historians who found a Lockean individualism at the heart of the nation's foundational document had carelessly or willfully misread it.[140]

Wills had always been interested in a usable past rather than one whose sheer strangeness distanced it from his own times. In his years as a classics professor he had edited an anthology of translated Latin poetry, prefacing it with the remark that the experience of imperial Rome, which it reflected, was particularly relevant to cold-war America. The Romans, like the Americans of the 1960s, "had their roots in deeply held agrarian principles but found themselves exercising world power through a cosmopolitan complex."[141] *Inventing America* was also meant to be didactic, to show Americans that their

139. The awards were the National Book Critics' Circle Award and the Merle Curti Award of the Organization of American Historians.
140. Garry Wills, *Inventing America: Jefferson's Declaration of Independence* (New York: Vintage, 1978), 167–75.
141. Garry Wills, *Roman Culture: Weapons and the Man* (New York: George Braziller, 1966), 24.

foundational documents were based not on individualistic liberalism, as generations of scholars had assumed, but on a much more communitarian tradition with strong natural law overtones. In Francis Hutcheson, Wills found a philosopher who, like himself, looked to the family rather than the individual as the basic unit of society, who argued for a government based not on contract but on natural sociability, "a more fraternal, communitarian basis for American democracy than a Lockean would ever admit." Some critics noticed this submerged contemporary agenda in *Inventing America*, and one remarked that it was the "individualistic cast of Locke's thought" which Wills disliked, "though he won't come right out and say it."[142] Even the historians most disturbed by Wills's conclusions, his rough way with opponents, and his meteoric rise in the field of Revolution historiography, had to admit that *Inventing America*, with its acute attention to nuances of language and its vast analytical range and power, could not be ignored by any serious historian of the era.[143]

As the 1970s came to a close, Garry Wills and Michael Novak both wrote autobiographies, and like John Lukacs, both chose titles that paid tribute to Saint Augustine. Wills's *Confessions of a Conservative* (1979) and Novak's *Confession of a Catholic* (1983) mark another of the several benchmarks for the comparison of these two gifted and prolific writers. Both showed that after two stormy decades they were finding ways of coming to terms with their country and making provisional peace treaties (or arranging armed neutrality) with their antagonists. Wills approached the task in his usual style of moving from the specific to the more general and abstract. Beginning with fond anecdotes about his early life with the anti-Communist conservatives at *National Review*, he explained his gradual detachment from their outlook, recalling with embarrassment that he had written a good deal of hair-raising anti-Communist rhetoric himself.[144] He moved next into reflections on the many politicians he had met and studied, showing how this experience fulfilled his earlier generalizations in "The Convenient State." Praising their skill in compromise, their willingness to "settle for less," Wills showed how the run of American politicians, along with most bureaucrats, should be welcomed, if not actually venerated, for their humble, down-to-earth efforts to assure social continuity (170–84).[145] The dan-

---

142. Richard Rabinowitz, "At Jefferson's Feet," *Nation*, March 31, 1979, 342–44.

143. See, for example, Edmund Morgan, "The Heart of Jefferson," *New York Review of Books*, Aug. 17, 1978, 38–40; Judith Shklar, "Inventing America," *New Republic*, Aug. 26, 1978, 26–30. For a comparable review of Wills's sequel, *Explaining America: The Federalist* (New York: Penguin, 1982), see Gordon Wood, "Heroics," *New York Review of Books*, April 2, 1981, 16.

144. Wills, *Confessions*, 51.

145. See also Wills, *Lead Time*, 117–77.

gerous ones were those who would not conciliate and temporize, those like Woodrow Wilson who pursued their goals inflexibly from inside the government. New inputs to the system, he now recognized, originated in the work of "prophets" such as Martin Luther King, who would have made a hopeless congressman or senator because of his refusal to compromise but who, by his peaceful intransigence from the outside, forced changes in the system itself and enlivened community consciences (157–69).

From these personal reminiscences Wills moved to reflection on Augustine's *City of God*, his favorite compendium, to show how skillfully this father of the church had blended political and religious wisdom in outlining his own version of the convenient state. Augustine had recognized that since the Christian millennium was probably not imminent, sinners and saints must live together in the earthly community while they waited, accepting "an agnosticism about the mystery of each other person's destiny." This "theological humility" comparable to the uncertainty Novak emphasized in *Belief and Unbelief*, had "important political consequences":

> Even the true members of the City of God (who do not yet know that they are true members) must "settle for less" than the final order of things, or they would exclude erring members of the final city still on their way to Christ. . . . The test of secular citizenship, therefore, cannot be theocratic or even "just" in any ultimate sense. That would arrogate to man the right to distinguish members of the two cities, a right God has reserved to himself for the last Day of Judgment. (192)

Here, said Wills, was sound guidance for the present. Now that a large state apparatus and bureaucracy existed, it would contradict the conservative principle of gradualism to try sweeping reforms of government. "Conservatism is a title deserved by a view that tries to value and retain the politician as well as the prophet, the bureaucrat as well as the technocrat, the business elite as well as the unions, the poor and the oppressed as well as the elites" (210–11). So long as it was leavened with prophets, Wills found much to admire in the American system, whose slow and often ponderous workings "guarantee coherence and continuity; they soften difference and mute change, so it may enter the social body as nutriment, not as a knifeblade. These surely are conservative values" (210). Charisma, by contrast, the quality for which President Kennedy was often fondly remembered, seemed to Wills a dangerous quality in a political leader because it led to delegitimation of institutions and tended to undermine, rather than reinforce, political continuities. His dislike for the Kennedys, always acute, burned brightly into the 1980s.[146]

Novak's *Confession of a Catholic* paralleled Wills's *Confessions of a Conservative* by blending personal reminiscences with meditations on a crucial Christian document. Whereas Wills chose the *City of God*, Novak chose the Nicene Creed, and in chapters named for each of its phrases he dissected the malaise in American society and Catholicism as he saw it, and his own role in the formation and solution of such problems.[147] By now Novak was a fellow at the American Enterprise Institute in Washington, D.C. As the 1980s began, the auguries in *The Guns of Lattimer* were fulfilled, and Novak became an outspoken apologist for capitalism. He believed that the free market was consonant with his faith because "democratic capitalism" (he was careful to couple the terms throughout) is not an individualistic but a familial system, which, under the rule of law, nurtures this basic unit of society and can be entirely compatible with the message of the Gospels. Entrepreneurs, as Novak told it, while operating out of self-interest at first, discipline themselves to make a fortune not just for personal gratification but because of their vision of a future in which their families and, beyond them, their communities will benefit.[148] This system is politically benign, because it depends on a free flow of information; encourages the free press and the development of "mediating structures," professional organizations to assure high moral standards in business conduct; and inhibits violent social change. The Holy Trinity in religion could be matched by a secular trinity—political democracy, market economy, and pluralistic liberal culture—which stood or fell together.[149] Novak, recognizing as Wills had in *Nixon Agonistes* that the United States had never been an unregulated capitalist nation, showed that historically the rise of capitalism and the rise of democratic and liberal regimes were intimately linked. The marvelous wealth generated by democratic capitalism bespoke an almost miraculous providence, like the paradox of Christianity itself.

> Capitalist ideology is depressing to read . . . because it takes human beings quite in their weakness. It follows the paradox of Isaiah and

146. See in particular Wills, *Kennedy Imprisonment*, esp. 195–206. For an earlier unsentimental assessment, see Wills, "The Kennedy Cult," *NCR*, Dec. 9, 1964, 9.

147. In several places Novak admits indiscretions in his earlier work, but the mea culpa has to compete with reproaches to liberal and radical Catholics who did *not* change their ways. See, for example, the chapter "Apostolic Church," dealing with Catholic obedience and issues of sexuality: Novak, *Confession*, 109–30.

148. Michael Novak, *The Spirit of Democratic Capitalism* (New York: Simon and Schuster/Touchstone, 1982), 156–70.

149. Ibid., 337–40.

of Christ, that redemption should come in the most unlikely spot, through the weakest and poorest of persons, as in the carpenter from a very poor and undeveloped part of the Roman Empire. In a related way, capitalist thinkers discovered the dynamic energy to change the face of history not where it might be expected, in human nobility, grandeur, and moral consciousness, but in human self-interest. In the pettiest and narrowest and meanest part of human behavior lies the source of creative energy. . . . Where no one would choose to look the jewels are to be found."[150]

A sympathetic reviewer summed up Novak's argument in the apothegm, "Capitalism succeeds because it is an economic theory designed for sinners, of whom there are many, just as socialism fails because it is a theory for saints, of whom there are few."[151]

In defending democratic capitalism, then, Novak argued that its own practitioners often unnecessarily put themselves on the defensive, feeling forced to admit the sordidness of their work rather than acknowledging the elevated motives that were no less central to the system.[152] Thomas Molnar said that counterrevolutionaries usually lost the battle as soon as they opened their mouths. Novak here added that the same was true of traditional capitalist theorists, who gave away too much to their enemy, failed to fight for their own high ground, and had not yet grasped the importance of seizing a place for themselves in the media, currently dominated by the adversarial "new class."[153] Just as Garry Wills complained that the inheritors of the Declaration of Independence did not even know its true nature, so Novak complained in effect that the inheritors of a benign system that had made the United States the richest nation in the world did not even know how to praise it.

Both men found that, all things considered, there was much to praise in the United States so long as it was properly interpreted along lines consonant with their Catholic principles. Both continued to feel, all the same, that they were outsiders. Novak in particular ruminated darkly about the "hidden agenda of self-aggrandizement" which the "new adversarial elite" was pushing, with its plans for an ever-growing bureaucratically centralized state, and pictured himself, as before, as one of the small band of truth seekers ever journeying to new "horizons" despite the obstructions of hypocritical and self-serving opponents.

150. Michael Novak, *Capitalism and Socialism: A Theological Enquiry* (Washington, D.C.: American Enterprise Institute, 1979), 117.
151. Samuel McCracken, "A Theology of Capitalism," *Commentary* 74 (July 1982): 76.
152. Novak, *Spirit of Democratic Capitalism*, 19–28.
153. Ibid., 181–85.

In one respect, at least, Novak's *Confession* was a mea culpa. He admitted that he had been wrong about Vietnam, had quite failed to anticipate the boat people, Pol Pot's massacre in Cambodia, and the horrible Asian aftermath of the U.S. mission there. He grieved to have been so vocal an opponent of a war that retrospect seemed to justify. He grieved also to have been so outspoken in religious affairs.[154] Admitting his role as a young Catholic rebel in the early 1960s, he now wrote that unimaginable indignities and blasphemies had been committed against the church in the name of Vatican II. Although he remained at variance with church teaching on the one specific doctrinal issue of contraception, Novak now lined himself up behind Pope John Paul II, Cardinal Ratzinger, and the forces of ecclesiastical counterrevolution, against feminist and liberation theology, against gay priests, and against what seemed to him the breakdown of all lines of Catholic authority.

In 1980 Wills and Novak were in their midforties; both went on to enjoy productive and profitable work in the following decade. The Reagan and Bush years did not lack for controversies, of course, and these two Catholic authors joined in the fray with their usual brio, Wills against the Republicans, Novak very much for them (he became President Reagan's ambassador to the United Nations civil rights commission at Geneva in 1982 and 1983). But the social changes of the 1980s were less explosive than those of the 1960s and 1970s, in which each man had suffered successive shocks that forced him into reconsideration of his faith, his political principles, and his understanding of the world. Thus, the continued changes in each man's work became far less dramatic. Both remained faithful to Catholicism, but as an interpretive device for their political and social outlook it had none of the coherence Catholicism had enjoyed thirty years before. The paradoxes of fragmentation were never more apparent than when the American Catholic bishops set themselves the task of writing a pastoral letter on nuclear weapons.

154. Novak, *Confession,* 10–12.

Epilogue

Nuclear Weapons, Dissent, and a New Generation in the 1980s

This book has traced the involvement of American Catholic lay conservatives in events since World War II. The 1960s was the crucial decade of transformation and fragmentation for Catholicism and for conservatism, and the reverberations of that decade's events have continued to the present. One incident that demonstrates the new face of U.S. Catholicism, its intellectual life and its internal fractures, is the debate over the bishops' pastoral letter on nuclear weapons, well publicized in the early 1980s.

In November 1980, the same month that a conservative triumph at the polls won the presidency for Ronald Reagan, the National Conference of Catholic Bishops announced that it was studying the issue of nuclear weapons and that it planned to issue a pastoral letter on the subject. The American and European campaigns for nuclear disarmament were then at their height. Unlike previous pastorals, which the bishops had written for Catholics alone, this one was to be addressed to all U.S. citizens because all alike were bound by universal moral norms. Also unlike previous pastorals, it was to be written after extensive and open public debate.[1] The letter went through three draft stages in the course of the next two and a half years, each of which

1. On the developments that immediately preceded this new departure in episcopal conduct, see Francis X. Winters, "The American Bishops on Deterrence—'Wise as Serpents, Innocent as Doves,'" in *The Catholic Bishops and Nuclear War: A Critique and Analysis of the Pastoral "The Challenge of Peace,"* ed. Judith Dwyer (Washington, D.C.: Georgetown University Press, 1984), 25–36.

was discussed by the assembled bishops. They did not disguise their internal disagreements: views ranged from absolute pacifism, on the one hand (Archbishop Raymond Hunthausen of Seattle), to traditional nuclear-based deterrence, on the other (Archbishop John O'Connor of New York), with a large middle ground opposing use of nuclear weapons in almost all circumstances (Archbishop Joseph Bernardin of Chicago).[2] No longer were Catholic leaders united behind the policy of "massive retaliation" as they had been in the 1950s when they had taken second place to no one in their espousal of tough measures in the cold war. Religious leadership of the conservative political resurgence of the 1980s was everywhere attributed not to Catholics but to evangelical Protestants.[3]

The final version of the bishops' letter, *The Challenge of Peace: God's Promise and Our Response* (May 1983), condemned a defense policy based either on first use of "counterforce" nuclear weapons or on second-strike "countervalue" attacks, each of which, said the bishops, by threatening the lives of millions, violated Jesus' peaceable injunctions and the principles of Catholic just-war theory. One historian of the process summarizes: "Although the bishops did not flatly reject the possible retaliatory use of small-yield nuclear weapons against clearly definable military targets, they believed that the burden of proof rested on those who asserted that limiting a nuclear war was possible. On this 'centimeter of ambiguity,' as Father [Bryan] Hehir subsequently called it, deterrence would have to rest."[4] If the government had put the letter's recommendations into practice, it would have had to restructure defense policy radically at a time (the gloomy twilight of the Leonid Brezhnev era) when an end to the cold war was not yet in sight.

Turnover in the episcopate since 1960 had been extensive. Although earlier generations of Catholic bishops had questioned certain aspects of government policy, none had previously made so drastic a challenge as this new group, for many of whom the cold war, Vietnam, and the

---

2. For the evolution of Catholic teachings on war and peace and the bishops' use of it, see George Weigel, S.J., *Tranquillitas Ordinis: The Present Failure and the Future Promise of American Catholic Thought on War and Peace* (New York: Oxford University Press, 1987), 257–85. See also William Au, *The Cross, the Flag, and the Bomb: American Catholics Debate War and Peace, 1960–1983* (Westport, Conn.: Greenwood, 1986).

3. One principal Moral Majority strategist in 1980 was Paul Weyrich, a former Roman Catholic who had adopted Eastern Rite Catholicism in 1965 as a protest against the vernacular liturgy. In general, however, the Catholics kept at arm's length from the strident evangelical idiom of Moral Majority. See Mary Hanna, "Catholics and the Moral Majority," *Catholicism in Crisis* 1 (Nov. 1982): 10–11. As Hanna shows, Moral Majority was instrumental in aiding antiabortion Catholic congressional and senatorial candidates in the 1980 election. Tensions between Protestants and Catholics in the group nevertheless remained.

4. Weigel, *Tranquillitas*, 271.

events of the 1960s had been crucial formative experiences. Although in this context the language of left and right is prone to mislead, because the Catholic political spectrum did not tally with the range of secular political views, it is worth echoing a media perception that the bishops had moved far to the left since the early 1960s on many social and political questions.[5] Another commentator noted: "In a sense the American Catholic community 'comes of age' with this Pastoral Letter. Addressing the sociopolitical arena, the Bishops do not hestitate to challenge certain key aspects of official United States policy regarding nuclear weapons."[6] In this instance "coming of age" (a favored Catholic phrase of the era) meant showing a greater willingness to criticize than to conform to government policy. The letter certainly indicated that the days were past when the government could rely on fervent official Catholic support for anti-Communist and military policies. It even granted intellectual and religious sanction to unilateral disarmament and radical pacifism, which earlier Catholic teaching had denied.[7]

The bishops said they welcomed input to their pastoral debate from interested parties and sought to generate rather than stifle discussion, but they may have gotten more than they bargained for. They were beset by a Catholic peace movement that deplored their temporizing between the second and third drafts of the letter (condemnation of nuclear weapons was softened) and by Catholic conservatives who were dismayed at their concessions to the peace movement.[8] William Buckley cautioned against a new era of appeasement, fearing that after forty years of holding out against communism the church was beginning to lose its stomach for the protracted cold war. He added that Christians must be willing to give up their lives even, if need be, in apocalyptic nuclear wars, mindful of Jesus' message that "His Kingdom is not of this world," rather than succumb to Soviet tyranny. Buckley was afraid that the widespread Christian antiwar sentiment of the early 1980s bespoke a veneration of life as a supreme good in itself. For Christians who aspire to Christ's Kingdom, he believed, it should ever remain no more than a contingent good.[9]

Michael Novak, by then religion editor of *National Review,* was simi-

5. Jay P. Dolan, *The American Catholic Experience: A History from Colonial Times to the Present* (Garden City, N.Y.: Doubleday, 1985), 452.

6. Judith Dwyer, S.S.J., Preface to *Catholic Bishops and Nuclear War,* ed. Dwyer, vii.

7. Wiegel, *Tranquillitas Ordinis,* 145–46, 248. On the efforts of isolated earlier Catholic pacifists, see Gordon Zahn, *War, Conscience, and Dissent* (New York: Hawthorne, 1967).

8. For the pacifist position, see Francis X. Meehan, "Nonviolence and the Bishops' Pastoral: A Case for Development of Doctrine," in *Catholic Bishops and Nuclear War,* ed. Dwyer, 91–107.

9. William F. Buckley, Jr., "Dubois Memorial Lecture," in Buckley, *Right Reason* (Garden City, N.Y.: Doubleday, 1985), 111–20.

larly alarmed by the bishops' letter. He had joined Notre Dame professor Ralph McInerny in founding a new journal, *Catholicism in Crisis*, at the end of 1982. The title paid tribute to Reinhold Niebuhr's *Christianity and Crisis*, which the eminent Protestant theologian had founded in 1941 as a forum for realpolitik approaches to foreign policy and to advocate early U.S. entry into World War II.[10] American Catholicism, Novak believed, now faced a crisis comparable to that of Protestants in 1941, with utopian-pacifist sentiment sweeping the nation just as a relentless adversary deployed new weapons in Europe, heightening the threat of aggression. *Catholicism in Crisis* portrayed itself as a voice of the "sane center" and said it hoped to "breathe life back" into a "liberal Catholic tradition" that had become moribund.[11] Despite this claim, the journal at once became home ground for Catholic conservatives with strong nationalist convictions and, in particular, for those who favored maintaining nuclear deterrence as a central support of American foreign policy. It showed a taste for polemics from the start; John Noonan was among its original editors but soon left the board because "its first few issues were far more vituperative than I want to be."[12] It also claimed, contrary to the conventional wisdom of postconciliar Catholics, that the role of the laity, far from expanding, was becoming steadily more circumscribed as bishops and priests made declarations on political issues (read: nuclear policy) for which they had neither training nor competence.[13]

Novak responded to the pastoral letter with an open letter to the bishops on behalf of a group of prodeterrence Catholics, which he published in an early edition of this new journal.[14] William Buckley was so taken by the force and cogency of Novak's open letter that he decided to reprint it in *National Review;* indeed, he devoted an entire issue to the letter, where it appeared just a month before the bishops published their own final draft.[15] Novak's open letter was then published as a book, *Moral Clarity in the Nuclear Age,* with an introduction by Buckley and—more illustrative of changed times—a foreword by Billy Graham. Graham's phrases were chosen to be inoffensive to all

10. Acton (pseud.), "The Present Crisis," *Catholicism in Crisis* 1 (Nov. 1982): 1–2. On the foundation of *Christianity and Crisis*, see Richard W. Fox, *Reinhold Niebuhr: A Biography* (New York: Harper and Row, 1985), 196–97.

11. Ralph McInerny, "The Lay of the Land," *Catholicism in Crisis* 1 (Feb. 1983): 1–2. *Commonweal* denied the claim: editorial, "Sane Center, or Just Anti-Left?" *C*, March 11, 1983, 131–32.

12. Personal interview with John T. Noonan, Jr., Berkeley, Calif., June 10, 1985.

13. Acton, "The Present Crisis," 2.

14. Michael Novak, "Moral Clarity in the Nuclear Age: A Letter from Catholic Clergy and Laity," *Catholicism in Crisis* 1 (March 1983): entire.

15. Michael Novak, "Moral Clarity in the Nuclear Age," *NR*, April 1, 1983, entire.

Christians who supported deterrence; Buckley, too, was careful to give no offense. He maintained that, while both he and Novak were devout Catholics, their remarks deserved universal attention. In emphasizing the point, he made a revealing and accurate remark about the recent past: "*National Review* is not a 'Catholic' publication. Indeed its editor, although he is most emphatically a Catholic, has from time to time been criticized by some Catholics who have reprimanded as ventures in indocility some of his positions."[16] Like the bishops themselves, in other words, and still in the tradition of John Courtney Murray, Novak and Buckley saw themselves as writing from their Catholic tradition but for the edification of all who would listen and learn.

Novak's open letter followed the bishops' letter almost point by point. Its repeated exhortations for "moral clarity" and calm reflection insinuated that the peace movement in general and the bishops in particular had given way to fear and frenzy, losing their reasoning ability along the way. Consonant with the declarations of the Second Vatican Council, both letters began with an explanation of the church's mission and its role in the world. Novak singled out a passage on the laity from the Vatican II declaration *Lumen Gentium*: "Every layman should openly reveal to [his pastors] his needs and desires with that freedom and confidence which befits a son of God and a brother in Christ. An individual layman, by reason of the knowledge, competence, or outstanding ability which he may enjoy, is permitted and sometimes even obliged to express his opinion on things which concern the good of the Church."[17] Here was the authorization he needed; Novak was not going to expose himself to criticism by deviations from church practice.

Next, in both letters, came a survey of relevant biblical passages (a rhetorical device more common in postconciliar Catholic literature than previously), with the bishops emphasizing the peaceful teachings of Jesus and Novak dwelling on such passages as "I have not come to bring peace, but a sword."[18] Novak also argued that the idea of apocalyptic destruction is thoroughly familiar in Judeo-Christian tradition and not a novelty of the post–World War II era, as devotees of the peace movement and even the bishops appeared to claim.[19]

16. William F. Buckley, Jr., Introduction to Michael Novak, *Moral Clarity in the Nuclear Age* (Nashville: Thomas Nelson, 1983), 14.

17. Novak, *Moral Clarity*, 23.

18. National Conference of Catholic Bishops (NCCB), *The Challenge of Peace: God's Promise and Our Response* (Washington, D.C.: U.S. Catholic Conference, 1983), 13–17 (numbers refer to pages, not paragraphs); Novak, *Moral Clarity*, 32–35.

19. Novak, *Moral Clarity*, 25–26, 41.

Then followed passages on Catholic just-war theory.[20] Just-war theory had evolved in the Middle Ages as the church attempted to mitigate the worst brutalities of war between Christians, and it remained the natural law framework within which Catholics discussed questions of war and peace, though its relevance in the nuclear age had recently come under scrutiny.[21] Just-war theory discusses the circumstances under which making war is legal and how war, once justly declared, can be conducted. Among the principles that allow for *declaring* war are a just cause, the intention to restore peace, declaration of war by a legitimate authority, self-defense, the prospect that a war will bring more good than ill, exhaustion of alternative means of conflict resolution, and the possibility of victory (forlorn-hope war being regarded as illicit). Among the principles for fighting a war are, noncombatant immunity and proportionality of means to ends.[22]

Central to the Catholic nuclear debate was the question of how (if at all) to apply rules drawn up in the age of crossbows to the deployment of nuclear weapons. The bishops' conclusion that "our *no* to nuclear war must in the end be definitive and decisive" suggested that there were virtually no circumstances under which the weapons could ever be used, that the idea of a just nuclear war was oxymoronic; hence, just-war principles enjoyed little practical emphasis in their pastoral. "Under no circumstances," they declared, "may nuclear weapons or other instruments of mass slaughter be used for the purpose of destroying population centers or other predominantly civilian targets."[23] Novak answered that the definition of noncombatants is no easy matter; twentieth-century wars had already demonstrated that entire populations and nations are mobilized, with the war's result often determined less on the battlefield than by economic outputs. Civilians working in munitions factories would clearly be "combatants" in the sense that their product facilitated prosecution of the war; the same could be said of farmers or almost any other population group. In other words, Novak came close to arguing that there are no noncombatants in a contemporary total war, and throughout his letter he emphasized that civilian deaths in conventional wars this century had been immense.[24] His entire letter stressed the concrete circumstances the United States currently faced. No doubt deterrence was far from per-

20. NCCB, *Challenge of Peace*, 26–34; Novak, *Moral Clarity*, 38–40.
21. On the history of just-war theory, see Weigel, *Tranquillitas Ordinis*, 25–45. John Courtney Murray, S.J., was among those who still considered it relevant and tried to adapt it to cold war issues: ibid, 122–38.
22. Novak, *Moral Clarity*, 39.
23. NCCB, *Challenge of Peace*, 46.
24. Novak, *Moral Clarity*, 67.

fect, but the particulars of the contemporary situation made it the least
of the available evils in the context of Soviet ambitions, ideology, and
the historical experience of Soviet respect for strength and contempt
for conciliation.[25] By contrast, the bishops left the question of the confrontation with the Soviet Union to the end of their letter; for them
the issue of nuclear weapons itself took precedence over the context
in which they had been built and deployed.[26]

The bishops and Novak also differed on the question of "use" of
nuclear weapons. The bishops assumed that using nuclear weapons
meant either firing them at the enemy or at least threatening to do so
while demonstrating a willingness to make good on the threat. Use of
this kind was bound to violate the proportionality principle since no
good could result from the ruinous destruction wrought.[27] Novak insisted that there is every difference between firing missiles and threatening to fire them and denied that the two possibilities were morally
equivalent. For him, nuclear weapons were "used" as deterrents by
not being fired. As soon as they left their silos their usefulness would
be ended. In a world where the knowledge and technology to build
nuclear weapons existed, Novak argued, they were in a sense the all-
but-perfect instruments of just war because they fulfilled the proportionality doctrine supremely well, killing and injuring no one and forestalling war because of the adversary's knowledge of their potential.
The bishops said they were "highly skeptical" about the idea that a
nuclear exchange could be controlled.[28] Novak in effect agreed, but
added the paradoxical qualifier that if nuclear weapons were exchanged they were no longer being used properly.[29] Novak never
looked for preemptive strikes or "rollback."

There was no coordinated political response to the bishops' pastoral
letter, and no policy changes. With far smaller conventional forces deployed on the ground in Europe than those of the Soviet Union and
Warsaw Pact, U.S. defense planners continued to rely on the threat of
first use of nuclear battlefield weapons in the event of war in that
theater; without it, they felt defeat was certain.[30] This was the policy
the Catholic bishops had supported in the 1950s, when the new conservatism began and when fear of communism had been the overrid-

---

25. Ibid., 49–56.

26. NCCB, *Challenge of Peace*, 76–80. For a critical evaluation of this organizational principle,
see Weigel, *Tranquillitas*, 282.

27. NCCB, *Challenge of Peace*, 46–50.

28. Ibid., 50.

29. Novak, *Moral Clarity*, 56–62.

30. See Daniel Charles, *Nuclear Planning in NATO: The Pitfalls of First Use* (Cambridge, Mass.:
Ballinger, 1987).

ing consideration, a policy they now repudiated. Following the bishops' lead, several other churches wrote their own declarations on the nuclear question (coming to similar conclusions).[31] As with the civil rights movement, so with nuclear weapons, it is hard to resist the conclusion that churchmen were responding to a popular social and political movement of the day rather than initiating debate, living off surplus political energy rather than generating their own, as Garry Wills had once aptly put it.[32] The practical outcome of the churches' protests was negligible. Only the end of the cold war in the years 1989–1991 would prompt a general review of U.S. nuclear weapons policy for reasons unconnected with the antinuclear movement.

In the mid-1980s, undeterred by the controversy generated by their nuclear weapons letter, the Catholic bishops completed a comparable letter on the economy, *Economic Justice for All*, emphasizing global economic interdependence and criticizing Americans' material overindulgence and their neglect of suffering elsewhere in the world. The letter implied that poverty and underdevelopment in the third world were actually caused by U.S. industries and banks, and that these institutions ought to accept an obligation of safeguarding basic human economic rights.[33] The 1983 furor was duplicated, and Michael Novak again led a group of influential Catholics, among them President Reagan's treasury secretary, William Simon, which publicly refuted the bishops' program point by point while arguing from the same premises. Novak's *Toward the Future*, his lay commission's economic manifesto, followed the pattern of *Moral Clarity* by laying out the same theoretical framework as the bishops had used and then arguing with a full show of syllogistic rigor to completely different conclusions. *Toward the Future*, like Novak's *Spirit of Democratic Capitalism*, provided a sterling defense of capitalism and free enterprise. Whereas the bishops emphasized issues of distribution, Novak emphasized issues of production and pointed out that equitable wealth sharing presupposes

31. See, for example, Episcopal Church, *To Make Peace* (Cincinnati: Forward Movement, 1982); David Gill, *Gathered for Life: Official Report, Sixth Assembly, World Council of Churches* (Grand Rapids, Mich.: Eerdman's 1983); United Methodist Church Council of Bishops, *In Defense of Creation*, in *Social Action* 14 (June 1986): 8–35. For a survey of other religious literature and church statements on the issue, see the review article by Allen Parrent, "Christians and the Nuclear Weapons Debate," *Anglican Theological Review* 67 (Jan. 1985): 67–92.

32. Wills used the expression in connection with the death of God movement. See Garry Wills, *Bare Ruined Choirs: Doubt, Prophecy, and Radical Religion* (Garden City, N.Y.: Doubleday, 1972), 95.

33. National Conference of Catholic Bishops, *Economic Justice for All: Catholic Social Teaching and the U.S. Economy* (Washington, D.C.: United States Catholic Conference, 1986), 67–78.

wealth creation, which can hardly be regarded as a matter of course.[34] Novak's many highly placed and wealthy supporters made the old "David and Goliath" treatment of this story implausible; newspapers no longer regarded the Catholic church as a monolithic force and no longer raised surprised eyebrows when laypeople challenged bishops. Moreover the bishops' letter on the economy received far less attention than had the nuclear letter; public perception and press treatment remained focused on abortion rather than the economy as the great "Catholic" issue of the period.[35]

John Noonan had remarked at the end of the 1960s that a natural law framework was proving an obstacle rather than a bridge to communication across devotional lines; at that point he had helped to turn the *Natural Law Forum* into the *American Journal of Jurisprudence*, opening it to a wider array of contributors, and had begun to supplement the natural law framework of his studies with a richer personalist approach. These confrontations between Michael Novak and the Catholic bishops in the early 1980s showed that even among those who still used a natural law framework there was no prospect of unanimity or even broad agreement. It was tempting to believe by then that the controversialists' convictions on the economy or nuclear weapons came first, and the natural law argumentation to back them up was fitted on after the fact.

Just as *Triumph* had criticized *National Review*'s belligerent nationalism in the 1960s, in the name of a Catholicism that transcended national loyalties, so in the early 1980s Novak and *Catholicism in Crisis* fell under criticism not just from the Catholic Left but also from a new generation of Catholic conservatives and traditionalists, who showed a continuing ambivalence about patriotism and capitalism.[36] Of these the most noteworthy clustered around the *New Oxford Review* and, like the *Triumph* group before them, were in many cases converts. The *New Oxford Review* grew out of a high-church Anglican journal, *American Church News*, but took on its distinctive characteristics under the editorship of Dale Vree, a Californian who led it briskly in the direction of Rome.

Dale Vree was a college senior at Berkeley during the 1964 Free Speech Movement, and was arrested and jailed briefly for his part in

34. See, for example, his tribute to entrepreneurs, Lay Commission on Catholic Social Teaching and the U.S. Economy, *Toward the Future: Catholic Social Thought and the U.S. Economy* (New York: Lay Commission on Catholic Social Teaching and the U.S. Economy, 1984), 28–29.

35. R. Bruce Douglass and William J. Gould, Jr., "After the Pastoral," C, Dec. 5, 1986, 651–54.

36. For an attack on Novak from the left, see Peter Steinfels, "Michal Novak and His Ultrasuper Democraticapitalism," C, Jan. 14, 1983, 11–16.

the Sproul Hall sit-in, which climaxed the movement. When parts of the new Left began to treat political activism as a therapeutic arena for self-fulfillment, Vree's puritanical side rebelled and he joined the ascetic, pro-Chinese Progressive Labor party, which shared his interest in politicizing the industrial working class. He next decided to try living out his socialism in a Communist country. East Germany (austerely unfashionable to the new Left) was his choice, but it did not take many months to disillusion him. He soon discovered that the same selfishness and materialistic banality against which he had revolted in the United States dominated the outlook of most East Germans.[37] Under this sobering realization, Vree abandoned communism but maintained his solicitude for the underprivileged working class and his contempt for capitalism.[38] The only group to win his admiration in East Germany was the Christians, for whom the practice of their faith entailed real costs, and it was in a shabby East German Lutheran church on Easter Day, 1966, that he experienced a forceful experience of conversion to Christianity.[39]

Returning to America, Vree studied for a Ph.D. in political science at Berkeley and became a professor at Earlham College, Indiana. His 1976 book *On Synthesizing Marxism and Christianity* (part of the gathering conservative critique of liberation theology) argued that these two great belief systems cannot be blended without violating the central principles of one or the other. Like Eric Voegelin and Thomas Molnar, Vree found a heritage of gnosticism in contemporary radicalism, notably in the work of Harvey Cox, Juergen Moltmann, and Roger Garaudy, three theological writers who had argued in favor of a Christian-Marxist reconciliation. And in a manner reminiscent of Frederick Wilhelmsen, Vree ended his analysis with an elegiac tribute to the defenders of orthodox Christianity. "Pity the orthodox, for alas, what they must defend—this present world, this frail body, this life so full of ugliness—is, as they supremely know, a lost cause."[40] It was, however, a lost cause to which he was fully willing to attach himself, and in 1983 he joined the ranks of converts by "going over to Rome."[41]

In a move that Catholic conservatives of William Buckley's stripe would never have made, Vree also rejected militant anticommunism as "one of the most insidious threats to the Church" and added that "it is folly to equate . . . the cause of Jesus Christ with the cause of

---

37. Dale Vree, "From Berkeley to East Berlin and Back," *NOR* 50 (Jan.–Feb. 1983): 12–23.
38. Dale Vree, "On Becoming a Roman Catholic," *NOR* 50 (Oct. 1983): 2–3.
39. Dale Vree, "God's Beloved East Germany," *NOR* 50 (March 1983): 10–22.
40. Dale Vree, *On Synthesizing Marxism and Christianity* (New York: Wiley, 1976), 180.
41. Vree, "On Becoming a Roman Catholic."

the West."[42] Militant anticommunism, after all, he reasoned, was based on fear of Communist conquest, but East Germany had showed Vree that persecution by Communists brought out the best in Christians, forced them to confront the imperious demands of their faith and to suffer for it. Suffering, if it be for God, was "a gift and a joy," but American Christians, he believed, had become too flabby and timid to relish this paradox of the gospel.[43] He did not mean that Christians should seek out suffering or throw themselves to the lions, but he did mean that they should forgo any intention of fighting to the destruction of the world in preference to conquest. "Christians have no business questing after martyrdom but neither are they entitled to threaten the annihilation of humanity and God's creation in order to avoid the martyr's crown of thorns."[44] Vree's willingness to suffer was another example of the "catacomb envy" that recurred among disaffected Catholics, left and right, throughout these decades. If he did not support Novak on nuclear weapons, neither would Vree support him on capitalism, for in his view, the sexual profligacy of the age was itself a baleful consequence of consumer capitalism: "The overall ethos of consumerist capitalism implies that pleasure is self-justifying and always to be maximized." He could never countenance such a view.[45]

One of Vree's fellow editors at *New Oxford Review*, James J. Thompson, Jr., was another convert, in this case from Seventh-day Adventism, who gave up a university professorship of history in dismay at what he saw as the secularization and trivialization of American education, becoming instead a freelance Christian writer.[46] A third of the *New Oxford Review* writers, Sheldon Vanauken, was, another convert from Anglo-Catholicism; these three and other like-minded traditionalists gave the journal its distinctive flavor. Like the *Triumph* group before them, they repudiated the Buckley-Novak style of nationalism.[47] But unlike the *Triumph* editors, they were ecumenical, welcoming the insights and opinions of all conservative Christians, not only on specific issues such as abortion but on the broader question of Christianity's

42. Vree, "God's Beloved East Germany," 18–19.

43. Ibid., 17.

44. Ibid., 20.

45. Dale Vree, "Sex in the Service of Capitalism," *NOR* 50 (May 1983): 8–23.

46. Thompson was author of *Tried as by Fire* (Macon, Ga.: Mercer University Press, 1982). On his decision to leave academic life, see Thompson, "One Christian's Life Witness," *NOR* 49 (Nov. 1982): 8–18.

47. For the critique of Novak, see Stuart Gudowitz, "Neo-Modernist Economic Theology," *NOR* 49 (Dec. 1982): 30–31; Robert Coles, "Conservatives Begin Rejecting Church Authority," *NOR* 50 (Jan.–Feb. 1983): 24, 26. The contrast between Vree's *New Oxford Review* and Novak's *Catholicism in Crisis* should not be exaggerated, however. Several writers (including Thomas Molnar, James Schall, S.J., and Christopher Derrick) wrote for both journals.

relationship to society. Anglican, Orthodox, even evangelical Protestant contributors appeared regularly in the pages of *New Oxford Review;* one evangelical argued that the Protestant churches owed a considerable debt to medieval Catholicism and that the rift of the Reformation was not so deep as polemicists on both sides had long assumed.[48] Anglican contributors likewise emphasized their membership in the worldwide Catholic communion.[49] James Thompson, noting that there was an honorable anticapitalist conservative tradition in America (he mentioned the southern agrarians and Russell Kirk, among others), declared that a political conservative can be a Christian. Capitalism was not *inevitably* anti-Christian. Nevertheless, "if there are no atheists in the foxholes, there are few good Christians in Bloomingdales." Christians must always remember to put their faith before their material and national interests.[50]

A younger generation of writers also took up the task of defending orthodox Catholicism in the 1980s. Michael Jones, for example, had been relatively untouched by the great political controversies of the 1960s. A high number in the lottery spared him the draft for the Vietnam War, and he spent his college years, 1966–1970, absorbed in the literature of James Joyce and Rainer Maria Rilke. Jones, from a Catholic family in Philadelphia, strayed away from his church completely for a time, noting that in that period "it seemed that all Catholics could do was bitch and moan about contraceptives." His education in a Catholic college (St. Joseph's, Philadelphia) paid scant regard to tradition or to the teaching of Aquinas and did nothing to vivify his faith. Later, however, while working as an English teacher in a German school, Jones read Thomas Merton's passionate spiritual autobiography *The Seven Storey Mountain,* and under its vivid guidance his faith revived. Having returned to the fold, he became a pillar of orthodoxy. Jones studied for a Ph.D. in English at Temple University and became an assistant professor of English at St. Mary's College in South Bend, Indiana, in 1979. His academic career, however, lasted only one year. A succession of op-ed articles in local newspapers, against abortion, feminism, and day care, made him highly unpopular with his departmental colleagues, and his department chair called him "an absolut-

---

48. Thomas O. Key, "Evangelicalism's Debt to the Medieval Church," *NOR* 50 (Oct. 1983): 10–16. Key was history department chair at Wheaton College, Wheaton, Ill.

49. See, for example, Tom Barnes, "On the Denver Consecrations," *NOR* 45 (June 1978): 4–13. Barnes, a Berkeley history professor and former Episcopalian, here justifies the formation of the orthodox Anglican Church in North America out of a breach occasioned by disputes on the ordination of women.

50. James J. Thompson, Jr., "Can a Political Conservative Be a Christian?" *NOR* 51 (Jan.–Feb. 1984): 14–22.

ist." His contract was terminated. Jones stayed in South Bend and turned to full-time writing, publishing the first number of the orthodox *Fidelity* magazine in December 1981.[51] He became the scourge of Notre Dame University, his near neighbor, and in a succession of biting exposés asked, "Is Notre Dame still Catholic?" His own answer was no; the theology department's abandonment of dogmatics, the university's willingness to give a platform to prochoice and gay liberation speakers in the name of academic freedom, and the use of material from aborted fetuses by campus scientists all convinced him that it was no longer an instrument for the promotion of Catholicism.[52]

Fidelity presented news of Catholic events plus long analytical articles, mostly by Jones himself, on the various aspects of modernity, whose effects on the church had been so grievous. The distinctive characteristic of modernity, Jones concluded, after studying modern artistic, literary, musical, anthropological, and architectural materials, was "rationalized sexual misbehavior." Thus the English art historian Anthony Blunt's acts of treason, Margaret Mead's deceptive conclusions about adolescence in Samoa, Freud's theory of the Oedipus complex, Picasso's Cubism, and Walter Gropius's theories of ideal living arrangements could all be attributed to their attempts to rationalize and generalize from their sexual deviancies.[53] The great moderns, Jones argued, were characteristically people who refused to repent when they sinned. Instead, they rationalized, creating either a theory to explain their misbehavior or else a "support group" of other people "involved in the same kind of perverted behavior."[54] Jones blamed Catholic intellectuals for leading the church into the corrupt orbit of modernity, using Vatican II merely as an excuse. The intellectuals who attended Vatican II, he said, such as Hans King from West Germany and Michael Novak from the United States, had felt inferior to their secular colleagues in the 1950s and early 1960s and had hoped to gain credibility by adopting the canons of modernity. In fact, said Jones, by adopting the modern outlook they had thrown fuel on a fire whose

---

51. Telephone interview with Michael Jones, Jan. 7, 1992.

52. Michael Jones, *Is Notre Dame Still Catholic?* (South Bend, Ind.: Fidelity, 1989), esp. chap. 1, "Is Notre Dame Still Catholic?" 1–19, and chap. 2, "The Strange Experiments of Dr. Basu," 20–41.

53. Michael Jones, "Sigmund and Minna and Carl and Sabina: The Birth of Psychoanalysis out of the Personal Lives of Its Founders," *Fidelity* 9 (Dec. 1989): 31–40; Jones, "Cubism as Sexual Loathing: The Case against Picasso," *Fidelity* 9 (Oct. 1990): 32–40; Jones, "The Future That Failed: Machines for Living and the Death of the Family," *Fidelity* 10 (Dec. 1990): 28–42; Jones, "Homosexual as Subversive: The Double Life of Sir Anthony Blunt," *Fidelity* 7 (May 1988): 18–31; Jones, "Samoa Lost: Margaret Mead, Cultural Relativism, and the Guilty Imagination," *Fidelity* 7 (Feb. 1988): 26–37.

54. Jones interview.

flames were consuming orthodoxy. The intellectuals "took the council as carte blanche to implement modernity in the Church," and in their reports and books on the council, they made flatly misleading statements about what it had intended. The infection was therefore worst at Catholic universities, which became havens of modernity and dissent: "From its inception dissent has had a sexual basis. . . . Dissent is not some disinterested pursuit of truth that hovers angel-like over academic life. It is desire at war with truth. It is the quintessential ideology, which chooses power over truth. Rather than attempting to conform its mind to reality through disinterested pursuit of truth, dissent seeks to remake reality in conformity to desire. Dissent is libido in academic regalia."[55] Combative and controversial, Jones enjoyed confronting professors at Notre Dame whom he considered modernists, men and women who had forsaken truth in pursuit of desire.[56]

Fidelity had a small readership, which periodically shrank when Jones took unpopular positions on issues in Catholic life. For example, he regarded the apparitions of the Virgin Mary in Medjugorje, Yugoslavia, as fraudulent, just when they were being celebrated in much of the Catholic press and prompting pilgrimages to the site. Jones went to Medjugorje, interviewed the priests and some of the children involved in the new cult, and wrote *Medjugorje: The Untold Story* to denounce it as a delusion brought about by the manipulation of the children's emotions in religious "encounter group" sessions.[57] Jones, a man of considerable intellectual power, wrote articles juxtaposing an ingenious analysis of modern phenomena with scorching polemics against those who, in his view, were denying God even, at times, in the name of Christianity itself.

A frequent contributor to *Fidelity* was James Sullivan, Jones's exact contemporary.[58] Sullivan, after fourteen years as a teacher in parochial schools, had become a local Connecticut organizer for Catholics United for the Faith, the orthodox lay Catholic organization that had been founded by Lyman Stebbins in 1968. From the outset CUF had pledged "unshakeable loyalty to the Pope, and thus to the Church, and thus to Christ."[59] A former reader of *Triumph*, which he had found "roman-

55. Jones, *Is Notre Dame Still Catholic?* vi.

56. See Michael Jones, "The Solitary Vice Goes Public," *Is Notre Dame Still Catholic?* 42–50, for his confrontation with Rev. Edward Malloy; and "Exegesis as a Weapon: An Evening with Professor Sheehan," ibid., 183–210.

57. Michael Jones, *Medjugorje: The Untold Story* (South Bend, Ind.: Fidelity, 1988).

58. See, for example, James Sullivan, "Catholic Neoconservatives," *Fidelity* 9 (Dec. 1989), 46–48; Sullivan, "Chill out with Bill," *Fidelity* 10 (Sept. 1991): 15–18.

59. James Likoudis and Kenneth Whitehead, *The Pope, the Council, and the Mass* (West Hanover, Mass.: Christopher, 1981), 19.

tic and intriguing" as a college student in the late 1960s, Sullivan had become dismayed by the decline of accurate dogmatic teaching and straight moral guidance in Catholic schools. "After being forced to sit through I don't know how many dreary catechetical days at school, where we would have constantly warm, fuzzy, touchy-feely, life-experience, no-doctrine, no-content workshops, I would writhe in agony," he recalled. Finally he decided, "I can't take it any more—I've been a Nicodemus too long"; he resolved to found a local CUF group.[60] From this start he joined the staff of CUF's journal, *Lay Witness*. When he rose to its editorship in 1990, he enlarged the magazine; he saw its mission as the teaching of the full church magisterium. Like Michael Jones at *Fidelity*, he was suspicious of such Catholics as William Buckley, Michael Novak, and Garry Wills, who, as he saw it, put their political or national interests before their faith.[61] "CUF," by contrast, he maintained, "is supposed only to echo the magisterium. We may have enemies to the left and to the right but we're supposed to keep our eyes on the Lord."[62] But this very insistence on orthodoxy in the environment of the 1980s made him appear, to many Catholics, conservative to the point of reaction.

The cumulative readership of these conservative Catholic journals was not great; none rivaled the "mainstream" status of *National Review* which, by the 1980s, was virtually the house organ of the Reagan administration. Prominent Catholic figures at the Reagan White House credited it with a large role in the formation of their ideas. Pat Buchanan (born 1938), for example, had discovered the journal in 1960 as he felt his way toward conservatism from an Al Smith Democratic family background, and he found that "there was nothing" in it "with which I disagreed." Buchanan thought that "it is difficult to exaggerate the debt conservatives of my generation owe *National Review* and Bill Buckley." "They not only wrote brilliantly. . . . they didn't give a damn who disagreed. I cherished their attitude. . . . When the sainted (but naive) Pope John XXIII issued his gauzy encyclical *Mater et Magistra*, Buckley headed his dissent, 'Mater Si; Magistra No!' That was just the right touch of faithfulness and fire, irreverence and spirit. That was

---

60. Telephone interview with James Sullivan, Oct. 8, 1991. The CUF characteristically mistrusted teaching based on experience because it privileged subjectivism. See, for example, Catholics United for the Faith, *Man Shall Not Live by Experience Alone* (New Rochelle, N.Y.: Catholics United for the Faith, 1977).

61. For remarks critical of *National Review* conservatives, see, for example, David M. Rooney, "A Commentary on Lamentations—over Papal Social Teachings," *Lay Witness* 11 (Feb. 1990): 1–6.

62. Sullivan interview.

what I felt too."[63] Likewise, Peggy Noonan (born 1950), third of seven children in an Irish-American Catholic family, who became a speech writer for Reagan and George Bush, recalled encountering the journal as a teenager in the late 1960s: "I started reading *National Review,* and it sang to me. They saw it the way I was seeing it: America is essentially good, the [Vietnam] war is being fought for serious and valid reasons, the answer to every social ill is not necessarily a social program . . . and God is real as a rock. I was moved. . . . Later I found that half the people in the Reagan administration had as their first conservative friend that little magazine."[64] If its days of offering companionship to solitary conservative youths had passed by the 1980s, *National Review* certainly kept alight the flame of religiously superheated anticommunism and the same old denunciations of liberalism, but without much attention to points of religious orthodoxy.

The diminution of the church as a disciplinary organization in the United States had, by 1980, ended the prospect of a united Catholic front on any major issue, and Catholics' attitudinal distinctiveness vis-à-vis other Christians had diminished steadily since 1960. To be sure, this outcome could be regarded as a healthy and long-overdue achievement, and in rhetoric, at least, many of the Catholic bishops and their supporters took exactly that view. For example, David Hollenbach, S. J., principal author of the bishops' letter on the economy, told me in 1985 that although there had been "a lot of upheaval" both in the U.S. church and in world Catholicism since Vatican II, still "I think on balance—in a major degree—that Vatican II was an extraordinarily good thing." He took the open controversy surrounding the bishops' letters as a sign of success and confidence rather than a confession of lost energies. Both Garry Wills and Michael Novak, said Hollenbach, along with many other conservative critics, had "picked up on some of the negative things" that had happened in the 1960s, but at least his own Jesuit order, and probably the church in general, "is considerably stronger, considerably more prayerful, considerably more intellectually serious in the main than it was twenty-five years ago."[65]

The Catholic community of the 1980s faced a new international configuration of forces. In the 1950s the American hierarchy had been docile toward directives from Rome; Cardinal Spellman had worked hand-in-glove with Pope Pius XII. The pontificates of John XXIII and Paul VI, however, had created something of an interregnum, during

---

63. Pat Buchanan, *Right from the Beginning* (Boston: Little, Brown, 1988), 221.

64. Peggy Noonan, *What I Saw at the Revolution: A Political Life in the Reagan Era* (New York: Random House, 1990), 14–15.

65. Personal interview with David Hollenbach, S. J., Cambridge, Mass., Nov. 12, 1985.

which a relative lack of strong direction from the center encouraged local initiatives or, when strong direction was given, as in *Humanae Vitae*, proved locally unacceptable and engendered widespread resistance. By the 1980s members of the hierarchy in the United States, as well as priests and laypeople, had a confident sense of their position and did not always take kindly to papal efforts to restore unity under John Paul II, whose pontificate began in 1978. John Paul II and Cardinal Ratzinger were not mere clerical reactionaries, as their opponents sometimes claimed, but they did believe in a coordinated and orthodox worldwide church. The pope's background in Communist Poland, where mere observance of the Mass constituted a subversive political act against an officially atheist regime, had made him unsympathetic to the experimental mood of many American Catholics and their praise for diversity and pluralism. Catholic conservatives lauded the new pope without always obeying him; liberal and radical Catholics, without always disobeying him, often expressed dismay.

The Catholic new conservatives of the 1950s had rallied around the principles of anticommunism and antiliberalism. The "liberalization" of the Catholic hierarchy; the liturgical, ecumenical, and intellectual reforms of Catholicism in the next thirty years; and the discrediting (for many Catholic Americans) of militant anticommunism in the Vietnam era made their once solidly respectable position in Catholicism increasingly marginal. Under the impact of the 1960s Catholic conservative intellectuals disagreed among themselves, dividing between those for whom the political issue of mobilizing conservative politicians was the most important and those for whom preservation of the church and its orthodoxy mattered more than the temporizing that practical politics made necessary.

The social and intellectual history of the American Left in the 1960s is an oft-told tale, but the odyssey of American conservatives in the same age is still known only to a few. Conservatives and leftist radicals of the 1960s disagreed on the issue of communism, but they shared many characteristics. Both confronted their age with a fervent moralism, drawn from classical, Christian, and American sources. Both rejected the regnant intellectual liberalism, dominant by the 1950s, which had spoken of "the end of ideology" and had regarded politics as the detailed adjustment of a smoothly advancing mechanism.[66] Conservatives and left-wing radicals alike, in startling, often theatrical ways, forced the nation to realize that fundamental questions were as

66. This view is embodied in Daniel Bell, *The End of Ideology: On the Exhaustion of Political Ideas in the Fifties* (Glencoe, Ill.: Free Press, 1960).

yet unresolved in the 1960s and that the passion could not be drained out of political life. They raised the possibility that the United States might be a source of moral corruption, not of salvation, and they insisted that a putative universalization of middle-class prosperity would not allay the spiritual cravings common to all ages of human history. As is so often the case in American history conservatives and leftist radicals alike prized their outsider status and made claims to the moral high ground. Even the pro-Reagan conservatives of the 1980s used "new class" rhetoric to depict themselves as an embattled minority rather than as the new establishment at the center of power.

As in politics, so in religion: the Catholic new conservatives, no less than radical evangelical Protestants of the Left and the Right, thought of themselves as a morally exalted outsider group, standing in judgment over a sinful nation and a slothful church, holding out the promise of salvation for the nation and its people and calling on them for repentance and transformation. As the Catholic church transformed itself internally at Vatican II and as the place of Catholicism in American society lost its old distinctiveness during the 1960s, they fragmented and lost whatever faint hope they might once have had of presenting a coordinated program of religion-based social reform. In most cases they exhibited a dignity in defeat and, already familiar with the idea of speaking up for lost causes, stayed at their task as doggedly in the "conservative" 1980s as they had done in the three previous decades. Meanwhile, their views remained attractive enough, even in defeat, to bring forth a new generation of forlorn-hope Catholic conservatives to carry on the struggle.

Index

Library of Congress Cataloging-in-Publication Data
Allitt, Patrick.
    Catholic intellectuals and conservative politics in America,
    1950–1985 / Patrick Allitt.
        p. cm.
    Includes bibliographical references and index.
    ISBN 0-8014-2295-7 (alk. paper)
    1. Catholics—United States—Intellectual life. 2. Catholics—
United States—Politics and government. 3. United States—Politics
and government—1945–1989. I. Title.
E184.C3A45 1993
320.5′2′08822—dc20   93-13515